D0183576

Plotting Hitler's Death
The German Resistance to Hitler 1933–1945

JOACHIM FEST
Translated by Bruce Little

PHŒNIX

A PHOENIX PAPERBACK

First published in Great Britain
by Weidenfeld & Nicolson in 1996
This paperback edition published in 1997
by Phoenix, a division of Orion Books Ltd,
Orion House, 5 Upper St Martin's Lane,
London WC2H 9EA

Originally published in Germany in 1994
by Siedler Verlag under the title
Staatsstreich: Der lange Weg zum 20. Juli.
Published in the USA in 1996
by Metropolitan Books, New York.

A CIP catalogue record for this book
is available from the British Library.

ISBN: 0 75380 040 3

Printed and bound in Great Britain by
The Guernsey Press Co. Ltd,
Guernsey, Channel Islands

'Only a very few books on this subject are valuable and readable at the same time. Fest's is the best'
Norman Stone, Observer

'Anyone interested in the debate over Europe's future and Germany's role within it should read this extraordinary book... the main part of the book may also be read as a gripping thriller, with twists and coincidences that even John le Carré might not risk... The story has often been told but never better and Joachim Fest has detail either new or unfamiliar'
John Keegan, Daily Telegraph

'The story of the German resistance to Hitler makes fascinating but terrible reading. It is a human tragedy, but also a political and moral lesson... This is a splendid book: complete, thorough and thoughtful, eloquently written and well translated. A memorable and chastening work'
Hugh Trevor-Roper, Sunday Telegraph

'A vivid and gripping account of the brave Germans who plotted Hitler's downfall in order either to prevent or end the war... Here is a fine read which makes one wring one's hands over the lost opportunity'
Spectator

'A fascinating story, well-told by an expert on the Nazi period'
The Express

'With his meticulous research and with the added perspective of time... [Fest] has assured an honoured place in history for these courageous people'
Christabel Bielenberg, Daily Mail

'He knows how to tell a good story, he throws in plenty of colourful detail... he is not afraid to make bold judgements... *Plotting Hitler's Death* can be recommended as a fluent, readable and well-informed introduction to a subject which still has the capacity to arouse passion and debate more than half a century after the event'
TLS

Joachim C. Fest was born in Berlin in 1926. After the war, in which he served and was taken prisoner, he joined the radio station RIAS-Berlin where he became the head of the Department of Contemporary History. In 1961 he became Editor-in-Chief of TV for Norddeutscher Rundfunk and published his highly acclaimed work *The Face of the Third Reich* in 1963. In 1973 he published the first comprehensive German life of Hitler since 1945. One of the world's leading authorities on the Nazi period, Joachim Fest lives in central Germany, near Frankfurt.

BY THE SAME AUTHOR

Hitler
The Face of the Third Reich

CONTENTS

PREFACE

On July 20, 1944, a powerful bomb ripped through Adolf Hitler's East Prussian headquarters during a briefing between the Führer and his senior officers. The bomb, planted by a dashing, highly decorated young count named Claus Schenk von Stauffenberg, blew pieces of wreckage and columns of smoke high in the air and completely destroyed the wooden barracks that housed the crowded briefing room. Although it miraculously failed to maim or kill Hitler, the explosion dramatically announced to the world the existence of a secret, indigenous opposition to the Nazi regime.

These events are, of course, quite familiar to most readers. But what is less widely known is that well before July 20 a substantial number of Germans had come to despise Hitler and his policies, even as the Führer racked up impressive victories at the ballot box and on the battlefield. This nascent opposition formed clandestine groups to help Hitler's victims escape from the country. Later, they plotted a coup d'état to rid Germany of Nazism and drafted plans for the society they wanted to create in place of the one they hoped to destroy. As many as fifteen assassination attempts were undertaken during the reign of National Socialism, but these efforts always failed: in some instances because of bad timing or poor planning; in others, because of the omnipresent scrutiny of the Gestapo or Hitler's own unerring instinct for danger.

It was only in the summer of 1944, when the wholesale defeat of the German army was already in sight, that the plot to kill Hitler finally came to fruition. The Allies had landed in Normandy a few weeks earlier, signaling a decisive turn in the direction of the war. This is why many historians have argued that Stauffenberg's bomb came too late to change the military and political course of the war, a fact of which the conspirators were only too well aware. Nevertheless, they wanted to send a message to the rest of the world that there had been men of principle in Germany who were prepared to lay down their lives to defeat Adolf Hitler.

There is ample reason to believe that the German resistance failed to achieve even this modest goal. The dark cloud of misfortune that hung over all of its endeavors has also cast a shadow on its historical legacy. Since the end of Hitler's reign many books have appeared on the subject—both in German and English—but none of these has managed to provide a full understanding of the conspirators and their actions.[1] The earliest accounts were personal reminiscences by resistance leaders who survived, such as Fabian von Schlabrendorff and Hans Bernd Gisevius, and extracts from the journals left by Ulrich von Hassel, a lawyer and diplomat executed in 1944. In 1948 an émigré historian, Hans Rothfels, wrote his classic *The German Opposition to Hitler: An Appraisal,* the first comprehensive scholarly history. The subtle pathos of Rothfels's book derived from his desire to make the public in the Allied countries aware of the history of the opposition movement, a history that had been largely suppressed.

A series of memoirs by less well known members of the resistance followed soon after the release of Rothfels's book, as did the first attempts to assess the historical significance of the opposition (many of which tended to glorify their subject) and several scholarly works. During the 1960s a group of young historians published critical studies that examined the differing philosophies of the major resistance factions, as well as their clandestine dealings with the Allies. At about the same time the first significant biographies of the leaders of the resistance appeared. As the literature expanded, its scope broadened to include previously unknown opposition figures, as well as the diverse forms of political dissidence. Lastly, research into the resistance among workers brought entirely new themes and perspectives to light.

By now the flood of literature has become so vast, however, that it threatens to submerge the real meaning and significance of the German opposition to National Socialism. Attention tends to focus on dramatic events like the idealistic and reckless actions of the White Rose, a group of students who distributed anti-Nazi leaflets in Munich; the courageous efforts of other groups are forgotten. Similarly, while the attempted coup d'état by a group of army officers on July 20, 1944, is quite well known, at least in its basic outline, little is remembered of the background: the various forces, motives, obstacles, and preparations that eventually culminated in Stauffenberg's deed. An undertaking of that sort is always more than a date and a sequence of events, and only a consideration of its historical context can reveal its meaning and importance.

Notwithstanding the celebrated events of July 20, the German public has long had difficulty acknowledging the resistance to Hitler and has never sufficiently appreciated the extent to which the existence of a relatively broad opposition helped ease Germany's acceptance back into the ranks of respectable nations. Foremost among the many reasons for this diffidence is the feeling—one deeply rooted in Germany's authoritarian heritage—that the opposition committed treason by abandoning the German people to its collective fate at a critical moment. This accusation has been leveled frequently and emphatically at opposition leaders like Brigadier General Hans Oster. Although it has been almost universally rejected in academic circles— no one charges Oster with deliberately seeking to harm his country— arguments such as this have done little to change received ideas and biases.

Perhaps a different approach to assessing the opposition's motives would succeed in convincing those who regard treason as an unpardonable offense. After several unsuccessful attempts to overthrow the regime, the conspirators' sole remaining ambition by July 20, 1944, was to save as much of Germany's "substance" as possible from the impending catastrophe. Recent evidence proves how well founded their motives were: one study shows that, while slightly more than 2.8 million German soldiers and civilians died during the nearly five years between the beginning of the war on September 1, 1939, and the attempt to assassinate Hitler on July 20, 1944, 4.8 million died during the nine and a half months before the war ended in early May 1945. These figures appear even more shocking if we calculate how many were killed on average every day during those two periods. Before the attempted coup some 1,588 Germans were killed daily; after it 16,641—more than ten times as many—perished, even though the war had obviously been lost.[2]

To this human cost must be added the destruction visited upon cities, industry, and cultural treasures. The cities of Stuttgart, Darmstadt, Braunschweig, Würzburg, Kiel, Hildesheim, Ulm, Mainz, Dresden, and Potsdam were all laid to ruin after the coup attempt, most of them having already suffered gravely in earlier bombing raids. The air war also continued virtually unimpeded against other cities, which were left defenseless following the complete collapse of German air power. Berlin did not suffer its most devastating attack until early 1945. Overall the destruction wrought in the last nine months of the war far exceeded that of the previous fifty-nine months, not to mention the countless casualties in other countries or the victims of Hitler's extermination policy, which continued to the very end.

One of the factors inhibiting appreciation of the German resistance has been the cacophony of voices in which it found expression. Opponents of the regime were motivated not only by a simple concern for human rights but also by Christian, socialist, conservative, and even reactionary beliefs. There is much truth to the claim that the German resistance to the Third Reich never existed in the sense of a unified group or movement sharing a common set of ideals.[3] In fact, the term *resistance*, which was not coined until after the war, encompasses numerous groups that acted separately and often held differing views. Although some of these groups eventually joined forces, for the most part they labored in isolation. Many organizations worked in such secrecy that to this day they are rarely mentioned in historical studies. The Solf Circle, which formed to assist the persecuted, is one such case, and others include the Stürmer group and the revolutionary left- and right-wing militants from the Weimar era who were brought together by former Freikorps leader "Beppo" Römer. We have some idea of the size of this last group only because nearly 150 members were tried before the so-called People's Court in 1942 and 1943. In its early days the German resistance was dominated by left-wing groups such as Beginning Anew, the Socialist Front, the Saefkow group, and the International Socialist Fighting League. Most important of all was the group led by the young Luftwaffe lieutenant Harro Schulze-Boysen, which joined with Arvid and Mildred Harnack and their friends in the early 1940s to form what become known as the Red Orchestra, a name given to it by the Gestapo.[4]

Of all the various resistance groups, however, only three were able to forge closer ties over the years and develop a strategy that posed a genuine threat to the regime. These were the conservative circle around Carl Goerdeler, a former mayor of Leipzig, and Ludwig Beck, who had resigned as army chief of staff; the Kreisau Circle, which was led by Count Helmuth von Moltke and dominated by a Christian and socialist philosophy; and finally the regime's opponents within the military. Around these groups moved a number of isolated individuals, including lawyers, former trade union leaders, businessmen, church officials, and state bureaucrats. Many developed resistance cells in their own offices, often with the tacit support of their superiors, such as Military Intelligence chief Admiral Wilhelm Canaris and Ernst von Weizäcker, the secretary of state in the Foreign Office. For a time, the Military Intelligence group actually played a leading role within the opposition.

It was this branch of the resistance whose motives were the clearest and whose efforts came closest to succeeding. And it was this branch that ultimately found expression in one symbolic act, for that is what the events of July 20, 1944, represented and how they were understood by most of the participants. The long road to this day, the internal tensions and setbacks, as well as the manifest futility of the effort are the subjects of this book.

Some might object that this is precisely the part of the resistance that has already drawn the lion's share of attention, to the neglect of other opposition efforts. It is all the more surprising, therefore, that of the literally hundreds of books that have been published on this topic not one both relates the fascinating story of the plotters and attempts to analyze it. Christian Müller's study of Stauffenberg, Peter Hoffmann's groundbreaking works, and those of Klaus-Jürgen

Müller, Helmut Krausnick, Hans Mommsen, and many others have made important contributions to our knowledge of the German resistance. All these works, however, are aimed at the limited number of experts in the field.

The present volume is intended for a broader audience with a general interest in history. Its purpose is not so much to convey new information as to recount an old story in the light of the latest research. It deals with folly and miscalculation, conflict and failure, human frailty and the ability to persevere in the face of adversity. The story is full of political and human drama that tends to be overlooked in strictly scholarly studies. What is new, here, above all, is the context in which this extraordinary drama was played out.

The lack of a comprehensive view, which is so integral to these events, has eroded the legacy of the German resistance. That legacy lies not in the political views of the opposition but rather in the insights that the plot to assassinate Hitler—like all momentous historical occurrences—offers us into the thoughts and actions of people operating under the most extreme circumstances. The fact that the subjects of this book failed in the end, after many attempts, does not in any way detract from their memory or from the example that they set.

1

THE RESISTANCE
THAT NEVER WAS

Essential to the history of the German resistance is the sense of powerlessness that defined it from the outset. How Adolf Hitler managed in a single stroke and seemingly effortlessly to seize power and construct an unconstrained totalitarian system is a question that has been raised frequently since the end of his twelve-year rule. But this question was also on the minds of Germans who lived through that period. Contrary to what most of the Nazis' defeated foes later claimed, it was not primarily by means of ruthless violence that Hitler rose to power, although terror and intimidation were certainly always present. Enabling factors far more complex were grasped relatively early on by astute observers of the Weimar Republic on the left as well as the right, who spoke not so much about how Hitler had overwhelmed the republic but about how the republic had caved in. The self-induced paralysis and shortsightedness of the democratic forces clearly played as great a role in the debacle as Hitler's tactical and psychological skills or his ability to seize the historical moment.

First of all, Hitler did not emerge out of nowhere to claim power. Rather, he worked away patiently in the background for years, overcoming many obstacles and awaiting the day when he could tout himself as Germany's "savior" from a parliamentary system entangled in countless intractable problems. The political parties of the Weimar Republic had long been set in their ways, embroiled in ideological disputes, and they were concerned much more with securing advantage for their members than with meeting the needs of the country. Years before, they had forfeited responsibility for forming governments and passing legislation to the president, who governed by emergency decree. It was precisely Hitler's promise of a return to parliamentary rule that induced Hindenburg, after long hesitation, to ask the Nazi leader to form a cabinet. Thus, on the morning of January 30, 1933, Hitler became chancellor of a new coalition government with the conservative German National People's Party.

No one could explain at the time how it had come to this. Hitler himself spoke of a "miracle" and interpreted his appointment as an "act of God."[1] Barely three months earlier he had suffered his first serious setback at the polls, losing over two million votes. Just two months earlier he had narrowly succeeded in holding his splintering party together with a dramatic appeal concluding in threats of suicide. Scarcely four days earlier, President Hindenburg had assured the army commander in chief, General Kurt von Hammerstein-Equord, that "he would not even consider making that Austrian corporal the minister of defense or the chancellor." The extraordinary reversal was brought about by ambition, a thirst for revenge, and what one contemporary observer saw as a "mixture of corruption, backstairs intrigue, and patronage."[2]

As if foreshadowing what was to come, Hitler's adversaries permitted him to outmaneuver them on the very day he was appointed. As evening fell on January 30 a few lingering parliamentarians sat together in the Reichstag. Still confused by the events of that morning, they had lost themselves in a lengthy discussion of the likely consequences when, from the darkness of the neighboring Tiergarten, movement and noise became perceptible, as if a great procession were under way. Outside, people streamed past the Reichstag in groups of varying sizes, heading toward the Brandenburg Gate. "Young people, all young people," remarked Social Democratic Party (SPD) deputy Wilhelm Hoegner of Bavaria as they passed on their way to a torch-light parade whose flickering lights illuminated not only the broad expanses around the Brandenburg Gate but also Unter den Linden and Wilhelmstrasse, casting a red glow on the skies above. Thousands of uniformed, hastily gathered marchers swept through the streets, while crowds of onlookers stood and watched. "But we just slipped away into the darkness," Hoegner later wrote, "crushed and wearied by the ferment of those days."[3]

The events in Berlin were echoed in dozens of other cities. Count Harry Kessler, a prominent diplomat, recalled "an atmosphere like pure Mardi Gras": Crowds, parades, bands, and flags filled the streets, though nothing more dramatic had happened than a change of government, like many others in the past. But there was undeniably a sense that a new era had dawned. A feeling of anticipation swept the nation, filling some with dread and others with hope. Hitler picked up on this mood in his radio address on the evening of February 1. Striking a moderate, statesmanlike tone, he recited the many hardships the people had known: the "betrayal" of November 1918, the "heartrending division" in the land, the hate and confusion. He described the self-inflicted "paralysis" of the multiparty state and held out the prospect of German society "coming together as one." He spoke of dignity, honor, tradition, family, and culture. He assured the nation, which felt reviled by the entire world and humiliated by the victorious powers, that he would restore the pride of old. At the end he appealed for divine blessing.

The majority of the population, however, remained uneasy about Hitler. Too much had been said in rabid speeches, and too much had been done in bloody street fights for his words to calm those who felt hostile toward or even just wary of the new leader. Furthermore, the much-maligned Weimar Republic was not without supporters. It had faithful champions among all the parties of the center, in particular among the Social Democrats and the trade unions. In the Reichsbanner, an elite paramilitary defense troop formed in February 1931, and the Iron Front, an alliance of the Reichsbanner, the SPD, and the unions that was formed the following November, the republic had two militant, prodemocratic organizations working to defend it against assault from the left or right. The Iron Front alone had three and a half million members, of whom 250,000 belonged to so-called protective formations, trained armed units that regularly carried out field exercises. Both of these organizations now awaited a signal to take action against a government that—with its party's million-strong militia, the Sturmabteilung or SA—they saw as threatening a coup of its own.

But the signal never came, no matter how much the local organizations and their individual members pressed their political leaders. Weakness, fear, and a sense of responsibility played their parts in this, of course. Even more decisive, however, were Hitler's tactics, which quickly undermined the willingness of the republic's supporters to take action. They had always assumed that the Nazi leader would stage a coup and had prepared themselves exclusively for this eventuality. But Hitler's experiences during his long rise to power, especially the well-remembered failed putsch of November 1923, had persuaded him that it was best not to be seen seizing control through overtly violent means. Having risen to chancellor through constitutional channels, he was not about to stigmatize himself as a revolutionary. The considerable forces still arrayed against him in the democratic fighting organizations; the cautious attitude of the majority of citizens, who remained hesitant amid all the stage-managed displays of jubilation; the respect Hitler felt compelled to show the president and the armed forces, the Reichswehr—all these factors forced him to continue ostensibly observing the rule of law while doing all he could to seize the reins of power. Later it would be said that the republic did not fight but simply froze helplessly—and then crumbled—in the face of these unexpected tactics.

Hitler's opening gambit in the struggle for power not only confused his avowed enemies but tended to reassure the wary in all social classes and organizations, overcoming or considerably reducing the apprehension they had always felt about him. A coup achieved through legal channels was something thoroughly unknown. The classical literature on resistance to tyrants, stretching back to the days of the ancient Greeks, dealt exclusively with violent seizures of power; there was no talk of silent takeovers through outwardly democratic methods, of obeying the letter of the law while mocking its spirit. By leaving the facade of the constitution in place, Hitler hopelessly confounded the public's ability to judge the legality of the new regime, to choose whether as good citizens they should feel loyal to it or not. Meanwhile, behind the scenes, radical change was under way.

The paradoxical idea of a legal revolution dumbfounded not only Hitler's opponents but his allies as well. The civil service was similarly perplexed but took comfort in the basically legal nature of the upheaval, despite its obvious excesses. Thankful to be spared the internal divisions and conflict that a revolution might have brought, the civil service willingly placed itself and its expertise at the disposal of the new government. As a result the Nazis eased smoothly into control of the entire apparatus of state. Indeed, since the days of the kaisers, civil servants had tended toward antidemocratic sentiments, but it was primarily the appearance of legality that won them over to the new regime or at least prevented any doubts from arising about the propriety of what the Nazis were doing. It is particularly significant that both the emergency decree (suspending virtually all major civil liberties) issued on February 28, 1933, the day after the Reichstag fire, and the Enabling Act wresting legislative authority from the Reichstag and conferring it on the government were crafted by loyal civil servants with no particular affection for the Nazi Party. The bureaucracy responded in the same acquiescent way to subsequent legislation, which led step by step to the demolition of the entire constitutional order.

The tactic of a "legal revolution" was complemented by another clever move, namely the depiction of the Nazi seizure of power as a "national revival." After all the humiliations of the Weimar Republic, many members of the middle class and other Germans understood this to signal a kind of liberation. The Nazis' single-minded pursuit of power did not, therefore, raise much protest and was even cheered as a sign of the nonpartisan resurgence of a country that had been divided against itself for too long and was finally gathering its strength. This confusion of the Nazi lust for power with the revival of Germany itself, encouraged by incessant, stage-managed festivities and the excitement generated by various plebiscites, led to a shift in mood that gradually enabled Hitler to shed any pretense of legality and boldly claim a right to govern in his own name.

Hitler's opponents were never allowed so much as a moment to catch their breath, consider their options, or prepare a counterattack. The new chancellor immediately set his sights on the innermost sanctums of power, working with stunning speed but with a highly effective overall plan to seize key positions one after the other or else to drain them of their importance so that little more than hollow shells remained. The opposition was left off-balance, discouraged, and demoralized. To fathom the speed and vigor of this operation one need only look at Italy, where it took Mussolini nearly seven years to accumulate the kind of power Hitler amassed in only a few weeks. Even then the monarchy still lay outside Mussolini's orbit, providing Italians with a legitimate alternative—whatever its weaknesses—for which there was no equivalent in Germany.

One cannot fully comprehend the ease with which Hitler seized power, however, without giving some consideration to the weariness of the nation's democratic forces after fourteen years of political life in an unloved republic that seemed fated to stumble from one crisis to the next. Most of the leading figures in the republic, men who shortly before had appeared so stalwart, simply packed their bags and vanished in a state of nervous exhaustion—Otto Braun, for example, the "Red Tsar of Prussia"; his minister of the interior, Karl Severing, who presided over the best-equipped police force in the Reich; the leaders of the Reichsbanner, and many others. Men who had always insisted that they would yield only to force melted before any heat at all was applied. It seemed as if the Weimar Republic never overcame the impression that it was somehow just a temporary phenomenon. Born of sudden surrender and tainted from the outset by the moral condemnations heaped upon Germany, it never gained the broad loyalty of the population. Their contempt only increased with the virtual civil war that raged during its early years, the inflation of 1923, which impoverished much of the traditionally loyal middle class, and finally the Great Depression, when confusion, mass misery, and political drift destroyed any claim the young republic might have had to being the kind of orderly state Germans were accustomed to. This series of disasters contributed enormously to the impression that such a republic would not long endure.

The feeling that major change was needed was not confined to the Weimar Republic, with the particular handicaps under which it struggled. Throughout the Western world a rising tide of voices decried parliamentary democracy as a system without a future. Such convictions were particularly widespread in nations with no indigenous history or tradition of civil constitutional government. All across Europe, in countries where liberal democracy had emerged only a few years earlier to the cheers of the throngs, its funeral was now announced and its tombstone readied. Feeding on this burgeoning mood, Hitler convinced millions that he represented the birth of a new era. His display of total confidence in his mission heightened his attractiveness to a fearful, depressed people without hope or sense of purpose.

And how could the Führer's opponents expect to counter such a powerful appeal? Divided among themselves, unable to muster their strength, and long plagued by feelings of impotence, many simply gave up in the spring of 1933, convinced that they had been defeated not only by an overpowering political foe but by history itself. This abstract way of thinking, inherent in the German intellectual tradition and therefore all the more easily adopted, advanced the Nazi cause by lending Hitler's conquest of power an air of grave inevitability. A higher principle seemed to be at work, against which all human resistance would be in vain.

Such feelings were encouraged by a numbing barrage of propaganda—an art at which the Nazis realized they were far superior to any of their opponents. This was not the least of the reasons why, from the very outset, Hitler strained his governing coalition to the limit by demanding new elections to the Reichstag (only four months had passed since the last elections, in November 1932). An electoral campaign, after all, would allow his propaganda experts to display their prodigious talents to the full, especially now that he controlled the resources of the state. More than anyone else, the Nazis recognized the power of the new medium of radio and immediately set about seizing control of it. As the state radio network was in the hands of the government, they managed to ensure that all electoral speeches delivered by cabinet members were broadcast. The commentary for Hitler's appearances was provided by Goebbels himself. This master propagandist usually began on a solemn, dignified note, drawing on pseudoreligious imagery as he built to a fervid climax: "The people are standing and waiting and singing, their hands raised in the air," he once intoned while waiting for the Führer to arrive. "All you see are people, people, people . . . the German *Volk* that for fourteen long years has waited and suffered and bled. The German *Volk* that now is rising, calling and cheering for the Führer, the chancellor of the new Reich."[4]

The Nazis' opponents had little to offset the verve and drama of shows like this. In early February the Social Democrats, the Iron Front, and the Reichsbanner responded to the spectacular Nazi parade of January 30 by organizing a mighty demonstration of their own in the Lustgarten in Berlin. Thousands came, but the speeches reeked so of the timidity, indecision, and impotence of the old-time leaders that the crowd listened apathetically before finally slinking away, disappointed and downhearted, as if from some kind of farewell. What a contrast with the self-assured, boisterous, optimistic gatherings of the Nazis, which reverberated in the mind for days afterwards! The difference lay not only in the rhetoric. Even more telling were all the symbols of a break with the past and an exciting new beginning. Columns of troops marching in close formation, brilliant pageantry, and oceans of flags contrasted with the aimlessness and anxiety of the Weimar years and transformed politics into liturgy and grand ritual.

At the same time, the Nazis did not hesitate to employ force to achieve their ends, beginning in Prussia, by far the largest of the states. Prime Minister Hermann Göring was given a free hand under an emergency decree issued on February 6 and immediately began to evict politicians and public servants from office. In less than a month the police chiefs of fourteen large cities were dismissed, along with district administrators, rural prefects, and state officials. The pattern was much the same at every level of government: masses of Nazi party members would take to the streets in a staged popular uprising that the authorities claimed they could no longer contain. Public security was then declared in jeopardy, and government officials or SA leaders, usually with no administrative experience, were appointed on a "temporary" basis to replace the people dismissed from their positions. In this way, first uncooperative mayors were forced out and then, one after the other, the prime ministers of all the German states.

On February 27, 1933, the day of the Reichstag fire, Hitler and Papen went to President Hindenburg and presented him with an emergency decree, prepared in advance, "for the protection of the people and the state." The decree rescinded all basic rights and became the main legal foundation of the regime. The rule of law was abandoned in favor of a perpetual state of emergency. Hitler remarked shortly thereafter that he no longer needed a pretext to crack down on his opponents. With this emergency decree, he could "try enemies of the state legally and deal with them in a way that will put an end to conspiracies."

This photograph of the Reichstag on the morning of February 28 is a fake that was probably produced at the time. The flames and smoke were added to the picture. According to the police report, the fire was already under control half an hour after midnight, well before this picture would have been taken.

On February 22, Göring appointed units of the SA, the SS (the Schutz-Staffel, Hitler's private army), and the nationalistic Stahlhelm movement to positions as assistant police. There ensued a wave of beatings, arrests, and shootings as well as raids on private homes, party offices, and newspapers. The socialist streak within Hitler's brown-shirted SA surfaced in the guise of "anticapitalist" acts of terror against banks and the directors of stock exchanges. Special SA "capture squads" ferreted out "enemies of the state," blackmailing, beating, and torturing them in bunkers and *Heldenkellern* ("hero cellars"). There were fifty of these torture chambers in Berlin alone.[5] At about this time, the first Gestapo chief, Rudolf Diels, moved his headquarters into a former school of applied arts at 8 Prinz-Albrecht-Strasse, which would soon become one of Germany's most notorious addresses. Diels assisted the SA in arresting political opponents of the regime. Soon the jails were filled to overflowing, and prisoners had to be held in specially constructed holding areas that became known as "concentration camps."

The vast majority of the population, which was not directly affected by these illegal activities, accepted them with almost unbelievable equanimity in view of the gaping holes in the Nazi veneer of legality. This widespread apathy is at least somewhat explained by the demoralization of what had by then been more than three years of continuous depression and widespread poverty, not to mention the daily routine of going from unemployment office to shelter to soup kitchen. Moreover, people had grown accustomed over the years to unruliness and violence in the streets and were not overly shocked by the activities of the SA gangs. The public had long been fed up with anarchy on the streets. It yearned for a return to law and order and tended to interpret the SA's activities as a sign of government vigor that had been sorely lacking during the death throes of the Weimar Republic. Many people construed Nazi violence as the last means of achieving the sort of profound change in which the only hope of salvation lay. When the multiparty political system was eliminated, it was not missed by a population that had grown accustomed over the previous years to strong presidential powers and a government little influenced by objections raised in parliament.

The lack of effective resistance to Hitler can also be attributed to the divided feelings that Hitler quickly learned to manipulate and exploit. Everything he did, including his surprise lunges for power and arbitrary acts, was planned in such a way that at least part of the population would have good reason to feel thankful to him. Often people were left feeling torn, as can be seen in records of contemporary reactions, which were often far more uncertain, vacillating, and contradictory than is commonly believed. Many Germans found their hopes raised one moment and dashed the next. Their fears, too, rose and fell.

This Nazi tactic was well suited to a sharply divided society in which many irreconcilable interests and ideologies clashed. The fruits could be seen in the almost immediate crackdown on Communists, whose persecution and arrest, often outside the judicial system, was greeted with relief by many people, despite their doubts about the justice and legality of it all. Similarly torn feelings surfaced at the time of the boycott of Jewish shops and department stores on April 1, 1933, even though the conditions were admittedly different. And again, in the summer of 1934, the public viewed with ambivalence the Night of the Long Knives, Hitler's purge of the SA, which seemed to suggest that the Führer shared the public's mounting disgust with SA hooliganism but which also showed, to the horror of many, his willingness to eliminate anyone who crossed him.

▪ ▪ ▪

Hitler's road to power was thus paved with a mixture of legality, anarchy, and arbitrary strikes at specific targets. The lack of strong public reaction to the numerous excesses and acts of violence was also related to the always widespread need to conform. There was a profound yearning for order, too, and a desire to identify with the state. In times of sweeping social change, opportunism and eagerness for advancement also figure prominently, hence the masses of new Nazi supporters who suddenly emerged from the woodwork in the first few weeks after Hitler came to power and who were referred to ironically as *Märzgefallene* ("those who fell in March").

Finally, one of the most striking features of the first six months of Nazi rule was the general eagerness to share in the sense of belonging and in the celebration of the fraternal bond among all Germans. Even intellectuals seemed to grow tired of the stale, stuffy air in their studies and to long to join the historic movement "down on the streets," sharing in the warmth and personal closeness of the "national revival." Among the curious platitudes making the rounds and gaining ever more converts was the cry that one should not "stand off aside" but "join the ranks" as the nation blazed a new trail. No one could say where this trail might lead, but at least it was away from Weimar.

■ ■ ■

Such were the tactical and psychological ploys that Hitler used to accumulate power. Also instrumental were what Fritz Stern calls the "temptations" of National Socialism: promises of a national rebirth, revision of the Treaty of Versailles, and a strong state.[6] All this was accompanied by Hitler's sonorous evocations of tradition, Germany's cultural roots, and its Christian values, each of which he repeatedly invoked in his rhetorical flights.

The Nazi movement was also surrounded by an aura of socialist ideas, which formed part of its appeal. Although the Weimar Republic had broken sharply in many ways with the Reich of the kaisers, it had clung to the past more closely than it should have. The republic paid dearly throughout its short life for failing to enact a social revolution in the wake of the postwar turmoil between 1918 and 1920 and for continuing to bear the legacies of the Germany of old. Many of the members of the conservative bourgeoisie also nursed unfulfilled desires for reform and a feeling that society desperately needed a thorough revamping. The vague but clearly radical program of the Nazis was interpreted as offering hope for the satisfaction of certain demands, such as greater social mobility, new economic opportunities, and social justice. Like all other mass movements, the Nazi movement owed at least some of its dynamism and vigor to this widespread desire for change.

These aspects of the Nazi movement were widely noted, and they appealed to the sentimental socialism of the German people. Despite its enormous contrasts with the traditional left, the Nazi brand of socialism stemmed from the same social and intellectual crisis of the first half of the nineteenth century. To be sure, the Nazi movement was not rooted, as traditional socialism was, in the humanist tradition.

But it did aim to create an egalitarian society and a sense of fraternity among its members, to be achieved through what it called the *Volks-gemeinschaft,* or community of the people. National Socialism rejected freedom, but the mood of the day placed more emphasis, in any case, on a sense of belonging and a place in the social order. The Nazis promised security and an improved standard of living, especially for working people and the petty bourgeoisie. The results included housing projects, community work programs, and the "beauty of work" plan, as well as social welfare programs ranging from subsidies during the winter months and "Nazi welfare" to the leisure cruises for workers organized by the Kraft durch Freude ("Strength through Joy") organization.

The Nazi brand of socialism was particularly attractive because of its appeal to nationalism. This, and virtually only this, was what concealed the real nature of the Nazi revolution, encouraging the mistaken but widespread view, at the time and later, that National Socialism was essentially a conservative movement. In reality it was egalitarian and destructive of traditional structures. However, in wrapping its radical core in a layer of German nationalism, it seemed not only to assert the long-neglected national interest, but also to meld the general desire for change with the equally strong need to preserve the familiar. People wanted a new, modernized Germany but they also feared it, and the cultivation of ritualistic Germanic theater, folklore, and local customs provided a comfortable setting for a radical break with the past. It was the combination of apparent conservatism with promises of change, the tempering of the one with the other, that brought National Socialism a level of popularity that Marxism's international socialism, with its adamant insistence on progress, could never achieve. Hitler's appeal to Germany's traditionally leftist working class cannot be understood if these factors are ignored—as they so often have been—or dismissed as mere demagoguery.

Increasingly convinced of the hopelessness of any opposition and hard pressed by the persecution and prohibitions they faced, many opponents of the Nazis—especially those on the left—decided to leave Germany. In so doing, however, they were abandoning the workers to their fates, as Carlo Mierendorff, later one of the leaders of the resistance group known as the Kreisau Circle, pointed out at the time. "*They* can't just all go to the Riviera," he replied when concerned friends advised him to flee.[7] Opponents of the Nazis who remained in Germany had only two options: they could attempt to influence the course of events from within the system, enduring all the illusions, self-deceptions, and unwelcome involvements that almost inevitably accompany such a double life, or they could accept social exclusion and often personal isolation, turning their backs on the "miracle of a unifying Germany," as the Nazis' self-laudatory propaganda described the emerging sense of community and revival.

Many people who felt torn by this dilemma have described what it meant for them. Wilhelm Hoegner, the future prime minister of Bavaria, recalled wandering through the streets of Munich feeling that all of a sudden they had become hostile and threatening.[8] Helmuth von Moltke's mother felt profoundly uprooted, as if she "no longer belonged to the country."[9] Others have spoken of losing old friends, of an atmosphere of suspicion, of spying neighbors and the rapid disintegration of their social lives even as the alleged brotherhood of all Germans was being celebrated in delirious parades and pseudo-religious services, mass swearings of oaths and vows under domes of light, addresses by the Führer, nightly bonfires on hills and mountains, secular chants and hymns. All this fervor was fueled by the intense sensation that history was in the making. For the first time since the rule of the kaisers, Germans seemed to be living in a country which celebrated both leadership and political liturgy.

In the week leading up to the March 5 Reichstag elections, the Nazis pushed both national exaltation and unbridled violence to new heights. Goebbels proclaimed March 5 the "Day of the Awakening Nation" and orchestrated nationwide mass demonstrations and parades, processions and carefully staged appearances. The brilliance and ubiquity of these events left the Nazis' coalition partner, the German National People's Party, completely overshadowed. Meanwhile, the other parties were subjected to every kind of sabotage and disruption, while the police sat idly by in accordance with their instructions. By election day fifty-one anti-Nazis lay dead and hundreds had been injured. The Nazis themselves counted eighteen dead. On the eve of the election Hitler appeared in the city of Königsberg. Just as he was ending his rapt appeal to the German people—"Hold thy head high and proud once more! Now thou art free once again, with the help of God"—a hymn could be heard swelling in the background, and the bells of the Königsberg cathedral pealed during the final stanza. Meanwhile, on the hills and mountains along Germany's borders, "bonfires of freedom" were lit.

Nazi expectations of overwhelming victory at the polls and at least an absolute majority in the Reichstag were to be dashed, however. Despite all they had done to intimidate their opponents, the National Socialists increased their vote by only about six points, to 43.9 percent of the total. The other parties suffered only minor losses. Having failed to win an absolute majority, the Nazis were forced to continue relying on the German National People's Party, together with whom they had a scant majority of 51.9 percent of the vote. Angered at the results, Hitler complained to his cronies on the evening of the election that he would never be free of that German National "gang" as long as Hindenburg was alive.[10]

As the election results showed, many Germans were still unwilling to embrace the Nazis and their new era—far more unwilling, indeed, than Nazi propagandists would admit. Many citizens reacted to the election with curiously mixed feelings: enthusiasm for the new regime alternated with anxiety; hope for more jobs gave way to renewed doubts; confusion was resolved by the sense of pride the Nazis so skillfully evoked. Occasionally, especially on the far left, entire street-fighting organizations such as the Communist Rotfrontkämpferbund switched sides, joining ranks with those who had been their bitter enemies only days before. On the right, many non-Nazi groups hastened to "get in line" or even disband before being forced to do so. All this is well documented, but far less is known of the countless opponents of the regime who simply "disappeared" during the first weeks and months of Nazi rule. Police records show that by mid-October 1933 about twenty-six thousand people had been arrested, while many more vanished without legal formalities into the hastily constructed concentration camps that were spreading across the land. According to official figures, some three million people were incarcer-

ated for political transgressions during the twelve years of Nazi rule;
another statistic, however, shows that only 225,000 people were actually brought to trial in political cases during the first six years.[11]

. . .

Our picture of these years would not be complete without mention of
how all established political formations, on both the left and the right,
melted away without resistance. Nothing so reveals the exhaustion of
the Weimar Republic as the pathetic end of its political parties and
organizations. Even Hitler was astonished: "Such a miserable collapse
would never have been thought possible," he said in Dortmund in
early July 1933.[12] Prohibitions, seizures of buildings, and confiscations
of property that a short time before would have brought Germany to
the verge of civil war now elicited only shrugs. A "Potsdam Day"
ceremony on March 21, 1933, celebrated the inauguration of the new
parliament with a review of troops, organ music, and gun salutes.
Former chancellor Heinrich Brüning commented that when he
joined a column of deputies headed for the garrison church, where
the ceremony took place, he felt as if he were being taken "to the
execution grounds."[13] There was more truth to this than he realized.

It could even be said that Brüning and his companions had sentenced themselves to their fate. They were not single-handedly responsible for the decline of the republic, even if they had hastened its
demise through their weakness and blindness; the republic had had to
face far too many opponents at home and abroad throughout its short
life and was hardly blessed by good fortune. But the men who served
it in high office were thoroughly lacking in judgment when they failed
to recognize the extreme danger that Hitler posed to the German
republic and to themselves and failed to take any measures of self-
defense.

The Weimar leadership had been seeking to evade responsibility
since 1930, with the SPD leading the way, attempting to recover its
status as the "glorious opposition of old" while pointing ever more
urgently to the mounting "threat to democracy."[14] In December 1932
Major General Kurt von Schleicher, who immediately preceded

After Hitler seized power in January 1933, the number of people who had been arrested for political reasons was far greater than the staged jubilation in the streets and squares might have indicated. By mid-October the police had recorded about twenty-six thousand arrests. Many more victims, however, were dispatched without official proceedings to one of the many concentration camps spreading across the land. Official figures show that only 225,000 people were actually brought to trial during the first six years of National Socialist rule.

Above: Inmates of the Sachsenhausen concentration camp near Oranienburg during a roll call.

Hitler as chancellor, made a final stab at saving the republic, but that effort foundered, undermined by the cold indolence of the leaders who, while talking passionately of their commitment to democracy, abandoned the nation to its fate. Even after Hitler gained control of the "fortress," as the republic was often called, they failed to recog-

On March 21, 1933, known as Potsdam Day, Hitler staged an elaborate ceremony celebrating the reconciliation of the old and new Germanys. His partners on this occasion were conservatives who imagined they could "tame" him. Their illusions, however, would soon be dispelled. Above: Hitler with Vice-Chancellor Franz von Papen and Defense Minister Werner von Blomberg.

nize what was right before their eyes. When news arrived that Hitler had been named chancellor, Rudolf Breitscheid, the Social Democratic leader in the Reichstag, clapped with joy that Hitler would now show himself for what he really was. He did, of course, and Breitscheid met his end in Buchenwald. Julius Leber, who would become a leading figure in the resistance, commented disdainfully at the time that he, like everyone else, was looking forward finally to seeing "the intellectual foundations of this movement."[15]

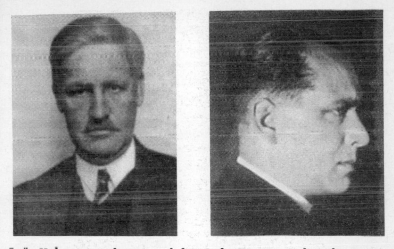

Left: *Hitler was underestimated during the Weimar era by politicians on both the left and right. Rudolf Breitscheid, the leader of the Social Democrats in the Reichstag, reportedly clapped with joy when he heard that Hitler had been named chancellor, believing that Hitler would now be exposed for what he really was. Just two months later Breitscheid was driven into exile in France. He was then extradited back to Germany by the Vichy government after the conquest of France. He died in August 1944 during an Allied air attack on the Buchenwald concentration camp, where he was interned.*

Right: *Julius Leber was one of the most charismatic and determined figures in the German resistance. A Social Democratic Party deputy in the Reichstag, he barely escaped being murdered by the National Socialists the day after Hitler seized power in January 1933. He spent the next four years in a concentration camp. In 1943 Stauffenberg drew him and his friends into the inner circles of the conspiracy, thereby opening the entire resistance movement to the political left. When Hitler became chancellor, Leber commented, "We're not afraid of these fellows. We are determined to take up the struggle against them."*

The miscalculations of those on the right, a result of arrogance and a lack of political instinct, were even more appalling. Their ideological affinities with the Nazis, their assumption of commonality on national issues, and their aversion to both democracy and Marxism led many to conclude that Hitler was just a radical version of themselves. The vast majority believed that conservative interests were safe in Hitler's

hands despite his distastefully rough, vulgar manner. In their condescending way, they assumed that they would soon be able to take this
demagogue in hand and tame him. They confidently imagined they
could restrict him to delivering speeches, staging Nazi circuses, and
venting his "architectural spleen," while they steered the ship of state.
Although it should have been obvious to anyone who looked beneath
the nationalistic, conservative surface, what the right failed to comprehend was the revolutionary essence of Nazism, bent on destroying
the traditional bonds, loyalties, and outmoded social structures that
the right-wing parties were so eager to restore. Hitler was no mere
rabble-rouser whose popularity conservatives could exploit to solve
their old problem of being a self-appointed ruling class without a
following. It would be some time before they understood this. By
1938 Hjalmar Schacht, whom Hitler had reappointed to his old position as president of the Reichsbank, was overheard commenting to a
table companion, "My dear lady, we have fallen into the hands of
criminals. How could I ever have imagined it!"[16]

Hitler's right-wing coalition partners owed their sense of security
to two factors: their "strongmen" in the cabinet—Vice-Chancellor
Franz von Papen and Alfred Hugenberg, leader of the German na-
tionalists—and the army, which they envisioned would soon clamp
down on the rowdyism and lawlessness that they saw as the only
blemish on the Nazi revolution. The supreme commander of the
armed forces was, after all, none other than that conservative stalwart
President Paul von Hindenburg. The right-wing parties were certainly not misguided in claiming him and the clout of his office as
their own; they failed, however, to consider the frailty of the old man.
He may still have cut a fine figure, but he was by this point little more
than a majestic-looking marionette, easily manipulated by self-serving
interests lurking in the background.

Hitler fully intended to take advantage of the weakness and tracta-
bility of the president, and success was not long in coming. Papen was
inordinately proud of a concession he had obtained that stipulated he
be present whenever Hitler met with Hindenburg. The president,
however, soon informed Papen that this arrangement betrayed a distrust that his "dear young friend," as he sometimes called Hitler,

could not long be expected to endure. Hitler managed to get his way time after time in the selection of the cabinet by playing his conservative coalition partners off against each other. On the afternoon of January 29, for instance, the day before he became chancellor, he let it be known in preliminary discussions that he would be prepared to accept as minister of defense the outgoing chancellor, his old and hated foe General Schleicher. But at literally the last minute, he abruptly changed course, managing with the help of Hindenburg and Papen to slip General Werner von Blomberg into the post. Impulsive and easily influenced, Blomberg was given to flights of fancy, earning among his army comrades the nickname "the rubber lion." Hitler went back on other agreements as well: he insisted, despite a previous understanding, that a Nazi be appointed Prussian minister of the interior; most importantly, he managed, once again with Papen's help, to push Hugenberg into agreeing in principle to new elections on March 5, 1933, though Hugenberg remained extremely reluctant and was still resisting in the president's antechamber until just before the swearing-in ceremony. All these steps were further moves toward disarming and quashing the conservative forces.

Even before the new government had taken power, the conservatives' plan to "tame" Hitler had begun to look shaky. Papen was warned of this repeatedly but maintained that the doomsayers were in error: "You're wrong," the vice-chancellor stormed, "we have his solid commitment." Papen even went so far as to boast that he would soon have Hitler backed so tightly into a corner that he would "squeak."[17] Instead, Papen was blindsided by the new chancellor, who toured the country making triumphant appearances, a performance that the vice-chancellor could hardly hope to match. Although Papen must have realized by this time that Hitler was not about to be tamed, he still failed to perceive that he had gotten himself into the untenable political position of opposing both the democratic, constitutional state and Hitler's mounting autocracy. The haughty simplemindedness of the conservative members of the cabinet was on full display in their eagerness to see the constitution set aside, even though it was the foundation of their own power and security. They looked forward just as eagerly to the passage of the Enabling Act on March 23, which freed

Hitler from the last remaining constraints of constitutional law and cleared the way for him to seize virtually unlimited power. By late June 1933 the German National People's Party was forced to dissolve despite its insistence on its rights as a coalition partner in the "cabinet of national revival." Its powerful leader, Alfred Hugenberg, was made to resign from the government by Hitler, in contravention of all the Führer's earlier assurances.

The venerable Social Democratic Party met an equally pathetic end. "A signal will come," the party's leader, Otto Wels, had assured restless members who were eager to rise up against Hitler. As time passed, though, it became increasingly apparent that no one had any idea where the signal would come from and what it would mean.[18] The SPD leadership had no ready response either to Hitler's accession to power or, once he was in office, to his tactics. It was especially in the tactical arena that it utterly failed to match him. Some of the befuddled SPD leaders, still enmired in theories of class struggle, continued to see Hugenberg as the real foe and Hitler as a mere front man or "agent of the reaction." The SPD leadership was inundated with demands that it organize resistance activities, but instead it sought to calm the waters by pointing to the guarantees in the constitution, though the constitution was clearly being disassembled. From January 30 on, the SPD issued repeated statements that it would not be the *first* to overstep the bounds of legality. This seemed to be a threat to fight fire with fire, but such hints were far too mild to make much of an impression on Hitler; indeed, they did not even move him to scorn. The chief effect of the statements was to demoralize the party rank and file, which could not help noticing the leadership's lack of backbone and its readiness to capitulate. In February and March 1933 the first wave of resignations from party organizations began, presumably registering members' fear, disappointment, or acceptance of the inevitable. In May many of the SPD's local associations voluntarily disbanded, anticipating in their confusion and sense of isolation the ultimate dissolution and prohibition of the SPD itself on June 22.

The once mighty trade unions came to similar if not even more pitiful ends. As early as the end of February 1933, union leaders had already abandoned the SPD's principled opposition to the regime in an attempt to preserve their "influence over the structuring of social life," not to mention their union halls, hostels, and charitable institutions.[19] In March they began signaling their allegiance to the new authorities and even issued declarations of loyalty despite the harassment and arrest of union leaders all across Germany. True to form, Hitler correctly perceived these attempts to appease him as signs of weakness. The reliability of his instincts was confirmed shortly thereafter by the union leadership itself. When Hitler acceded to the old union demand, which had never been granted by the Weimar Republic, to make May 1 a national workers' holiday, union leaders summoned their members to participate in the official ceremonies, and the world was treated to the spectacle of unionized blue- and white-collar workers marching in parades beneath swastika flags and listening bitterly but with forced applause to the speeches of their triumphant foes. This humiliating experience did more than anything else to break the will to resist among millions of organized workers. Just one day later, on May 2, union halls were occupied, their property was confiscated, and union members were swallowed into the newly established Nazi workers' organization, the German Labor Front.

The Communist Party, too, disappeared with barely a whimper, in an atmosphere of quiet terror, flight, and quick reversals of old allegiance. Right up to the brink of Hitler's "new age," it had stood its ground as a powerful foe not only of the Nazis but of the entire established order. For years the Nazis had fed on fears that the Communist movement sowed among the middle classes and had welcomed them as they fled its predictions of catastrophe. The image Hitler liked to project of himself as a savior was based largely on the great showdown that he sought with the Communists, and he saw the struggle to which he now dedicated all the powers of the state as only the prelude to a worldwide battle for supremacy.

But the Communist opponent, like other opponents, failed to materialize. Rosa Luxemburg's famous question of 1918, "Where is the German proletariat?" once again went unanswered. Seemingly unimpressed by either the persecution and flight of its leading members or the mass desertions among the rank and file, which began immediately upon Hitler's appointment as chancellor, the Communist Party persisted in its dogmatic belief that its most dangerous enemy was the Social Democrats. Fascism and parliamentary democracy were viewed as the same at bottom, and Hitler only a puppet of powerful interests. A resolution passed by the executive committee of the Comintern on April 1, 1933, insisted in rigid, ideological fashion that Hitler would sooner or later open the gates to the dictatorship of the Communist Party. "We're next," was the steadfast Communist refrain of those weeks, as well as *"Hitler regiert—aber der Kommunismus marschiert!"* ("Hitler rules but Communism is on the march!") The party still had not come to its senses by the summer of 1933, when it announced that its main task was to "train our fire more heavily than ever" on the Social Democrats.[20]

The Communists paid dearly for their blindness. The party evaporated without any sign of defiance, act of resistance, or even parting message to its militants. Its officials were arrested and its subsidiary organizations crushed. Those members who escaped became fugitives. Some took to plotting in nameless conspiracies that were usually quite local in nature. It is true that many Communists sacrificed their lives resisting the Nazis long before military, church, or conservative circles got into the act. But the Communist Party itself was responsible for the isolation in which its members found themselves and from which they never escaped; it was responsible as well as for the impotence of their "silent revolt," which has faded, therefore, from memory.[21] Over the years, Communist resistance cells occasionally approached other resistance groups, Social Democrats in particular, with offers to join forces, but the distrust sown between 1930 and 1934 never dissipated and these feelers were generally ignored. When one such offer was actually listened to and considered, it resulted in one of the most devastating setbacks in the history of the German resistance, as we shall see.

The crushing of left-wing parties and the trade unions left the working class without an organizational framework. Individuals who resolved to continue the struggle found themselves alone or in league with just a few close friends. Many working-class leaders were imprisoned. Others withdrew into their private lives and a few went underground. But most left Germany to live in exile, continuing to send messages home, encouraging and advising those who remained behind. It soon became clear, however, that very few of the former rank and file were still listening. The sharp decline in unemployment, the improving economy, and the social programs of the new regime had produced a sense of general well-being, even pride, among the working class. Memories of their socialist days, especially given the disappointments toward the end, faded fast. The enormous self-confidence of the Nazis in their handling of labor is suggested by the release from concentration camps in 1937 and 1938 of three once popular labor leaders—Julius Leber, Carlo Mierendorff, and the last acting chairman of the General German Trade Union Federation, Wilhelm Leuschner.

Not only did the Social Democrats, Communists, and German Nationals accept their fate quietly, so did all other political parties, leagues, professional organizations, and civic associations, though they often had long, proud histories. The Protestant Church alone successfully resisted Nazi co-optation, albeit at the price of constant disputes and schisms. It succeeded because the regime made the mistake of openly attacking it too soon, having assumed that it would fall easily into line because so many of its pastors leaned toward the German Nationals. The church rallied its forces and asserted its independence at a synod held in Barmen in May 1934. Barely two years later, however, Protestant unity broke down; the majority formed a purely religious wing and, motivated by the Lutheran tradition of deference to authority, sought an arrangement with the state, while the remainder continued the struggle, emphasizing their rejection of the totalitarian and neo-pagan proclivities of the regime. The central figure in this minority wing was Pastor Martin Niemöller, who had been a submarine captain in the First World War. Niemöller was arrested on July 1, 1937, and sentenced, after a show trial, to seven months' imprisonment. At Hitler's express orders, he was then rearrested and incarcerated as a "personal prisoner of the Führer" in the Sachsenhausen concentration camp, where he remained until April 1945.

Relations between the Nazi regime and the Catholic Church developed in virtually reverse order. At first the church was quite hostile and its bishops energetically denounced the "false doctrines" of the Nazis. Its opposition weakened considerably, however, when, at Papen's initiative, the Nazis undertook negotiations with the Vatican and successfully concluded a concordat on July 20, 1933. In the following years, the chairman of the Conference of Bishops, Cardinal Bertram of Breslau, developed an ineffectual protest system that satisfied the demands of the other bishops without annoying the regime.[22] Only gradually did the Catholic Church find its way back to a firmer brand of resistance in the efforts of individual clerics such as Cardinal Preysing of Berlin, Bishop Galen of Münster, and Bishop Gröber of Freiburg, although even their work was attenuated by internal disputes and tactical disagreements. The regime retaliated with occasional arrests, the withdrawal of teaching privileges, and the seizure of church publishing houses and printing facilities.

Resistance within both churches therefore remained largely a matter of individual conscience. In general they attempted merely to assert their own rights and only rarely issued pastoral letters or declarations indicating any fundamental objection to Nazi ideology. More than any other institutions, however, the churches provided a forum in which individuals could distance themselves from the regime. Because the Nazi policy of *Gleichschaltung*, or conformity to the party line and codes of behavior, encountered such forceful opposition from the churches, Hitler decided to postpone a showdown until after the war.

The various militant wings of the old parties, the independent youth organizations, and universities fared no better than the official political groups: they, too, were dissolved or co-opted without much sign of resistance. Any remaining assertions of autonomy were soon muted by countless qualms, attempts to appease the new ruling party, and timidity masquerading as respect for the law. The heavy-handed metaphors that the Nazis so loved—the images Goebbels concocted of storms sweeping Germany, of emptying hourglasses, of faces rising to meet the dawn—may not have been aesthetic triumphs but they hit their mark precisely. In just a few feverish weeks a highly heterogeneous society with innumerable centers of power and influence, independent institutions, and autonomous bodies was reduced to "mere, uniform, obedient ashes."[23] The *Gleichschaltung* process was completed on July 14, 1933, with a burst of new laws, the most important of which declared the National Socialist German Workers' Party—the Nazis—to be the only legal political party.

. . .

There was that day no sense of break or rupture; it simply marked the legal end of the Weimar Republic. Feelings of regret were few. People felt, often for very different reasons, that the republic had meant nothing or very little to them. There was even a sense of relief that it was finally all over. The republic, basic civil rights, the multiparty system, and democratic restraints on the exercise of political power were all firmly relegated to the past. Barely five months after Hitler's appointment as chancellor, those days seemed very remote indeed. Robert Musil wrote at the time that he felt that "the things that were abolished did not really matter very much to people anymore."[24] The future did not lie there, whatever direction it might take. Perhaps the future did indeed lie with Hitler's new order, which as it expanded and gained converts suddenly seemed to have some rational arguments on its side as well.

One must remember that the people who looked with such equanimity on the demise of the Weimar Republic had no conception of what they were getting into or of the horrendous despotism, criminality, and deprivation of rights that awaited them under a totalitarian regime. Most thought that they would soon find themselves, after a draconian transitional period, living under an authoritarian government running a strict, well-organized state. The total failure to grasp what was at stake can be seen in the comments of one leading Social Democrat after Hitler first came to power. Even after having listened daily to terrifying reports about the fates of old political comrades who had been beaten or seized by SA raiding parties, arrested, and dragged off to concentration camps, the worst that he could imagine scarcely surpassed the persecution of socialists under Bismarck. "We took care of Wilhelm and Bismarck and we'll take care of today's reactionaries as well!" he confidently informed his audiences in campaign speeches.[25] Some believed that Hitler's star would eventually burn out. At the SPD's last mass rally in Berlin, Otto Wels assured his listeners that "harsh rulers don't last long."[26] Others expected Hitler would soon meet his comeuppance in foreign affairs, when the great powers of Europe turned on him.

Although the Weimar Republic was dead, its ambiguous legacies lived on. With the benefit of time and despite the stunning setbacks of 1933, people here and there began to find the courage and determination to resist. Only now did it become apparent, however, how burned out and useless the rubble of Weimar was. Scattered resistance cells sprouted across the land, but they found themselves unwilling or unable to build on alliances from an earlier period. Communist offers to work with the Social Democrats met, for example, with deep suspicion—yet another legacy of the past. The resistance to Hitler therefore had to be built anew, on fundamentally different foundations. The deep enmity between the various political camps toward the end of the republic left the budding resistance fractured into small circles and cells, which often had no contact with one another despite physical proximity. They all agreed that it was essential to resist but most were reluctant to join forces. The old tensions continued to affect relations among them as late as 1944 and even flared up after the war both in scholarly and in more politically driven disputes over the history of the resistance.

The memory of Weimar also shaped the conspirators' conceptions of the political order they hoped to institute. None of the surviving plans hold up liberal democracy as a desirable model. Some historians have severely criticized this failing, but in so doing they have tended to forget the experiences of the conspirators, who hoped to present the German people with "credible" alternatives to the Nazi regime and felt unable, wherever they stood on the political spectrum, to include the Weimar system among them.[27] They argued that among other things Weimar had fostered the rise of Hitler. Carl Goerdeler, a leader of the civilian resistance, spoke of the "curse of parliamentarism," which almost always placed "party interests above the good of the nation."[28] In endless debates, whose intensity and poignancy are mirrored in the surviving documents, the members of the resistance devoted enormous efforts to developing evermore cumbersome and peculiar political models that wavered between restoration of the past and social utopianism; only occasionally is there evidence of a truly forward-looking idea.

The ease with which Hitler triumphed in Germany, the string of international political victories that the European powers soon permitted him, and the omnipresence of his secret police combined to convince anti-Nazis that there could be no question of a mass uprising or general strike like the one staged thirteen years earlier to thwart the Kapp putsch. There was also little hope for a coup from above by powerful elites in society and the government bureaucracy, so quickly and thoroughly had Hitler penetrated all social organizations.

One institution, however, had managed to preserve most of its traditional autonomy and internal cohesion: the army. As Hitler himself said at the time, half indignant and half impressed, it was "the last instrument of state whose worldview has survived intact."[29] The army alone also possessed the means to overthrow a regime so obsessed with security. Its great dilemma was that any coup it staged would put an enormous strain on long-standing loyalties and would necessarily threaten the continued existence of the state, to which it was deeply committed by tradition and professional ethic.

Nevertheless, whenever individuals or small groups came together to discuss conspiracy against the state, regardless of their background or concerns, their gaze turned almost inevitably to the military. Equally inevitably, for the reasons outlined above, all thought of resistance became part of a vicious circle, which determined the events of the next few years.

2

THE ARMY SUCCUMBS

In the early evening of February 3, 1933, only four days after becoming chancellor, Hitler hurried to 14 Bendlerstrasse to pay a first formal call on the leaders of the Reichswehr. The military commanders were reputed to be remote, secretive, and arrogant, and Hitler had gone to the meeting with some trepidation, because he knew they would play a key role in both his immediate schemes to seize power in Germany and his more long-range plans for expansion abroad.

Hitler understood well that many of the younger officers sympathized with him and his movement, albeit in a rather vague way. They felt that the Weimar Republic had suffered in both its internal and foreign dealings from a lack of courage and resolve, and they looked now to Hitler to cast off the Treaty of Versailles, restore the prestige of the army, improve their chances for personal advancement and promotion, and bring about real social change. Hopes for a renewal so sweeping that it could be deemed a revolution were common, especially among the younger officers who later joined the resistance. Henning von Tresckow, for instance, campaigned for the Nazis in the officers' mess in Potsdam as early as the late 1920s, dismissing detractors as hopelessly reactionary. Soon after the Nazis seized power Albrecht Mertz von Quirnheim had himself transferred to the SA. Helmuth Stieff and many others also threw in their lot with the new cause. There is apparently no truth, however, to the tale that an enthusiastic Stauffenberg placed himself at the head of a crowd surging through Bamberg in celebration of Hitler's nomination as chancellor.[1]

Senior officers took quite a different view, though the Weimar Republic had always seemed alien to them as well. They had high hopes that an authoritarian regime would not only wash away the "shame of Versailles" but also help reconcile the state and the army, thereby returning to them the influence they had once wielded in the corridors of government. Hitler's talk of party and army as the "twin pillars" on which the National Socialist state rested seemed to imply that they would regain the political leverage they had lost under the republic. Senior officers also imagined themselves powerful enough to determine the bounds of their own authority, within which Hitler would be prevented from interfering. But even so, they had serious reservations about the Nazis' rowdy, anarchistic behavior, their undisguised contempt for the law, the terrorism of the SA, and last but not least, the personage of the Führer himself, whose vulgar, hucksterish ways prompted one senior officer to say what they all more or less felt: Hitler was "not a gentleman but just an ordinary guy."[2]

In his official quarters on Bendlerstrasse, General Kurt von Hammerstein-Equord, the army commander in chief, greeted Hitler with obvious skepticism. An officer who was present reported that Hammerstein introduced the chancellor "in a benevolently condescending fashion; the assembled phalanx of generals were coolly polite, and Hitler made modest, obsequious little bows in all directions. He remained ill at ease until after dinner, when he was allowed an opportunity to speak for a longer period at the table."[3] Drawing on all his skills of persuasion, Hitler did his best to win the officers over. He promised that conditions within Germany would be "completely reversed," military preparedness would be improved, and—according to the notes of another of the participants—there would be "no tolerance of any views that run counter to the objectives [pacifism!]. Those who do not convert will have to be bent. Marxism will be eradicated, root and branch." On the subject of foreign policy, Hitler referred primarily to abandoning the terms of the Treaty of Versailles and mentioned only in passing "the conquest of new Lebensraum in the

East." The latter comment did not arouse any particular surprise or doubts among the generals, who were skeptical about politicians to begin with and did not pay especially close attention to their exact words. More important to the assembled officers was Hitler's assurance that, in contrast to developments in Italy, there would be "no amalgamation of the Reichswehr and the party-affiliated SA" and that the army would remain "apolitical and nonpartisan."[4] Many of the officers came away with the impression that Hitler would prove a more congenial chancellor than any of his predecessors over the previous few years, although opinion was divided. Applause was only polite, and Hitler himself remarked afterwards that he felt as if he was "talking to a wall the whole time."[5]

The cracks that the Führer nevertheless found in this wall were the newly appointed minister of defense, Werner von Blomberg, and the head of the Bureau of Ministers, Colonel Walter von Reichenau. Confounding the expectations of the German Nationalist leaders who helped make Hitler chancellor, these two military men would soon become enthusiastic supporters of the Nazi cause, though for very different reasons. Blomberg was an impulsive, unsettled figure, who in the course of his life had embraced in quick succession democracy, the anthroposophy of Rudolf Steiner, and Prussian socialism, then had come close to accepting Communism after a trip to Russia, and eventually had endorsed the authoritarian state, before falling for Hitler with all the exuberance of his nature. Later he said that in 1933 he was suddenly filled with feelings that he had never expected to experience again: faith, reverence for a leader, and total devotion to an idea. Hitler, he once remarked, acted on him "like a great physician."[6] According to Blomberg's intimates, a friendly comment from the Führer was enough to bring tears to his eyes.

Reichenau, on the other hand, was the very embodiment of the modern officer, devoid of prejudice or sentiment. With the cool calculation of one lacking strong political sympathies of his own, he perceived the new men in government simply as the leaders of a mass movement whose strength he would tap to improve the position of the army and enhance Germany's glory and prestige. A gifted man who combined elegance, toughness, and a taste for power, he was never personally tempted by National Socialism; he respected it as a

One of the most strong-willed and inscrutable German military leaders was Walther von Reichenau. The very essence of a modern officer, devoid of prejudice, sentiment, or conviction, Reichenau saw National Socialism as little more than a mass movement that he could exploit to enhance the status of the army and the prestige of Germany. He contributed even more than his superior, Minister of Defense Blomberg, to delivering the army into Hitler's hands.

political force without taking its ideology seriously. Reichenau believed that the Reichswehr, with its "seven antiquated divisions scattered across the entire country," was totally incapable of asserting itself. To expect it to do so was a "daydream" suitable only to the realm of "fiction." Hoping to cement the army's relationship with Hitler, marginalize the Nazi Party, and edge out its paramilitary wing, the SA, he proposed that the Reichswehr adopt the motto "Forward into the new state."[7]

Reichenau was relatively undisturbed by the excesses that accompanied the Nazi seizure of power. It always required an element of terror, he said soon after assuming his new position, to purge a state of all its rot and decay. What did cause him considerable dismay, however, was the mounting power of the SA. Its ranks had swollen to over a million since the mass conversions of the spring of 1933, and it was expressing its dissatisfaction ever more vehemently. Hitler's brown-shirted legions took a dim view of his legal revolution, which seemed to be undermining their interests, and they looked on bitterly as conservative politicians, aristocrats, capitalists, and generals—the very men whose worlds they wanted to smash—began assuming places of honor at celebrations of the national revival, while they, the eternally mistreated foot soldiers of the revolution, were expected simply to parade by.

The brownshirts felt they were the vanguard of the revolution, not just extras. They had learned from their slogans and songs how revolutions had been carried out since time immemorial: the fortresses of the old order were stormed in a torrent of bloodshed and plunder and the new order raised on the wreckage of the old—with the greatest rewards going to the most loyal soldiers. They could not understand Hitler's sly concept of revolution by infiltration and ruse, and their rugged leader, Ernst Röhm, was particularly lacking in the patience and cunning required. And so, while the SA continued, in the disorderly style it had adopted in the spring of 1933, to sow terror in the streets, to open up its own "wildcat" concentration camps, and to disrupt trials and legal proceedings—occasionally going so far as to beat up fellow party members who showed too much restraint— Röhm reminded his followers with mounting anger of the sacrifices they had made and the dead they mourned. When his demands on the government went unheeded, he found himself increasingly driven to take the stance of the betrayed revolutionary.

Bitterly disappointed by the course of events and spurred by the agitated masses, who were eager for the spoils of victory, he whipped up his followers in the SA with speeches and harangues, insisting that "the national revolution must end now and become a National Socialist revolution." Talk began to circulate in SA circles of the need for a "second revolution" to boost the Nazi movement fully into the saddle, to free it from its wretched mire of half

Ernst Röhm was a fanatical soldier with prodigious organizational talents. By early 1933 he had built the SA into a Nazi Party army of nearly a million men. Their uncontrolled, terroristic conduct frightened the general public, while the Reichswehr was annoyed by their demands for greater power. The situation was headed toward open conflict, which was "resolved" in the summer of 1934 during the Night of the Long Knives, when Röhm and his most important associates were murdered.

Above: Röhm in August 1933 during a parade at the Tempelhof airfield in Berlin.

measures, and to sweep Röhm and his organization to the top. When Minister of the Interior Wilhelm Frick warned in the summer of 1933 that he would take "severe measures"—at the very least putting disorderly SA members in "protective custody"—and followed through by clamping down on SA activities, Röhm threatened to march two brigades up to Frick's headquarters in the Vossstrasse and give him a public whipping.[8]

But Röhm did not confine himself to making extravagant remarks before cheering supporters. His slogans promising a "second revolution" were aimed first and foremost at the Reichswehr, which had so far successfully resisted *Gleichschaltung* and, in Röhm's view, epitomized the "forces of reaction" and the official tolerance of them. Röhm felt that the planned expansion of the Reichswehr, and the countless openings it would create for officers in particular, should be directed at satisfying the career ambitions of SA leaders. The logic of the situation led naturally, in his view, to the conclusion that all the armed forces should operate within the framework of the SA and gradually be molded into a National Socialist people's army. "The gray cliffs must inevitably be swallowed by the brown tide," Röhm proclaimed as he forged ahead with plans to take the much smaller army, with its gray field uniforms, into the embrace of the brown-shirted SA, transforming it into a popular militia.[9]

The generals of the Reichswehr were understandably protective of its traditions and prerogatives; Röhm's increasingly urgent and imperious designs alarmed them and confirmed their worst fears. As if to bring matters to a head, in the fall of 1933 Röhm incorporated another right-wing paramilitary organization into the SA, the Stahlhelm ("steel helmet"), which had originally been founded as a First World War veterans' group. At a single stroke he raised the strength of his domestic army to nearly three million men. At the same time he began building the SA into a state within the state, enhancing its military aura, creating a network of offices to oversee a little of everything—including paramilitary sports, gymnastics, and life in the universities—setting up an SA police force and judicial system, and establishing liaisons to industry, government, and the press. Despite his strident, relentless insistence on the unsatisfied demands of his followers, Röhm continued to have confidence in Hitler and considered him merely indecisive and susceptible to "stupid and dangerous" characters like Göring, Goebbels, Himmler, and Hess, who were blocking the way to the real revolution and the dawn of an SA state.[10]

Hitler probably basically agreed with Röhm's ideas. The Führer certainly shared his distaste for the officer caste, with its monocles and starchy mannerisms. If Hitler had exhibited any support for Röhm's demands at this juncture, however, he would have not only aroused the animosity of the Reichswehr and President Hindenburg but also jeopardized his alliance with the conservatives, undermined his basic tactic of "legal revolution," endangered the incipient economic recovery, and possibly even invited intervention by foreign powers. In short, supporting Röhm would have sabotaged his entire strategy for seizing power. At least for the moment, Hitler remained reliant on the expertise of the senior Reichswehr officers as he set about the pressing military tasks he had designated for himself, above all the rebuilding of the army.

Nevertheless, Hitler did not want to dismiss Röhm's demands out of hand. He even quietly encouraged the SA leader on the theory that all obstacles put in the path of the Reichswehr would ultimately make it more amenable to his will. At a conference of army commanders in December, Blomberg expressed great concern about "attempts within the SA to establish an army of its own." Six weeks later he received a memorandum from Röhm in which the SA chief flatly declared "the entire realm of national defense falls within the purview of the SA." The next day, as if not wishing to leave the slightest doubt about his plans, Röhm added comments that the generals took as an open declaration of war: "I now consider the Reichswehr to be only a military training school for the German people. The conduct of war and therefore also the mobilization [of troops] are henceforth the concerns of the SA."[11]

Blomberg and Reichenau responded by insisting on "a clear decision." Just as Hitler had expected, they made numerous attempts at accommodation to curry favor with him. A preliminary concession had already been made. The commander in chief of the army, Kurt

Kurt von Hammerstein-Equord (right), *the chief of army command from 1930 to 1934, made no effort to conceal his distaste for the Nazis from the moment they seized power, referring to them as "that gang of criminals." This outspokenness angered the newly appointed minister of defense, Blomberg, who relieved Hammerstein of many of his responsibilities. In the fall of 1933 Hammerstein capitulated and submitted his resignation.*

Above: *Hammerstein with General Kurt von Schleicher at a military inspection in Berlin in the summer of 1932.*

von Hammerstein-Equord, was an aloof, sarcastic man, who punctuated his principles with cutting displays of disregard.[12] He made no secret of his aversion to the new rulers, even speaking of them in wider circles as "that gang of criminals" or "those filthy pigs," the latter an allusion to the homosexual tendencies of the SA leaders. As a result, more and more of Hammerstein's responsibilities were assumed by Blomberg, for whom the duties came more easily than for Hammerstein, who had neither talent nor desire for intrigue and insisted on straight dealings. By the spring of 1933 it was already being rumored that the commander in chief of the army would last, at most, until the summer. Though somewhat passive, Hammerstein ultimately held on until the fall before submitting his resignation. Within the officer corps, hardly an eyebrow was raised. Things finally seemed to be improving, and "everyone was happy to be rid of Hammerstein."[13] Blomberg even went so far as to order his department head in the ministry to forbid any further contacts with the former army commander in chief.

This initial attempt to appease Hitler was soon followed by a second. Just a few days after the commanders' conference in early February, Blomberg ordered that Nazi insignia henceforth be the official symbol of the armed forces. Somewhat later he mandated that the officer corps adopt the so-called Aryan paragraph of the Act to Restore a Professional Public Service of April 7, 1933, requiring, among other things, that civil servants of non-Aryan descent be retired.[14] Shortly thereafter Blomberg issued orders making "sympathy with the new state" the decisive criterion for promotions and, still at his own initiative, introduced a program of "political training" for soldiers. Hitler, who was well versed in reading omens, may have viewed these gestures as the first sign of impending capitulation, despite all the grumbling about them in the Reichswehr.

To entice the army further down this path Hitler himself offered a concession: at the army's Bendlerstrasse headquarters on February 28, 1934, Röhm was forced to sign a paper in Hitler's presence that confirmed all the prerogatives of the Reichswehr and delegated only supporting military-training duties to the SA. The dispute between the two military forces was then officially washed away in a "reconciliatory breakfast," at which, according to Blomberg, the Führer delivered a "stirring" appeal to keep the peace.

Hardly had the ceremony ended, the table been cleared, and the guests departed, however, before Röhm exploded in a tirade of rage and frustration. He called Hitler a "ridiculous corporal," accused him of disloyalty and shouted, "If it can't be done with Hitler, we'll do it without him!" One of the witnesses, SA leader Viktor Lutze, scurried away from the champagne breakfast in the Huldschinsky Palace, Röhm's headquarters in Berlin, to Hitler's camp at Berchtesgaden to report what had happened. The Führer curtly informed him, "We'll just let this ripen."[15]

■ ■ ■

In the meantime Röhm carried on as if the agreements, assurances, and solemn handshakes of February 28 had never occurred. He purchased arms abroad, displayed SA muscle in gigantic military parades, held public flag-consecration ceremonies and reviews of his troops, and rode, mounted high on his steed, before the brown-shirted hordes. Still, Hitler waited, for the balance that had been achieved seemed to hold the SA and the Reichswehr in check, each in its own way. Finally, it was the many enemies Röhm had accumulated in the course of his career who decided to pounce, beginning with such people as Rudolf Hess and Martin Bormann in party headquarters and extending all the way to the SA division heads. Most important was Hermann Göring, who felt driven into an alliance that he would have preferred to avoid. He joined forces with Heinrich Himmler, the chief of the SS, turning control of the Gestapo over to him. In aligning himself with Himmler he was also taking on Himmler's assistant, Reinhard Heydrich, who had always struck him as eerie and sinister. By early May Heydrich had assumed responsibility for the operation against Röhm.

The change in the atmosphere was immediately palpable, as a veritable campaign was launched, complete with intrigue, rumors, and hit lists. Amid all the planning and plotting, the gray shadow of an officer's uniform appeared time and again. A vague aura of unease

Of the many titles bestowed upon Hermann Göring (right), none pleased him more than that of "Master Huntsman of the Reich," an honorific created especially for him. He felt that his passion for the hunt bolstered his self-image as the "last Renaissance man." Shortly after the Night of the Long Knives, in which he played a prominent part, he was invited to dinner by the British ambassador to Germany, Sir Eric Phipps. When Göring arrived late, offering the excuse that he had just returned from hunting, Phipps responded curtly, "For animals, I hope."

Above: Göring and Lord Halifax, who would later become British foreign minister, riding through a bison preserve near Berlin that Göring himself had designed.

began to spread, as if Germany was once again coming to its senses and beginning soberly to assess the changes that had taken place, whose true nature had been veiled by the inebriating spectacle of parades and by the Führer's speeches. Many of the intolerable conditions of the Weimar Republic had indeed disappeared, but only to be replaced by new horrors: the persecution of helpless minorities, a muzzled press, conflict with the churches, mounting suspicion of Germany from abroad, and much more. A showdown with the SA loomed nearer, heightening apprehensions, and the Young Conservatives, another group interested in sharpening antagonisms, began to make its presence felt. Egged on by certain of its members in his entourage, Vice-Chancellor Papen now sensed an opportunity to emerge from the background into which he had been forced and to steer Germany back to being an orderly nation. A revolt of the SA was rumored to be imminent and could perhaps be used, he calculated, to induce President Hindenburg to declare a state of emergency. Papen felt encouraged by the president himself, who commented as he set off in early June for a vacation on his Neudeck estate in East Prussia, "Things are going badly, Papen. Try to restore order."[16]

With this piece of encouragement ringing in his ears, Papen delivered a dramatic speech (written for him by the conservative writer Edgar Jung) at the University of Marburg on June 17, 1934. As if he had not been partially responsible for government decisions all along, Papen spoke out against the spread of violence, the extremism of the Nazis, the scramble for sinecures and easy money, the suppression of free speech, the mania for *Gleichschaltung,* and the "unnatural, totalitarian demands" of the state. Hitler was dismayed and bewildered for a fleeting moment, apparently assuming that the rather careless Papen had blurted out the details of a secret agreement that was being forged by the president, the Reichswehr, and the still influential conservative forces. There is much evidence to suggest that this was the moment Hitler finally decided to deal with the SA.

Feverishly but with great calculation, the stage was set for Röhm's demise. Public warnings were issued almost daily to those who advocated a "second revolution." The Reichswehr was tipped off that the SA seemed to be planning an operation. Secret but widely circulated reports advised that the brownshirts were on the verge of staging a revolt. Leading politicians from the Weimar Republic, such as Heinrich Brüning and Kurt von Schleicher, who had preceded Hitler as chancellor, were quietly advised to disappear for a few days or, better yet, to leave Germany entirely. The command posts of certain military districts were informed that, whatever happened, the SS would be on the side of the legal authorities and should be furnished with weapons, if necessary. Once again, a "hit list" of the SA made the rounds, landing on the desks both of Reichswehr officers and of some of those whose names it featured prominently. In the middle of the cleverly orchestrated agitation stood the unsuspecting Ernst Röhm, who had just completed arrangements to send his units on their regular leave. On June 29, 1934, the evening before the summer holidays were to begin, SA units in some cities were put on routine alert. Their commanders checked their readiness for action and sent them out to protest on the streets.

In the early morning hours of June 30 death squads began to fan out. Trucks of SS men and police roved the streets of Berlin, cordoning off the Tiergarten district, which housed the SA leaders' quarters as well as Papen's office on Vossstrasse. Hitler himself went to Bad Wiessee, where Röhm was holding a congress of SA leaders, and arrested him in his bed. Together with other SA commanders, Röhm was taken to the prison in Stadelheim. The executions began that morning, both there and in the SS barracks in Berlin-Lichterfelde. To take advantage of the "unique opportunity," as one participant phrased it, the hit list was expanded to include not only alleged "SA plotters" but also erstwhile opponents of the regime, including the circle around Papen and a number of leading conservatives. Exemplary terror would teach all such people to refrain from any hint of revolt.

General Schleicher, who had turned a deaf ear to various warnings, was shot in his apartment in Neu-Babelsberg, together with his wife. One of his closest associates, General Ferdinand von Bredow, the former chief of the Bureau of Ministers in the Ministry of Defense, was also slain, as were Edgar Jung, Erich Klausener (the head of Catholic Action), and many others. At around 9:00 a.m., three Gestapo officials accompanied by thirty SS men stormed into Papen's offices. They searched the rooms, finally discovering Herbert von Bose, the head of the press office and a close associate of Papen. They asked him his name and then, without another word, shot him. All this was done without judicial proceedings, judgments, or the slightest semblance of legality. Hitler seemed intent, in fact, on delivering these blows completely in the open so as to leave a deep and abiding impression, as if proclaiming from the rooftops his immutable will and the earnestness of his statement on the evening of January 30,

1933, as he entered the Reich Chancellery, that no power on earth would ever dislodge him alive.[17]

- - -

The public was horrified by the butchery, which continued into the evening of July 1. People seemed to realize instinctively that a line had been crossed. Leaders who permitted—or indeed engineered—such abominations were clearly capable of even more disturbing and frightful deeds. These fears were mitigated, however, by a sense of relief that the depredations of the SA, and the threat of chaos and mob rule that it embodied, had come to an end. For a brief moment a tear had appeared in the veil of the "legal revolution," revealing a Hitler stripped of middle-class airs, a man whose thirst for power knew absolutely no bounds. But a public relations campaign was immediately launched to calm the waters, and soon the public was prepared to dismiss the two days of massacres as representing "the [Nazi] movement's sowing the last of its wild oats" and the triumph of Hitler's forces of order over the savage energies unleashed by any revolution.

Nevertheless, Hitler's power hung in the balance for a time. Everything depended on how the Reichswehr would react. Certainly it had participated in the intrigue against Röhm; it had been more complicit and had provided far more assistance than its good name would allow. The ensuing bloodbath, however, far exceeded anything it had imagined and clearly violated the most basic legal norms. If the social order had truly been under the threat of an imminent uprising by the SA, as Blomberg claimed in an attempt to justify Hitler's action, then the Reichswehr would have been duty-bound to intervene; but everyone knew that this was not the case. If the social order was not threatened, then the army should have acted to put down the lawless outburst. Instead the Reichswehr had fanned the conflict and helped bring it to a head, making weapons available and finally giving the SS free rein, all to ensure its own victory.

Uncertainty about the reaction of the Reichswehr was not the least of Hitler's reasons for leaving Berlin immediately after the massacre and lying low for a while. Not until ten days later did he surface and return to the capital. After all, two generals—former chancellor Kurt von Schleicher and Ferdinand von Bredow—had been murdered in the wave of violence. No self-respecting army, let alone an officer corps that believed it had a right to participate in the affairs of state, could let such acts pass without account. In a tense and often contradictory speech before the Reichstag on July 13, 1934, Hitler offered the official explanation that Schleicher had been in contact with the ambassador of a foreign power, an assertion that failed to convince or satisfy anyone.

A few senior officers, including Erich von Manstein, Gerd von Rundstedt, and even Erwin von Witzleben (who had greeted the news of the murder of the SA leaders with a curt "Splendid!"[18]) insisted that a court-martial be convened to investigate the charge. Blomberg mollified them with the promise that proof would soon be provided. But the results of the investigation were suppressed, and there the situation remained. Eventually, in response to the concerns voiced by a few other officers, General Werner von Fritsch (who had, in the meantime, relieved Hammerstein as commander in chief of the army) demanded an explanation of Blomberg. But the minister evaded the issue, and in the end Fritsch allowed it to die.

These evasions and prevarications on the part of the minister of defense were rooted, of course, in his own complicity. Blomberg had even approved the orders for General Schleicher's "arrest," while Reichenau formulated the official announcement that Schleicher was shot while resisting arrest (an assertion disproved by the criminal investigation).[19] As chief of army command, Fritsch may well have felt that he could not afford to expose his political superiors; as the sources unanimously show, however, like most other senior officers he was horrified by the bloodbath despite feeling satisfaction at the taming of the SA.

Nevertheless, Fritsch rebuffed all demands for a protest by pointing to his low position in the hierarchy. He could not take action "without explicit orders," he later said. "Blomberg was vehemently opposed, and Hindenburg could not be reached and was apparently misinformed."[20] Be that as it may, the fact that the chief of army command did not insist on a military investigation plainly indicates that other factors were also at work. When the aged field marshal August von Mackensen took steps to restore the honor of the murdered generals, Fritsch distanced himself from the attempts. To crown it all, he meekly informed the troops of Blomberg's "muzzle edict," which forbade them to make any personal statements about the purge. Furthermore, neither Fritsch nor the officer corps at large raised any objections when Blomberg ordered that they not attend Schleicher's funeral. Those seeking the first signs of the army's retreat to a narrow, formalistic emphasis on a soldier's duty to obey—an emphasis on which all will to resist ultimately foundered in the following years—will find it here.

Fritsch's evasiveness cannot, however, be explained solely by his sense of loyalty and his belief in military obedience, though he did feel very much bound by these concepts. Nor can it be fully accounted for by his career-long adherence to the ideal of an apolitical army, which had been introduced by General Hans von Seeckt under the Weimar Republic. At least as important as these factors was the feeling that the army had many interests in common with the new regime; as a result, its commanders were inclined to restraint even in the face of obvious crimes. Defeat in the First World War and the harsh burdens imposed on Germany by the Treaty of Versailles had instilled in the officer corps an obsession with redress—not only for their military defeat but, more importantly, for the moral stain that had marked Germany ever since. In Hitler the officer corps perceived a man who could succeed on both these counts. Some officers even deluded themselves into believing that now, after the bloody break with Röhm, they could lure Hitler away from National Socialism and the narrow convictions of his youth; by offering ever-greater blandishments and concessions, they hoped to win him over to their views and perhaps even make him their lackey.

Such dreams were as vain as Papen's long-defunct hope of "taming" Hitler, though the ghost of that hope seemed to be reemerging in some army circles. With his highly developed sense for almost imperceptible shifts in the balance of power, Hitler immediately grasped that an army that had closed its eyes to the murder of two of its generals would not block his breakthrough to unfettered domination. Just three weeks later he moved to exploit the obvious weakness of the army leadership. On July 20 he recognized the "great accomplishments" of the SS, "particularly in connection with the events of June 30," by conferring on it the status of an independent organization directly responsible to him. Blomberg was required to provide "weapons for one entire division." Instead of a state built on the SA, as the impatient, ham-handed Röhm had insisted on, there now began to emerge, bit by bit, a state built on the SS.

At the same time the tightly closed ranks of the army began to crack. A number of officers who later joined the military resistance pointed to the events of June 30 and July 1, 1934, as the beginning of their break with the Nazis, among them Henning von Tresckow, Franz Halder, and Hans Oster, who even in the interrogations following July 20, 1944, denounced the "methods of a gang of bandits." Erwin Rommel also became disenchanted with the Nazis, saying that the Röhm affair had been a failed opportunity "to get rid of the entire bunch."[21] These officers remained isolated individuals, however, and none of them was in a position of real power. The army commanders, by contrast, were overjoyed that they had achieved their great objective, dealing the SA a death blow without attracting much attention to themselves. They failed to understand that the cleverness of Hitler's ploy had been to involve them in the massacre just enough to taint them but not so much that he owed them his success. Although once more his fate had lain in the hands of the Reichswehr, that would never be true again, as Hitler already knew during those critical days of June and July. The army's moment of opportunity had come and gone.

* * *

Hitler made his next move much more quickly than expected, when fortune handed him the opportunity to complete his seizure of power by taking over the last independent position in the government. In mid-July President Hindenburg's health went into steep decline, and his entourage expected his death at any moment. Until shortly before

The army contributed considerably to Hitler's success by overestimating its own strength. Above: The minister of defense (and now also commander in chief of the Wehrmacht), Field Marshal Blomberg (left), with the commander in chief of the army, Major General Werner von Fritsch, at a Nazi Party rally held in Nuremberg on September 13, 1937. In the background is the commander in chief of the navy, Admiral Erich Raeder.

this time disappointed conservatives had still imagined the president as a possible rival to Hitler. Elard von Oldenburg-Januschau, Hindenburg's clear-sighted friend from the neighboring estate, had, however, been speaking for quite some time, in the bluff manner he liked to affect, of the president "whom we actually no longer have." In any case, the office still existed and was the last institution of government that had not fallen into Hitler's hands. Furthermore, the president, as commander in chief of the armed forces, was the only remaining authority to whom the army could appeal over the head of the government—the presidency was thus the last bastion of army independence.

This office and the powers attached to it were all that separated Hitler from outright dictatorship. On August 1, 1934, though the news from Hindenburg's estate in Neudeck seemed more hopeful, Hitler moved with unseemly haste, presenting to the cabinet for immediate signature legislation that would merge the offices of president and chancellor, to take effect when the old marshal died. The proposed law was based, to be sure, on the Act for the Reconstruction of the Reich of January 1934, which gave the government authority to pass new constitutional laws, but it deliberately ignored article 2 of the Enabling Act, which enjoined the government from making any changes to the office of Reich president. Hitler thus concluded his putative "legal revolution" with an open violation of constitutional law, a move emblematic of his duplicitous intentions all along.

When Hindenburg died early the next morning, on August 2, 1934, Hitler's goals were all achieved. In the rush of events, the Reichswehr seemed most concerned about not being left out of the action. Blomberg attempted a coup de main of his own. Solely on the basis of his power to issue ministerial decrees, he ordered all officers and enlisted men to swear an oath of allegiance to their new supreme commander, the "Führer Adolf Hitler," that very day. The wording of this oath violated both the Oath Act of December 1, 1933, and the constitution by requiring soldiers to swear unconditional obedience to Hitler personally, not just to the office he held. The consequences of this fateful step would continue to make history long after the illusions of those days had been dashed.

A premonition seemed to sweep the ranks the day that the oath was administered. Numerous memoirs speak of the "depressed mood" in the barracks after Blomberg's surprise maneuver. The radical break with military tradition made apparent by the oath led General Ludwig Beck, head of the troop office and still one of Hitler's declared supporters, to call it the "blackest day of his life,"[22] while Baron Rudolph-Christoph von Gersdorff, then regimental adjutant in a cavalry unit, spoke of the oath as something "coerced." For the first time doubts had been sowed in the minds of younger officers, who had hitherto been unstinting in their trust and confidence.[23] Once aroused, these doubts would eventually lead some of them to distance themselves from the regime and a few to resist it, despite the numerous obstacles in their way—not the least of which was the oath of personal loyalty they had sworn to the Führer.

Blomberg himself was not at all troubled by such doubts, but the Reichswehr would never recover from the blow he delivered, with no outside prompting, by the introduction of the oath. Henceforth the army would be in Hitler's pocket. Blomberg and the military commanders, feeling quite pleased with what they thought they had accomplished, namely boosting the army to a position of unquestionable power, happily set about trying to extend their newfound influence to the political realm as well. They urged an initially hesitant Hitler to forge ahead with rearmament and to accelerate his plans for the army. When concerns were voiced in the Foreign Office that such a policy would heighten diplomatic tensions, the officers managed to dispel them. Their success in doing so may have encouraged them in their erroneous belief that the army would indeed play a major role on the political stage. Shortly thereafter, brushing aside economic objections raised by the president of the Reichsbank, Hjalmar Schacht, the army succeeded, this time with Hitler's help, in establishing the fundamental primacy of military objectives.

Anticipating Germany's return to military might, though it was far from being realized, Hitler decided in early March 1936 to reoccupy the demilitarized zone in the Rhineland—another in the series of bold moves with which he continued to surprise the world. After the introduction of universal conscription one year earlier, the occupation of the Rhineland represented the final step in eliminating the shackles imposed by the Treaty of Versailles. This step, like all the preceding ones, was accompanied by much reassuring talk. However, when the Council of the League of Nations passed a resolution forbidding Germany to construct military fortresses in this zone, Hitler tartly replied that he had not restored German sovereignty in order to countenance immediate limitations on it. For the first time since the defeat of 1918, Germans began to feel a swelling sense of national self-respect; the moment had come to put an end to the era when the whole world could address Germany in the tone of the conqueror. The seizure of the Rhineland was accomplished with only a handful of semitrained units facing vastly superior French forces, and Hitler concluded from this startling victory that, in the words of André François-Poncet, the French ambassador to Berlin, he "could do anything he wanted and lay down the law in Europe."[24]

It was, above all, the senior officers who found the hopes they had placed in Hitler vindicated. They forged determinedly ahead with rearmament despite mounting concerns about the domestic reservations. The wisdom of rearmament from a foreign policy viewpoint was also questioned: people wondered, with increasing unease, how much longer the great powers of Europe would tolerate Hitler's breaches of treaty obligations, responding, as they had in the past year, with mere protests and empty threats. That the army overlooked these concerns and single-mindedly devoted its skills and energy to a task that would benefit only Hitler suggests not only the officer corps's lack of political acumen but also the extent to which its leaders had been traumatized by their helplessness after the war.

The top military leaders saw the consequences of their brilliantly successful rearmament campaign when Hitler delivered his famous address of November 5, 1937, in the Chancellery in Berlin, which was recorded by his aide Friedrich Hossbach. In a four-hour harangue, delivered without pause, Hitler informed them that the time pressures generated by the rearmament campaign had led him to the "immutable decision to take military action against Czechoslovakia and Austria in the near future." Foreign governments on all sides had begun to suspect the Reich and to quicken the pace of their own rearmament, and Hitler rightly feared that the balance of power would soon shift back to Germany's disadvantage. The previous two years had shown Hitler the astounding results that could be achieved by appealing to the pride of the officer corps. He let it be known, therefore, in what was clearly a psychological ploy, that he was still dissatisfied with the pace of rearmament. Under the right circumstances, he informed them, he might even be ready to launch the invasions the following year. The Führer also made it clear that he considered Czechoslovakia as a mere stepping stone toward his far more ambitious plans for dealing with the German need for territory.

Some of the officers present were openly aghast, and the ensuing discussion was marked at times by "very sharp exchanges."[25] Blomberg and Fritsch actively opposed Hitler as, to a lesser extent, did the foreign minister, Konstantin von Neurath, who had been summoned to the gathering. They warned emphatically against taking such an overt course toward war, which would inevitably jolt the Western powers to action and result in a global conflict. For the first time, on November 5, 1937, the scales seemed to fall from the eyes of the military commanders: they realized that Hitler was deadly serious about the objectives he had been proclaiming for years. He had not the slightest intention, furthermore, of seeking the army's counsel on decisions of war and peace, as Beck was still urging him to do in a memorandum written shortly thereafter. In short, the generals finally recognized that Hitler was no mere nationalist and revisionist like them but exactly what he had claimed to be.

As far as Hitler was concerned, November 5 only confirmed his suspicion that he could not rely on these anxious, overly scrupulous members of the old elite to carry out his plans for conquest; they were not the steely adventurers he needed. Although Hitler used to remark on occasion that he had always imagined the military chiefs as "mastiffs who had to be held fast by the collar lest they hurl themselves on everyone," he now recognized how mistaken he had been: "I'm the one who always has to urge these dogs on."[26] Although there was disappointment on both sides, it was felt most keenly by the generals, who now saw their hopes of being treated as partners in government go up in smoke. Hitler, on the other hand, only found his disdain for the military commanders confirmed. He was so vexed that his plans had been challenged in any way that all subsequent meetings with the military top brass took the form of audiences at which the officers simply received their orders. The Führer left Berlin for Berchtesgaden, where he nursed his anger, repeatedly refusing to receive his foreign minister and awaiting an opportunity to reap the benefits of the day's events.

■ ■ ■

Once again circumstances played into Hitler's hand, and he swiftly exploited them for political gain. Minister of War Blomberg, long a widower, decided to marry a woman whom he himself confessed was of "modest background." Hitler and Göring acted as witnesses at the ceremony in mid-January 1938. Just a few days later, however, rumors began to circulate that Blomberg's young wife was well-known in vice-squad circles, indeed that she had worked as a prostitute and even been arrested once. The officer corps was scandalized by such a misalliance at the highest levels of the German military. Beck went to see Wilhelm Keitel, who had taken over from Reichenau at the ministry, and informed him that it was unacceptable for "the leading soldier" in the land to have "a whore" for a wife. Hitler, too, reacted with rage when Göring presented him with the evidence. A farewell appointment was set up for Blomberg only two days later. "I can no longer put up with this," the Führer informed him. "We must part." When, at the end of their discussion, the subject of Blomberg's successor arose, Hitler flatly rejected the idea of promoting Fritsch to the post, referring to him as a mere "hindrance."[27] Göring, too, was excluded from consideration despite all he had done to fuel the intrigue that made the minister's fall inevitable and, in his insatiable thirst for power, position himself as successor. Blomberg finally took the opportunity to deal the army a fateful blow by suggesting that Hitler himself assume command.

There is much to indicate that Hitler was already leaning in this direction. And at this point, another explosive police record turned up thanks to the assiduous efforts of Himmler and Heydrich, who produced it, and Göring, who turned it over to the Führer. This one enabled Hitler to rid himself of the entire high command of the Wehrmacht, as the Reichswehr was now called, reducing the army to the purely instrumental role he required for his war policy. The record in question accused the commander in chief of the army of homosexuality. An unsuspecting Fritsch was summoned to the Chancellery, where, as if playing a part in a farce, he was confronted by a hired "witness" before a large audience presided over by Hitler. The accusations against Fritsch would soon be proved groundless, but in the meantime they had had the desired effect: instead of merely hurling the "evidence" at Hitler's feet, as the Führer himself had expected, Fritsch seemed bewildered and confused by the charges. Failing to see through the ploy, he devoted all his efforts over the next few days to erasing the stain on his honor and convincing the Führer that a terrible mistake had been made. Obsessed with his personal disgrace, he rejected all attempts to persuade him to assume a broader perspective and expose the underlying plot, especially by summoning Himmler and Heydrich as witnesses in a court of law. Only after his cause was irretrievably lost did Fritsch realize that the entire affair was aimed not at him personally but at the army as a whole. Thus Hitler spared himself the public confrontation with the armed forces that he had been so eager to avoid.

Fritsch was not the only officer who failed to see that this maneuver was Hitler's attempt to eliminate all opposition within the army. Lieutenant Colonel Hans Oster of Military Intelligence, who did realize what was going on, attempted to persuade several commanding generals who could mobilize their troops, to demonstrate the military's might and force Hitler to back down. Ulex in Hannover, Kluge in Münster, and List in Dresden listened in outrage when informed by Oster or his emissaries of the true background to the Fritsch affair; Kluge, it is said, even turned "ash-white." But no one would take action. The jeering and snickering of those who had plotted the intrigue were almost audible in the background, and it is no wonder that Hitler said he knew for sure now that all generals were cowards.[28]

Even more revealing, perhaps, was the reaction of Ludwig Beck, who served briefly as the interim head of army command after Fritsch's departure. Not only did he provide his former chief with scarcely any support, he forbade the officers in army headquarters to talk about what had happened. When Quartermaster General Franz Halder visited him on January 31 to inquire about the affair, which continued to be a closely guarded secret, Beck stonewalled him, claiming he was duty-bound to remain silent. When Halder demanded that Beck lead his generals in a raid on the Prinz-Albrecht-Strasse headquarters of the Gestapo, which Halder presumed was behind all the intrigues, Beck replied with considerable agitation that this would be nothing less than "mutiny, revolution." "Such words," he added, "do not exist in the dictionary of a German officer."[29] The following day Fritsch's resignation was announced.

Thus Werner von Fritsch, the commander in chief of the army, was disgraced and quietly driven from his post, though he still felt quite loyal to the Führer. It probably only dawned on Hitler gradually that all the fortuitous events, plotting, and farcical twists of the previous few days had left him with the great opportunity he had always craved: to take a stiff broom to the army. With the first sentence of a decree issued on February 4, 1938, he assumed "direct and personal" command "of the entire Wehrmacht." Blomberg's Ministry of War was dissolved and replaced by the Oberkommando der Wehrmacht (OKW), or high command of the armed forces. Henceforth the Führer would not have to contend with anyone who spoke for the combined armed forces, just with the commanders of the various branches. At the same time, Hitler took the opportunity to retire or transfer more than sixty generals, in most cases apparently not for any lack of loyalty to the regime but simply in order to bring younger officers to the top. A number of ambassadors received the same treatment. Hitler was certainly at least partially motivated by a desire to shroud the dismissals of Blomberg and Fritsch in a fog of change and reorganization. The extent to which he used this reshuffling to take retribution against those who had opposed him on November 5 of the previous year is indicated by the fact that Neurath, too, was dismissed, to be replaced by Joachim von Ribbentrop. Hitler also put an end to his tempestuous relationship with Hjalmar Schacht, his minis-

After Blomberg's downfall in the spring of 1938, Hitler placed the Wehrmacht under his own "direct and personal" command. Wilhelm Keitel (left) *was made chief of the OKW, or high command of the armed forces. Keitel proved to be a willing tool to the very end, although Hitler only despised him for it. Once, when Goebbels suggested that Keitel be called on to explain a military point, Hitler replied that Keitel possessed "the brain of a movie usher."*

Above: *Hitler and Keitel on their way to Munich on March 12, 1938, after the Austrian* Anschluss.

ter of economics, by appointing Walter Funk to that post. Finally there was the question of what to do with Hermann Göring, whom Hitler named field marshal in an attempt to appease him for having been passed over in this orgy of new appointments.

Thus the last people who could challenge Hitler were eliminated, having been systematically weakened and stripped of their authority. The new men recommended themselves to the Führer through their pliancy and submissiveness, and he expected them to be nothing more than executors of his will. Wilhelm Keitel was made chief of the OKW because Blomberg, during his final interview, had disparaged him as a mere "office manager." "That's just the kind of man I need,"

Hitler promptly replied.[30] Walther von Brauchitsch, who took over as commander in chief after Fritsch, accepted the appointment reluctantly and after long hesitation, more out of a sense of duty than out of ambition. He was apolitical, like many of his fellow generals, tended to avoid conflict, and in any case was much too weak-kneed to have any hope of defending the army's interests against Hitler, the Nazi Party, and the rising SS.

Hitler's impatience and the hectic pace of events are almost palpable in the extant documents from this period. Within days of issuing his February 4 decree, he ordered that the matériel needed for army mobilization be "fully" stockpiled by April 1, 1939. Furthermore, he ordered plans to be drafted for a far-reaching naval program that would enable Germany to compete with Great Britain on the high seas and for a fivefold expansion of the Luftwaffe. At the same time, great strides were made on the operational side. Hitler's heady restlessness of that spring suggests that he was deeply gratified to be free at last of the incessant obstructionism of the old-line generals, with their frowning brows and shaking heads. Now he could pursue his dreams of grandeur and glory unimpeded and "save" the world according to his own vision. On the evening of April 20, 1938, he asked Keitel to head up general staff preparations for the occupation of Czechoslovakia. At about the same time, the chief of general staff, Ludwig Beck, drafted the first of a series of memoranda composed with mounting alarm over the next few months in an attempt to dissuade Hitler from going to war and also to restore the military's political influence through internal reorganization. That was the beginning of a long, drawn-out duel between unequal opponents. In mid-June Hitler announced that he would take any opportunity that arose after October 1 "to solve the Czech question."

Although the period between the Röhm and Fritsch affairs was marked by error and blundering, what stands out above all was a lack of will and assertiveness. In its pedantic, exacting way, history almost always requites such failings with shame and humiliation. In the case of Fritsch, not a single general insisted with appropriate vigor on clarifying the circumstances surrounding his denunciation or even on knowing the reasons, which Hitler only vaguely hinted at, that Fritsch

General Walther von Brauchitsch, appointed commander in chief of the army in 1938, tried to protect its integrity but allowed himself to be drawn deeper and deeper into the crimes of the regime.

could not be fully and publicly exonerated. Still, Brauchitsch interceded persistently and quietly on Fritsch's behalf and, by pointing to the mounting disquiet in the army, eventually did persuade the Führer to explain himself to the officer corps.

The meeting was held on June 13 at the air base in Barth, where, according to all reports, Hitler delivered one of the most compelling speeches of his career. With an eye toward his ripening plans for military conquest, he was determined to forestall the looming crisis of confidence in the army. He spoke of his "regrets" and the "tragedy" of the Fritsch case and promised that a similar situation would never arise again. His every word implied that the army remained the unchallenged and unchallengeable bearer of arms in the Reich, and he concluded by announcing that General Fritsch would be appointed "honorary commander" of the Twelfth Artillery Regiment.

But the army's irretrievable loss of influence in the wake of the

Fritsch affair became apparent as early as the next March, when the German incursion into Austria was planned without the consultation of the general staff. As if freed of his bonds, Hitler dared for the first time to send German forces across international frontiers, in an operation planned largely by party circles and carried out with the support of Himmler and the SS, whose star was plainly in the ascendant.

Werner von Fritsch, though now cleared of all charges, was put through one final humiliation. Hitler delayed communicating with him until March 30, when a chilly letter was finally sent out, followed two days later by a curt announcement in the press that the Führer had conveyed to General Fritsch his "best wishes for the recovery of his health." Fritsch responded one week later in a letter to Hitler: "The criminal charges against me have totally collapsed. However the deeply hurtful circumstances surrounding my dismissal from the army linger on—all the more painfully since the true reasons for my dismissal have not remained unknown to many in the Wehrmacht and the general public." Fritsch pleaded that "those people be called to account who were officially responsible for my case and for keeping you fully and promptly informed" and entrusted the restoration of his honor "to your wise judgment as commander in chief." He never received a reply.[31]

■   ■   ■

The Fritsch affair marked one of the lowest points in the long history of the German military. It also marked a new departure in the history of the Nazi regime, for the events of the spring of 1938 prompted the first stirrings of underground resistance. Groups materialized in a variety of locations, largely the creation of individuals who recognized not only the threat Hitler posed to Germany but the extent to which his behavior fell short of civilized standards. They formed ties, attracted like-minded people, and even overcame deeply entrenched European chauvinisms by reaching out across national borders to seek support abroad. They still differed immensely in their hopes and intentions and their readiness to shed the prejudices of the past;

uniting them was little more than the conviction that things could not simply be allowed to take their course.

The most prominent figure in these opposition groups was indisputably Hans Oster, who became chief of the central division of the OKW Military Intelligence Office in the autumn of 1938. He had been skeptical of the Nazis prior to 1933 but, like most of his fellow officers, initially approved of Hitler's foreign policy and therefore hesitated for a time once the new regime came to power. The Röhm affair served to clear his mind. Though not particularly politically minded at first, he nevertheless possessed sufficiently strong values and clarity of vision to understand the devastating defeat that the Reichswehr had inflicted on itself. The despotism in the land, daily growing more palpable in countless ways, the curtailment of the rule of law, and the emerging struggle against the churches prompted this parson's son from Dresden to progress from mere reservations about the regime to fundamental hostility toward it. This inspired him to use the resources of Military Intelligence to build a far-flung network of conspirators. The disgraceful farce leading to Fritsch's dismissal fired Oster with a determination to resist, though he recognized that it was Fritsch's own weakness that had made his downfall inevitable. Nevertheless, Fritsch had been Oster's regimental commander for a number of years and Oster continued to hold him in the highest regard, almost revering him. Decisive, quick-witted, and diplomatically imaginative, Oster was an unusual blend of moral rectitude, cunning, and recklessness. During many long discussions with Beck, he pointed out all the inconsistencies in the chief of the general staff's position and sowed doubt about the formalistic concept of loyalty to which Beck always hewed when Hitler repeatedly forced tests of conscience on him. Constantly on the move, Oster cultivated contacts on all sides and forged connections between the civilian and military opponents of the regime that would later become very important.

The driving force of the civilian opposition was Carl Goerdeler, whom the military resistance also came over the years to recognize as a leading figure. The scion of a conservative family, he originally joined the German National People's Party but left because of its narrow, reactionary views. Goerdeler then earned a reputation for

Before turning to the resistance, Carl Goerdeler, the mayor of Leipzig, tried to civilize the regime by working with it. He is shown (center) in 1935 with Winifred Wagner, her son Wieland (standing), Hitler, and Goebbels at the ceremonial laying of the cornerstone of the Richard Wagner National Memorial in Leipzig.

being a broad-minded, socially progressive politician as mayor of Leipzig. In the Weimar period, under Chancellor Brüning, he had served as Reich commissioner for price control. Now, after the Röhm affair, he agreed to assume this position once again but soon found himself in conflict with both Hitler's economic policy and the party authorities. He was a "classic exemplar" of that opposition from within which seeks to civilize the regime by cooperating with it.[32] Whereas many people later claimed that they had cooperated with the Nazis in order to prevent even worse from happening, when they had actually demonstrated little courage and achieved virtually nothing, Goerdeler proved to be an indefatigable and public adversary of Nazi criminality in his attempt to bolster "the forces of good in the party."[33] In 1933 he refused to raise the swastika flag at the Leipzig city hall. After some vacillation he finally resigned in 1937, when, in his absence and contrary to his explicit instruction, a monument to Felix Mendelssohn, a Jew, was removed from its position in front of the Gewandhaus concert hall.

From this point on, Goerdeler devoted himself tirelessly to the resistance. He mobilized acquaintances from far and wide. Just between June 1937 and late 1938 he traveled to twenty-two countries, always seeking to persuade the major powers to adopt an unyielding posture toward Hitler. Within Germany he established contacts on all sides and in this way contributed immensely to rallying the conservative, nationalistic, bourgeois opposition to the regime. He was motivated in all this by an indomitable, almost pathological optimism and unshakable faith in the power of logical argument. Even as a condemned prisoner on the eve of execution, he remained true to this belief despite his experiences and his fits of resignation.

Oster and Goerdeler were just the pivotal figures among a rapidly expanding corps of people who were prepared to oppose the regime. Some were lone wolves unattached to any group. In addition to the major circle within the army was another, at the Foreign Office, led by Adam von Trott zu Solz, Otto Kiep, Eduard Brücklmeier, Hans-Bernd von Haeften, and the Kordt brothers. In the wake of the Fritsch affair, these conspirators were joined by Georg Thomas, the OKW armaments chief; generals Wilhelm Adam, Erich Hoepner, Carl-Heinrich von Stülpnagel, and Erwin von Witzleben; Chief of Military Intelligence Wilhelm Canaris; and numerous other figures. The Fritsch affair had proved a turning point for Hans von Dohnanyi and Fritz-Dietlof von der Schulenburg, too, and Henning von Tresckow even pondered quitting the army and its all-too-acquiescent generals.[34]

Ludwig Beck's behavior reveals how difficult many officers found it to cast military tradition and principle aside and enter an entirely new world. In his memoranda and the comments he made to those around him, Beck repeatedly and vigorously denounced Hitler's impatient warmongering. At the same time he struggled stubbornly, albeit in increasing isolation, to save the battered "two pillar" theory of the state and assert what was left of army influence over political life, now that Brauchitsch had clearly given up and was completely occupied with staving off further demands rather than with making ones of his own. When Oster approached Beck at this point and asked him to take action, the chief of general staff agreed to persuade Brauchitsch to support a mass resignation of generals. At the same time, however, Beck was concerned that his name not become associated with the things that were still unacceptable to him as a soldier, such as mutiny and government by South American–style juntas.

Mass action on the part of German generals was certainly not without incalculable risk. It would be taken as signaling an uprising, for which there was not the necessary broad support, in either the army, the middle class, or the working class. It might also play into Hitler's hands, providing him with an opportunity to flood the army with officers loyal to the regime, possibly even plucked from the senior ranks of the SS. Their resignations might enable the Führer to succeed even more swiftly in creating an army that conformed ideologically to his worldview, which was more obviously becoming his aim with every passing day.

For these reasons, Beck's plan was to present the idea of the mass resignation of the army as an attempt to save Hitler from the clutches of the party and the SS—a fiction, to be sure. The rallying cry he intended to issue was, "For the Führer, against war, against rule by the bosses, for peace with the church, freedom of speech, and an end to Cheka methods!"[35] This approach was based on the widespread impression that Hitler's entourage was split into "good" and "bad" factions struggling for the heart and soul of the Führer. Everyone must help, therefore, reduce the influence of the "bad" elements around Ribbentrop, Himmler, and Goebbels. This was certainly the thinking behind Beck's comment to Brauchitsch at the time that he was prepared to shoot at the SS but not at Hitler.

Beck's doubts about the generals' strike were, in fact, well-founded, supported as they were by his realistic assessment of the situation. Any plan would have had to come to grips with the fact that this was a popular regime, headed by a man who had proved successful, was widely admired, and had just seen his support driven to new heights by the triumphant annexation of Austria. The regime, in its populism, was not unlike many people: egotistical, ruthless, and unconstrained by traditional values. Against it stood an Old World, elitist and confined by outmoded conventions that even it was struggling to shake off. A case in point: when Fritsch learned more about the background of the charges levied against him, he complained bitterly about his treatment and finally even conceded that Hitler had been as involved as Himmler; nevertheless, he refused to protest because that would have been rude and inappropriate for a person of his social standing. Fritsch's inability to come to terms with the coarse new world in which he suddenly found himself is evidenced in his almost comic yet poignant plan, devised with Beck's approval, to challenge Himmler—whom Fritsch believed had engineered the scandal—to a duel.

Until that day in January when Fritsch was suddenly confronted with a bribed witness before a host of onlookers, he and his army had thought that their position in the Reich was unassailable, that they had emerged victorious from the power struggle or at least were coasting toward inevitable victory. Now all such illusions were shattered. Despite his assurances that the Wehrmacht was and would remain the sole bearer of arms in the land, Hitler moved in August to elevate the SS to a kind of fourth service alongside the army, air force, and navy, thus laying the foundation for the emergence of the Waffen-SS. Venerable institutions are much more commonly laid low by their victories than by their defeats, especially when the true nature of those triumphs is disguised—as it so often is—or when it transpires that they are not in fact victories at all.

3

THE SEPTEMBER PLOT

Scarcely had Hitler finished basking in the jubilation, the flowers, and pealing bells that greeted him on his triumphant journey through Austria to the Heldenplatz in Vienna, when he became impatient for new adventures. At that very moment, however, forces were beginning to stir that would work with great determination to change the course that Germany was taking. The Fritsch affair had demonstrated to Hans Oster just how difficult it would be to persuade the generals to mount the kind of resistance that he deemed necessary. Regardless of how alluring they may have found Hitler's increasingly open plans for military expansion, they feared his gambler's instincts and the recklessness with which he risked war, even with Great Britain. Most remained paralyzed, however, inhibited from taking serious action, partly by the personal oaths of allegiance they had sworn to the Führer and partly by their ingrained belief in such ideals as loyalty and obedience.

Oster and his friends realized that even though Hitler had already demolished any basis for such loyalty, it persisted and could only be uprooted through the threat of a major foe. Only if the British adopted a determined, unyielding stance that drove home the danger of another great war would the generals realize the seriousness of the threat Hitler posed to his own country. Finally they would be seized with their responsibility for the greater whole, regardless of their oaths of allegiance and traditional duty to obey.

Ewald von Kleist-Schmenzin (left), *a conservative Christian and the owner of a large Pomeranian estate, always loathed Hitler. To organize international opposition to the Führer and hasten his fall, he traveled to London in the summer of 1938 as one of the first emissaries of the resistance. There he met, among others, Winston Churchill and Sir Robert Gilbert Vansittart* (right), *the British Foreign Office expert on Germany. Although he opened his interview with Vansittart by saying that he came "with a rope around his neck," his mission, like those of so many others, proved fruitless.*

This was the thought that prompted the curious pilgrimage to London and Paris beginning in the summer of 1938. Envoys of the opposition hoped to inform the Western powers of Hitler's intentions toward Czechoslovakia and to elicit strongly worded declarations of Western determination to oppose such aggression. Driven by his own restiveness, Goerdeler had traveled to Paris in early March and then again in April, meeting with the most senior official in the Foreign Ministry, Alexis Léger, but failing to obtain much more than fine words. In fact, many comments made at the time suggest that the French did not know what to make of a German who would warn a foreign power about the designs of his own government. No one seemed quite certain that Goerdeler was not actually acting on behalf of the Nazi regime. He aroused the same irritation in London. The extent to which the nations of Europe were caught up in their own preoccupations in those years can be seen in the fact that Sir Robert Gilbert Vansittart, the chief diplomatic adviser to the British Foreign Office, felt called upon to point out during their first conversation that what his visitor was doing amounted to nothing less than high treason.[1]

Oster's chosen emissary was Ewald von Kleist-Schmenzin, a worldly, courageous, and selfless conservative from Pomerania. In mid-January 1933 he had sought an interview with Hindenburg in a vain attempt to prevent Hitler's nomination as chancellor and had subsequently withdrawn in disdainful rage to his country estate. On several occasions he had already approached English friends with warnings about Hitler's expansionist designs. Now he traveled to London with an assignment from Ludwig Beck: "Bring me back certain proof that England will fight if Czechoslovakia is attacked, and I will put an end to this regime."[2] Kleist began his meeting with Vansittart by informing the chief diplomatic adviser that he came "with a rope around his neck." Everything else he had to say, however, made as little impression as did his later interviews with Lord Lloyd and Winston Churchill. Fully misunderstanding Kleist's mission, Prime Minister Chamberlain described Kleist and his reactionary friends as nothing more than modern Jacobites hoping to spark a revolution and restore the past with British help, much as the original Jacobites had sought to undo the revolution of 1688 and restore the deposed monarchy with French assistance. Little did Chamberlain realize that the analogy, far from being grounds for objection, pointed to the last chance to save the peace.

It is hardly surprising, therefore, that Oster's next emissary, the industrialist Hans Böhm-Tettelbach, also returned empty-handed. Far from allowing himself to become downhearted, Oster hoped to make his messengers seem more reliable by seeking assistance from co-conspirators in the Foreign Office. He asked Erich Kordt, the chief of the Ministers' Bureau, to draft a message to the British government requesting a "firm declaration" of opposition to Hitler's warmongering, a statement whose meaning would be "apparent even to ordinary people." If such a document could be obtained, Oster added, there would "be no more Hitler."[3] It was too risky to carry a copy of the message, so one of Kordt's cousins was asked to memorize it and repeat it for his brother Theo Kordt, who worked in the German embassy in London.

Although Theo Kordt aroused greater interest than his predecessors had and was even admitted to 10 Downing Street through a back entrance for an interview with Lord Halifax, the foreign minister, his mission, too, proved futile. Halifax listened attentively, to be sure, and seemed impressed when Kordt reminded him that Great Britain might have averted war in 1914 by issuing a similar declaration. He assured his guest as they parted that he would inform the prime minister and certain cabinet members about the gist of their conversation, so that Kordt departed with his hopes high. Once again, however, Great Britain could not be persuaded to issue a public declaration. The only noticeable effect of the conversation came in a letter Chamberlain sent to Hitler just before the outbreak of war in late August 1939, in which he mentioned the parallel to 1914 and expressed his hope that this time "no such tragic misunderstanding" would arise. A few weeks later, when the die had already been cast, Halifax commented to Theo Kordt, with a note of regret, "We could not be as candid with you as you were with us," for at the time of their conversation Whitehall had already decided to yield to Hitler's demands.[4]

So it went, over and over again. By the time Erich Kordt was drafting his message, the secretary of state in the Foreign Office, Ernst von Weizsäcker, had already begged the high commissioner for Danzig, Carl Jacob Burckhardt, "with the frankness of a desperate man betting everything on one last card," as Burckhardt later described it, to use his connections to persuade the British government to make some definitive gesture, perhaps by "sending out a general with a riding crop," whose language Hitler would presumably understand.[5] But all efforts were in vain. In the summer of 1939, just before the invasion of Poland, when war again seemed imminent, Hjalmar Schacht met several times with Montagu Norman, the governor of the Bank of England. Fabian von Schlabrendorff, Helmuth von

Hjalmar Schacht (right) occupied a key position in the Third Reich as minister of economics and president of the Reichsbank. In 1937 he resigned from the ministry and shortly thereafter established connections with the conservative resistance circle led by Goerdeler. He remained an outsider, though, keeping one foot in the opposition camp while preserving his contacts with the regime. Arrested after July 20, he spent the rest of the war in various concentration camps.

Above: *Schacht with Admiral Erich Raeder in September 1938 at Tempelhof airfield, before their departure for the Nazi Party rally in Nuremberg.*

Moltke, Erich Kordt, Adam von Trott, and Ulrich Schwerin von Schwanenfeld all joined the procession. But the British remained impassive, stoic, and distrustful, offering little more than empty words.

British policy at this time has often been criticized as inadequate. The pitiful failure of the German opposition figures' forays was due in large measure to Chamberlain's appeasement policy, upon which all attempts ultimately foundered. Britain had emerged exhausted from the First World War, and the prime minister wished to spare his nation another passage at arms, which would overtax its remaining strength and, it seemed, inevitably bring about an end to the empire. Chamberlain was no sentimental pacifist; there was more cool realism and even hard-hearted calculation in him than was later generally realized. He believed that a policy of prudent step-by-step appeasement would have a literally disarming effect, even on a man such as Hitler, and he pursued this course with conviction and tenacity. It was the only way, Chamberlain felt, to secure the peace—a goal for which he was prepared to pay virtually any price that did not compromise British honor and patience.

This is the background against which all the forays made by Hitler's opponents must be seen. The tactics the opposition had adopted were the very opposite of the British cabinet's, for they sought confrontation where Chamberlain hoped to avoid it. All they wanted from the British were words and gestures which they erroneously believed that Whitehall could easily deliver, because they were convinced that the Western powers would never abandon Czechoslovakia. In fact, Chamberlain was secretly prepared to do just that. To satisfy the requests of the German conspirators, the British would therefore have had to reverse their entire policy of conciliation. Furthermore, the British feared that the statements requested of them might goad the irascible Hitler to make decisions that would inevitably lead to war. Eventually, in view of Berlin's constant exacerbation of the tensions, Lord Halifax did send a message to the German government on September 9, 1938, reflecting at least somewhat the posture urged on Whitehall by the conspirators. The British ambassador to Berlin, Sir Nevile Henderson, flatly refused, however, to deliver a message so clearly out of step with the official conciliatory approach. Similarly, when Vansittart had written a memorandum a few months earlier advising a firmer posture toward Hitler, it was suppressed from within the bureaucracy. Vansittart's arguments were based on information channeled to him from German opposition circles detailing the Reich's economic, psychological, and military unpreparedness for war.[6]

As carefully calculated as Chamberlain's policies were, there was one element in the equation that he failed utterly to comprehend because it lay so far outside the orbit of his experience. For the sake of peace he was prepared to see Germany annex the Sudetenland, then Bohemia, and then even the Polish Corridor and parts of Upper Silesia; the new government in Berlin, he firmly believed, would eventually become as "sated, indolent and quiescent" as even the most rapacious of beasts.[7]

But Chamberlain did not understand Hitler at all, and his incomprehension would prove the undoing of his shrewdly devised policy. As a European statesman of the old school, the prime minister thought in terms of national interest. He had some grasp of such imponderables as injured pride and honor and the redress that Hitler constantly demanded. What he failed to realize, however, was that Hitler was not really serious about such things, indeed that amid his extravagant racist fantasies of saving the world there was little room for such categories as "nation," "interests," or even "pride." Like the Germans themselves—and probably like everyone else—the prime minister failed to fathom the radical otherness that Hitler introduced into European politics. In the words of a deeply shocked German conservative during the early years of Hitler's chancellorship, the Führer did not really seem to belong in this world. He "had something alien about him, as if he sprang from an otherwise extinct primeval tribe."[8]

One cannot judge the efforts of the German conspirators at this time without considering several other factors as well, especially the confusion they spread when abroad, despite their agreement about the ultimate purpose of their trips. It was, of course, very difficult under the circumstances to meet and adequately discuss strategy among themselves. Böhm-Tettelbach, for instance, did not even know when he traveled to London that Ewald von Kleist had been there just two weeks earlier on the same mission. Even more disturbing were the contradictions in what the various emissaries had to say. For instance, Goerdeler demanded—like Hitler himself—not only the cession of the Sudetenland but also, as if anticipating the Führer, the elimination of the Polish Corridor and the return of Germany's former colonies. Meanwhile Kleist spent his time advocating the restoration of the monarchy. When Adam von Trott declared that a new German government would preserve Hitler's territorial gains, he was unceremoniously evicted from the home of an English friend.

The German emissaries, many of whom considered themselves particularly knowledgeable about Great Britain, believed that making material demands such as these would heighten their credibility with the British. It is certainly true that the conspirators would never have gained the necessary public support to overthrow Hitler if their new regime had begun by renouncing all that the Führer had achieved—for instance, by revoking the *Anschluss* with Austria—whether voluntarily or under foreign pressure. Still, it is hard to believe their foolishness in playing down the basically moral nature of the opposition to Hitler and emphasizing German territorial claims instead, all in the belief that they would be better understood by the materialistic British, who are moved not by theory but by practical considerations.

Further confusing the issue for the British was the fact that nearly all these self-declared opponents of the regime held posts within it, some of them quite senior. At the end of a trip abroad in 1938, Adam von Trott wrote to his friend David Astor that, after giving the question much thought, he had decided to return to Germany solely in order to combat the Nazi regime. Suspicion lingered and grew, nevertheless, often leading to the breakup of long-standing friendships. The British, so blessed by nature and history, could hardly begin to understand the pretenses and subterfuges to which opponents of a totalitarian system had to resort. In the end, many in Britain could hardly distinguish between Hitler and these self-described opponents of his who seemed to endorse so many of his demands. "There is really very little difference between them. The same sort of ambitions are sponsored by a different body of men, and that is about all," wrote Vansittart, even though he was quite sympathetic toward the main purpose of the emissaries, namely a firm stance toward Hitler. Hugh Dalton, future chancellor of the exchequer, remarked sarcastically that these German conservatives were nothing more than "a race of carnivorous sheep."[9] Finally, there was the conviction in Britain, by no means confined to readers of the gutter press, that Germans were innately evil, or at any rate inclined to be so, as a result of their historical and cultural heritage. Cast in this light, Hitler's conservative opponents did not seem much different from the Führer himself, and considering the sins of Germany's elites extending back to the days of the kaisers, they were certainly no better.

One additional consideration actually weighed in favor of Hitler against his opponents. It was well known that the Junkers had always been more strongly oriented toward the East than toward the West and had long had many interests in common with Russia, in addition to their neighborly, cultural, and even emotional ties; no one could rule out the possibility that this group would not one day come to an understanding with the Soviet Union—as they had before with Russia—ideological impediments notwithstanding. Hitler, on the other hand, clearly lay above all reproach in this regard. Whatever else might be said about him, he was genuinely opposed to Communism, which was spreading into Western Europe through the Front Populaire in France, the Spanish civil war, and countless activities, mostly underground. Hitler himself described Germany under his leadership as a bulwark against the tide of Communism. He told Arnold Toynbee that he had been placed "on earth to lead humanity in its inevitable struggle against Bolshevism."[10] To people who saw the world in such sweeping, categorical terms, Hitler's illegal acts and despotic style must have shrunk to relative insignificance, or at least seemed minor problems that the Germans themselves could handle. Hitler's alien, sinister aura only heightened his credibility as the commander of a last bastion of Western civilization against the Communist hordes.

The efforts of the German conspirators were stymied by these as well as many other misunderstandings and misconceptions, which replicated on an international level the same delusions about Hitler shared by his would-be partners in domestic politics. In the end, therefore, there were insurmountable obstacles to any meeting of minds with the British, and if anything, the distance between the conspirators and the British only grew. When von Trott tried to prod Chamberlain in the direction of the German opposition, his words were received "icily." The ultimate reason for the countless misunderstandings in which the talks finally bogged down was clearly the

Among the most radical minds in the resistance was Hans Bernd Gisevius, known to his fellows as the eternal man of action. He was one of the few to escape arrest after July 20, 1944. His autobiographical account, Bis zum bittern Ende (To the Bitter End), *was the first book about the German resistance to enjoy wide success.*

two sides' mutual lack of understanding. The Germans, especially those who had British ancestors, had studied in Britain, or took a particular interest in the country, greatly admired the vast British Empire. They invoked it frequently and, to the discomfort of their hosts, often expressed their hope that Germany might one day achieve for itself some modicum of the hegemony that Britain had over the world. The British tended to interpret this as a manifestation of the old Teutonic ambitions and the insatiable German desire for a "place in the sun" that had challenged Britain's own status in the world for generations. Neither side perceived that the era of the great empires was actually drawing to a close, that imperialism had already become a relic of the past.

In the end, all that remained was disappointment and bitterness, and there is certainly some truth in the description of all these futile efforts as an Anglo-German tragedy. However, it was not only clumsi-

ness and short-sightedness that led to failure; there were also conflicting interests at issue. With the signing of the Hitler-Stalin pact in
August 1939, the increasingly half-hearted contacts seemed to die
away. They flickered to life again here and there, before disappearing
completely toward the end of the war. Fifty years later British historians are beginning to speak of Whitehall's "needless war" against
Hitler's domestic opponents.[11]

* * *

Despite the setbacks suffered by the resistance during these weeks,
Oster remained undaunted. The clearer it became that Hitler was
leading Germany straight into another war, the more numerous and
open his opponents became. The opposition circles that had formed
in the Foreign Office and in Military Intelligence were now joined by
Hans Bernd Gisevius, a former assistant secretary in the Ministry of
the Interior with an extensive knowledge of all the cliques and cote-
ries in the corridors of power; Count Peter Yorck von Wartenburg, an
assistant secretary to the Reich price commissioner; and Helmuth
Groscurth, chief of the army intelligence liaison group on the general
staff. All of them had friends in whom they confided as well as superiors and subordinates whom they informed and drew into opposition
circles. Fritz-Dietlof von der Schulenburg, for instance, won over the
prefect of police in Berlin, Count Wolf-Heinrich von Helldorf; even
more importantly, Oster revived his old connections with Erwin von
Witzleben, the commander of the Berlin military district. Witzleben
was a simple, unpretentious man with clear judgment. During one of
his conversations with Oster in the summer of 1938, he did not hesitate to declare himself ready for action: "I don't know anything about
politics, but I don't need to in order to know what has to be done
here."[12]

Beck was continuing his efforts and for the first time he began to
break out of the realm of mere counterproposals. At a meeting with
Brauchitsch on July 16, he suggested that the generals join together
to form a united opposition front. If this failed to sway Hitler and he
continued on a course toward war, the generals should resign en

masse. "Final decisions" needed to be made, Beck wrote, arguing that if the officer corps failed to act its members would incur a "blood guilt. . . . Their soldiers' duty to obey ends when their knowledge, their conscience, and their sense of responsibility forbid them to carry out an order. If their advice and warnings are ignored in such a situation, they have the right and the duty before history and the German people to resign."[13]

Brauchitsch summoned the generals to a meeting on Bendler-strasse on August 4. It soon became apparent that all the commanding generals believed that a spreading war would prove catastrophic for Germany. Busch and Reichenau, however, did not think that an attack on Czechoslovakia would necessarily lead to war with the Western powers, and as a result the tormented Brauchitsch did not even mention Beck's proposal that the generals attempt to pressure Hitler by threatening mass resignation. At the end of the meeting Brauchitsch did, however, reconfirm their unanimous opposition to a war and their conviction that a world war would mean the destruction of German culture.[14] Shortly afterwards, Hitler was informed about the meeting by Reichenau and he immediately demanded Beck's dismissal as chief of general staff. To show his displeasure he invited neither Beck nor Brauchitsch to a conference at his compound on the Obersalzberg on August 10; there he informed the chiefs of general staff of the armies and the air force that he had decided to invade Czechoslovakia.

Eight days later Beck submitted his resignation. This step and the way in which it was taken revealed once again the submissiveness and political ineptitude of the officer corps. After the Fritsch affair Beck had declared that he must remain at his post in order both to work for the rehabilitation of his humiliated superior and to prevent the reduction of the army to a mere tool of the Führer. His ensuing dispute with Hitler, however, which took the form of a series of memoranda opposing the Führer's plans for war and for the reorganization of the high command, proved to be the "final battle" of the officer corps in its struggle to maintain a say in decisions of war and peace.[15] Now Beck cleared himself out of Hitler's way, as it were, becoming merely an outraged, and later despairing, observer without position or influence.

Ludwig Beck was the "philosopher general": clever, wise, and authoritative—as friend and foe alike were inclined to agree—but lacking determination. Appointed army chief of general staff in 1935, Beck became, three years later, the only general to resign in peacetime in protest of Hitler's policies.

Only a few days earlier Erich von Manstein, his chief of operations, had written him a letter urging that he remain at his post because no one had the "skill and strength of character" to replace him. Beck's authority was indeed widely acknowledged throughout the officer corps. He was a clear, imaginative, rigorous thinker of great integrity. Even Hitler could not shake the aura of easy superiority Beck projected in every word and deed. During the Fritsch crisis the Führer had confided in a member of his cabinet that Beck was the only officer he feared: "That man could really do something."[16] Later Beck effortlessly assumed a leadership role in the opposition. No one doubted that if a successful putsch was launched he would become chief of state. "Beck was king," a contemporary recalled.[17] If there was a flaw in his cool, pure intelligence, it lay in his lack of toughness and drive. He was "very scholarly by nature," one of his admirers commented. Other opposition figures also found that he provided more analytical acuity than leadership at crucial moments.[18]

Beck was also probably less of a political strategist than the situation required and was certainly not conversant with the kinds of maneuvers and ploys at which Hitler was so adept. That is why he readily acquiesced to Hitler's request that his resignation not be made public lest it provoke an unfavorable reaction. As a result, the decision he had made after so much painful reflection had no public impact. Beck later admitted that he had made a mistake, adding a revealing justification that illustrates the helplessness of his position: it was not his way, he said, to be a "self-promoter."[19] Hitler did not even bother to grant him an audience when he took his leave.

Nonetheless, upon his departure Beck commended his successor, Franz Halder, to all those with whom he was on confidential terms. Indeed, only a few days after assuming his new post, Halder summoned Hans Oster to an interview. After a few exchanges of views about Hitler's foreign designs, Halder asked his guest point-blank how the preparations for a coup were progressing. More clearly than Beck, Halder recognized that the ingloriously abandoned plan for a "generals' strike" would only make sense as the first step in a coup; otherwise it was better left undone. Hitler could easily have found replacements for all the seditious generals and knew far too much about power and how to keep it simply to back down in the face of such opposition. The historian Peter Hoffmann quite rightly points in this regard to Manstein's comment at the Nuremberg trials that dictators do not allow themselves to be driven into things, because then they would no longer be dictators.[20]

Halder was a typical general staff officer of the old school: correct, focused, and outspoken. Observers also noted a certain impulsiveness, which, for the sake of his career, he had learned to control, if not overcome. Not long after his meeting with Oster he spoke with Gisevius for the first time, soon turning to concrete questions about plans for the coup and describing Hitler as "mentally ill" and "blood-

Field Marshal Gerd von Rundstedt (left) *greets Field Marshal Erwin von Witzleben at Rundstedt's headquarters in France in 1941. Rundstedt avoided political issues and time after time took refuge in the claim that he was an apolitical, purely military man. When Witzleben, in contrast, was asked by Hans Oster in 1938 whether he would be prepared to participate in a coup, he replied, "I don't know anything about politics, but I don't have to in order to know what has to be done here."*

thirsty."[21] Here and elsewhere, he proved that he was a man far more capable of action than Beck, who immersed himself in philosophical contemplation. Halder had resolved the conflict between the loyalty traditionally expected of a soldier and the need to topple Hitler and no longer felt inhibited from taking action by his oath to the Führer. As early as the fall maneuvers of 1937, he had encouraged Fritsch to use force against Hitler, and after Fritsch's treacherous removal he had pressed for "practical opposition." More clear-sighted than most of his fellow conservatives and less compromising in his values, he realized that Hitler was a radical revolutionary prepared to destroy virtually everything. Despite the adoring crowds at Hitler's feet, Halder considered his rule highly illegitimate because it stood outside all tradition: truth, morality, patriotism, even human beings themselves were only instruments for the accrual of more power. Hitler, in Halder's view, was "the very incarnation of evil." By nature a practical, austere man, meticulous to the point of pedantry, Halder was not, however, cut out for the role of conspirator and the very perversity of the times can be seen in the fact that such a man felt driven to such an undertaking. He later said he found "the need to resist a frightful, agonizing experience."[22] Halder refused to be a party to any sort of ill considered action and insisted that a coup would only be justifiable as a last resort.

Upon assuming his new post on September 1, Halder informed Brauchitsch that, like his predecessors, he opposed the Führer's plans for war and was determined to "exploit every opportunity that this position affords to carry on the struggle against Hitler." If this comment illustrates Halder's own character, the reaction of the overly pliable commander in chief, who felt himself forced from one horror to the next, was perhaps even more revealing: as if in gratitude, Brauchitsch spontaneously seized both Halder's hands and shook them.[23] A series of discussions soon ensued that included Witzleben; Hjalmar Schacht; Beck; the quartermaster general of the army, Colonel Eduard Wagner; and, most important, Hans Oster, the indefatigable driving force and go-between of the opposition. The necessary preconditions for a coup were spelled out and the aims more precisely defined.

In the course of these discussions a perhaps unavoidable rift emerged between the methodical, deliberate chief of general staff and Oster's immediate associates. Halder was primarily concerned with finding ways to justify a coup morally and politically, not only for himself but also for the army and the general public. A coup would only be warranted, in his view, if Hitler ignored all warnings and issued final instructions to launch a war. At that point, but not before, Halder said, he would be prepared to give the signal for a putsch. Oster and the impetuous Gisevius, on the other hand, were far more radical in their thinking and no longer had any patience for tactical considerations. In their view the regime had to be struck down by any means possible. Hitler's warmongering may have provided an inducement and opportunity, but it was not the primary reason for taking action. Although this basic difference of opinion surfaced now and then, it was never really resolved, leading one of the more resolute opponents of the Nazi regime to speak, with some justification, of a "conspiracy within the conspiracy."[24]

This basic difference of opinion came to the fore only once, when Gisevius tried to persuade Halder to strike immediately rather than wait for an opportune moment. Halder was as convinced as Gisevius that Hitler meant war but insisted nevertheless on proof; he was incensed by Gisevius's suggestion that evidence of these plans and countless further indications of the regime's hideous nature could easily be obtained by seizing Gestapo and SS files. Gisevius believed that it was preferable to attack the regime on criminal grounds rather than on political ones and to produce "a few dozen airtight arrest warrants" rather than all sorts of tortuous political rationales. No army officer worth his salt, in Gisevius's view, could resist a command to restore order in the face of murder, illegal confinement, extortion, and corruption. To advance moral and political rationales would simply invite a lengthy debate over the legality of the coup.

This proposal, and indeed Gisevius's entire attitude, struck Halder as far too adventurist, smacking more of mutiny and unsoldierly willfulness than of responsible action. Under no circumstances would he lend the army to such an operation. Only when Hitler issued orders to attack, thereby revealing himself to the public as the "criminal" that Halder had long considered him to be, could the signal for a military putsch be issued. A few days later an impatient Gisevius accompanied Hjalmar Schacht uninvited to a meeting Schacht had arranged at Halder's apartment. He hoped to urge his plan on the chief of the general staff once again, but Halder lost all patience and thereafter refused to receive Gisevius.[25]

Soon afterwards Halder asked Oster to work out a detailed plan for a coup, and with Oster's participation the rather aimless and rancorous activities of the conspirators gained a focal point and took on a more concrete shape. The web of conspirators grew rapidly and many loose ends were tied up, creating a much more solid organization. Halder made contact with Ernst von Weizsäcker—although direct communications between the Foreign Office and the general staff were explicitly forbidden—and with Wilhelm Canaris, the chief of Military Intelligence. In August Halder met in Frankfurt with Wilhelm Adam, the commander in chief of Army Group 2. Both men were concerned that Hitler was headed for war. When Halder "abruptly" stated that if Witzleben, the commander of the Berlin military district, were to "strike, the commanders in chief of the Reich would have to go along with him," Adam replied, "Go ahead, I'm ready."[26] Then, on September 4, Halder met with Schacht, who agreed to become provisional head of the new government in case of a successful coup. At the same time, Halder was in contact with Oster, Oster with Gisevius, Gisevius with Schulenburg, and virtually everyone with everyone else in a continuous round of discussions, to plan movements during the coup and to coordinate and review possible scenarios. Witzleben visited Schacht at his country estate near Berlin, parting with the comment that this time they would go all the way.[27]

In the meantime Witzleben had won over to the cause a subordinate of his, Count Walter Brockdorff-Ahlefeldt, commander of the Potsdam Division. This unit was regarded not only as a "model division" but it was also the strongest military force in the Berlin area and therefore crucial to the success of the coup. Halder arranged to have the First Light Division, commanded by Erich Hoepner, which was on maneuvers in the border region between Thuringia and Saxony, put on alert to block the path to Berlin of SS-Leibstandarte Adolf Hitler, the SS troop that acted as Hitler's bodyguard. Just before midnight on September 14, after all operations had been spelled out yet again—especially the plans to seize police stations, radio transmitters, telephone installations, repeater stations, the Reich Chancellery, and key ministries as rapidly as possible—and after Brockdorff-Ahlefeldt had personally inspected all pivotal positions, including even the transmitters in Königs-Wusterhausen near Berlin, Witzleben declared all military preparation completed for a coup.[28]

One major question was what to do with Hitler himself. Gisevius and a small group of predominantly younger conspirators felt that he should be killed without further ado. Witzleben, Beck, and most of the other conspirators, including Canaris, who was on the fringes of this attempt, believed that Hitler should be arrested and put on trial. By using the legal system to expose the crimes of the regime, they hoped to avoid either making a martyr of Hitler or igniting a civil war. Halder pointed out that it was not the moral judgments of the elite that counted but the support of the general population, most of which was still very much in thrall to the Hitlerian myth. Hans von Dohnanyi and Oster argued that after Hitler was arrested he should be brought before a panel of physicians chaired by Dohnanyi's father-in-law, the celebrated psychiatrist Karl Bonhoeffer, and declared mentally ill. Halder, for his part, hesitated. He was not opposed to eliminating Hitler, he informed his fellow conspirators, but under the circumstances he did not approve of murdering him in the open—perhaps an accident could be arranged, or they could pin the assassination on a third party. The radicals among the conspirators, who had always considered Halder indecisive, felt their doubts about him confirmed, and they began to fear for the operation, especially since the chief of general staff had explicitly reserved to himself the right to issue the order for the coup. Witzleben stated that if necessary he would take action without orders from above, cordoning off the former quarters of the Ministry of War and army headquarters and putting Halder and Brauchitsch "under lock and key during the crucial hours."[29]

Around September 20, the innermost circle of conspirators met in Oster's apartment for a final conclave: Witzleben, Gisevius, Dohnanyi, and probably Goerdeler, as well as Captain Friedrich Wilhelm Heinz and Lieutenant Commander Franz Maria Liedig. Heinz and Liedig had recently been asked to assemble a special task force, whose precise mission the assembled group now determined. When Halder issued the signal for the coup, the task force, under Witzleben's command, was to overpower the sentries at the main entrance to the Reich Chancellery at 78 Wilhelmstrasse, enter the building, neutralize any resistance, especially from Hitler's bodyguards, and enter Hitler's quarters. The Führer would then be ar-

Captain Friedrich Wilhelm Heinz (left) never succeeded in making the transition back to civilian life after the First World War. He was introduced to resistance circles by Hans Oster (right). In the best-prepared and most promising of all plots to overthrow Hitler, Heinz was supposed to force his way into the Chancellery at the head of a task force on September 28, 1938, overpower the SS bodyguards, and shoot Hitler. Heinz and his men were waiting at the ready in Berlin when news of the Munich conference broke. Thus the coup attempt failed before it ever started.

rested, the conspirators agreed, and immediately transported by automobile to a secure location.

Oster had arranged for Heinz to come to the meeting with Witzleben. Molded by his experiences in the Great War, Heinz, like many of his counterparts, had never felt at ease in civilian life and had continued to live by military habits. Initially a member of the Ehrhardt Freikorps, a private army formed after the First World War, he was swept up by the mood of romantic-revolutionary nationalism and joined the Stahlhelm, the paramilitary association that provided a home for restless members of the political right during the days of the much-hated republic but that, like all other political organizations, was dissolved in the great *Gleichschaltung* of the fall of 1933. Through his many connections with comrades from those days, and with Oster's help, Heinz managed to assemble a commando of about thirty rough, brash young officers, students, and workers trained in the use of firearms.

Witzleben had scarcely left Oster's apartment when the remaining conspirators expanded the plot in one key way. Heinz argued that it would not suffice simply to arrest Hitler and put him on trial. Even from a prisoner's dock, Hitler would prove more powerful than all of them, including Witzleben and his army corps. Heinz's arguments seemed to strike home. In the wake of the nationalistic euphoria over Austria's "return" to the Reich, Hitler's position was stronger than ever; the regime's propaganda machine had succeeded in portraying the Führer as the stalwart champion of the national interest. It was only the malevolent or corrupt forces in his entourage, according to some critical voices, who occasionally led him astray. Heinz therefore argued that it was essential to engineer a scuffle during the arrest and simply shoot Hitler on the spot.

If the records are not misleading, Oster finally agreed, although he knew that both Witzleben and Halder were opposed on principle to murdering Hitler. And thus a third conspiracy arose within the already existing "conspiracy within a conspiracy." It comprised the most determined core of conspirators—those who would stop at nothing. In hindsight, they were perhaps the only ones who might have been a match for the Nazis. All the others, including Halder, Beck, and even Witzleben, were impeded by their notions of tradition, morality, and good upper-class manners, though there were considerable individual differences among them. The resistance was therefore never really able to match the ruthlessness of the regime. Indeed, a few days after this evening conference, Beck warned Oster that the conspirators should not defile their good names by committing murder. The debate surrounding this issue would continue unabated until July 20, 1944.

In hopes of saving the peace so threatened by Hitler, British Prime Minister Neville Chamberlain traveled to Germany twice in one week in September 1938. Although Chamberlain repeatedly yielded to the German chancellor, Hitler only raised his demands. Two days after his second trip Chamberlain described Hitler to the British cabinet as "the most ordinary little dog I've ever met."

The photograph, taken on September 22, 1938, in Bad Godesberg, shows Chamberlain with Hitler and legation counselor and interpreter Paul Otto Schmidt. In the background to the right is Foreign Minister Joachim von Ribbentrop.

Nevertheless, all now stood ready for the coup. What remained was the signal from Halder, to be given as soon as Hitler issued the orders to invade. But on the evening of September 13 stunning news arrived. The British prime minister had declared his willingness to hold personal discussions with the Führer, immediately, at any location and without concern for protocol. Hitler is said to have commented later that he was "thunderstruck" by Chamberlain's action. For the conspirators, it was as if the world had come crashing down around them. As one of their number later wrote, they each struggled to maintain their composure; those who had advocated a more cautious approach heaped scorn on the irresponsibility of the activists who once again had underestimated the genius of the Führer. Witzleben expressed doubts about the judgment of the conspirators who claimed to be political experts. Brockdorff Ahlefeldt voiced his concern that the conspirators would now no longer be able to count on the army troops that were crucial to a successful coup. In a mood of glum uncertainty, most of the conspirators began to fear that the ground had been torn out from under them once and for all.

Ultimately, the overture to Hitler only proved something that Chamberlain had never been willing to acknowledge but that certainly must have begun to dawn on him within a few bitter days: Hitler wanted not to resolve the crisis in Europe but to heighten it. The Führer felt confirmed in his belief that the Western democracies would yield in the end when Chamberlain accepted the transfer of the Sudetenland to Germany, a decision endorsed by the British and French governments after nervous negotiations, and even accepted by Prague, though it consented only under great pressure.

Hitler was nevertheless surprised when, one week later, on September 22, 1938, the prime minister flew to Bad Godesberg, near Bonn, to deliver a copy of the agreement personally and to discuss the modalities of the transfer. Paradoxically, such eagerness to appease actually complicated Hitler's plans for further annexations by ruining the triumphant march into Prague that he was already savoring. After an embarrassed pause, Hitler quietly informed Chamberlain that the agreement they had reached in Berchtesgaden just a week before was null and void. He now insisted not only on marching immediately into the Sudetenland but also on satisfaction of longstanding Polish and Hungarian claims on various border regions of Czechoslovakia. After an exchange of letters from the respective staffs failed to resolve these issues, the negotiations were broken off that evening. An enraged Chamberlain demanded a memorandum setting forth the new German requirements. According to Ernst von Weizsäcker of the Foreign Office, Hitler "clapped his hands together as if in great amusement" when he described the course of the conversations. Three days later he issued an ultimatum: he would only hold his divisions back if his new Godesberg demands were accepted by 2:00 p.m. on September 28. "If England and France want to attack," he told the British emissary Sir Horace Wilson, who had come to Berlin on September 26 in a final attempt to reach an agreement, "then let them do so. I don't care. I am prepared for all eventualities. Today is Tuesday. Next Monday we'll be at war."[30]

Just as news of Chamberlain's trip to Berchtesgaden had virtually paralyzed the conspirators, Hitler's additional demands in Godesberg infused them with new life. When Oster heard the details from Erich Kordt, he said, "Finally [we have] clear proof that Hitler wants war, no matter what. Now there can be no going back."[31]

Everywhere in Europe war preparations began, accompanied by the darkest forebodings. By the time the first news arrived from Bad Godesberg, Czechoslovakia had already ordered its forces to mobilize, not without some sense of relief. Britain followed suit, ordering the navy to make ready for war. In London, slit trenches were dug, gas masks distributed, and hospitals evacuated. France called up the reserves. In Germany, Goebbels's propaganda campaign about the suffering of the Sudeten Germans, which had been launched just weeks before, grew shriller and shriller. Hitler ordered the Wehrmacht attack units to advance from their assembly areas in the interior to the launch points on the Czech border. In an attempt to stir up war fever in Germany, Hitler ordered the Second Motorized Division to pass through Berlin on its way to the border. It rumbled down the Ost-West-Achse boulevard, before turning into Wilhelmstrasse, where he reviewed it from the Chancellery balcony. Contrary to all expectations, however, no cheering throngs lined the streets. Hitler noted with annoyance the solemnity of the passersby and the glacial silence with which they observed the troops before turning away. Visibly upset, he withdrew into the middle of the room. The American correspondent William Shirer observed that this was the most striking antiwar demonstration that he had ever seen.[32]

What disappointed Hitler only encouraged the conspirators, who now moved to their starting positions. They carried out the final military and police preparations and checked over their proclamations to the German people. Equipped with firearms, ammunition, hand grenades, and explosives, Heinz's task force waited at the ready in a number of private dwellings in Berlin, such as 118 Eisenacherstrasse. Helmuth Groscurth, who was spending the evening with his brother, suddenly broke off their conversation and asked him if he could keep a secret. After repeated assurances, Groscurth finally told him the news: "Tonight Hitler is going to be arrested!"[33]

In fact, the ultimatum did not expire until 2:00 p.m. the next day. That morning Oster forwarded to Witzleben a copy of the note that Hitler had sent to Chamberlain in Bad Godesberg abruptly rejecting the British offers. Witzleben immediately took it to Halder. As Halder read it, "tears of indignation" welled up in his eyes, and together the two decided not to wait any longer. Halder offered to inform Brauchitsch and rally him to the cause, if possible, especially since he himself did not have direct command over any troops in his position as chief of general staff.

Commander in Chief Brauchitsch was also outraged by Hitler's note. He, too, began to see through the Führer's duplicity. "So he lied to me again!" he roared. But Brauchitsch was not yet prepared to commit himself to a coup at this point. He would "probably" participate, Halder reported to the waiting Witzleben upon his return. Witzleben thereupon telephoned the commander in chief right from Halder's office and appealed to him—"virtually begging him," according to Gisevius, "to issue the order to go ahead." The indecisive Brauchitsch said, however, that he wanted first to stop in at the Chancellery to assess the situation personally. Upon returning to military district headquarters on Hohenzollerndamm, Witzleben called out to Gisevius, "Any time now, Doctor!"[34]

At eleven o'clock, Erich Kordt was informed by his brother in London that Great Britain would declare war if Czechoslovakia was invaded. Paris, too, seemed resolute. But German war preparations continued nevertheless. The previous evening Hitler had ordered the divisions on Germany's western borders to mobilize as well. Kordt

Erich Kordt (left) was the leader of the resistance circle in the Foreign Office. He sought to have the great double doors of the Chancellery opened from within on September 28, 1938, to allow Friedrich Wilhelm Heinz's task force to enter Hitler's chambers.

Above: *Kordt speaking with his minister, Joachim von Ribbentrop.*

met Schulenburg, and they agreed to clear the way for Heinz's task force by opening from the inside the guarded double doors at the entrance to the Chancellery. Everyone waited: Witzleben, Brockdorff-Ahlefeldt, Oster, Kordt, Gisevius, Heinz, and the others. Most important of all, Halder waited for Brauchitsch to return from the Chancellery. And then the clock stopped ticking.

■   ■   ■

At literally the last minute, Hitler decided to yield to pressure from Mussolini and agree to a conference in Munich to settle the Sudeten issue. The conspirators were aghast. After all their planning, this was clearly the end of their plots. The issue had been clear—either a coup or war—and now the Munich conference threw everything into question. Only Gisevius, arguing desperately, tried to persuade Witzleben to stage the coup anyway. But the general asked him sharply, as Gisevius later recalled, "What can the troops possibly do against a leader this victorious?"[35]

In an instant the situation was turned upside down. The dread of war that had haunted the morning hours gave way to jubilation and relief that afternoon. When the news was announced in the British House of Commons, there was a moment of stunned silence and then an outburst of joy. Everywhere the reaction was the same, and the few unhappy or chagrined voices were soon drowned out by cheers. When Winston Churchill denounced the Munich agreement as the "first foretaste of a bitter cup," he was shouted down by indignant members of Parliament.[36]

Among the few who took little joy from the news of this day was Hitler himself. He had seemed pale and agitated during the Munich conference, often standing with his arms crossed, staring darkly ahead. "This fellow Chamberlain has spoiled my entry into Prague," Schacht heard him say. Although historians now have little doubt that Germany would only have been able to hold out for a few days against an invasion by the Western powers in the fall of 1938, Hitler still felt that he had been cheated of his grand timetable. The depth of the rancor and disappointment he felt over the Munich conference is reflected in the thoughts he expressed while holed up in his bunker in February 1945: "We should have gone to war in 1938," he said. "That was our last chance to keep it localized. But they gave in everywhere. Like cowards they yielded to all our demands. So it was very difficult to initiate hostilities."[37] The general public, unaware of Hitler's determination to go to war—and even of Britain's successful efforts to get Mussolini to intervene—concluded that the Führer could master any situation. He seemed magically in league with chance, luck, with the very fates themselves.

Among the losers at Munich were Hitler's domestic opponents. In a single day, as one of them noted, they had been reduced from powerful foes of the regime to a "bunch of malcontents" whose ideas had been disproved by events time after time and who had now become nothing more than a police problem.[38] But worse yet, the Munich accord was a devastating indictment of their political judgment and could not help but tarnish their reputations. The conspirators fell into a mood of bitter helplessness, and the ties among them—already weak in many cases—slackened further or were severed completely. Feelings of mutual distrust began to arise, and many resistance leaders, such as the diplomat Ulrich von Hassell, began to doubt if it was still possible to save the situation "before it reached the abyss." Munich had "decimated" the opposition, Halder aptly commented.[39]

Perhaps even more important than the failure of the coup to get off the ground was the fact that the events of the last days of September destroyed the very premise on which the German opposition had based its strategy, and it is one of the curious aspects of the movement that this truth remained largely unnoticed. Despite all the uncertainties, no other attempt to strike Hitler down in these years would come close to having as good a chance of success. Thereafter the conspirators never ceased complaining about the "betrayal" of the Western powers, their feebleness and blindness. These oft-repeated reproaches surfaced just a few days after the Munich conference in a letter Goerdeler wrote to an American friend describing the accord as "outright capitulation" and predicting that war was now inevitable.[40] Yet these statements actually illustrated the conspirators' crucial strategic mistake, an error that was brought into stark relief by the debacle of September 28, 1938: they had made their actions dependent on events they could neither accurately foresee nor control—first, Hitler's actually ordering an invasion; second, the Western powers' then declaring war.

The conspirators would not overcome this basic flaw until shortly before July 20, 1944. Whereas in the fall of 1938 they made their coup contingent on Hitler's going to war and on a firm response from Britain and France, they later made their activities dependent on Hitler's victories and defeats: victories, they felt, made him popular with the people and therefore unassailable, while defeats laid them, his internal enemies, open to accusations of aiding and abetting the downfall of their own country. Most of the conspirators never escaped

Fabian von Schlabrendorff described Hans Oster (above) *as "a man after God's own heart." Oster, who worked in the Military Intelligence Office and was close to Wilhelm Canaris, its chief, was for many years one of the key figures in the resistance. A curious combination of moral rectitude and cunning, he followed simple maxims in thought and action. Just before being hanged on April 9, 1945, in the Flossenbürg concentration camp, he wrote to his son that he had always tried to remain a "decent man," for which he required only what he had learned in the nursery as a child and in his training as a soldier. He concluded, "All we fear is the wrath of God."*

this dilemma, and the infirmity of purpose that is often imputed to the German resistance stemmed to a large extent from this self-imposed dependence on external circumstances. The alternative to this approach was embodied by Gisevius, the "eternal plotter," as the other conspirators derisively called him. His radicalism, which so annoyed Halder, stemmed largely from his firm focus on the criminal nature of the Nazi regime. This enabled him to liberate action from all considerations of tactics, ultimate aims, and outside influences. Similar approaches were taken by Oster, Henning von Tresckow, Friedrich Olbricht, Cäsar von Hofacker, and Carl Goerdeler, who had warned repeatedly against waiting for the "right psychological moment" and now considered emigrating to the United States.[41]

One evening soon after the debacle of September 28, Oster and Gisevius somberly burned the plans and notes for the coup—all that remained of their daring dream—in Witzleben's fireplace. Many months would pass before the resistance began to recover from the blow it had suffered. Only a small, highly committed core of conspirators remained, and even they felt completely spent; their nerves were too frayed and their energy too depleted for them to organize another coup attempt, especially since to do so went against the grain of all they had been taught, their way of thinking and their traditions, which, though honorable, had been overtaken by the times. The industrialist Nikolaus von Halem, who maintained ties with a variety of opposition groups, had already dismissed the officers' ideas as "romantic" in the summer of 1938 and observed that Hitler, the "messenger of chaos," could only be removed from this world by a professional hit man, or at least some figure from the renegade old soldiers' organizations. For a long time he considered attempting to persuade the former leader of the Oberland Freikorps, Beppo Römer, to undertake such an attempt.[42]

But Halem's approach was ultimately just another brand of romanticism. Much closer to reality was Franz Halder, who steadfastly held to his highly negative view of the regime, refusing to allow himself to be seduced by any of Hitler's triumphs and finding in the mounting horrors new confirmation of his belief that Hitler was evil incarnate. His willingness to take action flared up once again, but weakly and only for a passing moment. For the rest of the time, he doggedly performed his duty, served his country, kept himself isolated, nursed his hatreds, and, despite the darkness and horror on all sides, would not be persuaded to act. At noon on September 28, when news of the Munich conference broke, he lost his composure after so many days of feverish preparation. According to one observer, he "utterly collapsed" on his desk, "weeping and saying that all was lost."[43]

It had been a trying time for Hitler, too, who also thought that all was lost, his life's work in ruins. But he set about searching relentlessly for ways to recoup the situation. That was the crucial difference.

4

FROM MUNICH TO ZOSSEN

While the opponents of the regime were in the throes of depression, wondering whether it was possible to take moral stands in such a fallen world or whether those who did so inevitably ended up looking like fools, Hitler forged resolutely ahead. Although still disappointed with the Munich agreement, he realized that an opportunity had arisen to resolve the smoldering conflict with the army once and for all.

Only two weeks after the Wehrmacht had marched into the Sudetenland through the cheering throngs in the second of its "flower wars," Hitler presented the OKW with the outline of an executive order that was dressed up in the form of an "Appeal to Officers." It denied military leaders the right to form political judgments, demanding instead "obedience," "rock-solid confidence," and "faithful, aggressive determination." The principle that the general staff should share in political decision making was eliminated, as was the traditional practice, extending back to the era of the kaisers, of registering dissenting views in writing. To the extent they could agree on anything, the generals had joined together from the very beginning in warning against virtually every political decision Hitler had made—and they had been proved wrong time and again. Now the Führer informed the commanders in chief, "I don't want any more cautionary memoranda."[1]

Under the pressure of this dispute, a split developed within the officer corps for the first time, or at least more visibly than before. On the whole, the officer corps had preserved a surprising degree of internal solidarity over the previous few years and possibly for this reason had managed to maintain a certain self-confidence despite all the setbacks. Hitler had long hoped to break this cohesion; he tested it with the sudden expansion of the Wehrmacht after 1935, which also enabled him to push a greater number of ideologically reliable officers into leadership positions in the military. For much the same reason, the exact responsibilities of the army, navy, and air force were never clearly defined. In addition, Hitler purposely sowed conflict between the high command of the armed forces (OKW), which reported directly to him, and the high command of the army (Oberkommando des Heeres, or OKH), led by the obstinate old officers' caste. Despite all this, internal cohesion remained solid. The only exception had occurred early in the year when Admiral Erich Raeder, commander in chief of the navy, rejected an appeal to help with the rehabilitation of Fritsch: "That's a mess that the boys in red pants got themselves into," he said, "and they can get themselves out of it."[2]

In the light of Hitler's foreign policy successes, however, the ranks now began to waver. For the first time, senior officers endorsed his rebuke of the army high command. They lamented the lack of faith and loss of confidence the OKH showed in the Führer. The full extent of the split is evidenced in a letter written by OKW general Alfred Jodl in which he describes the OKH as the "enemy side." The consequence was that no resistance was offered when Hitler took advantage of the situation to reshuffle personnel for a second time, dismissing a number of generals whose skeptical attitudes boded ill for the sort of unconditional obedience he now expected, including Wilhelm Adam, Hermann Geyer, and Wilhelm Ulex. Nevertheless, despite all the traps Hitler attempted to set within the officer corps and despite the tensions that did arise, the traditional esprit de corps remained quite strong. Those who opposed Hitler or even conspired against him over the ensuing years were generally safe from denunciation by their fellow officers. Among the rare exceptions to this rule were Erich von Manstein, who informed on Tresckow early in 1944;

Wilhelm Keitel, who threatened to denounce any officer who criticized the Führer, "including on church or Jewish questions"; and
Heinz Guderian, who only refrained from denouncing a fellow officer
when he was similarly threatened in return.[3]

The success of Hitler's initial attempt to repress army interference
in political affairs soon became apparent. On the night of November
9–10, 1938, which has come to be known as *Kristallnacht*, "spontane-
ous demonstrations," as Joseph Goebbels phrased it in his directive,
were organized all over Germany. Synagogues were burned, Jewish-
owned stores demolished, and large numbers of Jews arrested; some
were killed. It was plain to see that the government was as responsible as the hordes of SA men were for the arson, plunder, and murder
of that night. People were horrified and shamed but remained quiet.
Their feelings, however, were soon given voice at a conference of
army commanders, where a number of generals did not hesitate to
express their outrage. General Fedor von Bock even asked his fellow
officers excitedly whether someone couldn't just "string up that swine
Goebbels."[4]

Walther von Brauchitsch, the army commander in chief, remained
unmovable. After all the disputes and unpleasantness of the previous
weeks, he simply shrugged his shoulders at demands that he lodge a
protest. Raeder, on the other hand, backed the formal protests of a
number of senior naval officers, among them Admiral Conrad Patzig
and Captains Günther Lütjens and Karl Dönitz, and sought an audience with the Führer. The only response Raeder received, however,
was that the SA district leaders had gotten out of control, a fabrication
that satisfied him.[5] Meanwhile, at a general meeting in the Reichsbank, Hjalmar Schacht sharply condemned the events. In addition,
the senior SA commander and prefect of the Berlin police, Count
Wolf-Heinrich Helldorf, who had been absent from the city that
night, summoned high-ranking police officials to a meeting immediately upon his return and bitterly reproached them for having obeyed
the order to stand by and do nothing. If he had been in Berlin, he
told them, he would have issued orders to fire on the SA mobs. In the
gloomy silence of those November days, the sound of another voice
rose for the first time, that of a young captain named Count Claus

Schenk von Stauffenberg, who criticized the officer corps as seeming dumbstruck, adding that not much more could be expected from people who had already had their backbones broken several times.[6]

Hitler rarely missed an opportunity to demonstrate to those he had defeated the full extent of their loss. On the morning of March 15, 1939, he finally fulfilled his dream of taking Prague, sending motorized units into the city through swirling spring snow. He kept the officer corps in the dark about his exact plans until the last possible minute, however, at times going so far as to mislead it with placating words. Even the devoted Keitel, chief of the OKW, later complained that he knew nothing of Hitler's intentions and was left to guess.

The opposition to Hitler failed to realize the significance of the occupation of the western provinces of Czechoslovakia. Most thought of it as another Munich, confirmation of all they had learned about the weakness and perfidy of the Western powers. In reality, though, Prague was the turning point. Hitherto, Hitler had always justified ripping up treaties and breaking solemn promises by invoking the injustice of the Treaty of Versailles. He had defended German incursions by citing the right to self-determination of those territories under foreign occupation—a right that had been proclaimed by the Western powers themselves. Now, for the first time, he emerged clearly as an aggressor, going beyond anything he had done in the past. The occupation of Prague, therefore, provided an excellent opportunity for a coup. The opposition groups remained scattered, however, and instead of a revolt there was widespread rejoicing over the Führer's latest stroke of genius. Diaries and memoirs of the period record that even some opposition figures felt patriotic pride as well as depression at Hitler's latest success. Like Mussolini during the turbulent days of Munich, some even began to believe, though without his feeling of contempt, that the democracies were by their nature weak-willed and easily intimidated.

■ ■ ■

Scarcely had Hitler annexed western Czechoslovakia when he let it be known that he now intended to settle scores with Poland. This time—

The Ministry of War, the general staff, and the Military Intelligence Office were all originally located in this building on Tirpitzufer. In 1938, after the Blomberg and Fritsch affairs, the high command of the Wehrmacht, the OKW, moved into the former quarters of the Ministry of War, which had been dissolved. With the outbreak of war in 1939, the OKW moved into various headquarters on the fronts, while the general staff went to Zossen, just outside Berlin. Only Military Intelligence remained in the old location. It was here that Hans Oster created one of the hotbeds of the resistance, under the protection of the chief of Military Intelligence, Admiral Wilhelm Canaris.

as if he had somehow sensed the previous fall's conspiracy to overthrow him if he went to war—he seemed very much at pains not to
provide the generals with opportunities for collusion. He concealed
his decision to go to war, which had long been firm, and assured those
around him that he would resort to force only if all attempts failed to
reach an amicable settlement. "We have to be good now," he told a
visitor.[8]

And so the conspirators remained passive, clinging to the idea that
a coup would only be justifiable if Hitler expressed a clear determination to go to war and issued the corresponding orders. Under pressure from Oster, Goerdeler, Gisevius, Hassell, and others, Beck now
attempted to involve Halder, his successor as chief of the army general staff, in new plans. At a meeting in Beck's home in Lichterfelde,
the two conspirators readily agreed on the basic nature of the regime,
Hitler's thinly veiled determination to provoke war, and the need to
overthrow him. They disagreed sharply, however, on when to strike.
Halder remained convinced, as he had been before Munich, that they
could not act unless the Führer was clearly headed for war. As to
Hitler's present designs on the port city of Danzig, it was a German
city, as even the British allowed, and it was still quite possible that the
negotiations with the Poles would be concluded peacefully.

By now Beck had come to see things quite differently. He was no
longer willing to stand by while Hitler scored piecemeal successes, for
he saw that they hastened the inevitable catastrophe. War would
come at some point, making a coup even more difficult to carry out.
Once hostilities began, "other irrational, 'patriotic' laws" would be
implemented. Time was therefore short. Halder and Beck were engaged in the same dispute that had divided Halder and Gisevius a
year earlier, but this time it was inflamed by the tensions and strained
personal relationship between the current chief of general staff and
his proud but isolated predecessor, their mutual professional admiration notwithstanding. When the two parted, both felt deeply irritated,
with Halder having detected accusations of indecisiveness in virtually
everything Beck had said.

Although the core conspirators gradually came back together, they
soon got bogged down in their passionate debates on a welter of

issues that were better resolved by decisiveness than by argument. Meanwhile Erwin von Witzleben, the former commander of the Berlin military district, took matters into his own hands. A practical man with little patience for tortuous discussion, he had been posted to Frankfurt am Main, as commander in chief of an army group there. Far from the center of things, he felt condemned to inactivity, a trying condition for someone of his energetic nature. Although he, too, realized that a coup had little chance of success at the present time, he had no doubt that a man as manic and restive as Hitler would soon provide fresh opportunity and the conspirators had to be ready.

Together with Georg von Sodenstern, his chief of general staff, Witzleben developed a long-term plan to identify like-minded officers and systematically build up as solid a network as possible of commanders who were prepared to support a military coup when the time was ripe. All previous plans had indeed relied far too heavily on two conditions: the elimination of Hitler in a quick strike and the smooth operation of the regular chain of command. Witzleben believed that it was no longer possible to assume that orders for a coup would be followed automatically without objection or complaint, a conclusion based on the fact that Hitler had succeeded so thoroughly in widening the rift within the armed forces. It has been suggested that Witzleben's idea of forming a secret officers' cadre was an alien concept incompatible with German military tradition, but it was no more revolutionary than Hitler's own policies and constituted an apposite response to them. There is considerable truth to the argument that the coup of July 20, 1944, failed at least in part because the conspirators depended too greatly on the chain of command and, for whatever reason, were blind to the conclusions that Witzleben now drew.

At this time, many of the resistance connections that had been severed in the wake of the Munich agreement were reestablished, though only hesitantly and as the opportunity arose. Schulenburg paid a visit to Witzleben in Frankfurt, as did Gisevius. Most important, Oster arranged for Carl Goerdeler to meet Witzleben. Goerdeler immediately began pressuring Witzleben to carry through

his plan and promised to establish contacts with Christian and socialist trade unionists, thereby broadening support for the conspiracy
beyond what had existed at the time of the September plot, especially
in the political realm. Thus, through Witzleben's efforts, new links
between military and civilian opposition groups were forged and old
ties were restored.

Witzleben's initiative never amounted to much, however, because
he did not plan to have his network of conspirators completed until
the following year. The next day, when Gisevius returned to Berlin to
see if Beck, Canaris, and Oster were interested in a meeting with
Witzleben, all military commanders, including Witzleben, were summoned to a meeting to be held the following day, August 22, 1939, at
Obersalzberg. In an unusually harsh address lasting several hours,
Hitler informed them that he had decided to strike immediately because all considerations argued in favor of rapid action. As if attempting to screw up his courage, he hinted to the hushed audience of
generals sitting "icily" before him that a pact would soon be signed
with Stalin—a pact that Foreign Minister Joachim von Ribbentrop
was in fact negotiating in Moscow at that very moment. "Poland is
now right where I wanted to have it," he said, predicting that Britain
and France would once again shrink from war. "Our opponents," he
told the generals, "are little worms. I saw them in Munich." His only
concern was that "at the last minute, some bastard will produce a
mediation plan."[9] Hitler even named the prospective time of attack:
the morning of Saturday, August 26.

But once again, his schedule was disrupted. Britain reacted to the
German war preparations with stoical equanimity and, after months
of negotiations, transformed its provisional support for Poland into a
formal pact. Amid the blizzard of entreaties, bulletins, and miscom-
munications, Halder told the British ambassador, Nevile Henderson,
"You have to strike the man's hand with an ax." Great Britain now
moved to dispel any lingering doubts about its determination to fight.
On the afternoon of August 25 a message arrived from Mussolini
reminding Hitler that their agreements stated that a war would not be
launched until later and informing him that Italy was regrettably not
prepared to open hostilities at this time. Again Hitler hesitated; after

brooding nervously for a short spell, he came to a decision that left everyone agape: the order to attack was rescinded. "Führer rather shaken," Halder noted in his diary.[10]

. . .

As the order to attack was being canceled, Schacht, Gisevius, and General Georg Thomas were on their way to the Military Intelligence building on Tirpitzufer to pick up Canaris, with whom they intended to drive to general staff headquarters in Zossen, east of Berlin. There, in a final, desperate act, they planned to force Brauchitsch and Halder to choose between arresting the three of them or arresting Hitler and the government. Determined to stop at nothing, they had agreed to exert extraordinary pressure on the commanders: if Brauchitsch and Halder chose to arrest them, they would deem themselves released at that moment from their pledge of loyalty to their fellow officers and would reveal the army chiefs' involvement in the resistance.

When the three arrived at Tirpitzufer, they encountered Oster. "Shaking his head" and "laughing heartily," he told them that the order to attack had been rescinded. Gisevius, the eternal man of action, argued yet again that this provided a unique opportunity to eliminate Hitler. The others, however, could scarcely believe that he wanted to carry on. The normally implacable Oster maintained that a "war lord who can rescind within a few hours as far-reaching an order as that for war or peace is done for." In any case, Oster felt, the generals would no longer back Hitler. Only days earlier he had instructed the members of Friedrich Heinz's special task force to prepare themselves once again for the storming of the Chancellery. Now any such action would be superfluous, he thought, in view of the dramatically changed circumstances. Canaris, too, was in an exuberant mood and declared that peace was assured "for twenty years." Everything would unfold as desired if just allowed to develop, and there was no need in the meantime to raise the generals' hackles by making rash demands.[11]

Despite all that can be and has been said about Oster's surprise about-face, there is no minimizing the enormous sense of relief that must have been felt by all after so many months of continuous pressure. Not only Oster but Canaris, Hassell, and many others were so jubilant that peace had been preserved that their judgment was dulled. Even in the Chancellery it was "clear to everyone," as an officer on duty there noted, "that Hitler had suffered a major diplomatic defeat."[12]

But anyone who understood the Führer's obsession with prestige over the years should have realized that he would quickly go to whatever lengths necessary to repair the damage. "Führer still hopes to sock it to Poland," wrote Colonel Eduard Wagner, a general staff departmental head, in his diary.[13] The belief that war had been avoided was totally misguided, and Gisevius was clearly right. Indeed, the ensuing days brought the very situation the conspirators had always dreamed of. In their exhaustive debates, they had always come to the depressing conclusion that Hitler's victories were psychologically as disarming as his defeats. What they had therefore always hoped for (in various scenarios) but what never seemed to occur was a serious setback that could be blamed on Hitler alone and that exposed to all the world his unwavering determination to go to war.

During their debates, they also concluded that the time that elapsed between Hitler's order for an invasion and the actual onset of hostilities was of decisive importance. They worried that the interval might not be long enough for them to decide on a coup and carry it out. In the days before the Munich agreement, Halder had already sought to allay such fears, assuring his fellow conspirators that Hitler could never deceive him on this score: the order would have to be given at least three days before an attack. Now the conspirators had the luxury of an even longer time span. But nothing had been prepared, and nothing was done. Of course, the abortive September plot of the previous year had had a devastating effect on the conspirators' resolve. The written plans for a coup had gone up Witzleben's chimney in smoke, and another draft was at best in the early planning stages. Nevertheless the impression remains that for most of the conspirators waiting had itself become a kind of strategy. Commingled with their immense relief that the peace had been saved was a sense of deliverance from actually having to do anything.

After such misguided elation, the descent to reality was all the more devastating when, on August 31, Hitler reissued the invasion order for the following morning. That afternoon Gisevius ran into Canaris on a back staircase at army headquarters on Bendlerstrasse. "So what do you think now?" asked the admiral. When Gisevius failed to find the appropriate words, Canaris added in a flat voice: "This means the end of Germany."[14]

■ ■ ■

The outbreak of hostilities in the early hours of September 1, 1939, was an enormous setback for the military and civilian opposition, whose desperate efforts had all been directed at preventing war. Britain and France declared war on Germany two days later, confirming the predictions of the countless analyses, memoranda, and warnings that had been drafted by the regime's opponents. But all their activity had been in vain. Hitler had scarcely noticed the reports, and to the extent that the documents were intended for the opposition, little had been achieved, because the coup they were supposed to justify never got off the ground. Nothing so damaged the credibility and reputation of the regime's opponents in the eyes of their foreign contacts as their failure to take action on September 1.

All will to resist seemed to disappear for an extended period after the war began, in part because of the deep, irrational feelings of loyalty that the outbreak of war always arouses, regardless of right and wrong or whether the conflict is willfully unleashed in contravention of existing treaties. Considerations such as these may leave some lingering doubts, but once war breaks out, all efforts and activities focus on responding to the challenge and bringing the conflict to a successful conclusion. Customs and traditions play a role, of course, as do the powerful emotions surrounding such notions as patriotism, loyalty, duty, obedience, and their counterpart, treason. Although the world that generated such sentiments had become distant under the Nazis, people still felt them strongly even in the face of reason. Typical was the behavior of General Georg von Sodenstern, who ten days before the outbreak of war had conferred with Witzleben over far-reaching plans to topple Hitler. But in September, when war had been declared, he turned "to the military duties incumbent upon him and away from any thought of a violent uprising."[15] Because such responses were by no means unusual, the resistance lost much of its strength after war broke out.

The professional pride that many officers took in their work also tended to dampen their hostility toward the government. Even so steadfast an opponent of the Nazis as Lieutenant Colonel Helmuth Groscurth, writing in his diary at the beginning of the Polish campaign, expressed virtually daily his pride at the way countless individual orders fit together perfectly to produce a grand, victorious campaign. Oster, Henning von Tresckow, Rudolph-Christoph von Gersdorff, and others were caught up in the same dilemma. Many memoirs from the time illustrate how much easier it was to solve this conundrum in one's thoughts than in real life. For some, there was no way out of it.

Amid all the jubilant announcements of further German victory appeared a name from the past that had virtually been forgotten: General Werner von Fritsch, the former commander of the army, who had quietly been rehabilitated but never reinstated. In a final, quixotic appearance, he was killed during the last days of the Polish campaign while observing the attack on Warsaw from the suburb of Praga.

After little more than three weeks Poland had been taken. The opponents of the regime, whose disappointment with the Western powers had always been colored with contempt, felt confirmed in that feeling when Britain and France failed to intervene, giving Hitler a lightning victory. France, which was bound by treaty to launch between thirty-five and thirty-eight divisions against Germany within sixteen days of the outbreak of hostilities, delayed mobilizing its forces. Throughout the half-hearted *drôle de guerre*, the French sought to cling as long as they could to the glorious illusions of the age and to the mirage of a peace that had long since been lost.

* * *

On the day the war began, Brauchitsch released a declaration stating that the hostilities were not directed against the Polish people and that the conquered territories would be administered in accordance with international law. But only one week later, Hitler issued guidelines for governance indicating that he had no intention of leaving the administration of the Polish territories to the army. In keeping with his principle of divided authority, he created a civilian administration in addition to the military one and, as if to complete the confusion, sent in so-called Einsatzgruppen (or "task forces," the SS's notorious execution squads) behind the front-line troops. These Einsatzgruppen were technically subject to the military justice system but actually took their orders from Reich Security Headquarters and therefore from Reichsführer-SS Heinrich Himmler. They soon instituted a reign of terror. Even before the Polish campaign was concluded at the end of September, the first complaints had been lodged about "summary executions of Poles and Jews, arbitrary harassment, and indiscriminate arrests." And as early as September 9, Quartermaster General Carl-Heinrich von Stülpnagel went to see Halder at Canaris's request to inform him of Reinhard Heydrich's comment that everything was going "too slowly." Heydrich had declared, "These people have to be shot or hanged immediately without any sort of trial . . . aristocrats, clergy, and Jews."[16]

Three days later, on a visit to the Führer's train, Canaris himself informed General Keitel that he had learned that "widespread shootings were planned" in Poland and that "the aristocracy and clergy in particular" were to be "wiped out." Canaris pointed out that "in the end, the world will hold the Wehrmacht responsible as well." Typically, Keitel failed to address the substance of what Canaris said, confining himself solely to questions of jurisdiction and noting that "these things had already been decided by the Führer, who made it clear to the army high command [Brauchitsch] that if the Wehrmacht did not want to become involved in all this it would have to accept the presence of the SS and Gestapo," which would, together with civilian authorities, undertake "the 'ethnic exterminations.' "[17]

And so the situation remained. Brauchitsch was very consistent in complaining only when the SS or civilian authorities overstepped their authority, although he involved himself in many petty quarrels on this account. He never raised the far more telling question of the extent to which the brutal systematic slaughter besmirched the honor and reputation not only of the Wehrmacht but of Germany itself. Even though he had given his word to the Polish people in his declaration of September 1, he remained impassive. And while he did work tirelessly to keep the Wehrmacht from involvement in any atrocities, by so doing he only cleared the way for acts of breathtaking barbarity by the other branches. Attempts were soon made within the Wehrmacht to enforce discipline and proper conduct more rigidly and to punish transgressions severely, but these efforts were inevitably frustrated and could not later shield the organization from accusations of thinly veiled complicity in the slaughter.

For a time, Brauchitsch attempted to keep commanders in the conquered and occupied territories from realizing that the so-called land cleansing operations in the east stemmed from decisions made by Hitler himself to which Brauchitsch had acquiesced without complaint. As a result, it was widely believed that the atrocities were due to "excesses by lower-level authorities." General Walter Petzel and, even more emphatically, General Georg von Küchler demanded an end to the indiscriminate massacres, as did others. Küchler described one SS unit as a "disgrace to the army." When the senior band leader of SS-Leibstandarte Adolf Hitler ordered fifty Jews shot, General Joachim Lemelsen had him arrested and turned over to the army group for sentencing. General Wilhelm Ulex, who had been rehabilitated and returned to command, also demanded an end to the so-called ethnic policy, which he called a "blot on the honor of the entire German people."[18]

There was no doubt in Brauchitsch's mind that any intervention along the lines demanded by these generals would lead to a fierce confrontation since the policies involved were in fulfillment of some of Hitler's most basic aims in the East.[19] The commander in chief was simply not prepared for such a showdown. In vain did General Wilhelm von Leeb remind the army leadership that the "army, if resolutely led, is still the most powerful factor around."[20]

Far from heeding this call to action, Brauchitsch sought salvation instead in evasion and did all he could to shed responsibility for the administration of the occupied territories. On October 5, in response to a complaint from Albert Forster, a gauleiter, or district leader, that the Wehrmacht was demonstrating a "lack of understanding" of the regime's ethnic policies, Hitler fulfilled Brauchtisch's request by removing Danzig and West Prussia from the jurisdiction of the military. Twelve days later, army responsibility for all other areas was withdrawn. At a meeting in the new Chancellery with Himmler, Keitel, Martin Bormann, Rudolf Hess, and Hans Frank, who had been designated the future governor general of occupied Poland, Hitler remarked that the Wehrmacht should be happy to be rid of these tasks. Keitel made notes in pencil on the Führer's further comments: Poland was not to be turned into some kind of "model province"; the emergence of a new "class of leaders" must be prevented; his policy required "a tough ethnic struggle, which could tolerate no constraints"; and "any tendency toward a normalization of conditions must be stopped." Hitler concluded with his infamous remark about the "devil's work" to be done in the East.[21]

The abrupt end of the army's responsibility for administration resulted in a surge of arbitrary actions on the part of party, civilian, and police authorities, kangaroo courts, district commissars, auxiliary police, and others, who could now claim to be carrying out special assignments not subject to external oversight. The change in administrative responsibilities also heightened the conflict with the army units remaining in these areas. General Karl von Rundstedt left his post as commander in chief of the eastern districts in horror after a short period; his successor, General Johannes Blaskowitz, sent Hitler a memorandum in early November describing the abuses, crimes, and atrocities, expressing his "utmost concern," and pointing out the danger that these actions posed to the morale and discipline of the troops. Hitler rejected the "childishness" of the army command, saying, "You can't wage war with Salvation Army methods."[22]

Still the matter would not die. A little later Blaskowitz wrote to Brauchitsch of the "bloodthirstiness" of the Einsatzkommandos, claiming that it posed an "intolerable burden" for the troops and reiterating his demand that a "new order" be instituted soon. More important, officers who opposed the Nazi regime, Lieutenant Colonel Groscurth in particular, then distributed Blaskowitz's memorandum

In contrast to the army commander in chief, General Walther von Brauchitsch, who ignored the atrocities committed by the Einsatzkommandos in Poland, Johannes Blaskowitz (left) protested vehemently against the "bloodthirstiness" of the SS. He stated in a report that "every soldier is sickened and repelled by the crimes committed." In May 1940 the recently appointed head of the Polish government general, Hans Frank, arranged to have Blaskowitz dismissed.

to the commanders in chief of the western districts and their staffs, among whom it aroused "stupefaction" and "great agitation." General Bock and others demanded to know whether "the hair-raising descriptions" were accurate and whether those responsible had been called to account. Some even demanded that a state of emergency be declared in the occupied territories.[23]

Although Brauchitsch shared the generals' horror at what was happening, he once again stonewalled all requests to take action. Finding himself increasingly besieged, he continued his hopeless attempts to allay the widespread outrage by downplaying events and refusing to discuss them. When this failed, he delegated responsibility for resolving discord to the lower ranks, where, as it happened, the opponents of the Nazi activities were winning converts to their cause. When, in January 1940, Blaskowitz arrived in Zossen with another, still more sharply worded memorandum stating that "The attitude of the army to the SS and the police alternates between abhorrence and hatred" and that "Every soldier feels sickened and repelled by the crimes committed in Poland by agents of the Reich and government representatives," Brauchitsch flatly refused to forward it to Keitel or Hitler. General Ulex had no more success when he complained that SS and SD (Sicherheitsdienst, or Security Service) units demonstrated "an utterly incomprehensible lack of human and moral sensibilities" and had sunk "to the level of beasts."[24]

Brauchitsch apparently never even passed along the concern, expressed by nearly all the critics, about the threat to discipline and the danger posed to supply lines by the prevailing state of pandemonium. He certainly never contemplated organizing a common protest or rallying the army commanders to resign en masse, though it seems likely they would all have agreed to this step, given that even an admirer of the regime like General Reichenau had on occasion expressed his revulsion at what was happening. By May, Hans Frank had been appointed governor general of the conquered territories, and he succeeded in having Blaskowitz replaced. Shortly beforehand Himmler had also succeeded, despite bitter opposition from both the OKW and the OKH, in obtaining permission to further expand the armed SS units and to form new ones. Despite its efforts, the Wehrmacht was never able to discover the troop strength of these units. It no longer played much of a role in the political calculations of the Nazi leadership.

It is not difficult in retrospect to identify when this decline began: during the Röhm affair years earlier. In a little-noticed directive from that period, the Ministry of Defense had ordered that people perse-

cuted for political reasons should not be protected. It is arguable that
this restriction so compromised the morale and self-confidence of the
officer corps that decline was inevitable. In mid-January 1940 Halder
noted in his diary a terse comment Canaris had made while visiting
him. "Officers too faint-hearted," Canaris had said, aptly summarizing
the old—and now terrifyingly obvious—dilemma. "No humanitarian
intervention on behalf of the unjustly persecuted."[25]

■ ■ ■

The events in Poland belong to the history of the resistance because
they illustrate the importance of basic moral standards and reveal the
manner in which such standards were subordinated to the traditional
virtues of the soldier. By this time, if not before, any ability to claim
ignorance of the essential nature of the Nazi regime had evaporated
for good. In fact, the activities in Poland of the state-sanctioned "murder squads," as Henning von Tresckow called them, were a turning
point for many, even if these people did not necessarily proceed to
active resistance. There were of course many others, indeed a majority, especially among younger officers, who succumbed to "Hitler's
magic" in the wake of the overwhelming German victory and who
viewed the failure of the Western powers to intervene, despite their
declaration of war, as further evidence of the genius of the Führer.[26]
Nevertheless, the hemorrhaging that the resistance had suffered between Munich and the outbreak of war was stanched, and the movement slowly began to recover. More important, opposition to the
Nazis within the army was no longer based solely on Hitler's fool-
hardy foreign policy and the military risks he ran but also on fundamental moral questions.

The precise role played by each of these various issues is difficult
to determine, but they all came to the fore again in the protracted
dispute between Hitler and the Wehrmacht after the Polish campaign, leading to a quick revival of the previous autumn's plans to
overthrow the regime. On September 12, when victory over Poland,
though imminent, was still not complete, Hitler in his haste informed
his chief Wehrmacht adjutant, Colonel Rudolf Schmundt, that he had

decided to launch an offensive in the West as soon as possible and certainly by late autumn. Eight days later the Führer took Keitel into his confidence. On September 27, the very day that Warsaw capitulated, he finally summoned the commanders in chief of the three branches of the armed forces, informed them of his decision, and ordered them to begin working on plans for a western offensive. Once again he based his decision on the argument that because time was working against Germany, both politically and militarily, the offensive could not begin soon enough.

The army high command, in particular, was convinced that any attempt to "draw the French and English onto the battlefield and defeat them" within a few weeks, as Hitler had said, would be as hasty as it was hopeless. The entire corps of generals was incensed, and they deluged Brauchitsch with protests. On the basis of Hitler's intimations that a settlement would be reached with the Western powers at the conclusion of the Polish campaign, the OKH had already begun to plan for redeployment in mid-September. It hoped that by simply mounting a solid defense against this enemy who had demonstrated so little stomach for war, it could gradually put the conflict "to sleep," thereby clearing the way for a diplomatic agreement. Hitler reacted "bitterly" to these plans over the following weeks, partly because the commanders did not seem to share his elation over the victory in Poland but most importantly because their complaints during the campaign suggested that they still felt they had some right of consultation in political decisions, while he believed that this issue had been settled once and for all.[27]

Stung by Hitler's response to them, the commanders retreated once again to purely military arguments. They pointed out that the troops were too tired to turn around and fight in the West, that stores of munitions and raw materials were depleted, that winter campaigns were always perilous, that the enemy was strong. But Hitler overrode all objections, regardless of source or context. When one general described the rigors of a late-autumn campaign, Hitler replied that the weather was the same for both sides. Even Brauchitsch objected openly to Hitler's plans and asked Generals Reichenau and Rundstedt to speak to him. When this, too, failed, these political and military concerns, now sharpened by moral considerations, led to a revival of plots to stage a coup.

By the end of September Canaris had already visited the various western headquarters to explore the officers' attitudes about the planned offensive and, in some cases, to gauge support for the overthrow of the regime. At the same time, Brauchitsch and Halder held an "in-depth conversation" about the choices they faced: either to stage the offensive that Hitler wanted or else to do everything possible to delay operations. A third eventuality was also raised in this conversation and duly noted in the official diary, namely to work for "fundamental change," by which they meant nothing less than a coup.[28]

As might be expected, Brauchitsch shrank from such a radical solution and preferred instead to create delays attributable to technical problems. Hitler, however, was in no mood for such ploys. He informed his commander in chief two days later that no hope remained of reaching a settlement with the Western powers and that he had made an "immutable decision" to wage war. The new campaign would be launched sometime between November 15 and 20. Five days later, on October 21, in a speech to the gauleiters, Hitler suggested an even earlier date, assuring them that the "major offensive in the West" would begin "in about two weeks."[29]

Brauchitsch was in despair. Canaris, who visited him late in the evening, was "deeply shaken" by both the nervous exhaustion of the commander in chief and by his report, in which the words "frenzy of bloodletting" appeared for the second time in recent days, now applied to Hitler and his furious desire to attack.[30] In the continued hope of forcing a postponement, Brauchitsch decided to work out only a sketchy campaign plan. But Hitler allowed him no leeway and only a few days later demanded the necessary amplifications, setting November 12 as the new date for the invasion. He ordered Generals Kluge, Bock, and Reichenau to Berlin to help speed up planning in the high command. All objections raised by the commanders, of whom Reichenau was characteristically the most outspoken, were dismissed by Hitler as unfounded. Once again he urged Brauchitsch and

Halder to hurry and concluded by producing some new operational plans of his own.

The increasing pressure exerted by the Führer, coupled with his evident disdain for the military, prompted a group of younger general staff officers to renew their old connections with opponents of the regime in the Foreign Office and, most important, in Military Intelligence, where Hans Oster had continued to work away with the encouragement of Canaris, who was now impatient to proceed. Oster had recruited Hans von Dohnanyi into Military Intelligence, and Dohnanyi in turn had brought in a number of close friends who opposed the Nazis, including his boyhood companion Justus Delbrück, baron of Guttenberg, and the theologian Dietrich Bonhoeffer, Dohnanyi's brother-in-law, who provided a bridge to Christian opposition circles. At the same time, Helmuth Groscurth resumed close contacts with Beck, who rekindled the connection to Goerdeler. Gradually, through many more intermediaries as well, various old and new contacts were established.

The resumption of ties to an active opposition group seemed to save Goerdeler from a psychological crisis. In his isolation he had fallen in with a group of staid old national-conservatives who did nothing but meet, talk, draft reports, hope, and wait. He had become increasingly distraught and had lost himself in far-fetched revolutionary schemes. Over Beck's vehement opposition, he worked on the idea of asking Hitler to send him on a mission to Britain and France to discuss peace conditions that, he calculated, "Hitler would not swallow and that would then lead to his downfall."[31] Goerdeler originally envisaged a "transitional cabinet led by Göring" for the first weeks following Hitler's fall. Other opponents of the Nazis advanced similarly misguided schemes, such as working with "open-minded circles" within the SS and tossing Ribbentrop "like a bone" to the enemy.[32] They argued for hours over the restoration of the monarchy and who would be the best pretender to the throne. These ludicrous fantasies stemmed, for the most part, from an enervating lack of real activity. If it is true that absolute power corrupts absolutely, and with respect to Hitler's regime that is irrefutable, then absolute impotence has a similar effect, at least insofar as any sense of reality is concerned.

The resistance circle created by Hans Oster within Military Intelligence included the lawyer Hans von Dohnanyi (seated). *As chief of special projects, he recruited his closest friends, including Justus Delbrück, a son of the historian Hans Delbrück, in whose house Dohnanyi had grown up, and Baron Karl-Ludwig von und zu Guttenberg, who had been the publisher for many years of the Christian-monarchist* Weisse Blätter (White Pages).

Dohnanyi with Guttenberg (left) *and Delbrück* (standing) *in August 1942.*

To the great disappointment of all the plotters, Halder continued to insist in the last days of October that the time was not ripe. Even the far more decisive General Carl-Heinrich von Stülpnagel now accused Oster and Canaris of rushing things. Neither Halder nor Stülpnagel apparently knew anything about the resistance cell within the high command called Action Group Zossen, which had been formed in midmonth primarily by younger staff officers in Colonel Wagner's circle. This ignorance throws a telling light on the isolation of the opposition groups and the lack of coordination among them. More radical and concrete in its approach than other conspiratorial circles, Action Group Zossen had formulated plans for eradicating Hitler, eliminating the SS and Gestapo, cordoning off the main centers of power, and even forming a provisional government.

Appeals for action now rained down from all sides. In order to prompt the indecisive Halder and, even more important, Brauchitsch to make their move, the conspirators in Military Intelligence wrote a paper, with the help of Secretary of State Ernst von Weizsäcker in the Foreign Office, Erich Kordt, and Hasso von Etzdorf, in which they once again marshaled the arguments against the planned western offensive. In their view, Hitler's plans would bring about "the end of Germany," a belief confirmed by his announcement that he intended to invade through Belgium and Holland, thereby in all likelihood drawing the United States and numerous other neutral countries into the fray. Experience, they continued, showed that protests and threats to resign would not change Hitler's mind and would only confirm his conviction that all "ships must be destroyed and bridges burned."[33]

Finally, after long hesitation, worn out by his exertions and by Hitler's scornful impatience, Halder decided on the last day of October 1939 that action could no longer be delayed. The mounting concern among the generals, as well as the pressure from Etzdorf, the Foreign Office, and Action Group Zossen, may have helped convince him there was once again hope that a coup would succeed. In any case, he summoned Groscurth on the evening of October 31 and informed the surprised Military Intelligence officer that he, too, had finally concluded that violence was the only solution. Halder mentioned his earlier plan of eliminating at least some of the leading Nazis in a staged accident. He outlined a few details concerning the operation itself and the new regime to take power afterwards and then added, with tears welling up in his eyes, that "for weeks on end he had been going to see Emil [Hitler] with a pistol in his pocket in order to gun him down," as Groscurth recorded in his coded diary.[34]

As often happened when a decision was finally made, support arrived from unexpected quarters. Wilhelm Ritter von Leeb, the com-

The private diaries of Helmuth Groscurth (above), a career officer who joined Military Intelligence in 1935, were discovered in the 1960s, providing valuable new insights into the resistance. Groscurth was taken prisoner near Stalingrad and died of typhus in a Soviet camp in April 1943. A friend in Military Intelligence called him "one of the most determined and high-minded of the rebel officers."

mander of Army Group C, sent Brauchitsch a letter that ended with the comment that he was prepared "personally to stand fully behind you and to support whatever conclusions you reach or actions you deem necessary." Oster and Erich Kordt had spent the evening of October 31 visiting Ludwig Beck on Goethestrasse in Lichterfelde. After much debate over the attitude of the generals, they arrived at the same desperate conclusion on which all their discussions had foundered for months: the most important condition for a successful coup was to kill Hitler. The next morning, when Kordt arrived at Military Intelligence, Oster half-resignedly summarized their discussion with the comment that no one could be found "who will throw the bomb and liberate our generals from their scruples." Kordt told Oster simply and calmly that he had come to request permission to do just that. All he lacked was the explosives. After a few more questions, Oster promised to have the necessary materials ready on November 11.[35]

Everything was now rushing toward a final resolution. The very next day, when Brauchitsch and Halder visited the commanders in the West to canvass their views once again on the impending offensive, Stülpnagel invited Groscurth to come along and assigned him the task of "starting the preparations." He offered encouragement and concrete information, especially about the position of reliable units and the commanders who could be counted on, and asked that Beck and Goerdeler be informed. Beck himself was discussing with Wilhelm Leuschner, a former trade union leader, the possibility of a general strike. A day later Oster was summoned to Zossen and asked to get out the previous year's plans and update them if necessary. In his diary Gisevius captured the feeling of hectic excitement that filled him and the other conspirators, who had known nothing until then: "It's going ahead. . . . Great activity. One discussion after another. Suddenly it's just as it was right before Munich, 1938. I rush back and forth between OKW, police headquarters, the Interior Ministry, Beck, Goerdeler, Schacht, Helldorf, Nebe, and many others."[36] Meanwhile, in Zossen, arrangements were made "to secure headquarters."

Once again everything was ready. Much as the coup a year earlier was to be sparked by the order to attack Czechoslovakia, this time everything would be set in motion by Hitler's command to attack in the West. Since Hitler had set November 12 as the date of the offensive, the orders would have to be issued by November 5 at the latest. On that date Brauchitsch had an appointment to see Hitler in the Chancellery; he intended to make one final attempt to dissuade the Führer from this "mad attack" by underscoring the unanimous opposition of the generals. Halder's plans were based on the expectation that when the commander in chief returned from his meeting at the Chancellery, rebuffed and quite possibly humiliated as well, he would not hesitate, as he had in 1938, to issue the marching orders, which only he could sign.

At noon on the appointed day, while Halder waited in the ante-chamber, Brauchitsch began his presentation to Hitler in the conference room of the Chancellery. Although the commander in chief formulated his concerns more pointedly than originally planned, Hitler listened quietly at first. However, when Brauchitsch began arguing that an offensive was impossible at that time, not only for technical reasons but also because of the failings and lack of discipline that the troops had demonstrated in Poland—particularly while on the attack—Hitler flew into a rage. He hurled accusations at Brauchitsch, demanded to see proof of his allegations, wanted to know what had been done about them and whether death sentences had been imposed on soldiers guilty of cowardice. Hitler loudly summoned Keitel into the room, and as Brauchitsch fumbled for words and became entangled in contradictions, he raged against "the spirit of Zossen," which he knew all about and would soon destroy. Then he abruptly left the room, "slamming the door" and leaving the commander in chief standing there.[37]

Brauchitsch, who had turned "chalky-white . . . his face twisted," according to one observer, found his way back to Halder.[38] Together they set out for Zossen, Brauchitsch exhausted and in a state of collapse, Halder apparently composed. When Brauchitsch casually mentioned Hitler's threat about the "spirit of Zossen," however—he had not really made much of it—Halder's ears pricked up and he, too, was seized by panic. Just a few days earlier, he had been warned by the chief signal officer, General Erich Fellgiebel, that Hitler suspected something, or at any rate was making increasingly suspicious-sounding comments about the army high command. This, coupled with Brauchitsch's revelation, made Halder fear that the plans for a coup had been betrayed or been uncovered by Hitler in some way. As soon as he was back at headquarters, therefore, Halder ordered all coup-related documents destroyed immediately. Not long afterwards, the order to launch an offensive in the West arrived.

■ ■ ■

By late afternoon Brauchitsch had regained his composure. Hitler, he said, had simply caught him completely by surprise. Although the order to launch an offensive had once again created precisely the situation that was supposed to spark the coup, Brauchitsch now declared that the attack in the West could no longer be stopped. He added, "I myself won't do anything, but I won't stop anyone else from acting."

Halder, alternating between resignation and apprehension, expressed similar sentiments. He told Groscurth that now that their undertaking had been abandoned, "the forces that were counting on us are no longer bound to us." Halder felt that there was no one who could succeed Hitler and that the younger officers were not yet ready for a putsch. Groscurth insisted that they act, arguing that the factors cited by Halder had been just as true before the scene in the Chancellery and reminding him that Beck, Goerdeler, and Schacht were still on board, not to mention the determined Canaris. Halder responded angrily, "If they're so sure at Military Intelligence that they want an assassination, then let the admiral take care of it himself!"[39]

Groscurth immediately carried this challenge back to Military Intelligence on Tirpitzufer, infuriating Canaris. At this point the opposition forces began falling apart at a pace so rapid it was almost visible. Canaris took Halder's message, which was possibly exaggerated in the retelling, to mean that the OKH was foisting the assassination attempt off on him because it could no longer do it. One of the questions that remains unanswered to this day is why Oster, who witnessed Canaris's outburst, failed to point out that an assassin was now available in the person of Erich Kordt, who had relatively easy access to the Chancellery and Hitler, was prepared to put his life on the line, and awaited only the necessary explosives, which a section head named Erwin von Lahousen had promised to procure. Most likely Oster was all too aware of Canaris's long-standing antipathy toward political assassinations of any kind. But Oster's silence also highlights how contradictory and uncoordinated the plans of even the innermost core of conspirators remained until the very last moment.

Soon Oster and Gisevius received further evidence that the resistance was unraveling. For encouragement, they went to see Witzleben, who had heretofore been steadfast in his determination, at his headquarters in Bad Kreuznach. But even he expressed strong doubts that Hitler could still be stopped from launching the offensive. Witzleben believed that the only remaining possibility would be for the three army group commanders in the West—Leeb, Rundstedt, and Bock—to refuse to transmit the order to attack when the time came. On the way back from Bad Krenznach, Oster stopped in Frankfurt am Main to see Leeb and explore the potential for such a step. However, when Oster not only mentioned the names of many of the conspirators but also drew from his pocket two proclamations, both written by Beck, to be read during the military takeover, Leeb's first general staff officer, Colonel Vincenz Müller, responded with outrage. Müller castigated Oster for his recklessness and eventually persuaded him to "burn the two documents in my big ashtray." Witzleben, too, was indignant when he heard about Oster's indiscretion and announced that he would not see Oster anymore.[40]

Shortly before their departure on the evening of November 8, Oster and Gisevius heard news that Hitler had narrowly escaped an assassination attempt in the Bürgerbräukeller in Munich by unexpectedly cutting short a speech that was scheduled to last several hours. Gisevius immediately conceived the idea of blaming the assassination attempt on Himmler and using it to justify a coup, in much the same way as the fictitious attempt on the Führer's life discussed by several of the plotters in September, 1938. But the main consequence of the assassination attempt was the immediate tightening of security measures, which heightened the already considerable difficulties that Lahousen was experiencing in procuring explosives for Erich Kordt. Nevertheless, Kordt was assured once more on November 10 that everything would be ready the next day. There was a catch, however. Under the new restrictions, Lahousen was only able to acquire an extremely complicated detonator that required special training to operate. Kordt declared that he was still prepared to proceed, but now Oster got cold feet and backed out. Thus was Hitler spared thanks to the first of many "providential" events that would henceforth occur regularly, preserving him for the "Herculean tasks" that he believed himself destined to carry out.

In the meantime, Hitler postponed the launching of the offensive from November 12 until the fifteenth, then the nineteenth, and finally the twenty-second. The sense of relief produced by these postponements further weakened the conspiracy. Returning from a visit to the western border, Stülpnagel remarked to Halder, "You're right. It won't work. The commanders and troops would not obey your call." Halder himself commented spontaneously to General Thomas that a coup d'état would fly in the face of all tradition and that "it is quite intolerable that the Germans should come to be the slaves of the English." The helplessness of the opposition at this point is revealed by Halder's suggestion to Secretary of State Weizsäcker that a soothsayer be bribed to influence Hitler and by his offer to provide a million marks for this purpose. Meanwhile, the commanders in chief of the army groups held a meeting at which they agreed unanimously about the perils of a western offensive but rejected Leeb's suggestion that they resign en masse. At that, Leeb resolved to banish all thoughts of resistance from his mind.[41]

In Berlin, Schacht continued for a time to search out new conspirators who had not yet become cynical and weary, but he, too, eventually grew resigned. Beck continued to write "papers for his daughter," as one observer scoffed. Gisevius was sent as vice-consul and military intelligence officer to the German consulate in Zurich, Goerdeler returned to his bizarre schemes, and Canaris finally succumbed to his revulsion for the world.[42] He forbade Oster to engage in any further conspiratorial activities and demanded that he recall "Herr X," Munich lawyer Josef Müller, whom Oster had dispatched to Rome in an attempt to discover through the British ambassador to the Holy See how London would react to a coup and what peace conditions it might offer should Germany rid itself of Hitler. An embittered Groscurth wrote to his wife on November 16, "We carry on, but nothing ever happens . . . except fiascos." The same day he met with his immediate superior, General Kurt von Tippelskirch, who had attended a briefing in Brauchitsch's office concerning fresh atrocities in Poland. Tippelskirch commented with a sigh, "We'll just have to get through the valley of the shadow of death."[43]

At Hans Oster's request Josef Müller (above), a Munich lawyer, traveled to the Vatican a number of times in the early 1940s to attempt to contact the British government. Known to his friends as "Ochsen-Sepp" ("Joe Ox"), Müller hoped to discover whether the Allies would be willing to negotiate a peace treaty with a German government that had overthrown the Nazis. He was picked up by the police during their first raid on Military Intelligence, in early 1943. He was held in a number of different concentration camps until near the end of the war, ending up in Dachau.

Hitler's apparent sixth sense, which he often followed, now induced him to summon the officers once again and rally support for his plans. He knew enough about psychology to employ not only his own oratorical powers but also a measure of spectacle; on November 23, the extended leadership of all three services, the commanders and general staff officers, were invited to a glittering gathering in the Marble Hall of the Chancellery. For the first time since the victory over Poland, the army leadership came together, and the whirl of uniforms, gold braid, epaulets, and red trouser stripes seemed to cast an enchanting spell over the assemblage, so that much of their fear and concern had already evaporated when Göring and Goebbels made rousing appeals to the group. Then Hitler himself appeared, looking rather somber, and spoke at length with portentous solemnity about the thinking that underlay his convictions.

He opened with a historical and strategic overview, assuring the assembled throng that the Great War had never ended—the second

act was only just beginning—and that he had not rebuilt the Wehrmacht in order not to use it. "The determination to strike has always
lain within me," he said. Anyone who opposed him would therefore
be crushed, "regardless of who he is." He said he had been deeply
offended by what he saw as a lack of faith: "I cannot endure anyone's
telling me the troops are not all right." After reviewing once again the
necessity for the impending offensive, he declared himself "indispensable," for he alone could make the difficult but crucial decisions.
Hanging in the balance was not just a National-Socialist Germany but
the entire question of "who will dominate Europe and therefore the
world." The speech bristled with threats directed at "doubters," "de-
serters," and those who would foment "revolution." The struggle, he
warned, would be waged without quarter against anyone who failed to
embrace the will to victory. He himself was prepared "to die, if necessary, but only as the last one": "I will not survive the defeat of my
people." These remarks were enthusiastically received in the ranks of
the navy and air force, who had often been praised by Hitler. Within
the army, even many of the generals who had recently expressed
strong opposition to an invasion conceded that they were "greatly
impressed" by Hitler, despite his unmistakable criticism of the high
command. Oster commented incisively that accusations of cowardice
had once again made cowards of the brave.[44]

• ■ ■

For the second time in a year, a coup plot had sputtered and failed.
The conspiracy of November 1939 was more tragedy than farce, yet
there is indeed something farcical about a coup that was foiled simply
by the angry outburst of a tyrant. It would be easy, in judging these
events, to confine oneself to moral categories and point to the conspirators' indecision, spinelessness, and lack of resolve. Count
Helldorf was certainly justified in calling Halder a "heroic philistine,"
as was Groscurth in expressing his "loathing for the generals," and
Hassell in pointing bitterly to the contradiction between the "marvel-
ous discussions" that the generals—or "Josephs" as he scornfully (if
obscurely) dubbed them—conducted in lieu of action. For those

seeking the cause of the army's failure, such verdicts may reveal something about the strained relationships between Helldorf and Halder, Groscurth and Brauchitsch, or Hassell and the generals, but they illuminate virtually nothing about the real reasons for the repeated failures of the coup.

Somewhat more enlightening is the remarkable lack of realistic imagination on the part of the conspirators. In the fall of 1939, as in September 1938, they made the initiation of the coup totally dependent on events they could neither accurately predict nor control. The officers on the general staff were professional strategists who had demonstrated their skill on numerous occasions, but all the evidence indicates that on this occasion their planning was inadequate and probably even stunningly inept. Much remains unknown, for most of the relevant documents were destroyed and their authors perished in the war or on the gallows. One fact, however, looms so large that it cannot be overlooked: the conspirators plotted all this time to "do away" with Hitler without even the most resolute core of the resistance ever deciding exactly how this would be done, who would do it, and even if it could be done.

In contrast to the September conspiracy, it is impossible to determine which units were to have delivered the blow in November. Groscurth and Stülpnagel developed orders for the operations, but Halder spoke quite vaguely after the war about two "panzer divisions that had been held back" for this purpose but whose names and positions no one seems to remember. The orders launching the coup could only be signed by the commander in chief of the army, yet, as everyone knew, Brauchitsch was not prepared to do this. Among the more farcical aspects of the conspiracy was Stülpnagel's idea of presenting the orders to Brauchitsch in a sealed envelope so that he would not ask any more questions. Brauchitsch may have said on November 5 that he would do nothing to prevent someone else from "acting," but this hardly demonstrated a willingness to sign papers authorizing the coup. The conspiracy was riddled with such inconsistencies, which would reappear on July 20, 1944.

The conspirators were not hampered by any lack of seriousness or moral insight. If anything, the opposite was true. All the protests against atrocities in Poland, of which there were many more than have been mentioned here, show that the outrage at Nazi barbarism extended far beyond the circles of active conspirators. Their really decisive failing, it seems, was their lack of political will to commit an act that ran against the grain of all their traditions and patterns of thought. There is truth to the remark of the Italian ambassador to Berlin, Bernardo Attolico, that the German character, as he had come to know it in those officers, was deficient in the qualities needed for good conspirators: patience, a keen understanding of human nature, hypocrisy, psychology, and tact. "Where can you find that between Rosenheim and Eydtkuhnen?" he asked.[45]

The conspirators were acutely aware of this deficiency, and attempted to hide it by continually finding new reasons for their inaction: they were waiting for a swing in the public mood or for Hitler to suffer a setback; the younger officers, as Witzleben complained, were still "intoxicated" by Hitler; a civil war would break out or another "stab-in-the-back" myth—reminiscent of the army's putative betrayal at the end of the First World War—would arise if they acted now; it would be best first to explore the attitude foreign powers would adopt toward a new government; and finally, time and again, no one was prepared actually to throw the bomb. When Dino Grandi went to the meeting of the Fascist Grand Council at which Mussolini was to be overthrown on July 25, 1943, he took two hand grenades with him. At the entrance to the chamber in the Palazzo Venezia, the first member of the Grand Council he encountered was Cesare de Vecchi. Fearing that Mussolini would defend himself and open fire, Grandi asked de Vecchi on the spur of the moment if he would take one of the grenades and throw it at Il Duce if necessary. De Vecchi agreed immediately without any doubt or hesitation. A major weakness of the German resistance at this point was that it did not have a Grandi or even a de Vecchi.[46]

The Italian conspirators focused all their attention on carrying out the assassination and ensuring its success, allowing the next day to take care of itself. The Germans, on the other hand, struggled so long and hard with the preconditions and consequences of their plans that their will to act dissipated. A typical picture of the conspirators would

Franz Halder wrestled constantly with the basic conflict felt by many officers. He hated the Führer, calling him "mentally ill" and "bloodthirsty" in a private conversation immediately after being appointed chief of general staff in 1938. He participated in two failed coup attempts and never changed his mind about Hitler, but thereafter he closed himself off, did his duty, nursed his hatred, and refused to become involved in new conspiracies.

Halder (second from right) in 1941 at Führer headquarters with Hitler, Keitel, and Brauchitsch.

show them huddled together rehashing arguments and counterarguments and drafting extensive plans for the world of tomorrow. Even Erwin von Witzleben, the conspirator least prone to lose himself in ruminations, eventually succumbed to this tendency. In September 1938 he had declared that if necessary he would simply put Brauchitsch and Halder "under lock and key" for a few hours; by the next year, however, he was claiming his own subordinate position, his responsibility for his troops, and Oster's recklessness as reasons for postponing any decision.

In the bitter cold of mid-January 1940, Beck and Halder wandered together for hours through the deserted streets of the Berlin suburb of Dahlem, deep in a conversation that dramatically illustrated some of the antagonisms that plagued the opposition as a whole. When Beck, perhaps echoing the didactic tone of his predecessor in office, implied that the army command was wanting in courage, Halder retorted tartly that he had opposed Hitler from the very outset—unlike Beck—and was in no need of lessons. He refused to allow the army to become the "handmaid" of civilian opposition groups and said he was still prepared to lead the way in a "spearhead" role, but only if backed by a broad-based political movement, of which there was still no sign at all. The task of the civilian opposition groups was to create this movement and not issue "instructions" to the army, for which they bore no responsibility. Both men were clearly right, and it was indeed for this very reason that their conversation ended in a falling-out. They never saw each other again.[47]

Apart from this and a few other isolated cases, what was missing in the resistance on the whole was not passion, strength, or personal courage. There was no lack of conviction that "the wagon is headed for the abyss and has to be stopped," in the words of a common metaphor of the time. What the resistance did feel the want of, though, was a widely acknowledged central figure whose authority and confidence could draw together all these brooding individuals, estranged by contradictory goals and approaches and united only by their disgust for the regime. Beck was certainly not this person. He was too pensive, philosophical, and inclined to defer action. Hitler's opponents sensed this shortcoming, as can be seen from the diaries of Ulrich von Hassell, who often speaks of *the* officer or *the* man for whom everything lay waiting. Such a man would need a spark of "Catilinarian energy" to be able to depose Hitler and would need also to shed all the scruples and misgivings that repeatedly hobbled the conspirators during the first phase of the resistance. That meant, as one of the conspirators pointed out, a readiness to "do things that others might never understand or undertake themselves."[48]

5

THE NEW GENERATION

Among the consequences of the failed November conspiracy was a shift in the center of gravity within the resistance. It has been observed, somewhat simplistically, that the resistance was led, up to this point, by older men, some retired and some still holding senior positions, who were struggling to regain their waning influence. Beginning in 1940 a younger generation came to the fore, taking up the challenge of overthrowing the regime and casting about for suitable leaders of its own.[1]

Although this view glosses over numerous distinctions within the gathering "second generation" of opponents to the regime, there is no doubt that new faces and even a new type of person began to appear after 1940. The difference between the new conspirators and the "old school" had less to do with age than with the conclusions they drew from their experiences. This gulf was rarely bridged, despite the many similarities in the two groups' views. While the older conspirators wanted to renew Germany in accordance with timeworn principles that they felt were still valid—though admittedly in need of updating—their younger counterparts were captivated by the idea that a new era was dawning, necessitating a sharp break with the past. In general, this second group was more radical and less respectful than the older generation, which felt bound by traditions, oaths, obedience and inhibited by possible accusations of high treason. The new generation tended to scorn such notions as the "subtleties" of a dying world. They made snide remarks about "the old-timers' revolution." Adam von Trott occasionally remarked that for the sake of their credibility they needed to "avoid any hint of being reactionary, of gentlemen's clubs, or of militarism," all of which stubbornly clung to the older opponents of the Nazis.[2]

In social terms, the "notables" who had previously set the tone were overtaken by the "counts," although by no means did all members of this second group stem from the aristocracy. In military terms, the "colonels" took over from the "generals." But there was, in fact, a fair amount of overlap between the two groups, as can be seen in the case of one of the key players in the first phase of the resistance who also played an essential role in the second and whose opposition to Nazism led him to such extremes that his actions remain controversial to this day.

Hans Oster had decided after much mental anguish that all resistance of the kind practiced hitherto was doomed to failure. Not only was the conspirators' ability to act severely limited by traditional notions of gentlemanly behavior, but worse yet, they could not get around the objection that a coup would have little chance for success so long as Hitler suffered no political or military defeat severe enough to break his spell over the German people, at least momentarily. It seemed to Oster that such a defeat should therefore be arranged.

This was a perilous conclusion. But in his despair and helpless rage Oster realized much more clearly than most of his colleagues that National Socialism represented an entirely new phenomenon: an ideology of such sinister immorality that traditional values and loyalties no longer applied. For this reason, Oster commissioned Dohnanyi to gather information about the crimes of the regime both in Germany and, starting in September 1939, in Poland. Oster was hardly surprised when the misgivings he expressed about an offensive in the West through Dutch and Belgian territory were brushed aside by Hitler. With all these examples in mind, Oster forced himself to overcome his final inhibitions and take the step that led him to treason.

In the early 1930s he had made the acquaintance of a young Dutch officer named Gijsbertus Jacobus Sas. At the time of the 1936 Olympic Games, they became fast friends. When Sas, having risen to the rank of colonel, was appointed a military attaché to the Dutch embassy in Berlin, they renewed their friendship and grew increasingly close despite the enthusiastic admiration of Sas's wife for the German Führer. On the evening of October 8, 1939, Oster was on his way home to 9 Bayerische Strasse with his occasional driver, Franz Liedig. Silent and sunk in thought, Oster suddenly asked to be dropped off at Sas's apartment. When he returned a few minutes later and took his place beside Liedig, Oster blurted out that now there was no going back: he had just committed high treason and, if discovered, would be hanged. In an extremely emotional state, he revealed all that had driven him to this point, concluding with words that Liedig would never forget: "It is far easier to take a pistol and kill someone, it is far easier to charge into a hail of machine-gun fire when you believe in the cause, than it is to do what I have done. If things should ever come to this pass, then please be the friend even after my death who knows how it was and what moved me to do things that others might never understand or undertake themselves."[3]

Oster's "treachery" has fired a passionate debate in Germany, with one side claiming that under a criminal regime all notions of illegality are overturned while the other takes a more formalistic view, saying that deliberate, premeditated treason should always be a capital offense. A third group makes the point that Oster's deed was "basically of little import" because the Belgians, to whom Sas immediately forwarded the information provided by his friend, lent it no more credence than the Dutch had.[4] Furthermore, the Western powers reportedly already knew of Hitler's intentions through many other channels. But these and other attempts to diminish, excuse, or condemn Oster's decision fail to come to grips with its seriousness and true intent; they also overlook the fact that Oster had crossed a crucial dividing line: he was prepared to cause the death of German soldiers if necessary, a position that practically none of the other members of the resistance could accept, no matter how much they still respected him.

It is impossible to assess Oster's actions properly without considering that his intent was not to injure Germany but to spare it the catastrophe that would inevitably result, in the unanimous view of the generals, if the original plans were followed and Western Europe was invaded immediately after the Polish campaign. His motive was to do everything he could to prevent the impending catastrophe that Hitler, after successful invasions of Czechoslovakia and Poland, was determined to visit on the entire western half of Europe, Germany included. Just how close the military itself was to desperate action can be seen in the example of Walter von Reichenau, who, though he has frequently been decried as a "Nazi general," vehemently opposed Hitler's plans for another offensive at the conference of August 30. He then went so far as to meet with Goerdeler in the house of the former vice-mayor of Berlin, Fritz Elsas, on November 6 and encourage him in scarcely veiled terms to leak the date of the offensive to the British and Dutch so that they would begin their preparations, thus foiling Hitler's strategic plan.[5]

While Reichenau was motivated primarily by pragmatic concerns, Oster's intentions were much more far-ranging. He hoped, for example, to reveal, or rather highlight, a paradox that was often ignored: most officers—even those who were highly critical of the Nazis—tended to focus narrowly on their own military victories and thus found it difficult to accept that their successes redounded to Hitler's glory, augmenting his authority and power and, for the time being, his reputation for almost magical invincibility.

Oster clearly saw no way out of this dilemma without breaking free of traditional values and thought patterns. He was enough of an officer to understand how seriously his peers took their responsibility for the well-being of their troops. But the question was how that responsibility compared to the one they would bear for the millions of lives that would be lost in a world war unleashed by Hitler and whether it was even possible to address the real issues from the standpoint of individual nations and their legal systems, which protected each nation's self-interests and made "high treason" a heinous crime. Traditional values provided inadequate tools for understanding or combating Hitler's rule. Moreover, they failed to address the moral grounds on which, more than anything else, Oster's fierce opposition was predicated. Some doubt may still remain, but when all the philosophical arguments have been exhausted, one point stands beyond challenge in Oster's thinking. He himself alluded to it when he told Franz Liedig that he had made a decision on moral grounds, for which he alone was responsible and for which, if things turned out badly, he alone would pay.

Like all previous designs of the German resistance, Oster's action failed, even doubly so. Hitler did not suffer the expected setback, since the date of the western offensive was postponed twenty-nine times in total between the autumn of 1939 and May 1940, when Wehrmacht units that had recovered their strength and were well prepared and better equipped finally smashed across the borders. Furthermore, the never-ending series of new starting dates for the attack that Oster relayed to the West made his warnings seem unreliable. The Dutch high command never placed much stock in them in any case, as the original November date struck them as too foolish and irrational to be believed, even of Hitler. They soon wrote Sas off, suspecting that he was either being deliberately misled by his secretive informer or that he had become hysterical and hoped to appear more important than he really was. As a result, all his messages were simply filed away. When Oster warned the Norwegian ambassador in Berlin of Hitler's decision to seize Norway and Denmark the ambassador, concluding that it was a deliberate attempt to mislead him, did not even forward the information to Oslo. By the time Norway eventually mobilized, it was too late. Similarly, the British fleet, which set sail on April 7 to beat the Germans to the punch in Norway (Hitler invaded on April 9) had no idea it was in a race against time. As if to remind Oster that he had risked his life, honor, and reputation in vain, the Dutch commander in chief, General Winkelmann, told Sas that the German officer who was feeding him information must be "a pitiful fellow."[6]

On the evening of May 9, 1940, Oster gave Sas the code word for the imminent German attack in the West: "Danzig." Sas hastened to the embassy to forward this information. The Ministry of War in The Hague hesitated, however, calling the embassy back to express its doubts, and ultimately seemed unwilling, out of fear of the Germans, to give orders for the mobilization of troops. The reaction in Belgium was no different. Consequently, when the invasion finally began in the early hours of May 10, the German units took their opponents so much by surprise that "Fortress Holland" fell within five days and Belgium soon thereafter. German units poured into France, using what Churchill called a "scythe cut"—a strategy developed by Erich von Manstein in the face of opposition from the OKH and substituted by Hitler at the last minute for the traditional strategic plan, which the Führer disparaged as "that old Schlieffen thing" (a reference to the attack on France in World War I). Within just a few weeks, the Germans overwhelmed the still slightly superior Allied forces, and on June 14 they marched through the Porte Maillot into the heart of Paris. On the same day, Guderian's panzer units reached the Swiss border and broke into the Maginot Line from the rear. This line had not only dominated French strategic thinking but also had misled France into the deceptive, self-absorbed sense of contentment that now proved so fatal.

On June 17 the French government made its "melancholy decision" to capitulate. Four days later Hitler reached the apex of his career: In the forest of Compiègne, where the terms of the armistice had been dictated to the Germans on November 11, 1918, a French delegation now signed the surrender. With his sense for high drama, the Führer invested the occasion with all the signs of symbolic reparation. The railroad car in which the historic ceremony had been held twenty-two years earlier was retrieved from the museum in which it had been displayed. In the little clearing, a German flag was draped over the granite monument, whose inscription stated that at this place "the criminal pride of the German empire" had finally been broken. Hitler had sworn in countless speeches never to rest until the humiliation of November 11, 1918, had been erased. Finally his goal had been achieved. The "deepest disgrace of all times," according to the text of the truce, was expunged.

The outburst of joy that this triumph prompted in Germany far surpassed that surrounding any of Hitler's other successes, despite the fact that the decision to launch the western war had seemed senseless and obstinate to many when it started. Many lingering reservations, as well as new doubts about the Nazis, were allayed that day—or even transmuted into respect and admiration. The victorious generals, having "gorged on titles, Knight's Crosses, and grants for distinguished service to the state," as Gisevius remarked bitterly, had little desire to recall their dire predictions about the offensive and felt forced to acknowledge that Hitler had perceived the weaknesses of the Western powers much better than they.[7] In the years that followed, it was these brilliant successes, much more than opportunism or personal weakness (although they also existed), that generated the mysterious confidence in Hitler's genius that always seemed to resurface despite setbacks.

For the German opponents of Nazism, the victory in France brought profound discouragement. Their only, albeit paradoxical, consolation lay in the fact that Hitler did not crown his triumph with serious peace initiatives; he savored it greedily but only for a short time before turning to new ventures. At some point, they thought, even Hitler's luck must turn and Germany's strength be exhausted. As if taking his leave from the cause that had so consumed him over the years, Canaris said that the resistance had "shrunk to fewer than the five fingers on one hand."[8]

The Security Service (SD) reports on the mood of the general population in the second half of June 1940 speak of unprecedented social consensus. According to them, church groups were still making "defeatist" statements, but even the Communists had ceased their oppositional activities, thanks in large part to the Hitler-Stalin pact. The surviving remnants of the Social Democratic Party had disintegrated into nothing more than apolitical circles of friends who met to reminisce about the days when their cause had seemed to be the wave of the future. Occasionally they produced leaflets to stir fading memories. Those party leaders who had remained in Germany had withdrawn into their private lives or joined the various civilian resistance groups, which offered at least intellectual opposition to the regime.

Recognizing that it was nearly impossible to mount a broad-based coup, the plotters resorted to assassination attempts. In May 1940 Fritz Dietlof von der Schulenburg resigned as regional commissioner in Silesia and joined his reserve regiment, because he believed that he could serve the resistance more effectively from within the army.

Together with Eugen Gerstenmaier, a theologian and member of the Kreisau Circle, he attempted to form a commando unit to undertake Hitler's assassination. They failed, however, to assemble the nearly one hundred people required, and their plans were frustrated by transfers, orders to travel on official business at inopportune times, and Hitler's unpredictable changes of location.

Also busy conspiring, from their positions in Paris, were members of the staff of Erwin von Witzleben, commander in chief of the western army groups, who was promoted to field marshal after the French campaign. Two members of this group, Major Alexander von Voss and Captain Ulrich Wilhelm Schwerin von Schwanenfeld, hoped to have Hitler shot by sharpshooters during the repeatedly postponed parade of German troops down the Champs-Elysées. Schwerin was also determined to kill Hitler with a hand grenade upon his first visit to the western front. But Hitler never went to Witzleben's headquarters, and the parade down the Champs-Elysées was finally canceled once and for all on July 20, 1940, partly to spare the feelings of the French population and partly because Göring could not guarantee safety from British air attacks.

The Nazi regime exploited the victory over France and the distractions it afforded to advance its special agenda with less outside interference than ever before. In the sections of Poland under his administration, Governor General Hans Frank undertook a mammoth "security operation" in May involving widespread mass executions. These activities, he said, had been "intentionally" delayed until the world "lost interest in events in the government general."[9]

. . .

In the summer of 1940 the civilian opposition began to gather strength, a development that cannot be ascribed solely to the silence of the generals and their withdrawal into apolitical pride over their great victory in France. Civilians like Goerdeler, Beck, Hassell, and Moltke were no less impressed by the military accomplishments of the Third Reich, but at the same time they were increasingly certain of the regime's imminent collapse. Thanks perhaps to their greater remove from military events and their ability to think politically, they were convinced that Hitler had been carried away by his own successes and was hopelessly overextending Germany's resources.

It is an indication of this growing confidence that in the very hour of Hitler's greatest triumph, when he stood at the pinnacle of his power, Goerdeler was writing a paper predicting the quick end of the Nazi dictatorship. The Führer would prove incapable, Goerdeler argued, of ruling the conquered territories "in such a way that the honor and freedom of the peoples living there are preserved." He concluded with Baron von Stein's celebrated words of October 1808 urging Friedrich Wilhelm III to resist Napoleon: "The only salvation for the honest man is the conviction that the wicked are prepared for any evil. . . . It is worse than blindness to trust a man who has hell in his heart and chaos in his head. If nothing awaits you but disaster and suffering, at least make a choice that is noble and honorable and that will provide some consolation and comfort if things turn out poorly."[10]

By this time Goerdeler had indisputably become the central figure in the civilian opposition. Although he was always surrounded by some controversy, he had established over the years an extensive network of like-minded friends, including business people, government officials, professors, clergymen, and labor leaders. To be sure, individual members who objected to his "open risk taking" or, like Julius Leber, to his "illusions" about foreign policy, were always dropping out of the network. Others were put off by his peculiar combination of antimodernism and social progressiveness, practicality and naive idealism. Generally, though, Goerdeler managed to conciliate the many sharp differences of opinion within the network and succeeded in steadily increasing its members.

As a result Goerdeler was unanimously considered not only the hub of the civilian opposition but its driving force as well; he pushed ahead tirelessly, insisting on action and fostering confidence among the conspirators. In the end it was his indomitable spirit in the face of any adversity that most distinguished him from his associates, who were prone to feelings of hopelessness and dejection. It is still hard to say whether his curiously restricted view of people and the world around him stemmed from his ability to reduce problems to their most basic terms, a skill that all his associates found praiseworthy, or from the natural simplicity of a man who trusted all too readily that reason would ultimately prevail. Many saw in the former mayor of Leipzig a strange combination of city-hall pragmatism and Prussian enlightenment, seldom encountered in such arid purity. Darker, more complex phenomena were beyond his comprehension. The philosopher Theodor Litt, who was teaching in Leipzig at the time and had contacts with the Goerdeler group, remarked: "Goerdeler was a clear-headed, decent, straightforward kind of man who had very little or nothing about him that was somber, unresolved, or enigmatic. He therefore assumed that his fellow human beings needed only enlightenment and well-meaning moral instruction to overcome the error of their ways. . . . The eerie tangle of good and evil, the seductive ambivalence of certain kinds of mental gifts, the power of unacknowledged prejudices and secret desires, the entire shadowy area in which the inner lives of so many are played out—there was no room for any of this in his view of humanity."[11]

Even before the victory over France, Goerdeler had quickly turned out a series of memoranda for his colleagues from which he then distilled a coherent overview of the positive aims of the resistance. The outline of the new order that resulted from this effort, entitled "The Aims," was finished in early 1941 and reflected not only his own ideas but, even more important, those that emerged in the course of comprehensive discussions with Beck; Johannes Popitz, the Prussian minister of finance; former trade union leaders such as Wilhelm Leuschner and Jakob Kaiser; and many others. Later Goerdeler also drew on a group of Freiburg professors, including Walter Eucken, Constantin von Dietze, and Adolf Lampe, the founders of the social market economy, as well as historian Gerhard Ritter and others, who had come together out of disgust for the regime after *Kristallnacht*. To understand the political aims of the conservative resistance, one must also consider a draft of a constitution produced in early 1940, apparently under the leadership of Ulrich von Hassell and Johannes Popitz, which had an unmistakable authoritarian and statist cast and from which Goerdeler in all likelihood distanced himself. There were always clashes and shifts of opinions within these constantly changing

Left: *Johannes Popitz, the Prussian minister of finance from 1933 to 1944, was an exceptionally knowledgeable and cultivated man. He joined the inner circles of the civilian resistance in 1938. In response to repeated failed assassination attempts, he hit on the idea in the summer of 1943 of trying to drive a wedge into the Nazi leadership by playing Himmler off against Hitler. He managed to arrange a meeting with Himmler, who had recently been named minister of the interior, but was widely condemned within the resistance for taking this step.*

Right: *A professor of political science, Jens Peter Jessen was a member of the conservative resistance. In the late 1920s he had been a proponent of the "German socialism" of the Nazis, although he never became a member of the party. He was soon disillusioned but continued to attempt to save the "idea" of the Nazi movement, even encouraging his students to join the SS, because he thought that was where the key decisions would be made.*

opposition circles, which were only labeled a "group" in retrospect. Even among national-conservative opponents of the regime, there existed a broad range of thoughts and ideas about the new order that would emerge. This so-called group was therefore much more heterogeneous and riven by contradiction and contrast than a simplifying label would suggest.[12]

Despite their clashing views, however, all the opposition groups, from the conservative "notables" to the various left-wing factions, were indelibly marked by their common experience of the totalitarian dictatorship that erupted in the midst of the democracy of Weimar and by the inability of the political parties, whether on the left or the right, to deal with this disaster. Virtually all opposition circles tended to blame this breakdown on the unyielding antagonism among the parties, which was played out in terms of nineteenth-century slogans and popular platitudes that no longer bore a resemblance to reality. The opponents of the Nazis turned their attention to the structures that had encouraged this disunity. Sweeping critiques of modern civilization had long been fashionable in Germany, and they certainly played a role as well, with their indictments of "mass society," "urbanization," the original sin of "secularization," and the spreading "materialism" that undermined all sense of higher purpose. The fact that even Dietrich Bonhoeffer, who certainly did not move in conservative circles, spoke of a "trend toward mob tastes at all social levels" demonstrates the prevalence of the aversion to modernity implicit in these critiques.[13] Like most other people of his political persuasion, he interpreted National Socialism as an expression, albeit an extreme one, of such modernist tendencies.

Virtually all the internal opponents of Nazism believed that it had originated in the miseries of the Weimar Republic. Even former supporters of democracy were convinced that Germany must dispense with political systems based on parties and adopt instead a rigidly structured, if not authoritarian regime. In their search for a minimal political and moral consensus, without which they believed no state could survive, they frequently flirted with utopian, "conflict-free" notions that were disturbingly reminiscent of the Nazis' own ideology of a "people's community." Yet wherever their ideas led them, the members of these civilian opposition groups were united in their desire to bring the Nazi tyranny to a quick end and to reorganize social and political life from top to bottom.

Much criticism has been directed at the German resistance's persistent skepticism toward democracy, its desire to return to older ethical systems and human values that were eternally valid and only in need of a contemporary form of expression. Hannah Arendt, for instance, saw the German resistance as nothing more than a continuation of the antidemocratic opposition to the Weimar Republic. After the collapse of the republic, which was, she stated, partially brought on by their efforts, resistance leaders paradoxically invoked Hitler as well, in order to advance what Arendt viewed as their own reactionary objectives. Others have seen a connection between the resistance and the so-called conservative revolution, that restless movement of radical intellectuals from all sides of society who were united only in their distaste for the democratic order.[14]

It is true that resistance groups of all kinds, and not just national conservatives, considered the "Weimar experiment" a hopeless failure and basically differed only in the conclusions they drew from it. Significantly, there was not a single well-known proponent of the defunct republic in these various circles despite the profusion of views their members held.[15] It would be historically inaccurate to pin the resistance down to this initial position. Close examination reveals numerous conflicts, some of them never resolved, and continuous confrontations that led to fresh insights. The resistance was neither static nor monolithic. Its peculiarity and perhaps even its glory lay in the openness and intellectual ferment it created as its members moved, often with much soul searching, from their original views, which tended to be narrow and highly conditioned by a particular social and political background, to broader visions.

Carl Goerdeler himself can be taken to illustrate this phenomenon. There is every reason to believe that he was closely involved in the draft constitution put forward by Ulrich von Hassell and Johannes Popitz, both senior officials in earlier governments, in early 1940. Under this plan, a three-person council would assume executive power after the Nazi dictatorship had been overthrown, with Beck as its leader, and a constitutional council would be formed to restore "the majesty of the law." Although the draft constitution clearly stated that this regime, quasi-dictatorial at best, would only be temporary, no termination date was specified and no mention was made of elections.

Goerdeler's counterproposal illustrated his unmitigated but perhaps misguided faith in reason. He suggested holding a plebiscite as soon as possible so as to give the new regime a solid popular base. His friends firmly rejected this proposal on the grounds that the corrupting effects of the Hitler years would still be felt for a considerable period so that it would be foolish to submit the new order to the people's will too hastily. Once again, however, Goerdeler was dissuaded from an authoritarian approach by his stubborn belief in the good judgment of humankind. He continued to insist, despite well-founded doubts on all sides, that if the truth about the Nazis could be freely spoken for "only twenty-four hours" their myopic followers would suddenly see the light. The same kind of reasoning led Goerdeler to argue that the NSDAP should not be prohibited under the new order.

Differences of opinion about the transitional regime remained. The political scientist Jens Peter Jessen and the lawyer Carl Langbehn, who advised the conspirators on their plans, added a sharply worded clause to the draft providing for a time limit on the state of emergency. The conspirators generally agreed, however, that all criminal acts committed under the Nazi regime should be severely punished: the "sword of justice," as Goerdeler later wrote, adding to the typical bombast of the times his own touch of the country pastor, must "mercilessly strike down those who have corrupted the fatherland into a caricature of a nation." Mere membership in Nazi organizations would not be punishable under this plan, though, and anonymous denunciations would be inadmissible in court. The conspirators also planned a law to rectify past injustices, especially toward Jews. A dubious feature of this law, however, was a set of provisions that recognized the citizenship of Jews whose families had long been established in Germany but that called for every effort to be made to enable more-recent Jewish immigrants "to found a state of their own."

The modifications that the conspirators' thinking underwent over the years is also evidenced in the fate of a plan Goerdeler and some of his advisers originally advanced to restore the monarchy. They were by no means royalists; rather, their intent was to establish an institution that would be universally accepted and remain above the fray of daily political life as the British and Dutch monarchies were. It seems that tactical considerations also played a role in their proposal: the conspirators hoped thereby to win the support of conservatives, especially within the officer corps. In the course of many lengthy debates, various names were considered as possible pretenders to the throne, but in the end the entire subject was dropped when it met with passionate opposition from Helmuth von Moltke's Kreisau Circle.

Many variants of Goerdeler's constitutional plans have survived, indicating both his openness to new ideas and the influence of changing advisers. But the core of his plan, which eventually took shape after a rather nebulous start, was always a strong government in which various "corporatist bodies" played a leading role while the parliament was limited to a more or less supervisory function. This basic thrust found expression in a considerable expansion of self-government at even the lowest levels of society; not only municipalities but universities, student bodies, churches, and professional organizations would be involved. To the end of his life, Goerdeler clung to the belief that this was the genuine "German way" in politics, which had proved itself even amid the confusion of the Weimar years and despite "extreme democratization" and "extensive corrosion by political parties." The various states within Germany he reduced to little more than large administrative units, seeing them as an intermediate level of government that was not really close to everyday life and yet too far removed from the focus of real power.

In the same spirit, Goerdeler attempted to limit the influence of the general public, especially through political parties, and to turn the decision-making process over to indirectly elected bodies whenever possible. One of the clear contradictions between Goerdeler's theory and his practice was that, despite his belief in the power of reason, he never entirely freed himself from the fear he had acquired in the Weimar years of what ordinary people might do. Notions such as "the power of parties," "splinter parties," and "self-interested parties" continued to haunt his own constitutional thinking as well as that of the entire group.

The election process was therefore calculated to bring forth strong,

Carlo Mierendorff joined the socialist movement as a young literature student. He became one of the most colorful and passionate figures in the German resistance—a "born leader," in the words of one contemporary. Arrested in 1933, shortly after Hitler seized power, Mierendorff spent a total of five years in concentration camps, which he later called "the silent world."

Right: Mierendorff at the time of his release from the Lichtenburg concentration camp in early 1938.

experienced "personalities with roots in real life" by means of a complicated modified majority-rule system. It is noteworthy that all the opposition groups agreed on this, despite their strong differences on other questions. The socialist Carlo Mierendorff said "never again shall the German people lose their way amid the squabbling of political parties," and his fellow socialist Julius Leber called for an end "to the old forms of party rule." It was he who summarized as follows the argument against proportional representation, which he blamed most of all for creating political fragmentation: "It fails totally to carry out its real functions, namely, selecting suitable men and maintaining the trust between the people and the leadership. Instead, it simply imposes on politics the determined dullards who eventually rise to the top of party hierarchies."[16] Goerdeler even contemplated a drastic limitation on majority rule by restricting seats in the parliament to the three strongest parties.

Another suggestion for the new order would have conferred a double vote on fathers with at least three children. Other plans for reform reflected the strong corporatist tradition in German society. Goerdeler, for instance, wanted to see a *Reichsständehaus*, an upper house consisting of fifty respected appointees as well as representatives of the churches, universities, artists' guilds, and, most important, labor unions, for whom he had particularly high expectations, certainly far higher than he did for political parties. He had learned in his years as mayor of Leipzig that involvement in everyday life soon dispels the doctrinaire theories that in his view were badly damaging political life or even destroying it.

Goerdeler also advanced some suggestions about how the economy should operate: he advocated moderate liberalism, limits on the role of industry (a stricture that clearly reflected the influence of the Freiburg school), participation of workers in corporate management, and a sense of social responsibility on the part of the propertied classes. There were many thoroughly antimodern aspects to Goerdeler's proposals, which were as passionately opposed to the egalitarian tendencies of contemporary industrial societies as they were to pluralistic social and political interests. Goerdeler wanted to bring all these contending interests together within an idyllic, community based order that served the general interest. Thus there was a definite utopian cast to national-conservative thought, an inclination to idealize the "good old days" even though, as everyone knows, they were never all that good. Nevertheless, these efforts cannot be dismissed as mere attempts to restore the lost societies of the past. Goerdeler's close working relationship and even friendship with trade union leaders such as Wilhelm Leuschner and Jakob Kaiser points to the contrary. Indeed, the first people to accuse Goerdeler of being "reactionary" were, in a remarkable twist, the most conservative members of the group—Hassell, Jessen, and Popitz—who denounced Goerdeler's proposals for going too far toward restoring democratic "Weimar" conditions.[17]

These proposals, of course, were fragmentary. Many of them were inevitably driven by tactical considerations, and in any case,

One of the central figures in the opposition to Hitler was Count Helmuth James von Moltke, great-grandnephew of a famous Franco-Prussian War general. He was one of the founders of the Kreisau Circle, which took its name from the Moltke family estate. The group met primarily to discuss Christian and socialist ideas for the renewal of society. Moltke was opposed to overthrowing Hitler by violent means.

Above: Moltke in 1928 at the age of twenty-one during a visit to Austria.

there is always a great divide in politics between theory and practice. It is impossible to say whether Goerdeler's proposals would have been adopted if a coup had succeeded. Thus they are primarily of interest for what they reveal about the two primary goals of Goerdeler's group, namely the far-reaching depoliticization of government and the overcoming of political fragmentation by forging a new sense of community. The Weimar Republic cast as long a shadow over these objectives as it did over the Hitler years. An underlying feeling of helplessness pervades these proposals. When

Educator Adolf Reichwein (above) was a leader of the opposition's youth movement, a powerful influence on the Kreisau Circle. A devoted socialist, he advocated formation of a united front with the Communist underground. Although many of his colleagues disagreed strenuously, contacts were made in 1944. The Communists, however, had been infiltrated by the Nazis. At his second meeting with them on July 4, Reichwein was arrested, followed by Julius Leber the next day.

Reichwein is shown here with his students in Halle.

Goerdeler remarked that he wanted to pursue the "German way" in drafting his constitution and would not allow himself to be "led astray" by Western models, he inadvertently disclosed an intellectual detachment and isolation that the entire German resistance never overcame. In the end, however, Goerdeler was not motivated by the desire for social and constitutional change embodied in these proposals, nor did he justify himself by them. They were produced under great pressure and emotional stress and were often not fully developed. To understand Goerdeler we have to look to more compelling forces.[18]

Peter Yorck von Wartenburg was descended from an old Prussian family and counted among his direct ancestors a famous general of the Napoleonic Wars. His apartment on Hortensienstrasse in the Lichterfelde section of Berlin became a frequent meeting place for the resistance. While Helmuth James von Moltke has been described as the "engine" of the Kreisau Circle, Yorck was its "heart."

■ ■ ■

Quite different from the Beck-Goerdeler-Popitz group, and yet in some ways strangely similar, was the other important group of civilian opponents of the Nazi regime. It was founded and held together by Helmuth von Moltke, a great-grandnephew of the celebrated army commander of the Franco-Prussian War, who worked in the Wehrmacht high command as an expert in international law. His group was later dubbed the Kreisau Circle after the estate owned by the Moltke family in Silesia, although it met there only two or three times. Its intense discussions, conducted in working groups, took place more frequently in various locations in Berlin; beginning in early 1943 most were held on Hortensienstrasse in Lichterfelde, at the home of Peter Yorck von Wartenburg, another bearer of a famous name in Prussian history. Related to both Moltke and Stauffenberg, he was a lawyer and officer who had been assigned to the eastern department of the Defense Economy Office. While Moltke has been described as the "engine" of the group, Yorck von Wartenburg was its "heart."[19]

Around Moltke and Yorck gathered what at first glance appeared to be a motley array of strong-willed individuals with markedly different origins, temperaments, and convictions. Among them was Adam von Trott zu Solz, a descendant, on his mother's side, of John Jay, the first chief justice of the United States. Trott had been a Rhodes scholar and had many friends in England, including the so-called Cliveden set around David Astor. Like Hans-Bernd von Haeften, another member of the circle, Trott was employed in the Foreign Office. Striving to include experts from as many areas of political and social life as possible, the Kreisau Circle recruited Horst von Einsiedel, a Harvard graduate and an expert in economics. Carl Dietrich von Trotha, on the other hand, was a cousin of Moltke's, born in Kreisau, and had been, like some other members of the group, a student of the philosopher and sociologist Eugen Rosenstock-Huessy.

The most striking characteristic of this group, apart from its strong religious leanings, was its earnest and quite successful attempt to attract a number of devoted but undogmatic socialists. Among them was the educator Adolf Reichwein, who came from the Romanticist youth movement of the 1920s and had met Einsiedel and Moltke in one of the reform-minded volunteer work camps. Through Reichwein, Theodor Haubach also joined the group. A former student of Karl Jaspers and Alfred Weber, Haubach was nicknamed The General by his friends because of his expertise in military policy. He also had a deep interest in philosophy and the arts and had served as chief press officer of the Prussian government for several years.

Haubach, in turn, recruited the man who was possibly the most colorful, emotional, and powerful figure in the circle, Carlo Mierendorff, a close friend since their school days in Darmstadt. Like

Haubach, Mierendorff had a background in literature; before finally devoting himself entirely to politics, he had dabbled in the expressionist movement and edited a magazine. According to another acquaintance, the writer Gerhart Hauptmann, he was a "born leader." Within the Social Democratic Party he was one of the young rebels who took on the complacent party hierarchy and its outdated programs and slogans. Mierendorff was arrested shortly after Hitler took power and spent five years in concentration camps, where at one point he was delivered by camp authorities into the hands of Communist fellow prisoners, who beat him nearly to death. During this time Haubach sought constantly to obtain the release of his friend, succeeding even in reaching Adolf Eichmann. (Never, he later said of Eichmann, had he seen "such glassy green eyes."[20])

A number of figures from the Christian resistance also joined the Kreisau Circle, including the Jesuits Alfred Delp and Augustin Rösch, as well as prominent Protestants like the theologian Eugen Gerstenmaier and the prison chaplain Harald Poelchau. Fritz-Dietlof von der Schulenburg and Julius Leber were also loosely affiliated with this group. They were older and more experienced than the others, with too much of the politician in them to be interested in sharing the circle's passion for theoretical debates. "What comes later will take care of itself," Leber was fond of saying. True to type, he struck up an immediate friendship with Stauffenberg—who was always pressing for more action—when the two met in late 1943.

What brought the Kreisau group together was not principally a determination to overthrow the Nazi regime but rather the common project of planning, through their preparatory discussions, what a modern, post-Hitler Germany would look like. In this way "they kept themselves alive," according to a close observer.[21] There was a strong utopian streak in their thought and planning, which was infused with Christian and socialist ideals, as well as remnants from the youth movement of a romantic belief in the dawning of a new era. They basically believed that all social and political systems were reaching a dead end and that capitalism and Communism, no less than Nazism, were symptomatic of the crisis deep and all-encompassing in modern mass society.

This lofty radicalism, often quite remote from the real world, was the main source of discord between the Kreisau and Goerdeler groups. The former accused the "old-timers" of being stuck in outmoded patterns of thought. Instead of seeking a genuinely new beginning, the Goerdeler group wanted merely to avoid the missteps that had been revealed by the failure of the Weimar Republic. The birth of a "new age," on the other hand, required an entirely fresh approach. Moltke spoke contemptuously of "that Goerdeler mess" and, like Delp, cautioned opponents of the regime who were looking for like-minded contacts against any involvement with what he called "their reactionary Excellencies."[22]

The two groups had more in common, however, than they ever imagined. They were both deeply enamored of the curious German tradition of grand, sweeping critiques of entire civilizations. The main difference lay in the fact that the Goerdeler group translated its ideas into more or less practical programs for action (which were by no means free of inconsistencies), while the Kreisau group moved in more theoretical and idealistic spheres, launching ideas that only occasionally led to concrete solutions. Both groups considered mass society the great scourge of the time, and both sought to replace it with a "community" of some kind—markedly more Christian in the case of the Kreisauers, although still not without an authoritarian streak. Both groups were eager to recover the lost "organic" communities of the past, which in their view still retained something of the Garden of Eden, and both were appalled by the egalitarian tendencies of the time.

For all these reasons, their members repeatedly expressed the need for an "elite," which the Goerdeler group thought could be created by a stern government based on traditional values and which the Kreisau group believed would emerge from a return to "personal substance" based on Christian or socialist values. There were even similarities in their recipes for the new society. The Kreisauers, too, imagined a society constructed from the bottom up, beginning with simple units of local self-administration. They also had a deep distrust of professional politicians and aimed to replace them with individuals who had proved themselves in practical life and had strong local or regional roots. The greatest contrast between the two groups was in the field of economics, although even here the Kreisau group's distaste for Goerdeler's liberalism only brought them into line with Popitz and Jessen, who favored a highly interventionist economy in keeping with their authoritarian, state-driven view of society. Even corporatist ideas found eloquent advocates in the Kreisau group, especially among its Catholic members.

The Kreisauers suffered many internal differences of opinion over such issues as the nationalization of heavy industry, the division of landed estates, and the role of parochial schools. The question of redrawing the regional map of the Reich led to such bitter controversies that some of the inveterate Bavarians even left the group. Historical perspective tends to make many of the internal and external conflicts of these groups seem less serious than they in fact were. Goerdeler's dismissal of the Kreisauers as "armchair Bolsheviks," for example, reveals as great a misunderstanding of their basic intentions as Moltke's and Trott's remarks about reactionary "notables" do of Goerdeler's circle, however accurate these characterizations may have been in individual cases.

Another difference was far more telling. While the group around Beck and Goerdeler was committed to some form of coup d'état, violent if necessary, most members of the Kreisau Circle rejected any sort of violence. This stance largely reflected their religious convictions, of course. Almost equally strong was their belief that "demonic forces" were at work in Hitler, which neither could nor should be "simply swept aside."[23] All attempts to do so were, in their eyes, merely efforts to overcome the great crisis in world history through the same arbitrary and violent means that helped cause it in the first place. Instead, the demonic forces had to be allowed to burn out. This conviction led many within the circle to reject not only an assassination attempt but even the notion of a coup, for, as Moltke wrote to his friend Lionel Curtis, "we need a real revolution, not just a putsch." Only a complete collapse and widespread acceptance of the inevitability of defeat and the ensuing chaos could create the necessary preconditions for the great internal revival on which the future depended. Among the Kreisauers, Eugen Gerstenmaier most vehemently attacked this belief and what he termed its un Christian fatalism. But Moltke championed it energetically nevertheless, carrying most of the circle with him. The fervor with which he denied the possibility of a shift in Germany's ebbing military fortunes and forecast total destruction (with far more realism than his friends) indicated that he took a certain satisfaction in the approaching inferno, which alone could give rise to a radically new beginning. "My own homeland of Silesia will go to the Czechs or the Poles," he wrote before the battle of Stalingrad to his old friend George F. Kennan.[24]

The foreign policy ideas of these two groups also differed greatly. Beck and Goerdeler's circle still thought in terms of hegemonic power and regarded it as a matter of course that Germany would continue to play a major role in Europe. The Kreisauers adopted a more radical, utopian stance on this issue as well, their ideas focusing to varying degrees on a new brand of international relations that would do away with the "borders and soldiers" of the past. In the new age that they saw dawning, selfish nationalisms would yield to a pan-European unity. The germ of this idea came from Moltke and the socialist members of the circle—Haubach, Reichwein, and Mierendorff—but it was swiftly embraced by all the others. Even before the outbreak of the war, the only belief that all the members of the Kreisau Circle shared was this emphasis on the larger picture, on what Europeans had in common, the intellectual foundations of their history, traditions, and way of life, a shared desire to see neighbors no longer as foes but as family, as people who were similar to one another and yet different in interesting ways. Only in this manner, they thought, could there be a reconciliation of the nations in Europe that considered themselves hereditary enemies, and only in this manner could the problem of minorities finally be solved, an issue that seemed always to end in bloodletting, especially in the central and eastern parts of the continent.

There was much less unanimity among the Kreisauers on the consequences of their program. To be sure, they agreed that the old idea of dominant powers in Europe should be abandoned, that there should be no more territorial claims escalating into life-and-death issues, that a new understanding of national interest, the state, and national sovereignty must emerge. Once again Moltke proved to be the most radical member of the circle, advocating nothing less than the elimination of the nation-state and the reorganization of Europe into a multiplicity of regions that were historically and culturally related. In this he was returning to the idea of small self-governing units and applying it to Europe as a whole. These autonomous regions would exercise only limited powers, with the traditional jurisdiction of sovereign states transferred to a single European entity.

Most of Moltke's associates did not share his radical vision of a federated Europe. Adam von Trott, the circle's "foreign minister," saw the national characters that the European countries had developed in the course of history as a feature of the old continent that merited preservation. For much the same reason, he opposed the idea of simply squeezing Germany into a "Western" constitutional tradition, despite his high hopes for what Anglo-German cooperation could achieve. He shared, though, the conviction of almost all the members of the circle that the age of the nation-state had passed and that some measure of sovereignty would have to be surrendered to a federal European state if the survival of the various nations of Europe was to be ensured.

These ideas were obviously not fully thought out, but they pointed the way to the future. They attracted support for their own sake, not only because they were categorically opposed to Hitler's approach of conquest and subjugation but also because their vision of the future stood in stark opposition to the nationalistic fervor of the times. This vision, like all the other plans and designs of the German resistance, eventually faded from memory, and during the actual process of European unification after the war it was not even mentioned. For this very reason, however, it deserves to be recalled now.

■ ■ ■

It is hardly surprising that the "notables" around Goerdeler viewed the pan-European ideas of the Kreisau Circle as little more than idealistic or eccentric fantasies. They had grown up at time when Germany was rising into the ranks of the great powers of the world and to them such concepts as nation-states, great-power status, zones of influence, and national interest were like the laws of physics—they could not simply be abolished. Virtually all the members of the Goerdeler group thought that at least the "greater German territories" should remain within the Reich. This has given rise to accusations that there were strong underlying similarities with the regime—or even that the national-conservative opposition was simply striving to realize Hitler's aims without Hitler.

As far as the first revisionist interpretation is concerned, there is some truth to this accusation. When Hitler pointed time and again to the injustices of the Treaty of Versailles as the grounds for his demands, people like Beck, Goerdeler, and Hassell could only nod in agreement, all the more so as his arguments were widely shared abroad, especially in Britain. Those who most strenuously indict the Goerdeler group, however, ignore an essential distinction: although the national conservatives generally agreed with Hitler's border claims, they did not agree with his methods. Ludwig Beck, for instance, said as early as 1938 that war was not only militarily absurd but anachronistic, and he attempted to resist, though perhaps not forcefully enough. At about the same time, Goerdeler called Hitler a "national bandit" for risking Germany's honor and reputation on one adventure after another.[25]

The inconsistencies within the conservative position therefore became all the more apparent with the outbreak of the war. Although Goerdeler repeatedly called for peaceful cooperation in Europe after Hitler and a renewal of the League of Nations, the papers he wrote after the conquest of France spoke unabashedly of "German leadership" on the continent. Among other contradictory positions, he assured the Western powers that Poland would be restored but he insisted on Germany's eastern frontiers of 1914. Hermann Graml has demonstrated convincingly that the "notables" clung to the familiar. They could only imagine, for instance, a unification of Europe and a distribution of power that would resemble the unification of Germany under Prussia.[26]

The conservatives' reflexive belief in the concept of the great powers, so deeply rooted in their psyches, began to disappear, however, by the end of 1941—and not just because of the spread of the war to the Soviet Union and the entry soon thereafter of the United States. More important was the mounting awareness of the destruction wrought by arbitrary German policies in southeastern Europe after the Reich smashed Czechoslovakia and extended its dominance deep into the Balkans. Most important of all were the rampant reports of massive crimes in the East, which cast a pall over all talk of the "Reich's mission to bring order and peace."

Despite the persistent disagreements between the two main civilian opposition groups, contacts were gradually established. Ulrich von Hassell played an especially important role in this regard. Although he was always uneasy with the utopianism of the Kreisau Circle, he shared many of its objections to Goerdeler and believed that the two most important resistance groups should not waste their strength nursing differences when they were in such extreme danger. The rest of the work necessary for a rapprochement was accomplished thanks to his skill as a negotiator. There were also contacts between Yorck and Jessen, Schulenburg and Goerdeler, and Popitz and Gerstenmaier. After strained preliminary negotiations, the two groups met for the first time on January 8, 1943, in Yorck's house, with Beck serving as chairman. They made little progress in narrowing the differences between them, partly because Goerdeler "trivialized all attempts to get to the heart of matters," as Moltke noted with great exasperation. But in the end a majority of the Kreisau group supported the selection of Goerdeler as chancellor of a transitional government, despite some complaints that the decision represented a dangerous "Kerensky solution."[27]

Now, under the influence of the Kreisau Circle, the national-conservative resistance moved even more quickly to drop its insistence that Germany play a leadership role in the new Europe. By mid-1943 Goerdeler himself had discarded a number of hitherto cherished notions. With all the impulsive exuberance of his nature, he began to speak of a European "peace confederacy" that no nation would dominate and in which "inner-European borders" would play "an ever-diminishing role."

Similarly, the ideas of the Kreisau group were colored by its increasingly close contacts with the Goerdeler people. There is no convincing evidence, however, for the accusation raised from time to time that the Kreisauers became infected with old nationalist ideas. It is true that Adam von Trott began insisting somewhat more determinedly on a "reasonable peace plan" for post-Hitler Germany and warning against the ruinous consequences of a second Versailles. But an unbiased observer would have to acknowledge that both the Kreisau Circle and the Goerdeler group, as well as Oster, Leber, Gisevius, and many other opponents of the regime, rejected nationalism much more strongly than most of their contemporaries did, even if they were less than sure-footed as they ventured onto new terrain.

The progress they had made is evident when considered in the light of the fruitless efforts of the German resistance over the years to establish contacts with like-minded people in other countries through the World Council of Churches, Allen W. Dulles, head of the Office of Strategic Services in Bern, the lawyer Eduard Waetjen, Theodor Strünk, Ulrich von Hassell, Gero von Schulze-Gaevernitz, and numerous others. Most of the politicians and military leaders whom they unsuccessfully courted in London, The Hague, and Washington still believed, however, that these Germans were committing "treason" and therefore regarded them with contempt. There was no appreciation of the fact that the opponents of the Nazi regime felt guided by new principles and laws whose legitimacy did not end at national borders. Even after the failed coup attempt of July 20, 1944, the *New York Times* commented reproachfully that the conspirators had plotted for an entire year "to kidnap or kill the head of the German state and commander in chief of the Army," something one would not "normally expect within an officers' corps and a civilized government."[28] But the German resistance deserves to be remembered precisely because of this break with "normalcy," a feat achieved with great effort but one that only further reduced the already slim chances for success.

■ ■ ■

Out of the blue during the summer of 1941, alarm bells sounded at Military Intelligence, when the commotion attending the victory over

The Chief of Military Intelligence, Admiral Wilhelm Canaris (left), led a double life. Responsible on the one hand for running the secret service, he also maintained close ties with the resistance. For years he protected his close associate Hans Oster, the head of the Military Intelligence Office's central division, who turned it into a center of activity for opponents of the regime. At the same time Canaris was meeting regularly with his most dangerous adversary, Reinhard Heydrich (right), for morning horseback rides in Berlin's Tiergarten.

France and Hitler's celebration of himself as the "greatest general of all time" had not yet died down. The research office informed Canaris that the timing of the western offensive had probably been betrayed by a German officer. The monitoring service had taped Colonel Sas's telephone conversation with The Hague on the eve of the attack and decoded telegrams from Belgian ambassador Adrien

Nieuwenhuys, in which he mentioned an informant in Rome. Suspicion immediately fell on Josef Müller, whom Military Intelligence had sent to the Vatican, and then on Hans Oster himself.

In fact, it is remarkable that the constant bustle surrounding Oster and the other conspirators, their trips and often frantic telephone calls, as well as their unannounced visits and swiftly closed doors, could have failed to attract attention for so long in as highly organized a police state. Virtually none of the conspirators lived in a world of his own. Most worked in government departments where everyone was acutely aware of everyone else and where personal animosities and rivalries, ideological conflicts, and competition for positions abounded. Everyone in Military Intelligence would presumably have been aware of Oster's friendship with Sas and his continuing contacts with Beck, Goerdeler, Popitz, Kordt, and others. Oster once gestured toward the five telephones on his desk and commented to a visitor, "That's me. I'm the middleman for everything."[29] In his diary Hassell recorded numerous breakfast meetings in hotels with four or more people, as well as "gentlemen's evenings" and walks in the Tiergarten. Occasionally he remarked on having all met at Beck's apartment or Popitz's or Jessen's—and then gone together to Yorck's place. Most of the conspirators demonstrated a similar lack of caution for years on end and were quite careless about whom they revealed their plans to. The likeliest explanation for why they were not apprehended sooner is that the military and the civil service, having fallen quickly into line after 1933, were not regarded with much suspicion by the security apparatus, whose gaze was still focused on the Nazis' original foes—Communists, Social Democrats, labor union leaders, and church figures suspected of opposing the regime.

Canaris seemed to be deeply upset by the rising tide of evidence against Oster. Those who knew the admiral found him an enigmatic, inscrutable personality, who always maintained a certain distance from people as well as from his duties. Among all the competing elements of his nature there may even have been some part that could understand the treason of his closest collaborator, though there is no evidence of this. In any case, Canaris continued to protect both Oster and Müller despite the fact that Hitler himself had taken an interest in the issue and had ordered Canaris to join Heydrich in conducting the investigation. Canaris demonstrated great resilience and flexibility in drawing the inquiry into his own hands, leading it, and then letting it drop quietly, all at great personal risk. His performance revealed a poker-faced master strategist, cold-blooded, quick to react, and gifted with sure instincts. "He pulled the wool over everyone's eyes—Heydrich, Himmler, Keitel, Ribbentrop, even the Führer himself," a Gestapo official later lamented.[30]

Behind the cool mask lay a high-strung disposition; Canaris was agitated and tormented by fear after each passing danger yet was still addicted to new adventures. Like most cunning people, he hated violence. He was nimble in the face of danger, witty, and sardonic. During one of his trips to Spain he would spring to attention in his open car and raise his arm in the Hitler salute every time he drove past a herd of sheep. You never know, he said, whether one of the party bigwigs might be in the crowd. He called his immediate superior, Wilhelm Keitel—his total opposite in temperament—a blockhead. Some observers have deduced from all the incongruities in Canaris that he was an unprincipled cynic who sought only thrills from the resistance and who admired Hitler as an even greater gamesman than himself. These interpretations miss the mark. In his last years Canaris increasingly suffered from the conviction that he had served Hitler far too long and far too submissively, and he regretted not having turned the resources of Military Intelligence against the regime in a more determined fashion. It has been said that he was a master of the art of obfuscation, and his skill has tended to obscure his rigid adherence to a number of principles. He could not abide treason whatever the pretext, as his break with Oster shows, but neither could he bear the lack of basic humanity that made the Nazi regime so abhorrent in his eyes.

One of his colleagues recounted that while visiting the Military Intelligence offices in Paris on his way back from Spain, Canaris learned that Hitler had issued orders to have former French prime minister Paul Reynaud and General Maxime Weygand not just arrested but quietly killed should the opportunity present itself. At dinner with his colleagues, Canaris sat sunk in silence until his feelings

suddenly erupted in an angry denunciation of "these gangster methods of Hitler and his henchmen," who were not only committing
crime upon crime in the East but now bringing betrayal and murder
to the West as well. Germany would lose more than just the war, he
added before leaving the table, and its future would then be too
frightful to contemplate.[31]

Because Canaris understood the nature of the Nazi regime better
than most and yet never crossed irrevocably into the camp of its
enemies, he exemplified the dilemma of many torn between emotion
and reason. They felt proud of the restoration of German might yet
were well aware of the repellent ways in which it had been achieved.
They took great professional pleasure in their successes yet despaired
over the "gangster methods of the regime." They recognized that a
catastrophe was looming for which they bore some responsibility yet
felt paralyzed by such honorable principles as duty, loyalty, and a job
well done. On March 10, 1938, Chief of General Staff Ludwig Beck
was summoned to the Chancellery and asked to prepare mobilization
plans for the entry into Austria. Although he plainly foresaw the disasters to which Hitler's ambitions would lead, he threw himself into his
task when it turned out that no plans existed because Hitler had been
keeping the general staff in the dark. He spurred on his staff and his
chief of operations, Erich von Manstein, to produce plans as fast as
possible. Five hours later they lay ready. There was no escape from
the fact that if opponents of the regime wished to avoid serving Hitler
they had to turn their backs on all the values they believed in and
even on longstanding friendships. Hans Oster was prepared to do
precisely that. Franz Halder once remarked—half in grudging admiration, half in disapproval—that Oster was fired by a "burning hatred
of Hitler," which caused him to conceive notions "that the sober,
critically minded listener simply could not accept."[32]

6

THE ARMY GROUPS

The western campaign was barely three weeks old and still in full swing when Hitler turned his mind to new horizons. On June 2, 1940, he spoke in General Rundstedt's headquarters about his hopes of soon concluding a peace treaty with Britain in order to gain "a free hand" for what he considered his "great, true mission: the struggle against Bolshevism."[1] Shortly thereafter, on July 21, he ordered the army high command to begin "mental preparations" for renewed operations in the East, which he considered launching as early as the fall of that year. This time, however, in contrast to his stubbornness after the Polish campaign, he allowed himself to be easily dissuaded from such an early date.

Above all it was his concern about the difficulty of waging a two-front war that made Hitler more uncertain and receptive. He had once said that avoiding such a predicament was a fundamental principle of German foreign policy. To get around it, he now elaborated a risky plan to divide the war into two phases: first the Wehrmacht would turn on the Soviet Union and conquer it in a lightning strike, then, after gathering its strength, it would turn to the task of polishing off Great Britain once and for all. Hitler's confidence in his luck and invincibility, and his obsession with his "true mission," which now lay so tantalizingly near, eventually laid to rest most of his concerns, and any lingering hesitation was overcome by his anxiety about timing— "Time, always time!" as he later grumbled. In mid-December he informed Alfred Jodl that "all problems on the continent of Europe" would have to be ironed out in 1941 because by 1942 "the United States would be in a position to intervene." To Mussolini he said that he felt like someone who had only one shot left in his rifle as night began to fall. In his haste, before the final decision to invade had even been made, he ordered that suitable locations be found in the East for headquarters and command posts for the army groups and that construction begin "as quickly as possible."[2]

At the same time, he began to make his entourage aware that this would be no ordinary war waged according to the traditional rules; it was to be a war of annihilation. His annoyance at repeated complaints from military leaders about atrocities committed in the Polish campaign led him to summon nearly 250 senior officers to the Berlin Chancellery on March 30, 1941, in order to explain this new kind of warfare to them. Everything they had previously experienced—the "flower wars," the easy victories gained through happy circumstance and the battles fought on the wrong battlefields—was only a prelude, he told them, in a speech that was to last two and a half hours. The real war, *his* war, was about to begin. According to the notes taken by one of his listeners, it would be a "struggle of two ideologies." Bolshevism was "equivalent to a social criminality, a tremendous danger for the future," the Führer declared. "We must abandon the viewpoint of soldierly comradeship," he cautioned. "What is involved is a struggle of annihilation. The commanders of the troops must know what is at stake." He concluded by singling out Communist leaders and the secret police for special treatment. "Commissars and GPU men are criminals and must be treated as such. The fight will be very different from the fight in the West. In the East harshness is kindness toward the future. The leaders must demand of themselves the sacrifice of overcoming their scruples."[3]

When Hitler finished speaking there was a moment of stunned silence. But he had scarcely left the room before the marshals besieged Commander in Chief Brauchitsch, talking and gesticulating wildly. No one had any doubt, it seems, about the real meaning of Hitler's words. Brauchitsch stood firm against the waves of complaints and references to international law, saying he had already done all he could but Hitler was not to be dissuaded. According to a statement that Jodl made at the Nuremberg trials, Brauchitsch and Hitler did indeed have a number of "very heated conversations." Halder tried to persuade Brauchitsch that the two of them should resign together, but the commander in chief was incapable of making a decision of that magnitude.[4]

Hitler knew better than to rely solely on appeals for harshness. A number of preparatory guidelines were soon issued transferring the Wehrmacht's responsibility for the administration of the occupied territories to special Reich commissioners. Heinrich Himmler and four Einsatzgruppen were commissioned to undertake "special tasks" arising "from the final battle of two opposed political systems." The dry administrative language outlining directives for the planned "war of ideologies" could hardly disguise the extent to which the basic principles of international law and warfare were being thwarted. Two of the most infamous directives were the decree on military law and the so-called Commissar Order. The former transferred responsibility for punishing crimes against enemy civilians from military courts to individual division commanders, while the latter required that Red Army political commissars be segregated upon capture and, "as a rule, immediately shot for instituting barbaric Asian methods of warfare." When Oster produced the documents at a meeting in Beck's house, "everyone's hair stood on end," according to one who was there, "at these orders for the troops in Russia, signed by Halder, that would systematically transform military justice for the civilian population into a caricature that mocked every concept of law." They all agreed that, "by complying with Hitler's orders, Brauchitsch is sacrificing the honor of the German army."[5] In the first half of June, two weeks before the invasion was launched, the "Commissar Order" was issued to the staffs at the front as the last of a series of preparatory edicts.

■   ■   ■

Henning von Tresckow was the first general staff officer of Army Group Center, headquartered in Posen at the time. Those who were

Henning von Tresckow was the first officer at the front to contact the resistance about overthrowing Hitler. Tresckow, who served on the staff of Army Group Center, proved to be one of the most resolute adversaries of the regime. He organized several assassination attempts in the spring of 1943, all of which ultimately failed. Although Tresckow initially believed that eliminating Hitler could advance various political aims—especially a negotiated peace—he eventually abandoned such hopes, saying, "The assassination must be attempted, coûte que coûte. . . . The practical purpose no longer matters; what matters now is that the German resistance movement must take the plunge before the eyes of the world and of history."

close to him all recalled the strong impression he made, his "leadership qualities," "distinguished manner," "sense of honor," and "Prussianness." These descriptions do more, however, to obscure his character than to illuminate it.

Next to Stauffenberg, he was the most remarkable figure in the military resistance, displaying not only the mental discipline and passionate moral sense of the other conspirators but also great coolness under pressure, decisiveness, and daring. The so-called Kaltenbrunner reports of the interrogations carried out after the July 20 assassination attempt describe him as the "prime mover" and the "evil spirit" behind the plot.[6] Originally an admirer of National Socialism, Tresckow did not have to wait for Hitler's blatant warmongering to see the error of his ways. The continual illegal acts, the persecution of minorities, the suppression of free speech, and the harassment of churches had long since turned him against the party. Unlike many others, he realized early on that the "excesses" of the Nazi regime were not excesses at all but its real nature. And with the same frankness with which he had once supported Hitler, he now began to criticize him. When one of his army comrades defended the regime, Tresckow vehemently disagreed and ended by predicting that a dispute like this could easily lead to their taking up arms on opposite sides some day. Indeed, the commander of the First Regiment of Foot Soldiers had once prophesied that young officer Tresckow would end up as either chief of general staff or a mutineer mounting the scaffold.[7]

At the time of the dispute over the western offensive, Tresckow attempted "in total despair" to organize a revolt. He urged his uncle Fedor von Bock, commander in chief of Army Group B, as well as Rundstedt and his chief of staff Erich von Manstein, to take action. But the generals "did not want to hear about any schemes directed against Hitler." They were merely experts in military strategy, they replied, closing their minds to further persuasion. For the first time, Tresckow felt "contempt for the army leaders," according to his biographer, Bodo Scheurig, and steeled himself to take matters into his own hands. But ironically, it was probably he who ensured that Brauchitsch and Halder did not scuttle Manstein's "scythe-cut" strategy for penetrating deep into France with tanks and other armored vehicles, which later proved so successful. Tresckow's former regimental comrade Rudolf Schmundt was now serving as Wehrmacht adjutant at Hitler's headquarters, and Tresckow succeeded in persuading him to present Manstein's plan to Hitler, who immediately saw its daring ingenuity and revised the invasion strategy.[8]

Tresckow's own plans for a coup began to take shape after he was assigned to Posen and the preparations for war against the Soviet Union had begun in earnest. He systematically placed officers who shared his views on the army group general staff, eventually filling all the key positions. First, to the astonishment and probably also the chagrin of his colleagues, he hired the strictly "civilian-minded" lawyer and reserve lieutenant Fabian von Schlabrendorff. Tresckow valued Schlabrendorff's prudence and judgment and made him his closest adviser. Tresckow also had General Staff Major Rudolph-Christoph von Gersdorff transferred from an infantry division. Gersdorff was a cavalry officer who, as Tresckow had discovered in the course of a chance encounter, agreed with him about the contemptible nature of the Nazi regime. Gersdorff combined rectitude with great presence of mind and courage, as well as a charmingly adroit manner. Tresckow also attracted two other majors, Count Carl-Hans Hardenberg and Berndt von Kleist, and Count Heinrich Lehndorff, a lieutenant, all of old Prussian stock. Eventually they were joined by Lieutenant Colonels Georg Schulze-Büttger and Alexander von Voss, First Lieutenant Eberhard von Breitenbuch, Georg and Philipp von Boeselager, and a number of others. It was later observed quite correctly that the largest and most tightly knit resistance group of those years could be found right on the general staff of Army Group Center.

When the edict on the application of military law and the Commissar Order arrived at Army Group Center, Tresckow immediately had the commander in chief's plane prepared for takeoff and went, with Gersdorff, to see Bock. On a pathway through a small park leading to Bock's villa, Tresckow suddenly stopped. "If we don't convince the field marshal to fly to Hitler at once and have these orders canceled, the German people will be burdened with a guilt the world will not forget in a hundred years. This guilt will fall not only on Hitler, Himmler, Göring, and their comrades but on you and me, your wife and mine, your children and mine," he said to Gersdorff. "Think about it."[9]

Bock, who had attended the officers' meeting on March 30, 1941, must therefore have been expecting these orders, but he expressed outrage upon receiving them, repeatedly exclaiming "Unbelievable!" and "Horrible!" during Gersdorff's summary of their contents. Nevertheless, he turned a cold shoulder to the suggestion that he immedi-

Germany's generals faced a decisive moment when Hitler issued orders to escalate the Russian campaign to a war of annihilation. When Field Marshal Fedor von Bock (right) learned of these orders, he was outraged but refused to intervene with Hitler. Instead he sent one of his officers to the army high command. When the officer returned empty-handed, Bock declared in almost triumphant tones, "Let it be noted, gentlemen, that Field Marshal Bock protested."

ately fly to Führer headquarters with Gerd von Rundstedt and Wilhelm von Leeb, the commanders in chief of Army Groups South and North, and disavow obedience to Hitler. The Führer, Bock said, would simply "throw him out" and possibly install Himmler in his place. Tresckow answered coldly that he could handle that.

After reflecting for a while Bock decided despite Tresckow's constant objections to send Gersdorff to OKH (Army) headquarters in Berlin with the message that Field Marshal Bock vehemently protested the orders and demanded that they be rescinded at once. Since Brauchitsch was absent, Gersdorff met instead with General Eugen Müller, who informed him that the high command did not disagree with the army group. In fact Brauchitsch had already attempted on numerous occasions to have the orders canceled or at least amended. But each time, Hitler burst into a rage; during Brauchitsch's last visit, he had even "hurled an inkwell" at him. "He won't go see the Führer anymore," Müller concluded laconically. Returning to the army group that evening, Gersdorff found Bock dining with his chief of general staff, Hans von Greiffenberg, and Tresckow, Hardenberg, and

Lehndorff. When Gersdorff reported the failure of his mission a deep hush descended. Then Bock, who was the first to regain his composure, remarked "almost triumphally": "Let it be noted, gentlemen, that Field Marshal Bock protested."[10]

Gersdorff later pointed out that if the commanders in chief of the army groups had jointly refused to obey Hitler, as Tresckow suggested, the Führer would have been forced to yield. It would have been impossible to replace such key commanders just ten days before the start of the campaign. We also know through Gersdorff that all the senior officers, at least in Army Group Center, objected to the orders and did what they could to prevent their being carried out. Tresckow made some attempts to influence the other two army groups in this direction. Considerable controversy persists, however, as to the extent to which these and other such efforts were successful.

Tresckow realized, of course, that opposition from army commanders could do little to prevent the Einsatzgruppen from carrying out mass murders behind the front. Army Group Center could, however, bring some influence to bear. Arthur Nebe, the leader of Einsatzgruppe B in its area, had moved in opposition circles since 1938 and had only accepted his assignment after great emotional conflict and largely at the urging of Oster and Gisevius, who hoped that he would be able to supply the opposition with information from the innermost sanctums of power in the SS. Nebe hinted to Tresckow that he intended to report his missions completed when in fact they were not. Ultimately, Field Marshal Bock came to an agreement with Field Marshals Kluge and Weichs and General Guderian that it was "undesirable" for the orders to be carried out. In the spring of 1942, almost one year later, the Commissar Order was officially rescinded.[11]

Still, the army had hardly covered itself with glory. For the first time Hitler had tried to make it an accomplice in his crimes without receiving a clear refusal. Since the Röhm affair, the army had been careful not to allow itself to be drawn directly into criminal activities; at most, it exposed itself to accusations of standing aside and failing to help the victims. Now Hitler had succeeded on his first attempt in eliminating the distinction—still maintained in Poland up to this point—between military men engaged in traditional warfare and the murderous Einsatzgruppen. The one became caught up with the other in a war of annihilation that criminalized everyone who took up arms in the name of the German Reich. There could be no more talk of the sort that was common in the apologia written by former members of the Wehrmacht after the war, of having been "swept away" by events against one's will and without sufficient knowledge. Hitler had without a doubt been encouraged to believe that he could get away with this final step by the supine resignation demonstrated by the generals over the years, their occasional outbursts of indignation notwithstanding.

This failure meant that the last opportunity of demonstrating to Hitler the limits to his power had been squandered. Brauchitsch would later claim that he sabotaged Hitler's criminal orders by issuing special instructions stressing that a soldier's primary duty was to fight and move on, not to engage in search-and-destroy operations. This strategy, however, amounted merely to a repetition of the failed tactic that the army had already practiced in Poland of abandoning conquered territories to the violence of the Einsatzgruppen and conspicuously washing its hands of any responsibility for what would follow.

It is true, of course, that opposition would have had little more than a delaying effect. This is no excuse, however, for either Brauchitsch or the other commanders. They failed to see that the restoration of the long-lost moral integrity of the army was at stake. Their failure to act seems even more egregious in the light of the unanimous sense of outrage expressed by the officers, of which so much was made following the war. It illustrates not only the widespread awareness of criminal activity but also the broad support that a determined commander who refused to carry out orders would have enjoyed. It is difficult to comprehend why three or more commanding generals could not agree to protest the orders as a body. It has repeatedly been argued that such a gesture would have been pointless, but it must be said that it was never really tried. Rundstedt's aide, Hans Viktor von Salviati, remarked shortly before the Russian campaign began that almost all the field marshals were well aware of what was happening, "but that's as far as it goes."[12]

* * *

At 3:15 a.m. on June 22, 1941, Hitler launched the war against the Soviet Union under the code name Operation Barbarossa. He had enjoyed an unbroken string of victories, including the last-minute campaigns against Greece, Albania, and Yugoslavia and the brilliant expedition in North Africa, where Rommel had succeeded in less than twelve days in reconquering all of the Libyan territory lost by Germany's Italian allies. Although these victories had fueled a widespread feeling of invincibility, a nagging sense of foreboding began to arise for the first time. "When Barbarossa starts, the world will hold its breath and keep still," Hitler crowed just a few days before the invasion.

Most of all, though, it was the Germans who held their breath. Everyone sensed that the mission that had been embarked on was too ambitious even for Hitler's formidable nerves of steel, his keen intuition, and his eerie ability to stride from one triumph to the next. For the first time, the feeling arose that he was setting out to achieve the impossible. "Our German army is only a breath of wind on the endless Russian steppes," said a staff officer who knew the terrain well. Almost all contemporary reports of the mood of the German people speak of "dismay," "agitation," "paralysis," and "shock." Occasionally, as one of the secret agents noted, there were "references to the fate of Napoleon, who was vanquished in the end by the vast Russian spaces."[13]

As the German armies advanced, so did the Einsatzgruppen. They set about their work with such brutality that Colonel Helmuth Stieff wrote in a letter that "Poland was nothing by comparison." He felt as if he had become the "tool of a despotic will to destroy without regard for humanity and simple decency." A general staff officer with Army Group North reported that in Kovno, Lithuanian SS squads had "herded a large number of Jews together, beaten them to death with truncheons, and then danced to music on the dead bodies. After the victims were carted away, new Jews were brought, and the game was repeated!"[14] Officers in this army group besieged their superiors with demands that the massacres be halted. Similarly, the members of Army Group Center's general staff, who had by this time been transferred to Smolensk, urged Field Marshal Bock "with tears in their eyes" to put a stop to the "orgy of executions" being carried out by an SS commando unit about 125 miles away in Borisov and witnessed by Heinrich von Lehndorff from an airplane. Attempts were immediately made to stop the massacre, but they came too late. Bock demanded that the civilian commissioner in charge, Wilhelm Kube, report to him immediately and turn over the responsible SS commander for court-martial. Kube responded curtly that Bock ought rightly to be reporting to *him* and that he had no intention, in any case, of producing the SS commander. The army group could not even determine his name; the commandant of army headquarters at Borisov, whom the army group accused of failing to prevent the slaughter, committed suicide.[15]

As a result of the massacres in the East, relations between Hitler and the officer corps, which had always been cool, despite a momentary reconciliation at the time of the great triumphs in France, began to deteriorate rapidly. "By nature I belong to an entirely different genus," Hitler had once said—and the feeling was mutual.[16] Hitler's speech to the assembled officers on March 30 and the subsequent orders putting his message into legal language had conclusively refuted the belief that Nazi excesses were the work of "lower-level authorities" carrying on behind Hitler's back, a misapprehension that had long inhibited action. Now the resistance gathered strong new support. Yorck showed up at Army Group Center headquarters passionately voicing his anger; Gersdorff finally overcame his lingering abhorrence of treason; Stieff turned away from the regime, sickened by what was happening. And it was apparently at this time, too, that Stauffenberg resolved to do everything in his power to remove Hitler and overthrow the regime.[17] The biographies of several members of the resistance, especially the younger conspirators, show just how crucial the horrendous crimes in the East were in motivating them to act.

Differences of opinion over military operations soon erupted between Hitler and his army commanders, exacerbating the latent tensions that already existed. German units had succeeded, to be sure, in slicing deep into the Soviet Union and running up an impressive series of victories. Yet it was becoming increasingly apparent that each triumph only carried them further and further into the endless expanses of the Soviet Union, while the front was becoming more and more disjointed.

Attention therefore turned to how the army could use its available forces most effectively. Whereas the OKH and Army Group Center advocated a concentrated assault on Moscow, Hitler insisted on "pushing through the Ukraine into the Caucasus" and beyond to the oil fields of the Caspian Sea and Persian Gulf. At the same time he ordered the troops to advance in the north so as to cut the enemy off from the Baltic Sea. The fractious dispute that ensued did not revolve around two rival strategies so much as around one strategy and one fantasy, consisting of Hitler's faith in his own invincibility, concern about increasingly noticeable shortages of goods and raw materials, and an unrestrained lust for land. By August 1941 general staff officers were already muttering about Hitler's "bloody amateurism."[18]

After a long spell in the doldrums the resistance was buoyed by rapidly spreading rumors about the tensions in Hitler's headquarters. In the early autumn General Georg Thomas visited the army groups to assess their willingness to take action. He learned that the swift advance through the Soviet Union and the unease it was creating in the various headquarters prevented any serious planning for a coup. The idea of striking from France with Witzleben's help was raised briefly but soon dropped. In late September Tresckow decided to send Fabian von Schlabrendorff to Berlin to let the circle around Ludwig Beck know that Army Group Center was "prepared to do anything" if a coup was launched. There is no doubt that this message vastly exaggerated current sentiments in the army group and was more an expression of the sense of mounting exasperation in the face of the increasingly pointed conflict between honor and obedience, the oath of allegiance and the barbarous methods of war. Schlabrendorff conferred in Berlin with Hassell, who noted in his diary the one truly notable feature of Tresckow's project: for the first time in the history of the resistance "an initiative of sorts" for

Left: *To the surprise of many of the military conspirators, Fabian von Schlabrendorff, a civilian who became a reserve officer, emerged as the closest confidant and adviser of Henning von Tresckow, who organized a resistance group on the staff of Army Group Center. Tried before the People's Court following the failed coup attempt of July 20, Schlabrendorff barely escaped a death sentence when a falling beam killed Roland Freisler, the president of the court, during an air raid. After the war Schlabrendorff wrote the first book on the German resistance,* Offiziere gegen Hitler *(Revolt Against Hitler).*

Right: *The resistance was greatly strengthened in the spring of 1942 when Hans Oster forged close ties with Friedrich Olbricht. Soon after being named head of the OKW General Army Office in Berlin, Olbricht assumed responsibility for the conspirators' logistical planning. Having entered the inner circle of conspirators, he was one of the four officers executed on the night of July 20 in the courtyard of army headquarters on Bendlerstrasse.*

overthrowing the regime had come from the army rather than the civilian opposition.[19]

A few days later General Thomas and General Alexander von Falkenhausen, the military commander in Belgium and northern

France, went to see Brauchitsch. They both found him surprisingly receptive to their ideas, probably not least because he was exhausted from the interminable wrangling with Hitler. According to an entry in Hassell's diary, Brauchitsch acknowledged "what a bloody mess everything' had become and even came to see that he himself must be held partially responsible."[20] As if a signal had gone out, activity within opposition circles immediately picked up. At meeting after meeting, "the overall situation was discussed," Hassell recorded, "just in case . . ." Other preparatory steps were taken as well: ties were established with Trott, Yorck, and Moltke, and Hassell was requested shortly thereafter to visit Witzleben and Falkenhausen. After the somber mood of the previous months, spirits within the opposition finally began to lift. Tresckow even felt sufficiently encouraged to make a last, although ultimately futile, attempt to draw Bock into the resistance.

At this point the great Russian winter descended on the troops in the field, who were left without appropriate provisions, having charged ahead on the assumption that there would be "no winter campaign," as Hitler had assured skeptics only shortly before. The German offensive literally froze in its tracks, and confusion spread across the front. With every ounce of the general staff's strength devoted to dealing with the situation of the troops, all planning for a coup ceased. The members of the resistance fell once again into such despondency that they even interpreted Hitler's dismissal of Brauchitsch on December 19—undertaken in the hope of ending the festering conflict with the OKH—as a blow. The incessant swinging from high to low had so frazzled them that the few strong words Brauchitsch had spoken to Thomas and Falkenhausen had raised their hopes in him, making them forget the countless occasions when he had demonstrated his lack of courage and sown nothing but despair. Hassell gave the figures who appeared in his diary humorously appropriate aliases, and it was no accident that Brauchitsch's moniker was "Pappenheim," which means a habitually unreliable person.

As he had done in the past, Hitler attempted to solve his problems with the army by assuming supreme command after Brauchitsch's dismissal, thus making himself answerable only to himself twice over. The reasons he gave for this step are equally revelatory of his arrogance and his suspicion, as well as of his desire to bring about the ideological radicalization of the army, which had remained noticeably cool to his ideas. "Anybody can handle operational leadership—that's easy," he said. "The task of the commander in chief of the army is to give the army National Socialist training; I know no general of the army who could perform this task as I would have it."[21] Hitler used Brauchitsch's departure as an opportunity to clean house in the upper echelons of the army. A large number of generals and division commanders were ousted, and Bock was replaced as commander in chief of Army Group Center by Field Marshal Hans Günther von Kluge. Relieving Gerd von Rundstedt of command of Army Group South, Hitler installed Field Marshal Walther von Reichenau. For failure to comply with orders to stand firm during the winter crisis, General Heinz Guderian was dismissed and General Erich Hoepner expelled from the army entirely. The commander in chief of Army Group North, Field Marshal Wilhelm von Leeb, resigned voluntarily.

But Hitler's nervous interventions and the insults and abuse he heaped on his generals could do nothing to dispel the specter of defeat that suddenly hung over the German forces. After striding for almost twenty years from one political, diplomatic, or military triumph to the next, Hitler suffered his first serious setback in the winter of 1941–42. The aura of invincibility that had surrounded Hitler and his armies, keeping them together and holding uncertainty at bay, began to dissipate. Always a gambler, Hitler had bet everything on a single card, and with the defeat before the gates of Moscow, his entire plan collapsed. The blitzkrieg had failed, as he immediately realized, and with it his whole strategy for the war against the Soviet Union.

Each step in the plan was predicated on the success of the previous steps. Just a few weeks before the invasion stalled, the general staffs had been made aware of a "preparatory commando unit" whose task would be to slip through the lines after Moscow was surrounded and assume responsibility for certain "security duties" in the heart of the Soviet capital. The unit's leader reported to the army commanders that Hitler wanted Moscow razed to the ground. The eastern border of the German Reich would then be advanced to the Baku-Stalingrad-Moscow-Leningrad line, beyond which a broad, lifeless "firebreak" would extend to the Urals.[22]

Defeat also put an end to the mission of the commando unit. Hitler's daydreams of master and slave races, resettlement programs, mass exterminations, and the renewal of bloodlines were also shattered, as were increasingly monstrous and megalomaniacal visions of himself as a world savior, though he continued to propound them in his "table talk" and monologues over the ensuing years. His magic spell broken by this setback, Hitler realized much more clearly than ever before that time was working against him. There is every reason to think that his disputes with the generals had been prompted largely by his nagging fear that the hourglass was indeed running down. Judgment day was not yet at hand, as one contemporary observer noted, but "dark clouds were gathering."[23]

Ironically enough, the opposition, too, felt that time was working against them and deepening their dilemma. If they took action after a military defeat, such as had just occurred for the first time, they could probably count on more support from the populace, at least in the short term. But they also ran the risk of making a martyr of Hitler and so giving rise to another stab-in-the-back legend. None of the conspirators had forgotten the poisonous effect of this legend on the government that was established after the First World War. On the other hand, by launching the coup after a string of military victories the conspirators ran the risk of operating without popular support in Germany, even if their actions opened the prospect of negotiating satisfactory peace terms. When Tresckow asked a friend what he thought the solution was, the friend responded that risk was inevitable and that "the most favorable time externally" was necessarily "the least favorable internally."[24]

As 1942 dawned, the conspirators faced the increasingly pressing question of whether a Germany that had rid itself of Hitler would have any hope of negotiating an acceptable peace with the Allies. The answer was clearly crucial, especially as far as the generals were concerned, and it had become all the more urgent since Hitler's declaration of war on the United States on December 11, following Japan's surprise attack on Pearl Harbor. A colossal worldwide coalition of powers was emerging that would sooner or later overwhelm the Reich. Furthermore, Great Britain and the Soviet Union had signed a mutual-assistance pact as of July 12, 1941, according to which neither party would enter into cease-fire negotiations without the consent of the other. One month later Prime Minister Churchill and President Roosevelt had announced the Atlantic Charter, which, notwithstanding its ringing declarations about peace, made plain their intent to disarm Germany for many years to come. Thus, even before the formal entry of the United States into the war, Beck, Hassell, and Popitz began to discuss whether it was not already too late for a coup. Even a government formed by the resistance, they felt, might "no longer be able to obtain an acceptable peace."

The plotters were probably well aware of the tensions within the Allied coalition, but this only heightened their fears rather than diminished them. It seemed most inauspicious that the various attempts to resume contacts with London after the French campaign had met with no response, and it was easy to foresee that as time passed and more people were killed, attitudes would only harden. As the likelihood of an Allied victory increased, the prospect of negotiations would grow even dimmer. This would remain true, the conspirators felt, as long as Moscow, London, and Washington did not agree on a joint policy toward Germany. Even if the Allies did reach agreement, it was likely that every dispute would be settled at Germany's expense, for when coalitions of this kind seek a common denominator they usually find it in the harshest possible conditions for the vanquished.

■　■　■

Concern over the shrinking window of opportunity heightened the pressure on the opposition to act. During the summer of 1942, German forces again began scoring impressive victories, especially along the southern wing of the eastern front. This did nothing, however, to prevent heated controversies from erupting once more between Hitler and his generals. After an angry exchange, Halder was finally sent packing in September. Although he had long kept his mounting hatred of the regime to himself and no longer actively participated in the resistance, the opposition circles felt they were losing their last contact in the highest echelons of the military. In their notes from this period they write again and again of "little hope," "few chances for success," and "no initial spark." Their generally depressed state of mind was such that they developed no plans and lacked any real drive or even a leader whom they all recognized. Exhausted by the continual setbacks, they placed their hopes on the visibly worsening relations between Hitler and the army, which they thought might prompt some as-yet-unknown officer to lead a revolt, and on the stirrings within Army Group Center.

Considering that the movement was led by experienced officers, it is remarkable how little planning had been done by this point and how much better the conspirators were at theorizing than they were at organizing. It was by no means easy, of course, to put together a resistance organization in a police state. Under the constant supervision of a huge security apparatus, the movement faced countless dangers and difficulties: it had to keep to a manageable size and yet be broad enough to have players in all the key positions; it had to bring together large numbers of people who were both reliable and willing to run tremendous risks. As it grew, the danger of discovery through recklessness or betrayal mounted.

Enormous efforts were required just to build up and bring together the three main hubs of resistance: the field army, the home army, and the civilian groups. In March Beck's office was finally designated as the headquarters.[25] At about the same time the conspirators scored perhaps their greatest success so far when Oster managed to establish close ties with General Friedrich Olbricht, the head of the OKW General Army Office and the acting commander of the reserve army. By nature and in manner a prudent administrative officer, General Olbricht proved one of the most determined and resolute opponents of the regime. Perhaps because he lived by the maxim that "a general staff officer doesn't make a name for himself," he has never received the recognition he deserves for the role he played in the preparations for July 20 and in the actual events of that day.[26]

In contrast to many of his fellow officers, Olbricht had supported the Weimar Republic and never allowed himself to be seduced, after the Nazi seizure of power, by any of Hitler's successes or his hints of future rewards. It was typical of Olbricht that as early as 1940, at the height of Hitler's triumphs, he had reached the conclusion that the dictator would have to be overthrown in a violent coup. Olbricht was motivated primarily by religious and patriotic considerations but also by the profound distaste of a cultivated man for the primitiveness of the Nazis and their moral unscrupulousness. He became the de facto technical head of the conspiracy, and it was his task to lay the groundwork for the government takeover to follow Hitler's assassination. His removal would provide the much-discussed "initial spark" that would set the rest of the plan in motion.

With Beck, Tresckow, and Olbricht, the opposition at last had the foundation it had lacked for so long. Nevertheless, it was still very loosely organized, it faced enormous risks, and it had to follow many a circuitous path. The various resistance groups were continuing to operate largely on their own, and so, to bring them closer together and to facilitate coordination of their plans, Tresckow asked Schlabrendorff to act as a sort of permanent intermediary between Army Group Center on the one hand and Beck, Goerdeler, Oster, and Olbricht on the other.

■　■　■

Tresckow also placed high hopes in Kluge, the new commander in chief of Army Group Center. Tresckow's relationship with Bock had soured for good after the field marshal cut him short during a last attempt to bring him over to the opposition; Bock had replied sharply that he would tolerate no further attacks on the Führer. Initial inquiries showed Kluge to be more alert, concerned, and accessible. He had sufficient insight to realize that Hitler was leading Germany and the Germans straight to catastrophe, and he was morally sensitive enough to be shocked by the crimes of SS and SD units behind the front. Furthermore, he was by no means submissive, occasionally even speaking out against Hitler's interference in the struggle at the front and his increasingly obvious contempt for the officer corps.

Recognizing that any successful revolt would have to be led by an army group commander or at least by a well-known military figure, Tresckow from the very outset focused all his talent and persuasive powers on winning Kluge over. He ordered his staff to make sure that Kluge saw all negative information: horrifying reports about the Einsatzgruppen, news about fresh enemy units appearing on other parts of the front, and memoranda about the huge capacity of the United States for the production of war matériel. When, on the occasion of his sixtieth birthday, Kluge received a handwritten message from Hitler along with a check for 250,000 marks, Tresckow immediately suggested that he could only justify accepting such an amount in the eyes of posterity by claiming that preparations to overthrow the regime were already under way and he had to avoid raising the slightest suspicion.[27]

It was not for nothing, however, that Hans Kluge (whose surname means *clever* in German) was widely known as "clever Hans," a reference less to his raw intelligence than to the smoothness and presence of mind with which he escaped from any jam. In the "dogged, drawn-out struggle" that Tresckow waged for his soul, Kluge would seem to yield one minute, only to slip away the next, to agree and then to disagree, to provide assurances and then to express surprise that he had ever done such a thing. Schlabrendorff spoke of Tresckow as a "clockmaker" who wound Kluge up in the morning "so that he would run and chime away all day, until by nightfall he had wound down and everything had to be repeated all over again."[28] But Tresckow's indefatigable efforts and the political and moral intensity of his arguments gradually succeeded in drawing Kluge closer to the conspirators.

Tresckow's first major success was in persuading Kluge to receive Goerdeler in army group headquarters, a significant achievement as Goerdeler had never made any secret of his beliefs and virtually everyone knew why he was so conspicuously on the move at all times. Once, when General Thomas suggested that the chief of the OKW, Field Marshal Keitel, grant Goerdeler an audience, Keitel replied with horror, "Don't let the Führer find out you have connections with people like Goerdeler. He'll eat you up!"[29])

Field Marshal Hans Günther von Kluge (left) typified the inability of many senior German officers to break the bonds of tradition, obedience, and patriotic loyalty. Since childhood, he had been known as "clever Hans" for his smooth quick-wittedness. For months in 1943 Henning von Tresckow applied his celebrated persuasive powers to winning Kluge over to the conspiracy. But the field marshal would agree one minute, only to change his mind the next, an indecisiveness he carried with him to the end. When he resolved to commit suicide following the July 20 coup attempt, he wrote an effusive letter to Hitler proclaiming his faithfulness.

Using false papers provided by Oster, Goerdeler arrived at the army group after a daring eight-day journey. His enthusiasm and determination made a strong impression on both Tresckow and Kluge. One officer even claimed to see "the ice break" with the field marshal. In any case, Goerdeler and Kluge held several meetings, apparently considering, among other things, having Hitler arrested when he visited army group headquarters. Before Goerdeler had even had time to return to Berlin, however, Beck received a confidential letter from Kluge complaining that he had been "ambushed" by the visit and that "misunderstandings" may have arisen.[30] Kluge's attitude was succinctly described shortly thereafter by Captain Hermann

Kaiser, who kept the reserve army war diaries and wrote in his own journal: "First, no participation in any Operation Fiesco. Second, no action against Pollux [Hitler]. Third, will not stand in the way when an action begins."[31]

By the fall of 1942 at the latest Tresckow had resolved nevertheless to stage an attack on the regime from Army Group Center. Apparently he hoped to sweep the vacillating Kluge along when the time came. Their conversations had convinced him that it was imperative not only to arrest Hitler but to kill him. Like Bock before him, Kluge always reverted to the oath of loyalty he had sworn; even Tresckow had had some difficulty in finding his way out of the maze of scruples. Patriotic and religious motives finally helped him and many of his colleagues in the military resistance to overcome those feelings. Hitler, Tresckow concluded, was not only the "destroyer of his own country" but also the "source of all evil." Nevertheless, the issue continued to haunt Tresckow, and his insistence to the very last (he killed himself on the eastern front on July 21, 1944) that "we aren't really criminals" betrays his misgivings.[32]

For a time Tresckow apparently entertained the idea of simply taking a pistol to Hitler. He would either do the deed himself or assign a group of his officers to act as an execution squad. According to all indications, he never totally abandoned this plan, which seemed to him the bravest and most chivalrous form of tyrannicide. All the same, by the summer of 1942 he was asking Major Rudolph-Christoph von Gersdorff to procure a "particularly powerful explosive" and "a totally reliable, completely silent fuse." Although Gersdorff had to sign receipts each time he took possession of such materials, he was eventually able to accumulate dozens of different explosives, which he, Tresckow, and Schlabrendorff tested in the meadows along the nearby Dnieper River. Finally they selected a British-made plastic-explosive device about the size of a book with a pencil-shaped detonator.

In late 1942 Olbricht indicated that he still needed about eight weeks to complete preparations for the coup and to have reliable units standing by not only in Berlin but also in Cologne, Munich, and Vienna "when the first step against Hitler is taken from elsewhere."

Rudolph-Christoph von Gersdorff (right) was a close friend of Henning von Tresckow's at Army Group Center, and like Tresckow, he attempted to assassinate Hitler. Escorting the Führer through an exhibition of captured weaponry at a Berlin museum in March 1943, Gersdorff, who had concealed a bomb beneath his uniform, saw his plan foiled when Hitler abruptly left through a side door. Gersdorff rushed to a nearby bathroom to remove the fuse from the bomb.

Shortly thereafter Tresckow traveled to Berlin to clear up the last remaining questions with Olbricht and Goerdeler and, most of all, to emphasize that time was running short. Tresckow's impatience pervades the notes taken by one of the participants. There was "not a day to lose," he said. "Action should be taken as quickly as possible. No initial spark can be expected from the field marshals. They'll only follow an order."[33] Olbricht now gave early March as the target date and explained that Colonel Fritz Jäger would advance at the appointed time with two panzer units to deal with the guard battalion in Berlin. In addition, Captain Ludwig Gehre had assembled a task force for special assignments, and the new Brandenburg division that was being organized in the Berlin area under Colonel Alexander von Pfuhlstein would handle Nazi Party forces. Friedrich Wilhelm Heinz, who commanded the Fourth Regiment of this division, emerged from the shadows to which he had retreated in the fall of 1938. Gisevius was summoned to Berlin to assist Olbricht with the planning, and Witzleben, though seriously ill, agreed with Beck that he would assume supreme command of the Wehrmacht. This basic plan—an assassination attempt followed by seizure of key positions in Berlin and a few other centers—would be largely adopted once again on July 20, 1944.

Getting a bomb near Hitler proved to be far more difficult than originally imagined. The Führer was growing increasingly distrustful and solitary. He seldom left his headquarters and then often altered his travel plans without warning. Arrangements were made for him to visit Field Marshal Weichs's army group in Poltava, where a group of officers was also prepared to overpower him; he abruptly changed his route, however, and flew instead to Saporoshe. There, ironically, he barely escaped an attacking Russian tank unit that had run out of fuel at the edge of his landing field.

After turning down a number of requests, Hitler finally agreed to visit Army Group Center in Smolensk in the early morning of March 13, 1943, on his way from his headquarters in Vinnitsa back to Rastenburg. Shortly before the three aircraft carrying the Führer, his staff, and the SS escort touched down, Kluge suddenly sensed something and turned to Tresckow, saying, "For heaven's sake, don't do anything today! It's still too soon for that!"[34] In fact, Tresckow, believing that the most opportune time had already passed with the battle of Stalingrad that winter, had taken the precaution of developing a number of assassination plans simultaneously. One of them called for a bomb to be placed in Hitler's parked vehicle during the visit, but all attempts to slip through the phalanx of SS men to reach the car failed. A second plot was to be carried out if possible by Georg von Boeselager, who had begun assembling a unit near Army Group Center for use in the impending coup. Tresckow was apparently prepared to ignore Kluge's concerns— so long as there was some assurance that the field marshal himself would not be put in danger—and had positioned Boeselager's officers and soldiers near Hitler's SS units as additional "security." In reality, it seems that they were supposed to open fire on Hitler if an opportunity presented itself[35]

After a briefing in Kluge's barracks, Hitler's party headed for the nearby officers' mess. As one witness described the scene, Hitler was sitting with his head hunched over his plate, shoveling in his vegetables, when Tresckow turned to Lieutenant Colonel Heinz Brandt, who was seated next to him, and asked if he minded taking two bottles of Cointreau back to headquarters on the flight. When Brandt readily agreed, Tresckow explained that they were part of a bet he'd made with Colonel Stieff and that Schlabrendorff would hand over the package at the airfield. When the visitors left shortly thereafter, Hitler not only took a different route than previously arranged, but also invited Kluge to ride in his car, thus ruling out any further action at this point. Meanwhile, Schlabrendorff sent Berlin the code word signaling the beginning of the operation and drove off after the column of vehicles.

At the airfield he waited until Hitler had boarded one of three waiting planes, then squeezed the acid detonator and handed the package to Brandt. The bomb was set to go off in thirty minutes, and since the planes took off immediately, Schlabrendorff and Tresckow calculated that the explosion would occur just before Minsk. They returned to headquarters and waited for news of the Führer's plane from one of its fighter escorts. But nothing happened. Having carried out countless test explosions during the previous weeks, not one of which had failed they were certain of success. But now two hours passed and still there was no word. The conspirators were waiting with mounting anxiety when a message finally arrived from Hitler's headquarters: the Führer and his escorts had arrived safely in Rastenburg.

The reasons for the failure of the assassination attempt of March 13, 1943, have never been fully clarified. The major problem immediately facing the conspirators, however, was how to undo their plan and recover the package before an accident occurred or the contents were discovered. Tresckow decided to telephone Brandt. Coolly he asked him to hold on to the package—there had been an unfortunate mix-up. Schlabrendorff would come the next day on the daily courier flight to Rastenburg and exchange it for the right one.

Fortunately, Brandt still had the original package the next morning when Schlabrendorff arrived, and the exchange was made. Schlabrendorff headed for the waiting train, which was to take him to Berlin that evening. Once in a closed compartment, he opened the bomb with a razor blade and removed the detonator. He found that the capsule had broken, the acid had eaten its way through the wire holding the firing pin, the firing pin had struck as intended, and even the percussion cap seemed to have ignited. But the explosive had not gone off. Among the theories that have been advanced to explain this mystery, the most likely is that the heater in the plane's cargo hold had malfunctioned, as it sometimes did, and the explosive, which was sensitive to cold, failed to ignite as a result. The most promising assassination plot of the war years had come to naught.[36]

Schlabrendorff and Tresckow were "shattered" by the inexplicable outcome of their attempt on Hitler's life, for which they had run so many risks and spent so much time laying secret plans. Tresckow refused, however, to allow himself to grow despondent, nor did he following the failures that were still to come. Typically for him, he did not waste a single second bemoaning his ill fortune, and when another opportunity happened to fall into his lap just a few days later he seized it. News arrived from Führer headquarters that "Heroes' Memorial Day" would be celebrated on March 21 and that, after attending a service in the glass-roofed hall of the Berlin Zeughaus, Hitler wanted to visit the exhibition of captured enemy weaponry in the same building. Since Army Group Center had arranged the exhibition, Hitler expressly requested the attendance of Field Marshal Kluge.

It was much more important to Tresckow that Gersdorff be there, and since it was Tresckow's department that had actually put the exhibition together, he had a perfect pretext to seek an invitation for the staff intelligence officer. Gersdorff was immediately summoned back to army group headquarters. When he appeared, Tresckow spoke "with the utmost gravity" about the situation and the "absolute necessity" of saving Germany from destruction. Then he abruptly broached the question of whether Gersdorff would undertake an assassination attempt in which he would probably be blown up himself.[37] Gersdorff reflected briefly and agreed. Schlabrendorff was asked to remain in Berlin and turn over to Gersdorff the bombs he still had from the assassination attempt of March 13.

But from this point on, the plot as promising as it seemed—would be plagued by misfortune. At first, Brigadier General Rudolf Schmundt, Hitler's increasingly suspicious chief aide, refused to allow Gersdorff to take part in the visit or even know when the ceremonies were scheduled to begin (as Hitler's inner circle was constantly reminded, the divulgence of such information was punishable by death). Then Kluge had to be persuaded not to go to Berlin, even though he had been invited by Hitler himself, because Tresckow wanted to keep him away from the assassination. Furthermore, when the explosive was turned over to Gersdorff, he learned that in the rush of events the usual short fuses could not be procured. Oster was asked to help but could do nothing, so Gersdorff was forced to rely on the ten-minute fuses he had brought along just in case.

The memorial service began an hour later than scheduled. After making a short address Hitler walked over to the exhibition with Göring, Himmler, Dönitz, and Keitel. Waiting at the entrance were Gersdorff, Field Marshal Walter Model, acting as Kluge's representative, and a uniformed director of the museum. Gersdorff ignited the fuse when he saw the Führer approach and kept close to his side as the Führer went through the exhibition. But Hitler paid scarcely any attention to the explanations Gersdorff wanted to provide about the objects on display. Nervously, as if scenting danger, he hurried through the rooms. Even a standard from the Napoleonic Wars that German engineers had uncovered in the riverbed of the Berezina failed to capture his attention. About two minutes after entering the exhibition, as a radio broadcast reported, Hitler abruptly left through a side door by the chestnut grove on Unter den Linden. Here, outside the building, he finally discovered a captured Soviet tank and was so fascinated by it that he spent considerable time clambering around on it. In the meantime Gersdorff had rushed to the nearest washroom, where he ripped the fuse out of the bomb. To catch his breath he went to the Union Club where he ran into the Cologne banker Waldemar von Oppenheim, who blithely related that he had just been in a position to kill Hitler as the Führer "drove very slowly in an open car down the Linden right in front of my ground-floor room in the Hotel Bristol. It would have been child's play to heave a hand grenade over the sidewalk and into his car."[38]

• • •

While all this was occurring at home, the war on the fronts had reached a turning point. Three disastrous defeats in November 1942 made this abundantly clear. Early that month the vastly superior forces of General Montgomery broke through the German-Italian positions at El Alamein, only five days before Allied landings in Mo-

Erich von Manstein exemplified the conundrum facing the German officer corps. In the view of many experts, one of the most brilliant strategists of the Second World War, Manstein was not equal to the political and moral challenges of those years. In a conversation with Rudolph-Christoph von Gersdorff, he acknowledged that Hitler was leading Germany to ruin, but he nevertheless deflected all attempts to win him over to the resistance.

Above: Manstein with his staff at a briefing on the eastern front in the summer of 1942.

rocco and Algeria presaged the end of the African campaign. Also in November, it became plain that Germany's U-boats were losing the war on the high seas. And on November 19 two Soviet army groups launched an offensive around Stalingrad in raging snowstorms. Henceforth it would be the Allies who orchestrated the war, deciding where and when to attack.

On February 2, 1943, the bruised and bloodied remnants of the German Sixth Army capitulated in Stalingrad. While Hitler fell ominously silent and Göring conjured up a mood of impending apocalypse with dark references to the myth of the Nibelungen, many

Germans began to realize that Hitler was no longer master of events. His bullying, threats, and vicious outbursts—for years the trivial secrets of his success—did not serve him anymore. Now, if ever, was "the right psychological moment" for which so many of the generals claimed they were waiting. For the first time, as one observer noted, Hitler was unable "to shirk responsibility; for the first time the critical murmuring was directed squarely at him."[39] Beck sought out Erich von Manstein, commander in chief of Army Group South; Goerdeler contacted Olbricht and Kluge; and Tresckow attempted to win over Guderian and then spent some time on leave in Berlin to position himself near the center of activity. From inside besieged Stalingrad, the voice of Helmuth Groscurth was heard once again through one of his officers, whom he succeeded in having flown out. "Only an immediate attack against the Russians," the messenger informed Beck and Olbricht, could stave off disaster in that "city of fate." But Manstein refused, and the officer sent by Groscurth to Rundstedt found the visit so depressing that he abandoned all hope. Captain Kaiser succinctly summarized the commanders' excuses: "One will only take action if orders are given, and the other will only give orders if action is taken."[40]

A small group of Munich students were the only protesters who managed to break out of the vicious circle of tactical considerations and other inhibitions. They spoke out vehemently, not only against the regime but also against the moral indolence and numbness of the German people. Under the name White Rose they issued appeals and painted slogans on walls calling for an uprising against Hitler. They also established ties with like-minded students in Berlin, Stuttgart, Hamburg, and Vienna. On February 18, 1943, Hans and Sophie Scholl were arrested while throwing hundreds of leaflets from the gallery of the atrium at Ludwig-Maximillian University in Munich. Their motives were among the simplest and, sadly, the rarest of all: a sense of right and wrong and a determination to take action.

The Nazis, having long based their power on the assumption that self-interest and the fear of standing out would suffice to keep the population under control, were stunned by this effrontery. The People's Court, under its president, Roland Freisler, was sent to Munich for a special session. In a trial lasting less than three and a half hours, Hans and Sophie Scholl and Christoph Probst were sentenced to death. The executions were carried out later the same day. Their mentor, the philosopher of music Kurt Huber, suffered a similar fate a few days later, as did other members of the group. Although Hans and Sophie Scholl could easily have fled after dropping their leaflets, they submitted without resistance to the university porter who came after them shouting, "You're under arrest!" Apparently they hoped to set an example of self-sacrifice that would inspire others. "What does my death matter if by our action thousands of people are awakened and stirred to action?" Sophie Scholl asked after reading the indictment. The only visible result, however, was a demonstration of loyalty to the regime staged right in front of the university just two hours after her execution. Three days later, in the university's main auditorium, hundreds of students cheered a speech by a Nazi student leader deriding their former classmates. They stamped their feet in applause for the porter, Jakob Schmied, who "received the ovation standing up with his arms outstretched."[41]

In the meantime, back on the eastern front, Tresckow had so expanded his influence over Kluge that the field marshal had grown to tolerate conspiratorial activities in his immediate surroundings and not infrequently even supported them. As the military situation worsened, he seemed eager to discuss removing Hitler and overthrowing the regime, although he still preferred that the Führer be eliminated by "accident" or killed by an officer from far away, or even by a civilian. Tresckow resolved to go for broke. Strolling with Kluge and Gersdorff near army group headquarters, he suggested that "that man" finally be removed. When Kluge replied, as he had so often, that he agreed but could not bring himself to commit murder, Tresckow threw all caution to the wind. "Field Marshal," he said, "beside you walks someone who made an attempt on Hitler's life not so long ago." Kluge is said to have stopped in his tracks, seized Gersdorff by the arm, and asked in great agitation, "For heaven's sake, what did you do?" As Gersdorff replied that he had only done what the situation called for, Kluge took "a few more steps, threw his arms out in a theatrical gesture, and said, 'Children, I'm yours.'"[42]

The field marshal did more than ever to support the conspirators during the summer of 1943, although he never acted without Tresckow's prompting. He extended and strengthened his contacts with the civilian opposition, attempted to win the support of other military commanders, and dispatched Lieutenant Colonel Voss to see Rundstedt in Paris. Eventually he even sent Gersdorff to see Manstein in hopes of persuading him to take part in a joint action and asking if he would "assume the position of chief of the army general staff after a coup." The records of the discussion in Army Group South headquarters in Saporoshe speak volumes not only about Manstein but about the attitude of most of the officers: their indecision, their narrow-mindedness, their ambivalence, and ultimately their servility. Gersdorff's notes begin with the short summary he presented of his mission:

ME: Field Marshal Kluge is extremely concerned about the course of the war. As a result of the antagonism between the OKW and the OKH and Hitler's ever-clearer amateurishness as a leader, the collapse of the eastern front is only a matter of time. Hitler must be made to realize that he is headed straight for disaster.

MANSTEIN: I fully agree. But I'm not the right person to say so to Hitler. Without my being able to stop it, enemy propaganda has portrayed me as eager to seize power from Hitler. So he is now very distrustful of me. Only Rundstedt and Kluge could undertake such a mission.

ME: Perhaps all the field marshals should go together to the Führer and hold a pistol to his chest.

MANSTEIN: Prussian field marshals do not mutiny.

ME: There are enough instances of it in Prussian history. . . . In any event, Prussian field marshals have never been in a position like the one they're in today. Unprecedented situations require unprecedented methods. But we, too, no longer believe that a joint action would have any chance of success. In Army Group Center we have long been convinced that every effort must now be taken to save Germany from catastrophe.

MANSTEIN: Then you want to kill him?

ME: Yes, Herr Field Marshal, like a mad dog!

At this point Manstein leapt up and ran excitedly around the room shouting, "Count me out! That would destroy the army!"

ME: You said yourself that Germany will go down to defeat unless something is done. The army isn't the main concern. It's Germany and the German people.

MANSTEIN: First and foremost, I'm a soldier . . .

When, after a bit more discussion, I conceded that it was pointless to carry on, I remembered a modest proposal that Kluge had asked me to convey.

ME: Field Marshal Kluge also asked me to inquire whether you would agree to become chief of the army general staff after a successful coup.

Manstein bowed slightly and said, "Tell Field Marshal Kluge that I appreciate the confidence he shows in me. Field Marshal Manstein will always be the loyal servant of a legally constituted government.[43]

As it turned out, Manstein had had a similar conversation just a little earlier, in the days following the capitulation in Stalingrad. Visiting Count Lehndorff at his castle in East Prussia, Tresckow had met a lieutenant colonel on the general staff named Claus Schenk von Stauffenberg and had described to him several vain attempts to win Manstein over. Stauffenberg himself wanted to give it a try, and Tresckow arranged for him to meet Manstein. But then, too, the field marshal merely dodged the issue. In response to Stauffenberg's reproaches about the impending disaster and the responsibility of highly placed officers to consider the entire picture, Manstein recommended only that Stauffenberg have himself transferred to a general staff position at the front, in order to escape "the unpleasant atmosphere at Führer headquarters." Manstein subsequently told close associates that he had had a "very brilliant conversation" with Stauffenberg, "but he wanted me to believe that the war was lost."

Of their meeting, Stauffenberg remarked that, whatever Manstein's answers were, they "were not the answers of a field marshal."[44]

7

STAUFFENBERG

By 1943 the situation had grown more ominous—and not just at the battle fronts. Almost all the resistance groups sensed a gathering storm. Rumor had it that another Night of the Long Knives was in the offing.[1] Both Ulrich von Hassell and Hans von Dohnanyi were tipped off that they were being shadowed everywhere they went. In early March Colonel Fritz Jäger, who played a key role in Olbricht's coup plans, was arrested on allegations that he was "conspiring." Schulenburg also found himself in difficulty after he was reported to have said that he was on the lookout for reliable, young officers for a putsch. Admiral Canaris, too, was feeling the pressure, and when he was asked by a friend from his Freikorps days to save a Dutch Jew from deportation by claiming the man was needed by Military Intelligence—a favor he had occasionally extended in the past—he felt compelled to refuse. Himmler, he said, had informed him that "he knew full well that leading circles in the army were considering plans for a coup. But it would never come to that. He would intervene." Furthermore, Himmler professed to know who was "actually behind it"—and mentioned Beck and Goerdeler.[2] When the first blow fell, however, it was not on these men.

On April 5, 1943, senior judge advocate Manfred Roeder suddenly turned up at Military Intelligence on Tirpitzufer, accompanied by criminal secretary and SS Untersturmführer Franz Xaver Sonderegger. They asked to be taken to Canaris, to whom they presented papers authorizing both the arrest of special officer Hans von Dohnanyi and a search of his office. He was suspected, they informed Canaris, of numerous currency violations, corruption, and even treason. Stunned, Canaris neither objected nor contacted his superior officer, Wilhelm Keitel, though the search order violated all Military Intelligence secrecy regulations. Without a word he led the two agents to Dohnanyi's office, which was located immediately adjacent to Hans Oster's.

Canaris had been warned more than once, most recently that very morning, that trouble was brewing. And in almost every case the fingers pointed at Brigadier General Oster. His anxiety growing, Canaris had ordered that his closest associate immediately dispose of any incriminating documents. Whether Oster failed to realize the urgency of the warning or was simply too busy meeting endlessly with Olbricht, Beck, Gisevius, Schlabrendorff, and Heinz is not known; in any event he did not carry out his orders. In the course of their search Roeder and Sonderegger caught Dohnanyi trying to remove some papers from files that were being seized. When he was prevented from doing so, Dohnanyi was heard whispering "The notes!" to Oster, who also attempted to remove them. As the indictment later stated, Oster was "immediately asked to explain himself and required to produce the notes." Roeder ordered Oster out of the room and reported to his superiors what had happened. As a result, Oster was placed under house arrest, and a few days later he was dismissed from his position at Military Intelligence. Shortly thereafter Canaris called a meeting of department heads and "officially informed them of orders to avoid any contact with Oster."[3]

This was a terrible blow to the resistance—the worst it had suffered so far. In Schlabrendorff's words, it "lost its managing director." Gisevius spoke of a "psychological shock" that stunned everyone and left a "conspiratorial vacuum." Oster explained his admittedly foolish act by saying that he had assumed at first that Dohnanyi meant certain notes coded "U7," referring to a Military Intelligence operation to spirit Jews out of Nazi-occupied Europe by disguising them as agents. At least as disorienting as Oster's removal was the fact that, for the first time, the previously inviolable inner sanctums of Military

Intelligence had been invaded. To add to the grim news, Dietrich Bonhoeffer was arrested the same day, as were Dohnanyi's wife, Christine, in Sakrow, near Berlin, Josef Müller in Munich, and another Military Intelligence employee in Prague.

The papers for whose sake Dohnanyi and Oster had risked so much were actually totally unrelated to the U7 operation. They were hardly less compromising, however, and they prompted Roeder to announce triumphantly after reading them, "I'm going to clean up that shop!"[4] Most important, one of the seized "notes" contained references to an issue that was becoming of great concern to almost all opponents of the regime, arising repeatedly in the course of their discussions—namely, the relations between the German resistance and the Allies and the possibility of negotiating a last-minute peace agreement.

· · ·

Since the spring of 1942 the opposition had debated whether the Allies would be willing to negotiate a peace treaty after a coup in Germany and whether that would even be desirable. Some members of the Kreisau Circle in particular opposed any attempts to negotiate such a treaty. With their decidedly religious cast, they felt that Hitler and his minions should be dispatched, metaphorically, to the inferno that had spawned them. But most of the opposition figures agreed, though they might differ on the details, that it was their duty to save as much of the "substance" of Germany as possible from political and moral corruption and now, in the midst of the unprecedented Allied bombing campaign, from outright physical destruction. This group therefore insisted that everything possible be done to contact the Allies. They feared that time was running out: Germany's remaining bargaining power was quickly evaporating as its military strength declined and the ever more dominant Allies forged ahead.

This was the crux of the matter, the issue that many believed would make or break the resistance. If the leverage Germany still had, however weak it might be, could not be used to negotiate a peace treaty, then the resistance might as well avoid the extremely dangerous, if

Adam von Trott zu Solz was the foreign policy expert of the Kreisau Circle, but his views were respected far beyond that group. He was related through his mother's family to John Jay, the first chief justice of the United States Supreme Court, and had been a Rhodes scholar in England. Back in Germany, he took a position in the Foreign Office and sought repeatedly until the summer of 1944 to engage the Allies in a dialogue. All his efforts, however, were fruitless.

not suicidal, risk of a coup attempt and simply watch the regime go down in flames. The opposition's foreign policy experts—primarily Ulrich von Hassell but also Adam von Trott and others—decided after much deliberation that in view of all the Nazis' broken promises, violence, and crimes, there was no certainty that an "acceptable peace" could be negotiated, but that at the very least it remained a possibility.[5]

Such a hope was inconceivable unless the Allies were prepared to distinguish between Hitler and the German people. The conspirators based the plans for their own uprising entirely on the belief that this distinction existed and on the need to emphasize it for the benefit of everyone, so as to expose the falsity of the Nazi propaganda campaigns that depicted the Führer and the *Volk* as one. It is true that the hope for a negotiated peace revived many of the opposition's shattered illusions and unrealistic aspirations, but despite the criticism that has in hindsight been levied against it, the resistance did have a legitimate basis for the way it proceeded. Neither the keenness nor the morality of its opposition to the regime is diminished by the fact that it continued to take the national interest into account. One could even say that those who combined their moral outrage at Hitler with an awareness of the political disaster he was heaping on Germany understood more thoroughly than anyone else the nature of the regime and the possibilities of taking action against it.

From a practical point of view, this meant they needed to be clear about the prospects facing a German government once the Nazis had been overthrown. Realizing that many concessions and guarantees would inevitably be extracted from Germany, the members of the resistance wanted to find out what the Allies' maximum demands might be and to ensure that they themselves would be recognized, in theory at least, as equal partners in a European peace plan. What they did not want was to become the managers of a "liquidation commission" that simply carried out the dictates of the Allied powers. The opposition fully realized that such a situation would leave it standing "right in the middle of all the filth," in the dramatic words of one member.[6]

The resistance continued to pin its hopes on London, despite the misunderstandings, exasperation, and devastating setbacks that had characterized its overtures in the late 1930s. In focusing on this relationship, the German resistance considerably overestimated Britain's role and influence in the Allied coalition; for quite some time London had not had the power to sign agreements of its own with anyone. Most of the conspirators felt, however, that Britain was somehow closer to them—and not just geographically. In comparison with the other two great powers, the United States and the Soviet Union, Britain seemed to stand for a less foreign, more European world. Just

A prominent member of the Confessional Church, Dietrich Bonhoeffer (second from left) was, from the outset, one of National Socialism's most tenacious opponents. The son of a psychiatrist, he studied theology and, beginning in 1933, served for two years as a pastor in London. Drafted into Military Intelligence in 1940, he maintained close ties with both Hans Oster and the Kreisauers. He described Hitler as just one of the "disguises in which evil has appeared" in our century and declared at a secret church congress in Geneva in 1941 that he prayed for the defeat of his country.

The photograph shows faculty members from the theological college of the Confessional Church. It was taken in the winter of 1937–38 in Jershöft on the Baltic Sea.

as opposition emissaries had traveled to the British capital in the late thirties, they now sought to pave the way for talks with London through British posts in neutral countries.

Theo Kordt had already attempted to do so at the outset of the war, having been dispatched by the Foreign Office to Bern, Switzerland, for precisely that purpose. All his efforts came to naught, however, as did those of Josef Wirth, the former German chancellor, who had emigrated to Switzerland; Carl Jacob Burckhardt; Willem Adolf

Visser't Hooft, the secretary-general of the provisional World Council of Churches in Geneva; and many others. In May 1941 Goerdeler passed along to the British government a peace plan approved by Brauchitsch; the cabinet declined even to acknowledge it. The British middleman informed his German contact that he had been forbidden to accept any such documents in the future.

Another series of attempts to establish contact had been under way in Stockholm since the early 1940s and revolved largely around Theodor Steltzer, a key member of the Kreisau Circle. In May 1942 Bishop George Bell of Chichester met with Dietrich Bonhoeffer and his fellow clergyman Hans Schönfeld in Stockholm. Without knowing anything about the plans of the other, the two Germans had both decided to go to Sweden when they learned that Bell would be there. They told him about the opposition and the Kreisauers' ideas for peace and expressed the hope that some token of encouragement might be offered. Bell was quite well acquainted with Bonhoeffer, who had been a pastor in the German church in London during the 1930s, and knew that he was one of the leading figures in the Confessional Church in Germany. A man of radical religious conviction, Bonhoeffer had repeatedly insisted that Hitler had to be "exterminated" regardless of the political consequences. At a secret church conference in Geneva in 1941 he had gone even further, announcing that he prayed for the defeat of his country because that was the only way Germany would be able to atone for the crimes it had committed.[7] Schönfeld, on the other hand, brought only one question: Would the Allies adopt a different stance toward a Germany that had liberated itself from Hitler than they would toward a Germany still under his rule? Bell forwarded a report to the British Foreign Office, but Anthony Eden wrote back only to say he was "satisfied that it is not in the national interest to provide an answer of any kind." When Bell approached the British Foreign Office again, Eden noted in the margin of his reply, "I see no reason whatsoever to encourage this pestilent priest!"[8]

One year later Helmuth von Moltke went to Stockholm for a week, taking with him some information about the White Rose and one of its leaflets, as if he felt impelled to prove the seriousness of his opposition to the Nazi regime. Eugen Gerstenmaier, the theologian, and Hans Lukaschek, a lawyer who had joined the Kreisau Circle, also traveled to Stockholm, as on a number of occasions, did Adam von Trott, whose words sounded a desperate appeal for help: "We cannot afford to wait any longer," he pleaded to a Swedish friend. "We are so weak that we will only achieve our goal if everything goes our way and we get outside help."[9]

But there was to be no help or any sign of encouragement, just a deep, persistent silence. The Allies did not even trouble themselves to reject the various attempts to contact them, they simply closed their eyes to the German resistance, acting as if it did not exist. Men like Bonhoeffer, Trott, Gerstenmaier, and Steltzer felt united with the Allies in their abhorrence for their common "archenemy" and their realization of the danger that he posed. They therefore imagined themselves closely affiliated with the Allied struggle against this monstrous tyranny, which, in Churchill's words, had never been surpassed in the "dark, lamentable catalog of human crime." This was an illusion for which the conspirators would pay with countless humiliations. Perhaps they were ahead of the times in their moral internationalism, which had met with such deep incomprehension in the conversations of 1938–39. At any rate, the sense of common ground on which they based their appeals was not shared by the British, who could never free themselves of the suspicion that they were dealing with a bunch of traitors, or Nazis in disguise. The phenomenon of committing "treason" for high moral or philosophical purpose, which has become so characteristic of the twentieth century, was an enigma to them.

The extensive postwar literature justifying Britain's policy of distancing itself from the German resistance revives the very arguments on which the prewar attempts to make contact foundered. It points as well to the general lack of success with which the resistance did indeed seem cursed. Three further reasons are often adduced: with Winston Churchill's appointment as prime minister, Britain focused all its energy on the military effort, leaving no time for complicated political initiatives and prompting Churchill to call for "perfect silence"; in addition, the British were concerned that entering into negotiations with Germans, even anti-Nazi Germans, would jeopardize their alliance with the Soviet Union; finally London wished to avoid the error that the Allies had made after the First World War, when they forged commitments that later gave rise to demagogues like Hitler. Even if every possible allowance is made for these motives, however, something is still left unexplained—especially since the messages from the German emissaries provide no justification whatsoever for the most frequently mentioned concern, namely, the much-feared fracturing of the Allied coalition.

The real reasons for the attitude of the British probably lay in their lack of flexibility, their hostility, their blindness, and a political obtuseness that for all intents and purposes represented "an alliance with Hitler," to quote Hans Rothfels.[10] If a policy consisting of periodic cautious gestures of support had been pursued—which was, in fact, all that the German opposition now wanted—it might well have been possible gradually to drive a wedge between the Nazi regime and the people. Instead, Allied policy drove them into each other's arms. In early 1942 Goebbels noted in his diary with unmistakable satisfaction that this time the enemy had not set forth "any Wilsonian Fourteen Points" to sow unrest and confusion among the German public.[11]

Attitudes hardened even more after the United States entered the war in December 1941, and it was precisely the memory of Wilson's Fourteen Points that made America so unapproachable. The ill-fated promises of yesteryear seemed to be all that Roosevelt had learned and remembered from his nation's involvement in European affairs. The crude and narrow inference he drew was that even the most noncommittal conversation with Germans must be rejected, regardless of who they were or what the discussions were about. When an American correspondent in Berlin, Louis P. Lochner, returned to Washington in June 1942 with a secret code that German friends in the resistance had given to him in the hope of establishing a permanent link with U.S. government officials, the administration rejected the approach, saying that these contacts had put it in an "awkward" position.[12]

This attitude was strengthened with the Casablanca declaration of January 24, 1943, when Roosevelt vowed in Churchill's presence that the Allies would "continue the war relentlessly" until they achieved "unconditional surrender." The cold-shoulder approach to the resistance was thus given the seal of official strategy by both governments. Its effect would be to achieve the opposite of what Adam von Trott had said was the "primary purpose" of his last visit to the United States, namely, "to ensure that the planned war of annihilation does not drive those elements that have just begun to join forces against Hitler into the hands of the National Socialists." A furious Ewald von Kleist-Schmenzin said he would like to see both Hitler and Roosevelt roast, each in his own vat in hell.[13]

Casablanca therefore posed another serious setback for the resistance and was particularly troubling to those who still hesitated or had not quite made up their minds. The policy of unconditional surrender led many to feel that to oppose Hitler would be to betray their own country, and only a very few were prepared to go that far, especially in wartime. It was only with great difficulty that Helmuth von Moltke managed to carry on in the aftermath of Casablanca. On the other hand, like many of his friends, Trott never got over his bitterness and accused the Allies of indulging in "bourgeois prejudice and hypocritical theorizing." When he surfaced again in Stockholm in early 1944, still searching for influential intermediaries, he had developed, according to one of his Swedish friends, a look of "desperation."[14]

The lesson of Casablanca, as of all the vain attempts of these years to communicate with the Allies, whether through Spain, Portugal, Turkey, or the Vatican, was that the resistance was on its own. The conspirators grew accustomed to "staring into the void" when they contemplated the prospects for a coup—both the void within Germany and, as was now plain, the one beyond. This strengthened their resolve not to predicate their enterprise on any national, political, or even material interest. They carried on not in the hope of success but solely as an act of self-purification.

There are many reasons for the impending failure of the German resistance: errors, inhibitions, clumsiness, indecision, and the vastly superior power of the opponent. Any fair-minded assessment must, however, also take into account the brusque dismissal the resistance received from those with whom it believed—mistakenly, as it turned out—that it was safely in league.

■　■　■

After the near exposure of Oster, Canaris barely managed to slip out of the tightening noose. Roeder may have been a skillful, experienced investigator, but he never succeeded in penetrating the clouds of deception created by the masters of that art at Military Intelligence. Where he expected to find a massive political conspiracy with elements of high treason, he could only uncover evidence of questionable dealings in foreign currencies, bogus exemptions from military service, and lax handling of money. When a few unguarded comments escaped his lips, Military Intelligence counterattacked with a fog of accusations, complaints about the investigation, and counterinquiries. They finally prompted Keitel, the most highly placed official in the department's chain of command, to turn to Himmler. In the end, as the entire affair became hopelessly clouded and obscure, Dohnanyi and Bonhoeffer were merely indicted for a few nonpolitical offenses and Oster for being an accomplice.

Canaris sensed, however, that the fate of Military Intelligence was sealed, and that the bureau, with the maze of dark corridors that had been his fiefdom, could not long withstand the kind of scrutiny to which it would now be subjected by suspicious officials. In an early sign of what lay in store for it, Military Intelligence was ordered to relocate to Zossen. The official explanation was the disruption and destruction caused by the bombing of Berlin, but Keitel ordered simultaneously that the agency be reorganized and almost all its department heads replaced.

Only now did the severity of the blow suffered by the resistance on April 5 become clear. Along with its "managing director" it had lost its very core and with it went much of its internal cohesion. Months would be needed to repair the damage, but time was already short. There were further setbacks during that spring of 1943. Beck fell seriously ill and was incapacitated for several weeks. In addition, the opposition's troubled relations with the Allies became generally known, undermining its attempts to influence the generals, though there were a few individual successes. Once again, profound pessimism began to spread among the conspirators. The certainty that an indomitable fate was at work and would follow its predestined course regardless of what they might say or do gave rise to bouts of resignation. As General Fritsch had written years earlier, Hitler was "Germany's destiny for better or worse, and this destiny will run its course. If he tumbles into the abyss, he will take us all with him. Nothing can be done." Erich von Manstein, too, explained his refusal to join the conspirators with the fatalistic comment that it was impossible to resist Hitler. General Edgar Röhricht remarked to Tresckow that one could not escape one's fate, and even Canaris occasionally described Hitler as a "scourge of God" that must be endured to the end. General Adolf Heusinger, the chief of army operations, responded to invitations to join the conspiracy by claiming that an uprising would not change anything but only delay the inevitable and that Germans should simply resign themselves to the idea that there would be no rescue.[15]

The resistance experienced so many disappointments and anxieties, it saw so many valiant efforts turn to dust, that few of its members could help but be overcome by feelings of despair. Jens Peter Jessen, for instance, fell increasingly prey to such emotions and at times withdrew from society altogether. Tresckow, Olbricht, Hassell, and Johannes Popitz, by contrast, were less affected, while the irrepressible Coerdeler even began dreaming of what he called a "partial action," by which he meant the assassination of a more accessible Nazi of secondary rank or some other spectacular deed that, if accomplished at just the right moment, would bring "the whole house of cards crashing down." He was persuaded not to press ahead with his plans at a dinner in the home of former state secretary Erwin Planck, where the attorney Carl Langbehn, Hassell, General Thomas, and others argued that "Hitler's prestige is still solid enough that if he's left standing he'll be able to launch a counterattack that will end in at least chaos or civil war."[16]

At the fronts, the tides of war had now begun to turn. In early July Hitler attempted to regain the upper hand in the East through Operation Citadel, a massive panzer offensive against a Russian salient near Kursk; it ended in failure. A few days later the Allies landed in Sicily, creating a second front, and on July 25 Mussolini was overthrown. Tresckow, just released from his position on the staff of Army Group Center, canceled a vacation he had planned to take for health reasons and went to Berlin. Shortly after arriving he told Rüdiger von der Goltz, a cousin of Christine von Dohnanyi, that the war was lost and that "everything therefore must be done to end it soon." That meant "the leadership would have to go."[17]

At about the same time, Tresckow finally succeeded in convincing Colonel Helmuth Stieff, the only conspirator who had access to Hitler in the regular course of his duties, to keep his pledge to participate in an assassination attempt. This was a promising turn of events. Warned by Schlabrendorff that Kluge seemed to be backsliding in his absence, Tresckow then managed to persuade the field marshal to come to Berlin, where Tresckow sought to keep him in the conspiracy. He also arranged for Kluge to meet with Olbricht and Goerdeler, as well as with Beck, who had recently been released from the hospital. At the end of a long conversation about foreign affairs and the policy of the government to be formed after the coup, Kluge stated with surprising firmness that since Hitler would not make the necessary decisions to end the war and was unacceptable to the Allies as a negotiating partner he had to be overthrown by force. But now it was Goerdeler who voiced his adamant opposition, once again swept away by his optimism and his belief in the power of reason. He reminded the conspirators of the duty of the army commanders and the chief of general staff "to speak frankly with the Führer." After that, he said, everything else would fall into place: "Anybody can be won over to a good cause." Kluge and Beck could no longer be dissuaded, however, and shortly thereafter Goerdeler, suddenly fired with new enthusiasm, informed the Swedish banker Jakob Wallenberg that a putsch was planned for September. Schlabrendorff would then be sent to Stockholm to initiate peace negotiations.[18]

This announcement, like so many before it, was not to be fulfilled. First of all, Goerdeler probably cited far too early a date. The coup was apparently planned for the second half of October at the earliest. Then on October 12 Kluge was badly injured in an automobile accident and was laid up for a considerable period, which meant that no assassination attempts would be staged in the foreseeable future by the armies at the fronts. After so many failed attempts, Olbricht now turned with renewed vigor to an idea that had already been considered: using the home army for both the assassination and the coup.

■　■　■

What was lacking above all was an assassin. Around August 10, however, Tresckow had been introduced at Olbricht's house to a young lieutenant colonel who would be taking up the duties of chief of staff of the General Army Office on October 1. He had been badly wounded in a strafing attack while serving on the North African front in April. He had lost his right hand as well as the third and fourth fingers of his left, and he wore a black patch over his left eye. After a lengthy stay in the hospital, he had asked the surgeon, Ferdinand Sauerbruch, how much longer he would need to recuperate. On hearing that two more operations and many months of convalescence would be necessary, he shook his head, saying he didn't have that much time—important things needed to be done. While still in the hospital he explained to his uncle and close confidant Nikolaus von Üxküll, "Since the generals have failed to do anything, it's now up to the colonels."[19] His name was Count Claus Schenk von Stauffenberg.

Stauffenberg imbued the resistance with a vitality that had long been lacking but that now served to encourage Olbricht's cautious deliberations and heighten Tresckow's determination. He seemed to send an electric charge through the lifeless resistance networks as he quickly and naturally assumed a leadership role. This effect stemmed not only from the infectious energy that so many of his contemporaries have described but also from his unusual combination of exuberant idealism and cool pragmatism. He was familiar with all the complex religious, historical, and traditional reasons that had repeatedly stood in the way of action, but he had not lost sight of the far more basic truth that there are limits to loyalty and obedience. He was therefore able to put aside scruples about treason and the breaking of solemn oaths. Possessed of a finely honed sense of what was appropriate

Friends say that in the days leading up to July 20, 1944, Claus Schenk von Stauffenberg (right) liked to recite Stefan George's poem "The Antichrist." Having resolved to carry out the assassination attempt, Stauffenberg apparently found in the poem something that moved him, as it did many of his fellow conspirators: the projection of the enemy into the realm of myth, and hence the elevation of resistance into a sacred deed.

under the circumstances, he dismissed the foreign policy concerns of almost all the other members of the resistance, simply assuming that a German government that had overthrown the Nazis would be able to negotiate a peace treaty despite the Casablanca declaration. Most important, he was determined to act at all costs. Like Tresckow, he rejected the tendency of the resistance to make its actions contingent on circumstance—a failing that had first become apparent in 1938 and had resurfaced that spring in the collapse of the Oster group.

Stauffenberg was a scion of the Swabian nobility, related to the distinguished Gneisenau and Yorck families. When he was seventeen he and his brothers had joined the circle of intellectuals and students led by the famous poet Stefan George. Although he stood vigil at George's deathbed in December 1933, along with some friends, he was not a true disciple. Like many other young officers, he had welcomed Hitler's nomination as chancellor in 1933 and had agreed, in theory at least, with some of the Nazi platform, especially unification with Austria and hostility to the Treaty of Versailles. By the time of the Blomberg and Fritsch affairs, however, he had already begun to have serious doubts about the Nazis, doubts that Hitler's recklessness during the Sudeten crisis only hardened. "That fool is headed for war," he said. But when war was finally declared he threw himself into his chosen profession like a devoted soldier. His response to the numerous atrocities was that once the war was over there would be plenty of time to get rid of the "brown plague"—a reaction he shared with many of his colleagues.[20]

Stauffenberg proved to be a brilliant staff officer and was promoted to the army high command in June 1940. Since the launching of the Soviet campaign he had become familiar with the army's organizational inefficiency and the complicated tangle of competing military hierarchies. Moved by his sense of "outrage that Hitler . . . was too stupid . . . to do what was required," he strove stubbornly, though ultimately in vain, to form units composed of Russian volunteers so as to undermine the Nazis' senseless policies toward the "peoples of the East." At first his critical view of the regime was spurred by technical, military, and national concerns. Gradually, though, moral issues came more and more to the fore, and in the end all these considerations played their part in a decision best summarized by his laconic answer to a question asked of him in 1942 about how to change Hitler's style of leadership: "Kill him."[21]

The historian Gerhard Ritter has written that Stauffenberg had "a streak of demonic will to power and a belief that he was born to take charge" without which "the resistance was in danger of becoming bogged down in nothing but plans and preparations."[22] Once, when a member of the high command, appalled by the needless sacrifice of German soldiers and the staggering brutality being inflicted on the Soviet civilian population, asked Stauffenberg if it was possible to impress upon Hitler the truth of the situation, the young officer shot back, "The point is no longer to tell him the truth but to get rid of him," a remark that sharply repudiated Goerdeler's incurable optimism.[23] At headquarters in Vinnitsa in October 1942 Stauffenberg spoke out openly before a gathering of officers about the "disastrous course of German policy in the East," saying that everyone had remained silent even though it sowed hatred on all sides. Many witnesses have also reported his criticisms of generals who considered honor, duty, and service to be not binding ideals but simply grounds for making excuses; one report speaks of his contempt for all the "carpet layers with the rank of general."[24]

Stauffenberg's entry into resistance circles caused an enormous shift in the distribution of power and influence without his doing anything in particular. It was inevitable that he would spark conflicts as well as hopes. Goerdeler and his close associates were particularly vexed by the eclipse of the civilian groups, which they felt should dominate the resistance, and began to mutter derisively about Stauffenberg's lofty political ambitions and vaguely socialist tendencies. Soviet and East German historians later turned this grumbling to their advantage by depicting Stauffenberg as having moved close to Moscow in his political sympathies. But this myth, its somewhat grotesque origins, and the intentional exaggerations it underwent have all been investigated and disproved.[25]

What is clear is that Colonel Stauffenberg was far from the flunky whom the self-confident Goerdeler had always expected and previously always found in his collaborators from the military. In Stauffenberg a far more politically minded officer stepped forward, one who had no intention of simply putting himself at the beck and call of some group and its "shadow chancellor." What distinguished Stauffenberg from Goerdeler was less the former mayor's conservative, bourgeois values than his reluctance to employ violence and his rationalist delusion that Hitler could be made to see the error of his ways. Stauffenberg considered this as far-fetched as the highly contemplative opposition shared by many in the Kreisau Circle, which he derided as a "conspirator's tea party." As the man who would soon lead the actual coup attempt, he almost inevitably found himself at odds with both groups of conspirators, although for different reasons. On the whole, he felt closest to Julius Leber, the undogmatic Social Democrat with whom he shared the realistic political views and normative pragmatism of a man of action.

• • •

In early September 1943 Stauffenberg and Tresckow set about revising Olbricht's plans for a coup once again, with an eye to correcting

the inadequacies that had become apparent during the March attempt. Ironically, the original plans were based on a strategy that had
been designed by Olbricht's staff and approved by Hitler for dealing
with "internal disturbances"—that is, an uprising by the millions of
so-called foreign workers in Germany, possibly at the instigation or
with the help of the Communist underground or enemy paratroopers.
Under the code name Operation Valkyrie, the diffuse, scattered elements of the "reserve army"—trainees, soldiers on leave, and training
staff and cadres—would immediately be united and transformed into
fighting units. After the experiences of March Olbricht developed a
second stage of this plan and had it approved in late July 1943.
Henceforth "Valkyrie I" designated a strategy to ensure the combat
readiness of all units and "Valkyrie II" provided for their "swiftest
possible assemblage" into "battle groups ready for action."

Tresckow and Stauffenberg hit upon what many have called the
"brilliant" idea of further tailoring these official plans, which Olbricht
apparently considered adequate, to the specific needs of a coup by
adding a secret declaration, to be issued immediately upon Hitler's
assassination. It would begin: "The Führer Adolf Hitler is dead! A
treacherous group of party leaders has attempted to exploit the situation by attacking our embattled soldiers from the rear in order to
seize power for themselves!" The Reich government, the announcement continued, had "declared martial law in order to maintain law
and order." Simultaneously, government ministries and Nazi Party
offices would be occupied, as would radio stations, telephone offices,
and the concentration camps. SS units would be disarmed, and their
leaders shot if they resisted or refused to obey.

Thus the conspirators succeeded in standing Operation Valkyrie,
and the plan for dealing with "internal disturbances," on its head.
Stauffenberg and Tresckow's additional declaration would pin the
blame for the uprising that they themselves were staging on the Nazi
Party, a strategem intended to pacify those who would probably oppose the coup if they knew the true situation. The entire plan to
overthrow the regime, therefore, depended on an enormous hoax
carried out in large part by scores of officers and troops obliviously
following orders.

Since the success of the undertaking relied considerably on the element of surprise—which, in turn, would set in motion blind adherence to the automatic chain of command—secrecy was of the essence. All written information was handled by Tresckow's wife, Erika, and by Margarete von Oven, who had been Hammerstein's secretary during his days as chief of army command. Both women wore gloves when they worked so as not to leave fingerprints. All meetings were held out of doors at various locations in the Grunewald, but they often had to be canceled and then, with great difficulty, rescheduled because of Allied air raids, breakdowns in public transportation, or other unforeseeable events. One evening a group of conspirators were returning from one of their meetings in the Grunewald when an SS van came screeching to a halt directly beside them on Trabenerstrasse. Margarete von Oven was carrying all the documents about the uprising under her arm, and "when the SS men poured out, each of them thought the conspiracy had been discovered and they would be arrested at once. But the SS men paid no attention to the three passersby and disappeared into a house."[26]

Despite the conspirators' efforts, the Valkyrie plan had a serious and possibly fatal flaw: neither Olbricht nor Stauffenberg was authorized to order its implementation. Hitler had expressly reserved this authority for himself, with the commander of the reserve army, General Friedrich Fromm, authorized to give the cue only in an emergency. Therefore Olbricht or Stauffenberg had either to win Fromm over or else to usurp his position and set Valkyrie in motion in his name. Olbricht was prepared to take Fromm into custody if necessary and sign the orders himself, but that risked questions about the chain of command and delays that might imperil the entire enterprise. It has also been pointed out rightly that this was a tactic that could work only once. If the conspirators failed to usurp Fromm's position "the first time around, there would be no second chance."[27]

General Fromm was a large, shrewd man who liked to boast that he "always came down on the right side." When Halder asked him earnestly in the fall of 1939 to support the generals' coup that was being plotted, Fromm evaded the issue at first and then requested time to consider the matter. He was torn by doubts about the chances

General Friedrich Fromm (right foreground, in gray uniform) *liked to say that he "always came down on the right side" of every situation. Hitler disapproved of this kind of opportunism, and starting in 1942, Fromm fell increasingly into disfavor. As commander in chief of the reserve army, Fromm held a crucial position in Operation Valkyrie. He could not, however, be won over to the conspiracy, although he hinted that he might support the conspirators if they succeeded.*

Above: Fromm in October 1942 at the opening of an exhibition of works by Italian soldiers in the Berlin Staatsgalerie.

of success and tormented by the fact that he had compromised himself by responding to Halder at all. Finally he formally absolved himself of involvement by recording the affair in his official diary.

Fromm certainly did not number among "Hitler's generals," and to his friends he frequently expressed his distaste for the Nazis. He was also clever enough to deduce what Olbricht and Stauffenberg were up to from all the secretive activity in their offices and the visitors whom they received. He always acted, however, as if it was none of his business. He slipped up only once, in mid-July 1944, when, in a particularly buoyant mood, he told Olbricht to be sure, in the event of a putsch, not to forget Wilhelm Keitel, whom Fromm hated.[28] Although Fromm did nothing to hinder the uprising, no one who knew him had any doubt that he would not assist it either and, most important, that he would definitely not sign the Valkyrie orders. The question of how he should be handled therefore remained open. By the end of October all other preparations were ready. Tresckow gave Witzleben the orders declaring martial law, and Witzleben, who was to assume command of the Wehrmacht once a coup was under way, affixed his signature.

Scarcely had these preparations been completed, however, when Tresckow was ordered back to the front. Thus it was Stauffenberg who took on responsibility for igniting the "initial spark." It was hoped that Tresckow would again assume a pivotal position in the military command from which he could provide support from the front as soon as the home army initiated the uprising, but this was not to be. The army personnel office had recommended him, along with other candidates, to serve as chief of staff for Army Group South under Field Marshal Erich von Manstein, but Manstein rejected him. Instead, Tresckow assumed command of an infantry regiment in a division led by Manstein. Rumor had it that he was being put in "cold storage."[29]

The problem now as ever was to find an officer who had access to Hitler and was determined to kill him. Stieff had recently declared himself ready, but when Stauffenberg sought him out he stalled. He did, however, take possession of the explosives Stauffenberg brought him and finally demanded the assistance of an accomplice, apparently in order to help steel himself. Stauffenberg turned to Colonel Joachim Meichssner, the head of the organizational section of the OKW operations staff, who had tentatively promised in September to be the assassin. At the same time, Stieff was apparently considering making an attempt with two young officers on his staff, Major Joachim Kuhn and First Lieutenant Albrecht von Hagen; but after further consideration, he again backed out, explaining that it was impossible to carry

In late 1943 Axel von dem Bussche (above) was introduced to Stauffenberg by Fritz-Dietlof von der Schulenburg. At twenty-four he was already a highly decorated captain. His initial enthusiasm for National Socialism had been shattered in October 1942, when he witnessed the mass execution of Jews at the Dubno airfield in the Ukraine. Bussche later said that he regretted not having done the honorable thing: taking off his uniform and lining up with the victims. When asked by Stauffenberg if he would assassinate Hitler during a presentation of new uniforms and equipment, he immediately agreed.

explosives into a briefing without being noticed. In truth, it was probably fear that deterred this lively and somewhat unstable man from action.

These harrowing efforts to find someone who would set off the "initial spark" prompted Stauffenberg to make contact, through Fritz-Dietlof von der Schulenburg, with one of the "reliable young officers" he had heard about in the spring. Axel von dem Bussche was a highly decorated twenty-four-year-old captain. His initial naive enthusiasm for Hitler and National Socialism had already dimmed considerably when, in early October 1942, he happened to witness the mass execution of several thousand Jews at the Dubno airfield in the Ukraine, a shock he never recovered from. There were, he said, only three possible ways for an honorable officer to react: "to die in battle, to desert, or to rebel." When Stauffenberg now asked him if he would be willing to kill Hitler, Bussche accepted without hesitation.

The plan was to use a previously scheduled presentation of new uniforms and equipment to lure Hitler from his bunker at headquarters, where he increasingly ensconced himself. Bussche was to explain the features and advantages of the new items and then, at a suitable moment, to set the fuse on the bomb, leap on Hitler, and hold him tight for the three or four seconds until the explosion. Toward the end of November the presentation seemed likely to take place at any moment. Bussche traveled to Führer headquarters in East Prussia and waited. "The sunny late-autumn days amid the forests and lakes are imbued with the heightened intensity a soldier feels before an attack," he wrote.[30] But the presentation was postponed again and again. Finally Stieff informed the other conspirators that the model uniforms had been in a railroad car that was destroyed in one of the bombing raids on Berlin. Replacements would probably not be ready before January. Bussche returned to the front, where he was severely wounded early in the new year, losing a leg, which disqualified him from further attempts.

An unexpected complication now arose. Bussche was left with a bomb in his suitcase and no way of disposing of it. He found himself transferred from one hospital to another, all the while carrying his secret along with him. Not until the fall of 1944 did he finally find a sympathetic officer who threw it into a lake for him.[31] Stieff, too, had been left with explosives on his hands when he backed out of killing Hitler. He assigned the disposal of "the stuff" to Kuhn and Hagen, who came up with the ill-advised idea of burying the explosives and detonators in the woods under a watchtower within the boundaries of Führer headquarters. As it happened, a military police patrol spotted them, but they managed to escape without being recognized. Had the incident been brought to light it might well have had serious consequences for the entire resistance. Fortunately, however, the investigation was assigned to a close confidant of Hans Oster's named Lieutenant Colonel Werner Schrader, and thus a conspirator ended up investigating the conspiracy.[32]

In January, after Bussche had been wounded, Stauffenberg approached Lieutenant Ewald Heinrich von Kleist. Once again, the plan was to assassinate Hitler during the presentation of new uniforms. Stauffenberg did not press Kleist, saying only that the earlier attempt had failed. Kleist said he wanted first to speak with his father, the same Ewald von Kleist Schmenzin who in the summer of 1938 had traveled to London at the behest of Oster and Beck to meet with Vansittart and Churchill. When the son appeared at the family estate the next day and asked his father's opinion, the elder Kleist immediately responded that this was a task he could not refuse. The son pointed out that he was being asked to do nothing less than blow himself up with Hitler. His father stood up, went to the window, and after a moment's thought, replied, "You have to do it. Anyone who falters at such a moment will never again be one with himself in this life."[33]

But this brave resolution also failed, once again the date of the presentation was repeatedly postponed. Stauffenberg next turned to his adjutant, Werner von Haeften, who agreed in principle to carry out the task but was then dissuaded by his brother, Hans-Bernd, who raised vehement objections on religious grounds. These pangs of conscience, excuses, concerns about Hitler's security precautions, and struggles to procure explosives and then dispose of them generated anguish and despair in the ranks of the conspirators—while meanwhile the slaughter continued on all sides. All these pressures burst forth one day when Paul Yorck von Wartenburg screamed at Gersdorff, "That swine does, after all, have a mouth that somebody could just shoot into!"[34]

This very approach was adopted by Eberhard von Breitenbuch, a cavalry captain who now declared that he would do the deed

Tresckow had arranged for Breitenbuch to join Army Group Center, where he became adjutant to the new commander in chief, Field Marshal Ernst Busch, following Kluge's accident. On March 11 Busch was summoned to a briefing on the Obersalzberg and, as usual, took along his adjutant. Breitenbuch, not informed of the briefing until that very morning, agreed on the spot to make the attempt. While the participants in the briefing waited to see Hitler, Breitenbuch took the opportunity to write his wife a farewell letter and send her the few personal effects he had with him. Finally the door to the great hall of Hitler's Berghof swung open and an SS man invited the waiting party to enter. Keitel, Jodl, and Goebbels led the way, while Breitenbuch, as the lowest-ranking officer, drew up the rear. Just as he was about to step into the hall, the SS man intercepted him, announcing that the briefing would be held without adjutants. Busch protested that he needed his aide, but Breitenbuch, with the cocked Browning revolver in his pocket, was turned aside. Although he later had similar opportunities he turned them down, saying, "You only do something like that once."[35]

The preceding is only a condensed account of the best-known of the assassination attempts. Although there were many other clandestine discussions and a number of attempts that also failed, little is known about them, because virtually all those involved were discovered and executed. It is said, for instance, that Stauffenberg attempted to kill Hitler on December 26, 1943, in the "Wolf's Lair," as Führer headquarters at Rastenburg was called. Stauffenberg's original plan, apparently, was to blow himself up with Hitler, but Beck and Olbricht objected so vehemently that Stauffenberg agreed to spare himself. He was waiting in Hitler's antechamber for their meeting to commence when he was informed that it had been canceled.

Be that as it may, it was at about this time that Stauffenberg first began to consider taking the assassination into his own hands. Only in this way, he felt, could he break the curse that seemed to haunt the resistance.

■　■　■

In retrospect it may seem that the inner strength of the resistance had already begun to ebb by late 1943 and early 1944 and that Tresckow's failed plot in March 1943 was the turning point in this drama. If so, Stauffenberg joined too late, forced as he was to struggle not only against the Nazi regime but also, to a greater extent than any of his predecessors, against mounting exhaustion and pessimism among the conspirators. Moreover, the state security apparatus began taking greater interest in the opposition after the raid on Military Intelligence, and bad news seemed to pour in from all directions.

Tresckow, however, remained determined to escape the backwater in which he found himself as an infantry commander and to improve his chances of gaining access to Hitler. In December 1943 he contacted his old regimental comrade General Rudolf Schmundt with a proposal to establish a department of psychological and political warfare at Führer headquarters, with himself as head. Tresckow's "negative attitude" had become so widely known in the meantime, however, that Schmundt, the chief of army personnel, who was still well-disposed to his old friend, quietly let the matter drop. Tresckow also applied to become General Heusinger's delegate in the OKH operational section but failed at that, too, apparently for the same reason. Heusinger only glanced at the letter, which Schlabrendorff delivered to him, before saying, "It doesn't require an answer." Tresckow also wrote to Colonel Stieff, who was still hesitating, begging him to take action at last. When he read the letter, Stieff "burst into approving laughter" and promptly destroyed it.[36]

The conspirators suffered another blow in December when Carlo Mierendorff died in a building that collapsed during a bombing raid on Leipzig. According to witnesses, his final word, shouted from the burning cellar, was "Madness!"[37] At about the same time the Gestapo honed in on members of an opposition group that had formed around Hanna Solf, the widow of the former German ambassador to Tokyo, and that provided support for people who were persecuted or living underground. Suspicion was probably aroused by the involvement of three officers from Military Intelligence: Nikolaus von Halem, the former legation secretary Mumm von Schwarzenstein, and Otto Kiep. The Security Service had begun systematically to put all Military Intelligence officers under surveillance in the hope that Canaris's department would continue to crack and could then be absorbed into the expanding empire of the SS. On January 12, 1944, the members of the Solf Circle were arrested while at afternoon tea. One week later Helmuth von Moltke, who had attempted to warn Otto Kiep of the danger, was also picked up. The flood of bad news continued on February 11, when Canaris was dismissed from his job and imprisoned in the Lauenstein fortress, while Himmler's henchmen, Ernst Kaltenbrunner, Walter Schellenberg, and Heinrich Müller, began to dismantle Military Intelligence piece by piece.

The ascendancy of Heinrich Himmler and the SS state led to a bizarre episode that concluded just as the new year began. Spurred by the repeated failure to overthrow the regime by force, Johannes Popitz had hit on the idea of encouraging a "palace revolution" or at least of exacerbating the tensions that existed among the leading members of the Nazi Party in order to speed up the already perceptible disintegration process. At first Popitz considered approaching Göring, Hitler's designated successor and the prime minister of Prussia, in whose cabinet he still officially sat as minister of finance. He soon concluded, however, that Göring had become too self-indulgent and corrupt, too preoccupied with his flamboyant social life to function even as the figurehead of a serious uprising. Popitz turned therefore to none other than Heinrich Himmler in his perilous venture to destroy the regime from within.

Popitz had no reason at all to assume that Himmler would prove amenable. After a brilliant early career Popitz had become state secretary in the Ministry of Finance while still quite young, working for a time under the Social Democratic minister Rudolf Hilferding, whom he helped escape Germany after the Nazis seized power. His close bonds with Hilferding may explain why he leaned toward a policy of strong governmental control of the economy, which recommended him to some of the younger members of the Kreisau Circle despite his reputation as a "reactionary old Prussian." Having made friends with Hans Oster in 1935, Popitz had become deeply involved in the resistance to Hitler even before the war; indeed as a sign of protest against the persecution of Jews, he submitted his resignation as minister to Göring in November 1938, explicitly requesting that Hitler be informed of the reasons. He never received a response, however, and in the end remained in office.

Popitz was also acquainted with Carl Langbehn, who had joined the opposition in the late 1930s. It turned out that Langbehn knew Himmler personally both as a lawyer and as a neighbor in the Dahlem neighborhood of Berlin. Through this connection Popitz now contacted the powerful chief of the SS, who had recently been appointed minister of the interior. They met on August 26. In a conversation conducted with Machiavellian cunning, in which he skirted the edge of the abyss more than once, Popitz suggested that no one but Himmler could resolve the desperate situation that had befallen the regime both at home and at the front. Such a suggestion was not totally devoid of promise, as the clear-headed, coolly calculating SS leaders had themselves already begun to entertain serious doubts about whether Germany could win the war and to wonder how their interests might best be served. Popitz avoided referring directly to "overthrowing" Hitler, although that was his ultimate aim, instead making oblique references to "lightening the burden" the Führer had to bear. In general Popitz gained the impression that Himmler had long doubted that Germany could win the war. At the end of their conversation the two agreed to meet again soon.

This second meeting never took place. The next month Langbehn was arrested after his contacts with the Allies through Swiss intermediaries were exposed. Popitz found himself increasingly marginalized within the civilian resistance despite the leading role he had played until this point. His daring initiative was, of course, an act of desperation, predicated on the belief that Himmler could be elbowed aside after he had served his purpose. That idea seemed an eerie echo of the illusions of the spring of 1933, when it was thought that Hitler could be controlled once in power. But Popitz's greater error was his failure to realize that the SS leader did not act independently and exercised only delegated authority. Furthermore, he overlooked how damaging it would have been for the opposition to be maintaining contact, for whatever reason, with a man who was widely believed to epitomize Nazi terror. Gerhard Ritter was not far off track when he described Popitz as the type of intellectual who has "pure intentions but few sure political instincts." It was this shortcoming that gave rise to the general feeling within resistance circles that Popitz had overstayed his welcome in the role of leader. At any rate, Goerdeler felt that Popitz had gone too far and, after hesitating at first, decided that he didn't want to hear so much as a word about the conversation with Himmler. At Stauffenberg's urging Goerdeler, too, abandoned the finance minister. The circle had been "blown apart," Hassell wrote in late February. "Everything is going to hell."[38]

What tore this "band of brothers" apart more than anything else were their repeatedly dashed hopes for an assassination. In February Goerdeler wrote to Beck complaining about Stauffenberg's failure to keep his promises and proposing to revive his own pet project of a bloodless coup. Through a number of intermediaries Goerdeler managed to contact Chief of General Staff Kurt Zeitzler to request that Zeitzler arrange an interview with Hitler or even a debate between them to be broadcast over the radio, during which Goerdeler intended to "eliminate" the Führer by prompting him to give up or resign. When this initiative failed, Goerdeler wrote Zeitzler an epistle of more than twenty pages outlining his ideas. Fortunately, Goerdeler's staff did not forward it.[39]

Such initiatives aroused only scorn and contempt from Stauffenberg, and though they were a genuine expression of Goerdeler's irrepressible confidence and courage, they only served to widen the gulf between the two men. Differences in age and temperament figured, of course, in their disagreements, but so did the fact that Goerdeler was a skillful, cosmopolitan bureaucrat, and Stauffenberg an impatient and still young man of action. The deeper reason for the discord was that Stauffenberg, conscious of the key role he was playing and encouraged by Fritz-Dietlof von der Schulenburg, the former regional commissioner in Silesia, drew increasingly close to Wilhelm Leuschner and Julius Leber, without concerning himself with how much Goerdeler "suffered from his distant attitude," in the words of one contemporary. "Again and again Goerdeler complained, 'They're trying to cut me out. They don't tell me anything anymore.'"[40]

Stauffenberg was indeed becoming convinced that Leber would make "the better chancellor," although Leber himself, along with Wilhelm Leuschner and the trade unionist Jakob Kaiser, believed that the persistence of the stab-in-the-back myth from World War I made

As a young man Count Fritz-Dietlof von der Schulenburg took seriously the socialist pretensions of the Nazi program and even joined the party in 1932, although he soon turned against it. Although he had a highly successful career in various administrative posts, he was already considered politically unacceptable by the mid- to late 1930s. He was close to both the military and the civilian resistance circles and mediated between them.

Schulenburg had an engaging personality, and young people in particular gravitated toward him. He introduced Stauffenberg to Axel von dem Bussche and Ewald Heinrich von Kleist, both of whom agreed to attempt to assassinate Hitler. One contemporary wrote in her diary: "Everybody does what [Schulenburg] says, even though he looks neither rich nor powerful in his shabby blue suit or torn uniform, with his crooked nose and absurd monocle."

it inadvisable to place a Social Democrat or a labor leader "all too visibly in the front rank of those responsible" immediately following the removal of Hitler. Moreover, although Stauffenberg was closer to Leber on domestic policy, he knew that in foreign affairs he had more in common with Goerdeler, who had developed an eleven-point program that he wanted to present to the Allies, still believing, even in the summer of 1944, that a negotiated peace was possible. This program stipulated that Germany would retain its 1914 borders, as well as Austria and the Sudetenland, and that it might even secure the return of parts of South Tyrol.[41]

Julius Leber took a much more sober view. He thought that unconditional surrender was inevitable, and therefore adopted an ever-cooler attitude toward Goerdeler. The main points of contention reveal how pronounced the divisions within the resistance had become. Leber, for instance, who was no friend of conservatives, came quite close to advocating the strong authoritarian state that Jessen, Hassell, and Popitz envisaged for the transition period; he agreed with them that "a dictatorship cannot be put on a democratic footing over night."[42] Meanwhile, for this very reason, the conservatives distanced themselves from Goerdeler, whose blind faith in democracy and sympathy toward the trade unions made them distrust him as the leader of a strong interim regime. In foreign policy Trott may have shared many of Goerdeler's opinions, but Moltke and most of the Kreisau Circle did not. They continued to see Goerdeler as a man linked to business circles that would not be sufficiently accepting of a government that, in Yorck's words, "included the working class and even left-wing Social Democrats." And so, little by little, the resistance tore itself apart in controversies that bore little connection to the real world until everyone alternately agreed and disagreed with everyone else in one way or another, and the majority support for Goerdeler that had existed a year before was now gone. Indeed, the Gestapo agents who interrogated the conspirators after July 20 were not far wrong when they concluded that the attempts of the diverse resistance circles "to build a united front" had produced "a political monstrosity," and that the conspirators were united "only in a negative sense, in their rejection of National Socialism."[43] The ties that bound them had in fact been broken.

This state of affairs was not overly apparent in the early summer of 1944, however, because at that point the dominant concern continued to be foreign policy—specifically, how the Allies would respond to a coup. Most opponents of the Nazi regime still found it hard to accept that they did not have a shred of hope. Even Stauffenberg harbored illusions about a negotiated peace, hurrying off to seek solace from Trott after some particularly sobering conversations with Leber. And when an embittered Trott returned from a trip abroad convinced that there was "no genuine desire on the part of the British and Americans to reach an understanding"—especially since the demand for unconditional surrender first expressed in the Casablanca declaration had just been underscored at the Teheran Conference—dreams of a separate peace with the Soviet Union surged briefly to the fore.

The resistance based its hopes on Stalin's well-known comment of February 1942 that although individuals like Hitler might come and go, the German people would remain. If the Soviet dictator was hinting at some disagreement with the intransigent policy of the Western powers, he took a step further in this direction in the summer of 1943 when he began approaching the German opposition through their contacts in Stockholm and through the National Committee for a Free Germany established in Krasnogorsk, near Moscow, by German prisoners of war and emigrants. Like the attempts to forge ties in the West, however, these contacts were soon undermined by distrust and suspicion. Heretofore the activities of the Communist-inspired groups led by First Lieutenant Harro Schulze-Boysen and Arvid and Mildred Harnack had gone virtually unnoticed by the rest of the resistance, despite a few personal ties between them. The group known collectively as the Red Orchestra (after its Gestapo nickname) consisted of both hard-core Communist ideologues on one side and a motley assortment of dreamers and visionaries on the other. Their arrest in August 1942 aroused little more than feelings of empathy among the rest of the resistance, which cared little for their use of political theory to mask the many concrete similarities between Hitler and Stalin. The leftists' continued embrace of the old dream of a historic mission shared by the "profound" German and Russian cultures, as opposed to the "superficial" Western cultures, further alienated the other factions. As a result not even the loosest of ties were forged, especially as Moscow itself was apparently not interested in developing this group into a cell or even a center of political resistance. Rather, the inner circle of the Red Orchestra was used as an intelligence-gathering service for the Soviet Union.

Thus the question of establishing contacts with the Soviet Union arose at this point only as a tactical ploy to elicit more interest from the Western powers. But the resistance soon dropped this plan too. One of the strongest pieces of evidence against Stauffenberg's alleged Communist sympathies is that he turned down the appeals of the National Committee for a Free Germany with the comment, "I am betraying my government; they are betraying their country."[44] Stauffenberg not only supported the attempts of men like Goerdeler, Trott, and Gisevius to reach some kind of understanding with the Western powers but later joined in those efforts himself. Although the Gestapo was eager after July 20 to find some evidence of collusion between the conspirators and the Soviet Union or one of its agents, they failed to find any.

There was yet another aspect to this question—namely, the resistance's connections with the Communist underground. Only isolated remnants had survived the shocking announcement of the Hitler-Stalin pact, so that it was difficult to determine their strength. The uncertainty prompted Leber to respond positively to various Communist overtures. Although there was still no question of including the Communists in the conspiracy, there was talk of an "opening to the left," and of determining how the Communist leadership would react to a coup.

After much argument, a discussion of the issue was finally held in Yorck's house on June 21. There were violent differences of opinion. Leuschner opposed any sort of rapprochement, insisting that the Communist apparatus had been infiltrated by the Gestapo. The Kreisauers Theodor Haubach and Paulus van Husen were also dead set against establishing any contacts. Only Adolf Reichwein advocated "a kind of socialist solidarity," the outgrowth of his "almost embittered socialism." The reticence of many of the participants was greatly reduced, however, when Leber reported that he had been contacted by "two well-known Communists" and pointed out that "he had shared a bunk with the two men in a concentration camp for five years." Although the misgivings abated, it is still not clear whether they were totally dispelled. Stauffenberg, at any rate, seems to have favored a meeting.[45]

The next day, June 22, Leber and Reichwein went to meet two members of the central committee of the Communist Party, Anton Saefkow and Franz Jacob, in the apartment of a Berlin physician. When they arrived, however, they found that Saefkow and Jacob were accompanied by a third man, who had not been mentioned in the agreement. More disturbingly, one of the Communists greeted Leber by his full name, though this, too, ran counter to their agreement. Leber must have regarded their salutations as a sort of kiss of Judas. In any case, he apparently realized immediately that the meeting was a terrible mistake that posed an enormous danger not only to him but to the entire conspiracy, just as it was gathering its strength for another, perhaps final attempt on Hitler's life.

Although both sides had previously agreed to meet again on July 4, Leber did not attend. Reichwein showed up alone and was arrested along with Saefkow and Jacob. The next morning the Gestapo nabbed Leber in his apartment.

■   ■   ■

By this time the war was entering its final phase. On June 6, 1944, the Allies had begun their invasion of Normandy. Just over two weeks later they had firmly established a beachhead and shipped one million men, 170,000 vehicles, and over 500,000 tons of matériel across the Channel. What is more, on June 22 four Soviet army groups, outnumbering the Germans six to one, broke through the thin, porous line of Army Group Center between Minsk and the Beresina River. They drove deep behind the German positions, isolating three pockets containing twenty-seven German divisions—far more than at Stalingrad—which they surrounded and quickly destroyed.

Henning von Tresckow, who had been restored to his position as chief of general staff of the Second Army on the southern flank of Army Group Center, was once again pressing for immediate action against Hitler. Stauffenberg had always believed that the invasion of France was a point of no return, after which a coup would be only a futile gesture any hope for a negotiated "political" settlement would die. The fear of having arrived on the scene too late dominated all his thoughts and made him extremely impatient.

Stauffenberg sent Tresckow a message through Lehndorff asking whether there was any reason to continue trying to assassinate Hitler now, since they had missed their last opportunity and no political purpose would any longer be served. Lehndorff returned promptly with Tresckow's response, which signaled a final break from all concern with external circumstances, which had so often paralyzed the conspirators, as well as from political goals of any kind: "The assassination must be attempted, *coûte que coûte*. Even if it fails, we must take action in Berlin. For the practical purpose no longer matters; what matters now is that the German resistance movement must take the plunge before the eyes of the world and of history. Compared to that, nothing else matters."[46]

8

THE ELEVENTH HOUR

On July 1 Stauffenberg was promoted to the rank of colonel and simultaneously assumed his new duties as chief of staff to the commander of the reserve army. General Fromm had always been a vigilant, cautious, opportunistic man, whose suspicions that Stauffenberg and Olbricht were plotting a coup had long since hardened into certainty. It seems all the more curious, therefore, that he went to such lengths to have Stauffenberg appointed to his staff. Fromm may simply have wanted to use Stauffenberg, who had written a report that drew extremely laudatory reviews from Hitler, to escape the disfavor into which he had himself fallen. "Finally a general staff officer with imagination and intelligence!" Hitler is said to have remarked.[1] It is also possible that Wehrmacht adjutant General Rudolf Schmundt recommended the brilliant young officer—who had been widely noticed and even considered as a possible successor to General Adolf Heusinger, the chief of operations—in the hope of reviving Fromm, who had "grown tired." In any case, when Stauffenberg first met with his new boss and intimated that he was indeed considering a coup, Fromm merely thanked him for his frankness and let the matter drop. Stauffenberg's successor on Olbricht's staff was Colonel Albrecht Mertz von Quirnheim, whom Stauffenberg had known since their days together at the War Academy.[2]

Of crucial importance to Stauffenberg and to Olbricht, who now had to do without Stauffenberg's services, was the fact that the new position gave Stauffenberg the access to Hitler that the conspirators had long sought. No longer would they need to arrange presentations of new uniforms or other difficult events. On June 7, the day after the Allied invasion of Normandy, Stauffenberg had already accompanied Fromm to a discussion at the Berghof, Hitler's Obersalzberg headquarters. Stauffenberg recalled that Hitler seemed "in a daze," pushing situation maps back and forth with a trembling hand and casting repeated glances at him.[3] Now, barely one week after his new appointment, Stauffenberg found himself back at the Berghof once again.

It is not clear whether he intended to assassinate Hitler then, but he did take a bomb with him and the other conspirators were warned in advance. It had always been assumed in resistance circles that Göring and Himmler would also have to be killed in any attack on Hitler. As things turned out, they were not present at this meeting, which may explain why Stauffenberg did not set off the bomb. It may also be, however, that he was still counting on Helmuth Stieff, whom he went to see when he learned that Stieff would preside at the following day's long-postponed presentation of new uniforms at Schloss Klessheim—an occasion identical to the ones at which Bussche and Kleist had planned to blow themselves up with Hitler half a year earlier. But when Stauffenberg informed Stieff that he had brought "all the stuff along," Stieff declined the mission.

This response reinforced Stauffenberg's resolve to carry out the assassination himself. Upon learning of his new appointment in June, he had begun accustoming himself to the idea—over the objections of Beck—and had informed Yorck and Haeften of his intention. No one had ever proposed that Stauffenberg himself be the one to kill Hitler, both because of his severe war wounds and because the plans for a coup made his presence in Berlin indispensable. In view of what he termed "our desperate situation," however, he decided that there was no other way. In early July he began to make the necessary preparations (arranging, above all, for an airplane to fly him back to Berlin) and to think through the changes that would have to be made to the plan to accommodate his dual role as assassin and leader of the uprising in the capital.

In early 1944 Stauffenberg approached his adjutant Werner von Haeften (right) with a plan to kill Hitler during a ceremony to present new uniforms. Haeften agreed but was dissuaded by his brother, Hans-Bernd von Haeften (left), who objected vehemently, largely on religious grounds.

It is revealing that Stauffenberg's decision to take so much upon himself raised no practical objections from the other conspirators, though it considerably increased the hazards of their undertaking. Only the surgeon Ferdinand Sauerbruch advanced serious reservations following a meeting held at his house. Stauffenberg, who had stayed behind, told him about what was planned, at least in part. Sauerbruch's qualms at first focused on Stauffenberg's still seriously weakened physical condition but ultimately broadened to include many other concerns as well.[4]

Stauffenberg's fellow conspirators, by contrast, were troubled once again mostly by deep philosophical concerns. In lengthy discussions running from early spring until June, Stauffenberg finally managed to assuage the theological and ethical objections that Yorck and other members of the Kreisau Circle had to killing Hitler. He made especially great strides in this regard when he was able to confront the "hairsplitting scholars of the loyalty oath" with evidence of orders from Kaltenbrunner prescribing "'special treatment' for 40,000 or 42,000 Hungarian Jews in Auschwitz."[5] Nevertheless, Hans-Bernd von Haeften wrestled to the very end with his anxieties about assassination, tied in knots as he was by professional codes of honor, ethical maxims, and, most important, religious strictures. When, early in the year, his brother Werner returned from a meeting with Stauffenberg and announced that he had agreed in principle to be the assassin the conspirators needed, Haeften asked: "Are you absolutely sure this is your duty before God and our forefathers?" But then, as the daily toll of the dead and injured mounted, he was tormented by the thought that he had dissuaded his brother and saved Hitler.[6]

Hans-Bernd von Haeften thus became entangled in a hopeless web of philosophical and religious reflection. His confusion can be seen in the solution he ultimately embraced: that Hitler ought to have been killed *before* Stalingrad, "if at all," but that now that everything "was going downhill and luck was deserting him," there could be "no blessing in tyrannicide." Similarly, Moltke opposed murdering Hitler for a long time, then came to favor it, and finally, when he knew that the end of his life was near, expressed great joy that he had only "thought" about it. Men like Beck, Steltzer, and Yorck were also deeply religious. Their involvement in the resistance was based to a large extent on their spiritual convictions. Of course they wanted to save their country and mankind and to put an end to the unspeakable practice of mass murder, but they were equally or perhaps even more concerned with saving their own souls.

Stauffenberg, on the other hand, considered the oath of loyalty to have been invalidated countless times. His religious and ethical beliefs led him to the conclusion that it was his duty to eliminate Hitler and the murderous regime by any means possible. His friends recalled that in the days and weeks preceding the assassination attempt he liked to recite Stefan George's poem "The Antichrist," which speaks in broad, phantasmagoric images about the chaotic confusion of senses and reason that ushers in and accompanies the Antichrist's ascension. Although Stauffenberg was a great admirer of George, he always had an eye for simpler, rougher truths, and he led the debate within the resistance back to the political realm where it really belonged. Germans found themselves in a position, he argued, where they must inevitably commit some crime—either of commission or of omission. A few days before July 20 he added: "It's time now for something to be done. He who has the courage to act must know that he will probably go down in German history as a traitor. But if he fails to act, he will be a traitor before his own conscience."[7]

■ ■ ■

Speed was of the essence, although no longer just for military reasons. The so-called western solution, which called for the withdrawal of all German forces from France so as to strengthen the defense against the Soviets in the East, raised unrealistic hopes for Germany's strategic situation. Goerdeler, for one, volunteered to go to France, possibly accompanied by Beck, and use his talents of persuasion to convince the German commanders there to offer Eisenhower a truce and open the front, allowing the Western Allies to pour into the heart of Germany. Goerdeler envisioned an unconditional surrender to the Western Allies as not only saving the country from the advance of the Red Army but, more important, forestalling what he later called the "ill-starred assassination attempt." This, as it turned out, would be the last political proposal of Goerdeler's life.[8] Stauffenberg, too, had pondered the plan and, though tempted, discarded it as impracticable. Beck also distanced himself from any such endeavor. Hopes for a negotiated peace therefore faded to a faint glimmer, which was completely obliterated when Otto John, a lawyer who worked for Lufthansa, reported from Madrid on July 11 that the British ambassador had reiterated that hostilities would end only with simultaneous and unconditional surrender on all fronts. There was no avoiding total military disaster.

A far greater impetus to immediate action was the conspirators' concern about being discovered. Their ever-widening circle could not escape detection by the Gestapo forever. Furthermore, Leuschner, Kaiser, and Max Habermann, the president of the German Office Workers' Association, had been busy building an "invisible network" of opposition cells throughout Germany to provide broader support for the coup, which was being staged largely "from above." As soon as the new government was installed, these cells were to whip up the public support and cooperation that would be essential to its success.

Trade union leader Jakob Kaiser used his old connections to create small resistance cells throughout Germany beginning in 1943. Following Hitler's assassination these cells were to begin immediately mobilizing support among the general population for the new government. Kaiser was one of the few people involved in the coup attempt who managed to escape in the summer of 1944 and remain undetected.

He is shown here in a wanted poster issued by the Gestapo in 1939.

But these preparations also increased the number of people who were initiated into the conspiracy.

On top of this, in June news of the death sentences pronounced for Nikolaus von Halem, Mumm von Schwarzenstein, Otto Kiep, and other members of the Solf Circle had filtered down. At the same time the Gestapo arrested Colonel Wilhelm Staehle, a close contact of Goerdeler's. In early July Leber and Reichwein were arrested. No one could be sure how much police interrogators managed to pry out of them, but everyone knew, as a number of diarists noted, that the air in Berlin was thick with furtive confidences and hushed but unambiguous understandings. The nervous strain of all the months of waiting began to take its toll. Military Intelligence captain Ludwig Gehre, for instance, panicked and threatened "to blow that whole nest on Bendlerstrasse sky-high" if he fell into the hands of the Gestapo. Stauffenberg was under enormous pressure to move quickly, but it was above all the arrest of Leber that motivated him to take action. "I'll get him out. I'll get him out," Stauffenberg assured those around him on numerous occasions, and he also wrote Frau Leber saying, "We know where our duty lies."[9]

On July 11 Stauffenberg was once again at Führer headquarters on the Obersalzberg and once again he was carrying a bomb. He had summoned Goerdeler to Berlin to wait at the ready and had also informed others, including Witzleben, General Hoepner, Yorck, Count Helldorf, and a number of young officers in the Ninth Potsdam Reserve Battalion. Nevertheless, this day had the feel of a test run because many preparations that would have been necessary for the coup that was to follow the assassination were left undone. Furthermore, Himmler failed to show up yet again.

Stauffenberg's patience was wearing thin. Just before the conference was to begin, he asked Stieff, "My God, shouldn't we do it?" But Stieff pointed out Himmler's absence, thereby imposing, perhaps unwittingly, another difficult condition on an assassination attempt that he himself was still not prepared to carry out. In the end Stauffenberg abandoned his plan and decided not to detonate the bomb he had taken along. When the news reached Berlin, Goerdeler commented, "half laughing and half crying, 'They'll never do it!' "[10]

Three days later, Stauffenberg was ordered to report for another meeting, on July 15, this time at the Wolf's Lair, where Hitler had returned even though—or perhaps because—Russian forces were now only about sixty miles from the East Prussian border. Stauffenberg used the intervening time to review some of the technical and personnel details that would be crucial to the success of the coup. An agreement had been reached with General Erich Fellgiebel, the chief army signal officer, to interrupt signal traffic to and from Hitler's headquarters at a given moment. But Fellgiebel had pointed out on several occasions that little could be done in advance because although there was a central communications center, the army, the air force, the SS, and the Foreign Office each had their own signal lines. In addition, care would have to be taken not to cut off signals to and from the troops at the front. Thus, Fellgiebel maintained, Führer headquarters could only be isolated for a limited period, everything depended, he said, on doing exactly the right thing at exactly the right time. Meanwhile, however, improvements were to be made in communications with the liaison officers in the military districts, whose cooperation would be so essential to Operation Valkyrie; the preparedness of the army units in the Berlin area to take fast action had to be ensured; and numerous other aspects of mobilization, which were largely in Olbricht's hands, needed to be clarified. The final problem facing Stauffenberg was how to handle the pliers for igniting the bomb, which had to be specially constructed for him because of his mutilated hand.

The statements to be made to the public were also checked again. A number of versions are still extant, all of them rough drafts or working copies that contain repetitions and contradictions. Apparently the conspirators never managed to produce a text acceptable to everyone. One proclamation came from Goerdeler, who evidently drafted it in concert with Tresckow and the lawyer Josef Wirmer. Leber and Reichwein produced another, and Beck a third, which was specifically addressed to the troops. Stauffenberg also drafted a proclamation, which was discussed and amended on a number of occasions within his circle of friends. The original text did not survive the war, but his close friend Rudolf Fahrner wrote a short summary from memory in August 1945.

According to Fahrner, Stauffenberg's statement began by informing the German people "without further explanation that . . . Adolf Hitler was dead. Then came a few sentences condemning the party leaders," whose behavior had created "the need and duty to intervene." The head of the transitional government (whose name Fahrner never learned) provided "assurances that he and those who had placed themselves at his disposal wanted nothing for themselves. The nation would be summoned as soon as possible to freely determine the future constitution of the state, which would be new and innovative. The head of the transitional government," Fahrner wrote, "swore on behalf of himself and his colleagues to act in strict and complete accordance with the law and neither to do nor to tolerate anything that contravened divine or human justice. In return he demanded unconditional obedience for the duration of his government. It was then proclaimed that crimes and unlawful acts committed under party rule would have to be thoroughly atoned for, but no one would be persecuted for his political convictions. This was followed by an announcement that the transitional government would do everything in its power to reach a truce with the enemy as soon as

*Family connections contributed to the
creation and cohesion of the resistance.
Cäsar von Hofacker was a cousin of the
Stauffenberg brothers. While on the staff
of General Carl-Heinrich von
Stülpnagel, the military commander in
France, Hofacker became the chief
advocate of a military putsch in Paris.
He was arrested shortly after July 20. In
the ensuing interrogations he expressed
his view of Hitler in such resolute terms
that even the SS interrogators accorded
him a grudging admiration. He was
hanged on December 20, 1944, in
Plötzensee prison.*

possible" and that this could not be achieved "without great loss and sacrifice."[11]

On the evening of his return from the July 11 meeting at Berchtesgaden, Stauffenberg had met with his cousin Cäsar von Hofacker, who was on Stülpnagel's staff in Paris, to orchestrate plans for the coup. Hofacker informed him that Field Marshals Hans von Kluge, who had recently been named commander in chief in the West, and Erwin Rommel, the chief of Army Group B, had both said that Allied superiority, especially in the air, was so great that the front could be held for only two or three more weeks at best. The troops were "withering" under the incessant onslaught. Stülpnagel was most willing to assume an active part in the coup, while Kluge remained as coy as ever and Rommel basically kept his distance. Rommel had endured a tense confrontation with Hitler one month earlier at the Wolf Gorge II headquarters near Margival, north of Soissons, incurring Hitler's wrath by calling attention to the Allies' vast material advantage and advising that the war be ended. But Rommel was not prepared to resort to violence. A few days later he drafted an "ultimatum" telegram to the Führer, in which he begged him to draw "the political consequences" of the imminent collapse of the western front; but he

The conspirators never succeeded in winning Erwin Rommel (right) to their cause. He was not an opponent of the regime, but he thought that the military situation on the western front was hopeless and he seemed determined to open the front to the Allies in defiance of Hitler's orders. He has become associated with the resistance because of his forced suicide, but the connection is more legendary than real.

Above: Rommel with his chief of staff, Major General Hans Speidel, on July 16, 1944, one day before he was gravely injured in a strafing attack near the front in France.

was still unwilling to go any further. It remains an open question whether Rommel would ever have joined the opposition. The growing chasm between him and the conspirators in Berlin is apparent in the fact that he allowed his chief of general staff, Hans Speidel, to persuade him to remove the word *political* from his telegram before sending it, so as not to "annoy" the Führer unnecessarily.[12]

When Stauffenberg flew to Rastenburg in the early morning of July 15, along with Fromm and Captain Friedrich Karl Klausing, the coup was more thoroughly planned and the circle of supporters wider than four days earlier. Stauffenberg and Olbricht's determination to take the plunge that day is clearly evident in Olbricht's decision to issue the Valkyrie alert to the guard battalion and the army schools around Berlin at around eleven o'clock, or two hours before the earliest possible assassination attempt. In so doing, he risked squandering the only opportunity he would have to act on his own authority. Moreover, Stauffenberg had apparently abandoned his insistence that the attack be carried out only if Himmler was present.

Immediately on arriving at Rastenburg, however, Stauffenberg encountered Fellgiebel and Stieff, both of whom were adamant that the attack be canceled because of Himmler's absence. They also told Stauffenberg that Quartermaster General Eduard Wagner had been most definite the previous evening that the assassination ought only to be carried out "if the Reichsführer-SS is present." Both Olbricht's decision to issue the Valkyrie alert and Stauffenberg's evident exasperation with his own hesitation on July 11 seem to indicate, though, that this time Stauffenberg was determined to overcome any such objections.

But "it all came to nothing again today," Stauffenberg was forced to admit to Klausing after the briefing as they headed for dinner in Keitel's special train. According to one version of events, Stieff prevented the attack by removing the briefcase with the bomb while Stauffenberg was out of the conference room making a telephone call to army headquarters in Berlin. According to another version, Stauffenberg himself wavered, worrying that Stieff, Wagner, and Fellgiebel's vehement insistence that the attack not be carried out amounted to an abrogation of their agreement to participate. All that Stauffenberg ever said on the subject was that, to his surprise, "a meeting was called at which he himself had to give a report, and thus he never had an opportunity to carry out the assassination," his brother Berthold recalled.[13]

The real reasons the attack of July 15 was called off can no longer be determined with any certainty. Whatever they were, though, this failure highlighted the resistance's most serious deficiency. There is no doubting the moral integrity of the conspirators, their hatred of the Nazi regime, and their horror at the atrocities committed in Germany's name. But the distance between outrage and action is great. In his telephone call to Berlin, where Witzleben, Hoepner, Olbricht, Mertz von Quirnheim, Hansen, Haeften, and many others were gathered, Stauffenberg, faced with the opposition of Stieff, Wagner, and Fellgiebel to an attack that would not also kill Himmler, apparently intended to ensure that his fellow conspirators were still with him and

On July 15, 1944, Stauffenberg took a bomb into Führer headquarters in Rastenburg, East Prussia. Various circumstances, however, prevented him from carrying out the attack. The above photograph, taken that day, shows Stauffenberg (far left) with Hitler and Field Marshal Wilhelm Keitel (right).

to win a consensus for proceeding despite Himmler's absence. After a half hour of dithering, which wasted precious time and demonstrated to the impatient Stauffenberg how much his fellow conspirators relished endless discussion and debate, the answer came back that the majority of those assembled wanted to postpone the attempt. None of them, apart from Mertz von Quirnheim, seems to have appreciated the traumatic effect their response had on Stauffenberg. That evening Mertz spoke to his wife about the "deeply depressing feeling . . . of finding yourself all alone at a moment when great courage and determination are required to succeed." Of the abortive efforts to bring the bomb to Hitler one conspirator noted that for the third time in just a few days "Stauffenberg has gone down that terrible road in vain."[14]

According to one account, the news that the attack had been postponed once again eased the tension at army headquarters on Bendlerstrasse and gave rise "to an almost euphoric mood." This report may not be reliable, however, particularly with regard to General Olbricht. He knew only too well what consequences might attend his unauthorized issuance of the Valkyrie orders in Fromm's absence.[15] Olbricht departed at once to cancel the untimely alert. He drove to the affected units in Potsdam and Glienicke, and, concealing his involvement, expressed his "particular appreciation" to General Otto Hitzfeld, the commander of the Döberitz infantry school, who was partially initiated into the conspiracy. He also made note of the fact that the new commander of the Krampnitz panzer school, Colonel Wolfgang Glaesemer, probably could not be won over to the cause, and rescinded the alert.

The next evening Stauffenberg met for the last time with his closest friends. Gathered together at the house on Tristanstrasse in the Wannsee district of Berlin where he lived with his brother Berthold were Ulrich Schwerin von Schwanenfeld, Peter Yorck von Wartenburg, Fritz-Dietlof von der Schulenburg, Adam von Trott zu Solz, Cäsar von Hofacker, Albrecht Mertz von Quirnheim, and Georg Hansen. Once again they discussed ways of proceeding: the "western solution," outlined above, and the "Berlin solution," according to which the central signals system would be seized for twenty-four hours and Hitler's headquarters outmaneuvered by a number of irre-

Helmuth Stieff (center), *chief of the army organizational section, was deeply disturbed by SS atrocities during the Polish campaign. Since he was one of the few senior officers who had access to Hitler, Tresckow pressured him to undertake the assassination. Stieff finally agreed in August 1943. Soon thereafter, however, he again began to waver and turned down all further requests.*

Responding to the heavy casualties suffered by the Germans during the winter of 1942 outside Moscow, he wrote to his wife, "We have so laden ourselves with guilt—for we are all responsible—that I believe the punishment we are beginning to suffer is justified atonement for all the disgraceful things that we Germans have done or tolerated in the last few years."

This picture was taken on July 7, 1944, during the presentation of new field uniforms at Schloss Klessheim, near Salzburg. From left in the first row: *Hitler, Albert Speer, and Stieff.*

versible withdrawals of German forces. Both these ideas were rejected, as was the idea discussed occasionally of ending the war by means of a direct agreement between the commanders in chief of the various national armies, speaking as "one soldier to another" and circumventing governments entirely.

All these solutions ran aground on the hard fact that no progress

Stauffenberg's successor as chief of staff to General Olbricht was Colonel Albrecht Mertz von Quirnheim (right, with Stauffenberg). Unhappy at first to be transferred from the front to a desk job, he was overjoyed to discover that he could join forces with Stauffenberg and therefore with the conspiracy against Hitler. As one of the leading figures in the attempted coup, he was among those executed on the night of July 20 in the courtyard of army headquarters.

could be made in any of these directions—either with the Allies or with the German commanders—so long as Hitler was alive. The Allies had absolutely no intention of negotiating with him and the commanders little stomach for openly opposing him. The only option left, the conspirators on Tristanstrasse concluded, was indeed assassination. There is some indication that Stauffenberg was eager to hold this lengthy discussion, which stretched well into the night, in order to allay once and for all both his own qualms about doing "the dirty deed" and those of so many others. It was now clearly too late for the conspirators to turn the assassination of Hitler to advantage and negotiate better political terms with the Allies. All that remained was the possibility of reducing the number of war victims and sparing Germany some measure of humiliation by purging itself of the Nazis. In a subsequent conversation with Beck, Stauffenberg reviewed what had gone wrong on July 15 and pledged that "the next time he would act, come what may."[16]

. . .

As always happened when things were heading toward a climax, more bad news arrived—of precisely the kind that had repeatedly sapped the conspirators' resolve in the past. First, while returning from the front Field Marshal Rommel was severely injured when his car was strafed by an airplane. To be sure, he had never really figured in the plans for a coup, but when he had been asked the previous day how he would react if Hitler rejected his "ultimatum," he had coolly replied that he would "throw open the western front," thereby fueling the opposition's lingering hope of unilaterally putting a stop to the fighting on that front.[17] Furthermore, Rommel was extremely popular with the general public, and though he was certainly not an enemy of the regime, the insurgents hoped that he might join them if the circumstances were right. Rommel's participation would have helped prevent the creation of another stab-in-the-back legend, a concern that had so preoccupied the conspirators.

In the midst of all the other bad news, however, the loss of Rommel was scarcely noticed. Much more disturbing to the conspirators was a tip from Arthur Nebe that Goerdeler had been named by Wilhelm Staehle and was about to be arrested. Stauffenberg responded to the information by asking Goerdeler "to disappear as quickly as possible and not endanger the entire conspiracy by running around Berlin making telephone calls." Goerdeler, already bitter at having been pushed about for months and feeling increasingly squeezed to the periphery of the conspiracy, took this as another attempt to belittle him, especially since Stauffenberg did not mention that he had been summoned to report to Hitler's headquarters on July 20, just two days hence. Nevertheless, Stauffenberg did ask Goerdeler to remain ready for a coup, and Goerdeler let it be known that his hiding place over the next few days would the estate of his friend Baron Kraft von Palombini in Rahnisdorf.[18]

Possibly even more disconcerting was a warning delivered to Stauffenberg on July 18 by Lieutenant Commander Alfred Kranzfelder: a rumor was circulating in Berlin, Kranzfelder reported, that "Führer headquarters would be blown sky-high that very week." It seems that a young Hungarian nobleman had picked up this piece of information at the Potsdam home of the widow of General von Bredow, one of those murdered in the Röhm putsch. Later it turned out that the source was none other than one of the Bredow daughters, who was on friendly terms with Werner von Haeften, and it was reasonable to conclude that the information had thus far been confined to the Bredow household and had not actually spread to Berlin. But Schulenburg also informed the conspirators that day that "two men had been inquiring about him in his neighborhood" and that he did not think they were harmless visitors.[19]

These and other tips made Stauffenberg feel even more strongly that he had to act immediately. He felt driven as well—perhaps even more—by his chagrin at the delays and at the lack of resolve over the previous weeks. His exhaustion and his raw nerves, mentioned in various accounts, undoubtedly added to his sense of urgency. One observer spoke, with poetic overtones, of the "dark shadow" that seemed to have enveloped him since June. In any case, as Stauffenberg now said to Kranzfelder, "There's no choice now; we've crossed the Rubicon."[20]

The next day, July 19, was spent on preparations. By about noon Olbricht's and Stauffenberg's staffs were busy alerting Witzleben, Hoepner, Berlin city commandant Paul von Hase, Colonel Jäger, Major Ludwig von Leonrod, and the large number of other officers who had roles to play. In the early evening Stauffenberg called on Quartermaster General Wagner in Zossen, hoping perhaps to straighten out the difference of opinion that had arisen on July 15. At the end of their discussion Wagner arranged for a special airplane to be placed at

Stauffenberg's disposal for the return flight from Rastenburg. After Stauffenberg had taken his leave Wagner informed Stieff of the preparations.

Early on the morning of July 20 Wagner greeted Lieutenant Colonel Bernhard Klamroth by asking, "What are we going to do if the assassination really *is* today?"[21] Rarely had the conspirators' lack of confidence been so clearly expressed as in this naive-sounding question; it was almost as if an actual assassination was the last thing they expected. Perhaps the sense, reinforced over the years, that whatever they touched would inevitably turn to dust lent all their plans a noncommittal air, which could not help but affect their determination to act. Just a few hours later this ingrained skepticism would have fatal consequences.

First, however, the notion that nothing ever happened as a result of their efforts was about to be shattered. Wagner's query suggests he suddenly realized that Stauffenberg had brought to the resistance an unwavering determination to carry out the plot. One might wonder, as the historian Peter Hoffmann has, why Stieff, Wagner, Meichssner, Fellgiebel, and other officers who had access to Hitler palmed the assassination attempt off on Stauffenberg, whose physical dexterity was limited and whose absence from Berlin would seriously jeopardize the coup following the assassination. In all likelihood, they hadn't fully understood that they were now irrevocably implicated, and that if Stauffenberg failed their own ruin was assured as well.

All the conspirators wrestled with their doubts that the coup would be successful. Hofacker said he felt that the chances were very small, as did Schulenburg and Berthold von Stauffenberg. Tresckow stated that the attempt would "very likely go awry," and Beck expressed similar sentiments. Even Stauffenberg was apparently skeptical and told a young officer in early July that "it was questionable whether it would succeed." In his next breath he revealed how far he had moved from hopes of achieving any far-reaching aims, a feeling shared and in many cases expressed by his close friends. "But even worse than failure," Stauffenberg continued, "is to yield to shame and coercion without a struggle."[22] This was Stauffenberg's only certainty. Everything else that followed would be a "leap in the dark."[23]

9

JULY 20, 1944

Stauffenberg flew into the Rastenburg airfield shortly after 10:00 a.m. with Werner von Haeften and Helmuth Stieff, who had boarded the flight in Zossen. He immediately headed for the officers' mess in Restricted Area II, carrying in his briefcase only the papers he needed for the reports he was expected to give. Haeften, meanwhile, carried the two bombs in his briefcase and accompanied Stieff to OKH headquarters. The plans called for Haeften and Stauffenberg to meet shortly before the briefing in the Wolf's Lair to exchange briefcases.

At around eleven o'clock Stauffenberg was summoned by the chief of army staff, General Walther Buhle, and after a short meeting they proceeded together to a conference with General Keitel in the OKW bunker in Restricted Area I. Here Stauffenberg learned that on account of a visit by Mussolini what was to have been a noon briefing with Hitler had been put back half an hour to twelve-thirty. Immediately following the conference with Keitel, Stauffenberg asked the general's aide, Major Ernst John von Freyend, to show him to a room where he could wash up and change his shirt—July 20 was a hot day.

As Keitel and the other officers headed toward the briefing barracks, Stauffenberg met Haeften in the corridor. Together they withdrew into the lounge in Keitel's bunker, where Stauffenberg set about installing and arming a fuse in the first bomb. He had barely begun, however, when a most unfortunately timed telephone call came from

Werner von Haeften (above) accompanied Stauffenberg to the Führer's Wolf's Lair headquarters in Rastenburg on July 20, 1944. Haeften was with Stauffenberg in the lounge of Field Marshal Wilhelm Keitel's bunker when he armed the bomb that would explode in the conference room. Having returned to Berlin with Stauffenberg, Haeften was arrested that evening and condemned to death. He was shot in the courtyard of army headquarters.

General Fellgiebel, who asked to speak with Stauffenberg on urgent business. Freyend sent Platoon Sergeant Werner Vogel back to the bunker to urge Stauffenberg to hurry.

As Vogel entered the lounge, he saw the two officers stowing something into one of the briefcases. He informed them of the call, adding that the others were waiting for them outside. Meanwhile Freyend shouted from the entrance, "Stauffenberg, please come along!" With Vogel standing in the doorway, Stauffenberg closed the briefcase as swiftly as possible while Haeften swept up the papers that were lying around and stuffed them into the other briefcase.

Fellgiebel's telephone call and the intrusion of Sergeant Vogel may well have determined the course of history, for it is likely that they prevented Stauffenberg from arming the fuse on the second package of explosives. No one knows for certain why Stauffenberg did not place the second bomb in his briefcase alongside the one whose timer had already been activated, since the explosion of one would surely have set off the other as well. Some have claimed that both charges would have been too bulky and heavy to carry into the briefing room unobtrusively. This argument is hardly convincing, however, as the bombs weighed only about two pounds each, and Haeften had carried them both around in his briefcase earlier without any problems.

Stauffenberg was certainly nervous, and Vogel's sudden appearance in the room must have given him a fright, but the most probable explanation for his bringing only the one bomb is that he was not fully aware of how such explosives work. Believing that a single bomb would suffice, he probably did not adequately consider the cumulative effect of two bombs. It may be that the second charge was only taken along as an alternative in the event that something went wrong, especially since the two timers were set differently, one for ten minutes and the other for thirty. What is clear, according to all experts, is that inclusion of the second charge, even without a detonator, would have magnified the power of the blast not twofold but many times, killing everyone in the room outright.[1]

Together with General Buhle and Major Freyend, Stauffenberg hurried out of the OKW bunker, briefcase in hand. They crossed the three hundred and fifty yards to the wooden briefing barracks, which lay behind a high wire fence in the innermost security zone, the so-called Führer Restricted Area. After declining for the second time Freyend's offer to carry his briefcase, Stauffenberg finally turned it over to him at the entrance to the barracks, asking at the same time to be "seated as close as possible to the Führer" so that he could "catch everything" in preparation for his report.

In the conference room the briefing was already under way, with General Adolf Heusinger reporting on the eastern front. Keitel announced that Stauffenberg would be giving a report, and Hitler shook the colonel's hand "wordlessly, but with his usual scrutinizing look." Freyend placed the briefcase near Heusinger and his assistant Colonel Brandt, who were both standing to Hitler's right. Despite his efforts to edge closer to Hitler, Stauffenberg could only find a place at the corner of the table; his briefcase remained on the far side of the massive table leg, where Freyend had placed it. Shortly thereafter, Stauffenberg left the room whispering something indistinctly, as if he had an important task to attend to.

Once outside the barracks, he went back the way he had come, turning off before Keitel's bunker and heading toward the Wehrmacht adjutant building to find out where Haeften was waiting with the car. In the signals officer's room he found not only Haeften but Fellgiebel as well: as they stepped outside, Hitler was already asking for the colonel, and an irritated General Buhle set out to look for him. It was just after 12:40.

Suddenly, as witnesses later recounted, a deafening crack shattered the midday quiet, and a bluish-yellow flame rocketed skyward. Stauffenberg gave a violent start and simply shook his head when Fellgiebel asked with feigned innocence what the noise could possibly be. Lieutenant Colonel Ludolf Gerhard Sander hurried over to the two men to reassure them that it was common for "someone to fire off a round or for one of the mines to go off." Meanwhile, a dark plume of smoke rose and hung in the air over the wreckage of the briefing barracks. Shards of glass, wood, and fiberboard swirled about, and scorched pieces of paper and insulation rained down. The quiet that had suddenly descended was broken once again, this time by the sound of voices calling for doctors. Stauffenberg and Haeften climbed into the waiting car and ordered the driver to take them to the airfield. As they did so, a body covered by Hitler's cloak was carried from the barracks on a stretcher, leading them to conclude that the Führer was dead.[2]

When the bomb exploded, twenty-four people were in the conference room. All were hurled to the ground, some with their hair in flames. Window mullions and sashes flew through the room. Hitler had just leaned far over the table to examine a position that Heus-

When Benito Mussolini, who had been overthrown a year earlier, visited Hitler at the Wolf's Lair in the early afternoon of July 20, 1944, he was shown the devastated barracks from which his host had been saved as if by "a miracle."

inger was pointing out on the map when his chair was torn out from under him. His clothing, like that of all the others, was shredded; his trousers hung in ribbons down his legs. The great oak table had collapsed, its top blown to pieces. The first sound to be heard amid all the smoke and devastation was Keitel's voice shouting, "Where is the Führer?" As Hitler stumbled to his feet, Keitel flew to him, taking him in his arms and crying, "My Führer, you're alive, you're alive!"[3] At this point, Hitler's aide Julius Schaub and his valet, Heinz Linge, appeared and led the Führer away to his nearby quarters.

In the meantime Stauffenberg and Haeften had reached the Restricted Area I guardhouse. The lieutenant in charge, having seen and heard the explosion, had already taken the initiative of ordering the barrier lowered, but recognizing the striking figure of Stauffenberg, he allowed the car to pass after a brief pause. More difficulty was encountered at the outer guardhouse on the way to the airfield. By this time an alarm had been raised and all entry and exit forbidden. The staff sergeant on duty was not about to be intimidated by Stauffenberg's commanding bearing, and for a moment everything seemed to hang in the balance. Thinking fast, Stauffenberg demanded to speak by telephone to the commandant of Führer headquarters, Lieutenant Colonel Gustav Streve, with whom he had a lunch appointment. Fortunately, he could only reach Streve's deputy, Captain Leonhard von Möllendorff, who did not yet know why the alarm had been issued and therefore ordered the staff sergeant to allow Stauffenberg to pass. Halfway to the airfield, Haeften tossed the second package of explosives from the open vehicle. At about 1:00 p.m. the car reached the waiting airplane, and within minutes the conspirators took off for Berlin.

■　■　■

At just about this point, news of the blast reached army headquarters on Bendlerstrasse. Fellgiebel had taken steps about an hour earlier to block all signal traffic to and from both headquarters in Rastenburg, and he now received confirmation by telephone that this had been done. While the communications blackout was certainly part of the conspirators' plan, it would also have been a plausible reaction to the hastily issued instructions from Hitler's staff that no news of the attack be allowed to reach the public. As a result, suspicion did not immediately fall on Fellgiebel, who soon had the amplification stations in Lötzen, Insterburg, and Rastenburg shut down as well. As Fellgiebel had frequently pointed out, however, it was technically impossible to cut the headquarters area off completely from the outside world.

As a result, Fellgiebel himself managed to put through a telephone call to the conspirators' base of operations on Bendlerstrasse. But this call only caused more problems because the conspirators were faced with a situation that apparently none of them had foreseen and for which they had no code words: the bomb had gone off but Hitler had survived.

For the second time that day, then, General Fellgiebel found himself in a position to change the course of history. He basically had two options open to him. He could hide from Bendlerstrasse the fact that Hitler was alive and do everything possible to maintain the communications blackout of the Wolf's Lair, resorting to violence if necessary. However hopeless it might seem, this ploy would help heighten the general confusion and at least keep the coup attempt going. The personal risk he would run by taking this course was not particularly great, as his fate would be sealed in any case if the coup failed. On the other hand, he could tell Bendlerstrasse that Hitler had survived and try to abort the coup attempt, at least the communications component, before it had really gotten under way. After all, he understood better than anyone else the impossibility of maintaining a communications blackout under these circumstances.

In the end, however, Fellgiebel hit on a third course. He informed his signal corps chief of staff at Bendlerstrasse, General Fritz Thiele, a fellow conspirator, that the assassination had failed but gave him to understand that the coup should proceed nevertheless. He thus blew away the elaborate smoke screen shrouding the attempt to seize power and revealed it as a straightforward revolt. According to Stauffenberg's biographer Christian Müller this was a "major psychological blunder." By informing Bendlerstrasse of the true state of affairs, Fellgiebel left it to the weak-willed group assembled there to decide what to do, at least until Stauffenberg's arrival.[4] Shortly after 3:00 p.m., Fellgiebel's order blocking signal traffic was rescinded by Himmler, who had been summoned to Rastenburg, and Hitler began to swing into action, inquiring how soon it would be technically possible for him to address the German people directly over all radio stations in the Reich.

Meanwhile the hunt for the would be assassin was launched. Initial suspicions fell on the construction workers employed at Führer headquarters. But then Sergeant Arthur Adam came forward to say that he had seen Stauffenberg leave the briefing barracks before the explosion without his briefcase, his cap, or his belt, but little attention was paid to this information at first. Lieutenant Colonel Sander even shouted at Adam that if he really harbored "such monstrous suspicions about so distinguished an officer" he should go directly to the

Security Service (SD).[5] Instead, Adam approached Martin Bormann, who took him to see Hitler. One piece of evidence quickly led to the next, leaving little doubt among the Führer's confederates that Stauffenberg was the culprit. They did not yet realize, however, the enormity of the conspiracy or that a coup d'état was under way in Berlin.

Shortly after hearing of the attack, Himmler had ordered the head of the Reich Security Headquarters (RSHA), Ernst Kaltenbrunner, and the superintendent of police, Bernd Wehner, to fly from Berlin to Rastenburg to take over the political and technical investigation of the assassination attempt. When Wehner arrived at Berlin's Tempelhof airport, the plane was ready for takeoff. The waiting Kaltenbrunner, who was not privy to the latest information, stunned his companion by announcing, "The Führer is dead!" Before the superintendent could regain his composure, Kaltenbrunner asked calmly whether he might like to play a few games of skat to while away the time.[6]

■　■　■

Somewhere in the skies between Berlin and Rastenburg the two planes must have crossed paths. It is not difficult to imagine the emotions Stauffenberg must have been feeling or the questions racing through his mind, in contrast to the icy calm of his adversary in the other plane. Having succeeded in igniting a bomb at Hitler's feet—the event that had always been thought of as the "initial spark" that would touch off the great upheaval by which the entire Nazi regime would be overthrown—he now found himself condemned to more than two hours of anxious waiting. He could only pin his hopes on others: on Olbricht and Mertz, who alone held the levers of power; on reliable friends like Yorck, Hofacker, Schwerin, and Schulenburg, as well as on Jäger, Hoepner, Thiele, Hase, and many others, including the liaison officers in the military districts. He could only assume that orders would be followed unquestioningly down the chain of command—perhaps even with the acquiescence of General Fromm—after Olbricht issued the Valkyrie II code word.

The reality that awaited him was far different. As his plane neared Berlin, the coup had not advanced at all. Fellgiebel's indecisive and

rather vague message—"something terrible has happened: the Führer is alive"—left Thiele unsettled and confused. To clear his mind he
decided abruptly to go for a walk, apparently without bothering to
inform Olbricht, and for nearly two hours he was nowhere to be
found. Olbricht, too, had received a telephone call, probably around
2:00 p.m., from General Wagner in Zossen, and in view of the puz-
zling information from Rastenburg, they agreed not to act for the
time being. After all, Fellgiebel's message might have meant that the
bomb had failed to go off or that Stauffenberg had been discovered
and arrested, or that he was fleeing or that he had already been shot.
Just five days earlier, Olbricht had issued the Valkyrie orders prema-
turely, and he knew that any repetition of that fiasco was bound to be
fatal. This time, furthermore, in contrast to July 15, Fromm was present and would have to be dealt with.[7]

As a result, precious hours slipped away. Thiele returned around
3:15 p.m. and, after another conversation with Rastenburg, reported
that there had been an "explosion in the conference room" at Hitler's
headquarters, which had left "a large number of officers severely
wounded." He thought that his source at Rastenburg may have "implied between the lines" that the Führer was "seriously injured or
even dead." This was what prompted Olbricht and Mertz to decide
finally to take the decisive step of issuing the Valkyrie orders, on their
own initiative if necessary.[8] Shortly thereafter, Haeften telephoned
from the airport to announce that he and Stauffenberg had just
landed, the attack had been successful, and Hitler was dead. When
Hoepner suggested that the conspirators at Bendlerstrasse should
wait for Stauffenberg to arrive, Olbricht retorted indignantly that
there was no more time to lose. He got the deployment orders out of
the safe for Fromm to sign. Meanwhile, Mertz called the senior officers of the Army Office together and informed them that Hitler had
been assassinated. Beck would take over as head of state, he continued, while Field Marshal Witzleben would assume all executive functions of the commander in chief of the Wehrmacht. Major Harnack
was ordered to issue Valkyrie II to all military districts; to the city
commandant, General Paul von Hase; and to the army schools in and
around Berlin. It was shortly before 4:00 p.m.

Everything now depended on Fromm. But when Olbricht approached him to report that the Führer had been assassinated, and asked him to give the orders to implement Operation Valkyrie, Fromm hesitated at the very mention of the word. He had received an official reprimand from Keitel for the alert issued on July 15 and was worried lest he fall back out of favor with Hitler, having just returned to his good graces. He therefore telephoned Keitel to ask whether the rumors in Berlin about the death of the Führer were true. The OKW chief replied that an assassination attempt had been made but that Hitler had escaped with only minor injuries. Where exactly, he wanted to know, was Fromm's chief of staff, Colonel Stauffenberg? Fromm answered that the colonel had not yet returned, and he hung up. He decided simply to do nothing.

It is not clear whether Olbricht had already sent the orders for Valkyrie II out over the lines before he went to see Fromm. At this point he presumably still thought that Hitler was dead, and he had good reason to expect that Fromm could be won over. When he returned to his office to announce, "Fromm won't sign," he discovered that Mertz had plunged feverishly ahead, carrying the plans a step further. Although "Olbricht had once again grown hesitant," he was "stampeded" into continuing.[9] Captain Karl Klausing already had his orders to secure army headquarters; four young officers, Georg von Oppen, Ewald Heinrich von Kleist, Hans Fritzsche, and Ludwig von Hammerstein, had been summoned from the Esplanade Hotel to serve as adjutants; and Major Egbert Hayessen had already set off for the city commandant's offices. Olbricht now leapt in, helping to organize matters and speed them along. He contacted the other commanders who were privy to the coup and called General Wagner in Zossen and Field Marshal Kluge in La Roche-Guyon, while Klausing was asked to send off the teleprinter message that began: "The Führer Adolf Hitler is dead! A treacherous group of party leaders has attempted to exploit the situation by attacking our embattled soldiers from the rear in order to seize power for themselves!" Klausing finished typing and handed the message to the signal traffic chief, Lieutenant Georg Röhrig, but Röhrig immediately noticed that it did not contain the usual secrecy and priority codes. He chased after Klaus-

Three officers at the heart of the conspiracy. Major Egbert Hayessen (above, left) was the liaison officer between army headquarters on Bendlerstrasse and the city commandant's headquarters at 1 Unter den Linden. Captain Friedrich Karl Klausing (below) accompanied Stauffenberg to Führer headquarters on July 11 and 15, 1944, when the planned assassination attempts were aborted. Hans-Ulrich von Oertzen (above, right), who had served on Tresckow's staff for several years, tried in vain to win over the commanders of the Berlin military district. Arrested on July 21, he killed himself with two hand grenades. Klausing and Hayessen were arrested and sentenced to death by the People's Court in August 1944.

ing, reaching him at the end of the hall, and inquired whether the message should not have the highest secrecy rating. Without much thought, Klausing replied with a nervous "Yes, yes," a decision that would have enormous unforeseen consequences. For only four typists were available at Bendlerstrasse who were cleared to send secret teleprinter messages, and it took them close to three hours to transmit the text. Without the secrecy requirements, the messages could have been sent out at much greater speed over more than twenty teleprinter machines.

The first message had barely begun to be transmitted when Klausing reappeared in the traffic office with another. It consisted of a number of instructions that hinted at the true nature of Valkyrie. The new communiqué ordered not only that all important buildings and facilities be secured but also that all gauleiters, government ministers, prefects of police, senior SS and police officials, and heads of propaganda offices be arrested and that the concentration camps be seized without delay. Following an injunction to refrain from acts of revenge came the sentence that unmasked the real intentions of the conspirators: "The population must be made aware that we intend to desist from the arbitrary methods of the previous rulers."[10]

Since this message bore Fromm's name, the conscientious Olbricht felt obliged once again to go and seek the consent of the chief of the reserve army. Hitler was truly dead, he assured Fromm, informing him that therefore "we have issued the code word to launch internal disturbances." Fromm jumped to his feet. "What do you mean 'we'?" he bellowed indignantly. "Who gave the order?" he shouted, insisting that he was still the commander. Olbricht said that Mertz was responsible, and Fromm ordered that the colonel be brought to him immediately. When Mertz confirmed what he had done, Fromm replied, "Mertz, you are under arrest!"

On the way back to his office, Olbricht peered out through a window overlooking the courtyard and saw Stauffenberg's car pull up. It was 4:30 p.m., almost four hours after the explosion in the Wolf's Lair. Stauffenberg gave Olbricht a short, hurried report on the assassination, and the two men decided to return together to see Fromm. Stauffenberg insisted once again that Hitler was dead: he had witnessed the explosion himself and had seen Hitler being carried out on a stretcher. Fromm remarked that "someone in the Führer's entourage must have been involved," to which Stauffenberg coolly responded, "I did it."

Fromm was flabbergasted, or at least seemed to be. With mounting rage, he told Stauffenberg that Keitel had just assured him the Führer was alive, to which Stauffenberg replied that the field marshal was, as always, lying through his teeth. Unconvinced, Fromm asked Stauffenberg whether he had a pistol and, if so, whether he knew what to do with it at a moment like this. Stauffenberg said he did not have a pistol and in any case would do nothing of the sort, adding that the attack on Hitler was not the final goal but merely the first strike in a general insurrection. Unimpressed by this news, Fromm turned to Mertz von Quirnheim and ordered him to get a pistol. Mertz replied astutely that since Fromm had taken him into custody he could not carry out orders.

With mounting anger, Fromm now declared that Olbricht and Stauffenberg were under arrest as well. But as if he had been waiting for these words to be uttered, Olbricht turned the tables on the general by informing him that he was mistaken about the balance of power: it was up to them, not him, to make arrests. Fromm leapt up and rushed at Olbricht with clenched fists but Haeften, Kleist, and several officers from the map room next door separated the two and held Fromm off with a pistol. Resigned, Fromm announced, "Under the circumstances, I consider myself out of commission." He offered no further resistance and, having requested and received a bottle of cognac, prepared himself to be led away to the office of his aide, Captain Heinz-Ludwig Bartram.

In the meantime, Beck, Schwerin, Helldorf, Hoepner, Gisevius, and the chief administrative officer for the Potsdam district, Gottfried von Bismarck, had assembled in Olbricht's office, and Olbricht now told Hoepner that he was to assume Fromm's duties immediately. Ever the pedant, even in the midst of a coup, Hoepner demanded to have his appointment in writing. The formalities were being completed when Hoepner ran into Fromm in the hallway as he was being taken to his aide's office. Bowing slightly, Hoepner said that he regretted having to take over Fromm's office. The deposed general replied, "I'm sorry, Hoepner, but I can't go along with this. In my opinion, the Führer is not dead and you are making a mistake."[11]

It had by now became clear to those at the Wolf's Lair that the assassination attempt signaled the start of a general uprising. They could hardly fail to notice since, due to a switching error, telegram dispatches from army headquarters on Bendlerstrasse were arriving at Führer headquarters as well. By about 4:00 p.m. Hitler had named Reichsführer-SS Heinrich Himmler the new commander in chief of the reserve army. Soon thereafter, Keitel instructed the military districts not to obey the orders they were receiving from Bendlerstrasse. Hitler's counterattack was gathering momentum. As a result of Klausing's error in giving the orders the top-secret rating, some military districts even received counterinstructions from Führer headquarters before the original orders from Bendlerstrasse arrived, sowing great confusion at first. In Breslau, the military district commanders decided against a coup before they even knew it was under way. In Hamburg, party and SS officials went to the office of the district commander, General Wilhelm Wetzel, to drink sherry and vermouth, raise toasts, and swear that they were not about to shoot one another.

In all the bewilderment over conflicting reports, Beck declared that he did not "care what was being said, he did not even care what was true; for him, Hitler was dead," and he urged his fellow conspirators to adopt the same attitude lest they spread confusion in their own ranks. He had begun dictating an address for broadcast in which, anticipating a counterbroadcast, he argued that it "does not matter whether Hitler is dead or alive. A Führer who engenders such conflicts among his closest associates that it comes to an assassination attempt is morally dead."[12] The only chance that the conspirators still seemed to have was that the fictions they had invented would be widely believed. The key question was whether this makeshift justification would have enough force to insure that orders passed down the chain of command would be strictly obeyed. Anything less and the coup would not succeed.

That the course of events still depended on the courage and determination of a handful of officers could be seen on a number of occasions during that chaotic day. Among the outposts that received early warnings was that of the Berlin city commandant, General Paul von Hase. As Operation Valkyrie was launched, he called the head of the army ordnance school, Brigadier General Walter Bruns; the head of the army explosives school, Colonel Helmuth Schwierz; and the commander of the guard battalion, Major Otto Ernst Remer, to his headquarters at 1 Unter den Linden, where he gave them their orders. By 6:00 p.m. the Ministry of Propaganda had been cordoned off, two sentries had been posted in front of Goebbels's house, and Goebbels himself, having seen what was taking place on the street, had disappeared into a back room to get a few cyanide capsules.[13] Half an hour later the government quarter had also been surrounded by the guard battalion. Only the units from the ordnance school in the Berlin suburb of Treptow, which were supposed to occupy the city palace, were delayed, because their trucks did not arrive on schedule to transport them.

Elsewhere, too, things were going according to plan. Units of the elite Grossdeutschland reserve brigade stationed in Cottbus, near Berlin, occupied the radio stations and transmitters in Herzberg and Königs Wusterhausen and seized control of the local Nazi Party offices and SS barracks without encountering resistance. When news of Hitler's assassination reached Krampnitz, the senior officer at the post, Colonel Harald Momm, shouted, "Orderly! A bottle of champagne! The swine is dead!" Although there were some delays there, the Valkyrie units were finally mobilized. Those in Döberitz, too, were ready to go, and Major Friedrich Jakob had orders to seize the main broadcasting center on Masurenallee in Berlin, block all transmissions, and then rendezvous with a signal officer who would be dispatched by headquarters. Bendlerstrasse issued a list of targets to be seized, ranging from SS and party offices down to various ministries and finally the city administration; the explosives school contributed by forming thirty task forces of ten men each to help. Helldorf alerted the security police to be ready for a wave of arrests.

But from this point on, things began to go awry. Helldorf received no further instructions. Major Jakob succeeded in occupying the broadcasting center on Masurenallee, but the signal officer failed to appear because General Thiele had vanished. In his absence, Jakob relied for technical information on the station manager, who assured him that broadcasting had stopped when, in fact, it was continuing. Back on Bendlerstrasse, Beck urgently awaited news that the station had been occupied. The units that seized the Nauen and Tegel transmitters on the outskirts of Berlin had experiences similar to that at Masurenallee. At 5:42 p.m., and in quick succession thereafter, a series of communiqués was broadcast from Führer headquarters announcing the attack and the serious injuries suffered by Schmundt, Brandt, and the stenographer, Berger, but also reporting that Hitler himself had escaped injury and "resumed his work" immediately.

At the conspiracy's headquarters on Bendlerstrasse, signs of uncertainty were beginning to appear. When SS Oberführer Humbert Pifrader arrived, on Himmler's orders, at 5:00 p.m., demanding to see Stauffenberg, he was arrested with no fuss. But when the commander of the Berlin military district, General Kortzfleisch, appeared shortly thereafter and was similarly arrested after flatly refusing to join the coup, he was belligerent, roaring at Hammerstein, who was standing guard over him, that he wanted to know to whom exactly he had sworn his oath of loyalty. Kortzfleisch eventually calmed down and complained that he just wasn't prepared to participate in a coup; he had always considered himself nothing but a soldier and was now "interested only in one thing: going home and pulling weeds in my garden." The conspirators replaced him with General Karl von Thüngen, but even the new man hesitated, feeling that the situation was still far too murky. He lingered for a long time at Bendlerstrasse talking things over before finally proceeding reluctantly to his command post on Hohenzollerndamm, where the chief of staff, General Otto Herfurth, ruminated over the onerous decisions that had fallen to him. Herfuth repeatedly requested more information and delayed the implementation of the orders he was receiving. Finally he sank down onto his field cot and declared himself ill.[14]

Although the inner circle of conspirators still held firm, Major Remer, who commanded a guard battalion in Berlin, had figured out by this time that he was risking his neck. Urged on by a suspicious propaganda officer, but in defiance of explicit orders from his superior officer, General Hase, he decided to seek the advice of Goebbels. Remer arrived at Goebbels's apartment at about 7:00 p.m. to find Major Martin Korff of the explosives school attempting to arrest Goebbels. The minister was clever enough to recognize that Remer felt torn between his oath of allegiance and his orders, and he quickly telephoned Führer headquarters in Rastenburg.

Hitler himself came on the line and asked Remer if he recognized his voice. When Remer said he did, the Führer conferred on him plenary powers to put down the uprising. Remer scarcely had time to think. Overwhelmed by the discovery that Hitler was still alive and by the magnitude of his new responsibilities, he immediately removed the cordon that had been set up around the government quarter and gradually took command of the units and task forces already in the city center and those arriving there. When Colonel Jäger came to take Goebbels away, the sentries on duty already had orders to protect the minister. The uprising had begun to collapse.

Those conspirators who had insisted that killing Hitler was the crucial prerequisite for a coup were proved right, though now it was too late. The decisive importance of the Führer was most powerfully evinced by Remer's actions but could also be seen in the reactions of Fromm, Thüngen, Herfurth, and others and in the endless, paralyzing debates that took place in many barracks after the initial radio broadcasts reported Hitler as alive. The fact that Olbricht and Stauffenberg were issuing orders that exceeded their authority—a fact certainly noted with suspicion by some officers—did not itself jeopardize the coup, because the Wehrmacht command structure was confusing to begin with and, in any case, all power was finally centralized in the hands of Adolf Hitler. It did, however, mean the chain of command would not function automatically.

But by this time it was not just the chain of command that was coming apart. Already that afternoon Fellgiebel had despondently refused to speak with Olbricht, informing him in a message that "there's no reason for all that anymore." Perhaps Fellgiebel realized what a horrendous error he had made in reporting that the assassination had failed. He saw that the only chance the conspirators had ever really possessed was to forge ahead single-mindedly and to play the one card they had held from the outset. In any case, on hearing that Thiele had disappeared (it later turned out that he had gone to see Walter Schellenberg at Reich Security Headquarters), Fellgiebel remarked that Thiele was "making a big mistake if he thinks he can extricate himself like this."[15] Stieff, too, tried to defect. Meanwhile Hoepner sat in his office and stared darkly and irresolutely ahead, responding lamely to requests for information. If Hitler really was alive, he told Beck, then "everything that we're doing is senseless." It would all come down, he added, "to a test of strength." To which Beck replied acidly, "That's for sure."[16] But where was Witzleben, his fellow conspirators wondered, and where, for that matter, was General Lindemann, who was supposed to read the conspirators' grand proclamation over the radio?

Only a few of the plotters refused to give up: Mertz, Olbricht, Beck, Schulenburg, Haeften, Schwerin, Yorck, and Gerstenmaier, who had by now arrived at army headquarters. And then, of course, there was Stauffenberg, hurrying back and forth through crowded offices and hallways from one incessantly ringing telephone to the next, convincing skeptical callers, issuing orders, coaxing, pressuring, reassuring. Even Gisevius, who had always disliked him, was forced to admit that Stauffenberg was the only person "on top of the situation." Gisevius overheard Stauffenberg tell callers that Hitler was dead. The operation is in full swing, he insisted, the panzers are on their way . . . Fromm is not available . . . Of course Keitel is lying . . . Orders must be obeyed . . . Everything depends on holding firm . . . The officers' time has come.

Away from the maelstrom sat Beck, asking time and again when news would arrive that the broadcasting center had been occupied. Since Lindemann had the only copy of the proclamation, Beck began working on a new version. Then he spoke with Kluge in France, but Clever Hans, true to form, refused to commit himself. Beck also made contact with the chief of staff of the army group that had been nearly cut off by the advancing Red Army in Courland and issued an order to withdraw the troops; he took the time to write a small note to this effect at the top of the proclamation "for future historians." The order was to be the only one he would issue in his new position.

At about 8:00 p.m. Witzleben appeared at Bendlerstrasse. Everyone realized that the moment of decision had come. Witzleben had just paid General Wagner a visit and knew that the assassination attempt had failed. His cap in one hand and his marshal's baton in the other, he strode into the cluster of waiting conspirators. Stauffenberg rushed up to deliver a status report but Witzleben brushed him aside, barking, "What a mess!" and proceeded with Beck into Fromm's office. Beck attempted to calm the furious Witzleben and to give him some idea of the difficulties that had arisen; the field marshal was not, however, in a forgiving mood. Stauffenberg and Schwerin were summoned, and one witness was able to discern through the glass of the sliding door that an angry debate had broken out, with Witzleben periodically banging his fist on the table.

There was no disputing that, for whatever reason, neither the government quarter nor the radio stations had been brought under the conspirators' control; nor were there even any battle-ready units standing by. Apparently Witzleben made no attempt to seize the initiative and save the situation. He had come, it seemed, solely in order to take command of the Wehrmacht from the conspirators. Stauffenberg and Schwerin stood by "like marble pillars." After three-quarters of an hour, a red-faced Witzleben burst from the room, stalked through the throng of officers waiting outside, descended the stairs, and drove off. And, as if these events were of no relevance to him, he returned to Zossen and coldly announced to General Wagner, "We're going home."[17]

Only Stauffenberg still appeared unwilling to admit that the coup was doomed. After Witzleben's departure he hurried back to his telephones, shouting out encouragement with a fervor born of desperation. Even he must have sensed, however, the growing coolness and distance on all sides. At about this point, Fromm discovered that a side door to Bartram's office had been left unguarded, and he succeeded with his aide's help in contacting the branch heads of the reserve army and ordering countermeasures. Increasingly convinced that the coup was doomed, some of the branch heads went to see Olbricht and demanded to know what was happening. Told that the Führer was dead, one of them, General Karl-Wilhelm Specht, replied that the radio was reporting just the opposite. He had sworn an oath of loyalty to Hitler, Specht said, and could not act on the basis of mere rumors of the Führer's death. All the other heads supported Specht's decision. Two hours earlier Olbricht would simply have placed them all under arrest, as he had Fromm and Kortzfleisch. Now, though, they were quietly allowed to depart.

Outside headquarters, other officers who had gone along with the conspirators were beginning to switch sides as well. At 9:00 p.m. Kleist returned from the city commandant's headquarters and reported that the guard battalion had defected. General Hase had been to see Goebbels and, after a short discussion, accepted his invitation to dinner. This tête-à-tête with the minister had soon been interrupted, however, by the arrival of the Gestapo, who carted Hase away. Fromm, still under guard at Bendlerstrasse, asked Hoepner if he could be moved to his private apartment, one floor above where he was being held. He would do nothing, he promised, to hurt the cause of the conspirators. Hoepner agreed, perhaps simply as a courtesy to an old army comrade but more likely because he had long since abandoned hope and was trying to curry favor with someone who might intercede on his behalf.

Everywhere there were signs that the Nazis were regaining the upper hand. When Gisevius called on Helldorf and Nebe and learned that Himmler was flying back to Berlin, he, like them, became convinced that the coup had failed. At army headquarters, Colonel Glaesemer, the commander of the armored unit from Krampnitz that had taken up position in the Tiergarten in the early evening—who had been placed under arrest by Olbricht for refusing to carry out orders once the tide began to turn—now simply stood up and walked out. Similarly, Mertz attempted to arrest Lieutenant Colonel Rudolf Schlee of the guard battalion, who, under orders from Remer, was trying to withdraw the sentries from in front of army headquarters. But Schlee escaped easily and soon returned at the head of a detachment to begin countermeasures. Having surrounded army headquarters, Schlee stationed guards with machine guns at every entrance and locked away in the porter's room all those who attempted to oppose him. Even the valiant Mertz gave up, telling Schulenburg that the "cause is lost."[18]

Earlier, Olbricht had called a meeting of those officers on his staff who had not been informed about the conspiracy: Franz Herber, Karl Pridun, Bolko von der Heyde, Fritz Harnack, and Herbert Fliessbach. Although they had all come to realize during the course of the afternoon that they were being swept up in a coup, they had continued to carry out their orders correctly, if unenthusiastically. Perhaps it was a mistake for Olbricht not to have taken them into his confidence earlier. In any case, they now displayed the kind of resentment felt by those who have been ignored, a class of people that has more than once been the undoing of tottering regimes. Moreover, these officers were understandably reluctant to be invited onto a sinking ship. When Olbricht withheld information that they demanded to know, evaded their questions, and then ordered them to take over the defense of the building and stand guard, they decided to confer with one another in Heyde's office. Meanwhile, some distance away, in Mertz's office, Gerstenmaier was suggesting that the conspirators should ready their weapons. But Yorck objected, saying that if it came down to a direct confrontation, Göring could simply bomb army headquarters to oblivion.

While the officers in Heyde's office were discussing why they were defending army headquarters and against whom, the weapons Olbricht had promised arrived. Taking pistols, submachine guns, and grenades in hand, they decided to go see Olbricht once again and get some answers. They set off down the hall with a great clatter, sweeping the officers they found along the way into Olbricht's office. Herber demanded, "Herr General, are you for or against the Führer?" When Olbricht failed to reply, Herber insisted on seeing Fromm. Olbricht referred him instead to Hoepner.

At this moment Stauffenberg entered the room. Pridun and some other members of the group attempted to grab him, but he managed to pull free and escape through the adjoining suite of rooms to Mertz's office. As he tried to reenter the hall, shots suddenly rang out. No one could later say who fired first. Stauffenberg had managed to load his revolver by using the three fingers of his remaining hand and clamping the stump of his other arm against his hip. He got off a shot at Pridun, but then he himself was hit in the upper left arm and dodged back into the office, leaving a trail of blood.

The shooting stopped as abruptly as it had started. While Olbricht, Herber, and the others set off to find Hoepner, Stauffenberg remained behind and asked one of the secretaries to contact Paris. He still clung to the dim hope that Stülpnagel, Hofacker, and possibly Kluge had finally made their move and that even now the troops were rolling in from the west. All day he had worn his black eye patch, but now he took it off, as if in a gesture of capitulation. The connection with Paris was never established.

In the meantime, Herber and his group were joined by others at Bendlerstrasse who had been waiting to see how events would unfold and who now emerged from hiding places all over army headquarters and headed for Hoepner's office. Everyone passing through the corridors was confronted at gunpoint with the question "Are you for or against the Führer?" It was shortly after 11:00 p.m. Fully aware of the authority with which he had suddenly been invested, Herber loudly demanded of Hoepner, "What game are you trying to play?" and insisted on speaking with Fromm himself. Hoepner replied that the general was in his private apartment. And while one member of the group set out to get Fromm, the others began to disarm all the conspirators they could find in the offices and hallways.

Within minutes General Fromm appeared, strutting at the head of a retinue of armed supporters. For a moment he halted in the office doorway, obviously savoring the scene before him. Olbricht was standing at the map table with Stauffenberg beside him, Beck sat in the foreground at a small table, and Mertz, Haeften, and Hoepner stood off to the side. Taking a few steps into the office, Fromm remarked, "So, gentlemen, now it's my turn to do to you what you did to me this afternoon."[19]

In fact, however, Fromm proceeded much more decisively. Wasting no time, he placed the six main conspirators under arrest and demanded, pistol in hand, that they relinquish their weapons. Beck asked to keep his pistol "for private purposes," to which Fromm replied gruffly, "Go ahead, but be quick about it!" Wishing to make a final statement, Beck raised his revolver to his temple and began, "I think now of earlier times—" But Fromm cut him off impatiently. "I told you, just do it!" he shouted. Beck paused for a moment and then, in front of several onlookers, squeezed the trigger. The bullet merely grazed his head. Fromm ordered two officers to take Beck's revolver away, but Beck resisted clumsily, firing and wounding himself once again and collapsing in a heap—still alive.

Leaving the former chief of general staff dying on the floor, Fromm turned to the other conspirators: "If you wish to make a statement or write something, you can have a moment to do so." Stauffenberg, Mertz, and Haeften remained silent, though Hoepner tried to assure Fromm that he had had nothing to do with the entire affair. Fromm remained unmoved. Only when Olbricht asked to be allowed to write a few lines did Fromm show some sign of compassion. "Come to the round table," he said, "where you always used to sit across from me."[20]

But time was pressing. A unit of the guard battalion, it was reported, had arrived in the courtyard. Fromm must also have known that Himmler was on the way and that every one of the arrested officers, with the exception of Hoepner, was in a position to testify against him and had to be silenced. He therefore urged them again to hurry and finally declared, "In the name of the Führer, I have convened a court-martial that has pronounced the following sentence: General Staff Colonel Mertz, General Olbricht, the colonel whose name I will not speak, and First Lieutenant Haeften are condemned to death."

Stauffenberg spoke out, claiming in a few clipped sentences sole responsibility for everything and stating that the others had acted purely as soldiers and his subordinates. Fromm said nothing in reply, merely standing aside so that the prisoners could be taken out. Glancing down again at Beck, who was still in his death throes, Fromm ordered an officer standing nearby to put him out of his misery. The officer refused, protesting that he was incapable of such an act, and passed the order along to a staff sergeant. The sergeant dragged Beck into an adjoining room and shot him. It was just after midnight.

In the courtyard outside, several military vehicles pulled up, their headlights glaring. Along all the sides of the square, groups of curious onlookers gathered. In the middle stood an execution squad consisting of Lieutenant Werner Schady and ten noncommissioned officers.

On the night of July 20, 1944, Hitler addressed the German people by radio, claiming that "a very small clique of ambitious, wicked, and stupidly criminal officers forged a plot to eliminate me and, along with me, virtually the entire leadership of the Wehrmacht." He said that he saw his survival as a sign from Providence that he should continue pursuing his life's goal. He concluded with these words: "We will settle accounts the way we National Socialists are accustomed to settling them."

The photograph shows Hitler making his address, surrounded by supporters. In front of the curtain is SS Obergruppenführer Julius Schaub, Hitler's personal aide; in the first row are, from right, Major General Hermann Fegelein of the Waffen-SS, General Alfred Jodl, Admiral Karl Dönitz, and Martin Bormann.

As the prisoners emerged from the staircase, they were positioned in front of a small pile of sand. Olbricht was the first to be shot. Next it was Stauffenberg's turn, but just as the squad fired, Haeften, in a defiant gesture, threw himself into the hail of bullets. When the squad again took aim at Stauffenberg, he shouted, "Long live sacred Germany."[21] Before the sound of his voice died away, shots resounded. The last to die was Mertz.

Fromm immediately dispatched news of the executions by teleprinter: "Attempted putsch by disloyal generals violently suppressed. All leaders shot."[22] Then he descended to the courtyard, passed the crumpled bodies without a glance, mounted one of the vehicles, and delivered a rousing speech celebrating the Führer, his miraculous deliverance, and the works of Providence. He ended with three "Sieg Heils," joined enthusiastically by the soldiers and onlookers.

Meanwhile Beck's bloody body was being dragged down the stairs. It was thrown with the others into one of the trucks and carted to the nearby cemetery of St. Matthew's Church in the Tiergarten. The custodian was instructed to inter the bodies secretly that very night, but the next morning Himmler ordered that they be exhumed and burned, and the ashes scattered "in the fields."

The other conspirators at Bendlerstrasse—Schulenburg, Schwerin, Yorck, Berthold Stauffenberg, Robert Bernardis, Gerstenmaier, and others—were locked up in the old offices of Stauffenberg and Mertz. For a while it seemed as if another round of executions was imminent. Then, half an hour after midnight, Sturmbannführer Otto Skorzeny, who had been summoned to Berlin by Walter Schellenberg, arrived with an SS unit. Kaltenbrunner also appeared, as did Remer, who forbade all further executions. Skorzeny approached the prisoners and without a word tore off their medals and decorations and tossed them into a steel helmet on the floor behind him. Then the radio was switched on and the silent, heavily guarded prisoners were forced to listen to the speech that Hitler was delivering over all stations.

Satisfied with himself and convinced at the end of a long and confusing day that he had once again managed "to come down on the right side," Fromm went off to see Goebbels. He wanted to be the first to report in person that the conspiracy had been crushed and the ringleaders executed. Then, perhaps, he would even deliver the news to Hitler himself. Instead, upon his arrival at Goebbels's office, he was immediately arrested.

■　■　■

The collapse in Berlin was not the end of the coup. Particularly in Prague and Vienna the commanders of the military districts had car-

On the morning of July 21, one day after the abortive coup, SS troops occupied army headquarters on Bendlerstrasse. Himmler's units can be seen moving into the courtyard where four of the leading conspirators had been executed the night before.

ried out the instructions from Bendlerstrasse with considerable alacrity, arresting most SS and Security Service (SD) officials and occupying the main public buildings. Now they expressed their regrets to their captives, explaining that it was all a great mistake. The jailers and their erstwhile prisoners raised a few glasses together, and everyone departed.

In Paris the day's events were much more dramatic. Around 2:00 p.m. Quartermaster General Eberhard Finckh, who had been privy to the secret plot, was alerted by telephone from Zossen that Hitler had been assassinated. About three hours later Stauffenberg himself came on the line to inform his cousin Cäsar von Hofacker that Hitler was dead and the uprising had begun. General Stülpnagel called a meeting of his officers, issued the prearranged orders, and distributed maps to the city commandant's staff showing the residences of the two most senior SS and SD officials, Carl-Albrecht Oberg and Helmut Knochen, as well as the location of their units. The arrests were planned for 11:00 p.m. so as to cause as little commotion as possible.

While the preparations went ahead, Kluge contacted Stülpnagel and invited him to his headquarters in La Roche-Guyon. In view of the hopelessly superior firepower of the Allies, Kluge had come to share Rommel's view that Germany could not hold out much longer. He therefore resumed wavering between halfhearted support for a coup and timid opposition. His hopes had initially been raised by the news from Bendlerstrasse but soon grew shaky with the denials from the Wolf's Lair. After hesitating for a while between the conflicting reports from the two camps, he finally got in touch with Stieff, who confirmed that Hitler was alive and well.

When Stülpnagel and Hofacker arrived in La Roche Guyon, Kluge, who was by then fully apprised of the situation, showed little patience for their passionate appeals and denied any knowledge of a conspiracy, commenting coolly, "Well, gentlemen, just a botched assassination attempt." Stülpnagel and Hofacker argued that the apparent failure of the attempt only increased their own responsibility. The uprising could still succeed if the three of them refused to obey Hitler and unilaterally brought the war in the West to an end. But Kluge would not be swayed. Acting as if they had not just been discussing an issue of the highest importance, their last chance to avoid horrific devastation, Kluge invited his guests to a gracious candle-lit dinner, at which he droned on incessantly about his war experiences. His table companions stared glumly into space.

To end this intolerable scene, Stülpnagel finally asked Kluge to step out onto the terrace and told him about the arrests they had planned. Kluge was horrified, summoned his chief of general staff, General Günther Blumentritt, and ordered the immediate cancellation of the measures. He then dismissed Stülpnagel from his position and calmly returned to dinner. The atmosphere now, according to one witness, was "eerie—as if in a morgue."[23] Once again Stülpnagel and Hofacker begged the field marshal to reconsider but all he would say was, "If only that swine were dead!" As they parted, he gave Stülpnagel a piece of well-intentioned advice: "Put on civilian clothes and disappear somewhere."[24]

As Stülpnagel took his leave of Kluge, without a parting handshake,

Left: *General Carl-Heinrich von Stülpnagel, the military commander in France from 1942 to 1944, was initiated into the resistance in the fall of 1943. His staff headquarters in the Hôtel Majestic in Paris soon became the center of the military resistance in France. Ordered back to Berlin after July 20, he broke off his journey near Verdun in order to take his life on the great battlefield of the First World War. He succeeded, however, only in mutilating one side of his face and blinding himself. He was transported back to Berlin, where the People's Court sentenced him to death. On August 30, 1944, the executioner in Plötzensee prison led him by hand to the gallows.*

Right: *General Günther Blumentritt was involved in one of the most remarkable episodes to occur on July 20. The senior SS and SD commanders in Paris, Carl-Albrecht Oberg and Helmut Knochen, were arrested by the army conspirators that evening but released when the coup failed. Sent to Paris by Field Marshal Hans von Kluge, Blumentritt managed that night to come up with an arrangement with Oberg and Knochen that allowed many of the conspirators in Paris to go undiscovered.*

at around 11:00 p.m., the task forces in Paris were just setting out from the Bois de Boulogne. Quickly and without encountering resistance, they arrested some twelve hundred members of the SS and SD

in their quarters near the Arc de Triomphe. They also took into cus
tody both SS Obergruppenführer Oberg and Security Service chief
Knochen, who had first to be located in a nightclub and then summoned to return to his headquarters on avénue Foch. Meanwhile, in
the courtyard of the Ecole Militaire, a detachment under the city
commandant, Hans von Boineburg, was piling up sandbags for the
expected executions. Lawyers on his staff had already drafted indictments accusing Himmler's subordinates of deporting Jews, blowing
up synagogues in Paris, and confiscating "enemy property" in contravention of all legal principles.[25]

Shortly after midnight Stülpnagel returned to his headquarters in
the Hôtel Majestic. Defying Kluge's orders, he did not immediately
release the arrested officials and troops. Instead he went to the Hôtel
Raphaël next door, which served as the officers' mess. The rooms
were packed, and in the great din there was much clinking of glasses.
Officers and their civilian co-workers—people who were privy to
what was going on and people who had had no idea—were all celebrating the arrests and the apparently imminent end of the war. Suddenly a voice from the radio room rose above the general clamor,
announcing that the Führer was about to speak.

The room fell silent. Stülpnagel entered, took a few steps forward
toward the radio, and then remained there, still as a statue, as Hitler
began to speak. The Führer raged about "a very small clique of ambitious, wicked, and stupidly criminal officers," thanked Providence for
his survival, and condemned the "coterie of criminal elements which
is now being mercilessly rooted out." One officer noted that
Stülpnagel was under "tremendous tension" but "showed no sign of
emotion as he stood there, his hands crossed behind his back, twisting
his gloves." When Hitler finished, Stülpnagel turned on his heels and
strode from the room without a word.[26]

Outside he was informed that the commander in chief of Naval
Group West, Admiral Theodor Krancke, was threatening to march on
Paris with more than a thousand men to free the interned SS and SD
troops. In addition, the Luftwaffe commander in Paris, General
Friedrich-Karl Hanesse, had put his forces on alert. Then
Stülpnagel's chief of staff, Colonel Hans-Ottfried von Linstow, re

ported that Stauffenberg had called earlier in the evening to say that all was lost and that his killers were already prowling the hall outside his office. But still Stülpnagel did not give up. Even when notified that Kluge had put through his dismissal as military commander and that General Blumentritt was on his way to relieve him, he carefully considered his next move and even discussed with Hofacker and Finckh the possibility of forcing Kluge's hand by taking the decisive and irreversible step of executing the SS commanders. In the end, though, Stülpnagel abandoned all hope and gave the order to release the prisoners. "Providence," he said, "has decided against us."[27]

With the release of the SS commanders, a very delicate and dangerous situation arose. It was handled with aplomb, however, by the reliable Hans von Boineburg. A small, bald man with a hoarse voice and a monocle, Boineburg proved that night that he was far more than the mere caricature of a German soldier whose persona he liked to affect, albeit somewhat ironically. He set out resolutely for the rue de Castiglione, where Oberg and Knochen were being held prisoner in a suite at the Hôtel Continental. In his charmingly blunt manner he announced that they were now free to go and delivered to the outraged Oberg an invitation from Stülpnagel to return to the Hôtel Raphaël. Boineburg managed to mollify the SS commander to such an extent that he eventually agreed to come. Knochen, however, went back to his quarters.

A bizarre scene then unfolded in the Salon Bleu of the Hôtel Raphaël, as the conspirators and the executioners sat down together. Just minutes before, they had been deadly enemies, some planning the murder of the person next to them, others feeling stunned and vengeful, and all brimming with suspicion. In the halting conversation that ensued, each player was keenly aware that any misstep could easily spell the death of Stülpnagel, Boineburg, Hofacker, Linstow, and the other members of Stülpnagel's staff on the one side or Ambassador Otto Abetz and SS Obergruppenführer Oberg on the other, not to mention Knochen, Krancke, and Blumentritt, who joined the group somewhat later.

Stülpnagel had ordered a round of champagne in an effort to create a relaxed, friendly atmosphere despite the heavy shadow cast by recent events. Abetz arrived first, in an angry mood, but he had grown much more conciliatory by the time Oberg appeared soon afterward. Still uncertain as to how to proceed, Oberg immediately declared that "investigations" would have to be conducted. But Abetz intervened, managing to persuade the still-furious SS commander to shake hands with his adversary. Abetz assured Oberg that Stülpnagel had been given contradictory orders, and gradually he led the conversation toward the conclusion that, in view of the approaching Allied forces and the mounting threat from the French underground, Germans had no choice but to stand together, shoulder to shoulder.

Oberg, who of course suspected that Stülpnagel had known exactly what he was doing, was hardly deceived by the game that was being played. "So, Herr General," Oberg said in response to Stülpnagel's greeting, "you seem to have bet on the wrong horse." Oberg also realized, however, that his own carelessness and imprudence would make him an object of scorn within the SS. He was therefore by no means immune to the attempts of the army commanders to paper over the entire affair. Thus, as the evening wore on, he grew more approachable, the conversation picked up, and an atmosphere of friendly camaraderie began to develop. Champagne flowed in great quantity, and by the time Blumentritt and his two aides arrived, those gathered, though still somewhat distrustful, seemed in remarkably good spirits—as if at "a party that was in full swing."[28]

On his way to the Raphaël, the ever-resourceful Blumentritt had hinted that a certain "arrangement" might be arrived at—a suggestion that was eagerly seized on by Knochen. Now Knochen reintroduced it, cautiously testing the waters by tentatively describing his notion, then retreating, then stating it a little more clearly, and then backing off behind a fog of words. Eventually he and Oberg decided to step outside for a moment. Back in the Salon Bleu, Blumentritt finally came out with the proposal, which everyone present seemed to find convincing except Admiral Krancke, who suddenly erupted in a tirade about "Stülpnagel, treason, and perfidy." For a moment the whole fabric of half-truths seemed about to fall apart, but then opinion rallied around Blumentritt's story of "mistakes" and "false alarms." Considerably relieved, the partygoers returned to their

Police authority in France lay in the hands of two men, Carl-Albrecht Oberg and Helmut Knochen. Condemned to death in Germany in 1946 by the Allies and then again in France in 1954, they were both pardoned during the 1960s by President Charles de Gaulle.

Above: *Oberg* (left) *and Knochen before a military court in Paris in September 1954.*

champagne, drinking toasts to one another and celebrating into the early hours of the morning. The author Ernst Jünger, who was on Stülpnagel's staff, wrote of this day, "The big snake [Hitler] was in the bag, but then we let it out again."[29]

Stülpnagel presumably only participated in the game in an attempt to protect his staff, which had always gone along with Hofacker's and his wishes. (In fact, a relatively large number of his officers did survive the ensuing purge.) For himself, Stülpnagel realized, there was no hope—even though he did not yet know that he had already been betrayed to Keitel by Kluge, who brushed Blumentritt's astonishment aside with the comment, "Things will now take their course." Early in the morning orders arrived from Keitel: Stülpnagel was to return to Berlin at once. He took leave of his colleagues and set out by car. Near Verdun, where he had fought in the First World War, Stülpnagel had his driver drop him off and proceed ahead a little. With Mort-Homme Hill rising before him, he climbed down the embankment of the Meuse canal. The report of a pistol split the air. Stülpnagel's two traveling companions hurried back and dragged his body out of the swirling waters. He was still alive, having succeeded only in blinding himself. Nursed back to health under constant guard, Stülpnagel was arraigned before the People's Court on August 30. He refused to name any accomplices, and when Roland Freisler, the judge, asked specifically about Rommel and Kluge he answered tersely, "I will not discuss the field marshals!" Later that day the executioner led the blind man to the gallows.[30]

. . .

Many factors led to the failure of the July 20 plot. Among those most frequently mentioned is the "amateurism" of the leading conspirators, insufficient planning, blind trust in the chain of command, and poor coordination among the participants, which led to the bedlam that broke out at army headquarters. As Admiral Canaris observed, not without a certain cynicism, to an acquaintance he met on the street two days later, "That, my dear fellow, was not the way to go about it."[31]

In any event, many important aspects of the plan did indeed go awry, from the failure to establish the loyalty and presence of the Döberitz and Krampnitz commanders to the defection of the task forces, which caused Colonel Jäger so much grief, to the absurd deception practiced on Major Jakob after he seized the broadcasting center on Masurenallee. Numerous other oversights and blunders—and simple human frailty—played a role as well, which is all the more surprising because the coup was planned and carried out by experienced officers of the general staff. The uprising lacked drive, but perhaps even more fatal was the fact that the staff officers who planned it did not have proven commanders at their disposal—resolute, careful officers experienced at overseeing troops and accustomed to bearing complete responsibility. Goebbels was amazed, for instance, to discover on the evening of July 20 that although the government quarter had been surrounded and two sentries posted in front of his apartment his telephone line had not been cut.[32]

Nevertheless, it was not these obvious weaknesses that ultimately caused the uprising to fail. Strictly speaking, success or failure hinged on just two things: the assassination of Hitler and the interruption of all communications from the Wolf's Lair. When the first of these conditions was not fulfilled, the second could not be maintained for long. One can hardly fault General Fellgiebel, who, astonished to see Hitler walk by him right after the explosion, made the fateful decision to call Berlin and pass along the news.

But however damaging the "logistical" failure, it does not capture the essence of the problem. Far more decisive on July 20, as on so many other days, were deeply ingrained attitudes and behaviors that inhibited any kind of revolt. Although criticism of Hitler and his regime was widespread within the army, not a single officer who had not been privy in advance to the plans for the uprising decided to join the rebels on the spur of the moment. The radio broadcasts in the early evening proclaimed not only that Hitler had survived but, even more important, that "legal" authority remained in his hands. Thereafter, most officers almost instinctively dismissed the rebels as insurgents or traitors.

The enormous respect accorded "legality" greatly impeded the conspirators, stifling any questions as to why they were acting as they were. It was precisely in order to circumvent the army officers' profound aversion to mutiny and broken oaths that the conspirators had planned to dress the coup up as a "legal" takeover. With the failure to assassinate Hitler, however, their reliance on legality was turned against them. This shift was clear in the initial reluctance and then the quite open defiance of the department heads on Bendlerstrasse, as well as in the passionate arguments that broke out in the Döberitz mess and prompted Colonel Wolfgang Müller to report that evening, "The troops cannot possibly be persuaded to fight against Hitler. They refuse to obey me against him." Even among units that were deployed according to plan, a reference to "personal orders from the Führer" worked "like magic," so that the troops turned around and headed smartly back to barracks.[33] Thiele and Thüngen reacted the same way and, most critical of all, so did Kluge. After his telephone conversation with Stieff, he was totally impervious to all appeals or attempts at persuasion, despite his previous close affiliation with the rebels.

It is here that the weakness of the Valkyrie plan—its reliance on orders being followed unquestioningly down the chain of command—clearly emerges. Even if the attack on Hitler had been successful, many generals with troops at their command would still have had to decide to obey the new government. A few examples suggest that this decision was far less certain than the conspirators imagined: on receiving instructions from army headquarters in Berlin, the commanders of military districts in Hamburg, Dresden, and Danzig immediately contacted their regional party commanders or local Gestapo officials for clarification. They may have been exceptions, but they illustrate the extent to which innumerable individual decisions would have had to go the right way in order for the rebels to pose a serious challenge to the logistical might of the established legal authorities. In his complex combination of contempt for the regime and submissiveness to it, indecision and legalism, Field Marshal Kluge illustrates better perhaps than any of his fellow officers the problem that would likely have doomed the coup even if the attack on Hitler had succeeded.

As always in human history, only a small minority of men were willing to raise moral principle not only above the traditions with which they grew up but above life itself. When Henning von Tresckow discovered in the early hours of July 21 that the attack on Hitler had failed, he said to Schlabrendorff "in a totally calm, collected way" that he would now take his own life because he feared what would happen when he was pressured to reveal the names of his accomplices. The next morning, as he took his final leave of his friend and prepared to drive out past the German lines into no-man's-land in order to end his life, he added another reason for his actions: "The whole world will vilify us now, but I am still totally convinced that we did the right thing. Hitler is the archenemy not only of Germany but of the world. When, in a few hours' time, I go before God to account for what I have done and left undone, I know I will be able to justify in good conscience what I did in the struggle against Hitler. God promised Abraham that He would not destroy Sodom if just ten righteous men could be found in the city, and so I hope that for our sake God will not destroy Germany. None of us can bewail his own death; those who consented to join our circle put on the robe of Nessus. A human being's moral integrity begins when he is prepared to sacrifice his life for his convictions."[34]

A far more typical example of human behavior, however, was the expedient set of actions taken by Kluge—though in his case it was writ particularly large. Late in the evening of July 20, shortly after dismissing Stülpnagel and Hofacker with a resounding "No!" he sent a telegram to Hitler expressing his devotion: "The attempt of villainous murderers to kill you, my Führer, has been foiled by the fortuitous hand of fate."[35] Kluge knew full well that he still could not escape Hitler's longstanding suspicions of him. Five days later, when the great Allied offensive in the West began with General Patton's armored breakthrough in the area around St. Lô and Kluge could not be reached all day because he was directing the German troops from right behind the front, Hitler immediately suspected him of attempting to negotiate a surrender. In any case, the Führer believed that Kluge "knew about the assassination attempt," as he remarked to Guderian. The reprimands and interference of a suspicious Führer soon culminated in Kluge's being told where he should station himself in battle. They continued with specific orders as to when to attack and where to hold the line—even though no troops were available for the maneuvers that were demanded. The ultimate humiliation came on August 17, after the fall of Falaise, when Field Marshal Walter Model suddenly appeared at Kluge's headquarters and announced that he was the new commander in chief in the West. The letter from Hitler confirming Kluge's dismissal ended with the ominous words "Field Marshal Kluge shall keep this office advised of where in Germany he intends to go."[36]

The "master of tactical improvisation," as Kluge liked to be known, was forced into something he had always avoided; an irrevocable decision. He also had an opportunity to soften, at least for posterity, the memory of his indecisiveness, his pathetic "Children, I'm yours!" outburst, his constant evasion of and faithlessness toward Beck, Tresckow, Rommel, and Stülpnagel. Once again, however, he failed to take a stand, even though he had already resolved to put an end to fear and anxiety. He remained his guarded self in a farewell letter to Hitler and, while he did call for peace, he also wrote of the Führer's "grandeur" and "genius" and concluded by writing, "I take leave of you, my Führer—to whom I have always stood closer than you perhaps realize—in the firm conviction that I did my duty to the absolute best of my ability."[37] Kluge then set out on the road back to Germany. Near the place where Stülpnagel had tried to end his life, Kluge ordered his car to stop and swallowed poison.

As it happened, only days before, Rudolph-Christoph von Gersdorff had visited Kluge, like a ghost from the past, and attempted to persuade him to negotiate with the Allies, withdraw his troops to Germany's prewar borders and, with the help of a few reliable units, try to overthrow the Nazi regime. "If that should fail, Gersdorff," the commander retorted, "Field Marshal Kluge will go down as the biggest swine in world history." Gersdorff continued to press, arguing that "every great man in world history" has faced a decision that would cause him to be remembered either as a criminal or as "a savior in times of dire need." Kluge simply laid his hand on the colonel's shoulder and remarked, "Gersdorff, Field Marshal Kluge is no great man."[38]

10

PERSECUTION AND JUDGMENT

By the night of July 20, widespread manhunts were already under way. Besides those arrested on Bendlerstrasse, anyone who had had personal or professional dealings with the known conspirators or who had attracted the earlier attention of the security authorities was investigated. Around midnight Helmuth Stieff was taken into custody at headquarters. At about that time Erich Fellgiebel was engaged in a lofty philosophical debate with his adjutant, First Lieutenant Hellmuth Arntz, about the afterlife, which Fellgiebel did not believe in. When the long-awaited call came he replied simply, "I'm on my way." Arntz asked if he had his pistol, but Fellgiebel said, "One doesn't do that. One takes a stand."[1]

The next day SS Obersturmbannführer Georg Kiessel was appointed head of a special board of inquiry, which soon numbered four hundred people. Hitler held a briefing to announce guidelines for the judicial proceedings against those involved in the failed coup. Denouncing the conspirators as "the basest creatures that ever wore the soldier's tunic, this riff-raff from a dead past," he declared: "This time I'll fix them. There will be no honorable bullet for . . . these criminals, they'll hang like common traitors! We'll have a court of honor expel them from the service; then they can be tried as civilians. . . . The sentences will be carried out within two hours! They must hang at once, without any show of mercy! And the most important thing is that they're given no time for any long speeches. But Freisler will take care of all that. He's our Vishinsky."[2]

As the days passed, the number of suspects grew larger and larger. Witzleben was among the first to be arrested. Popitz was picked up in his apartment at about five o'clock on the morning of the twenty-first and was soon followed by Oster, Kleist-Schmenzin, Schacht, Canaris, Wirmer, and many others. Only shortly before July 20 the Gestapo officials responsible for surveillance of the military had reported no particular activity, noting only in passing a certain "defeatism" in the circles around Beck and Goerdeler.[3] That was the reason Hitler apparently believed at first that the attack was the work of a "very small clique of ambitious officers," as he said in his radio address to the German people. Now, to the astonishment of virtually everyone, it turned out that Stauffenberg and his immediate accomplices represented only the tip of the iceberg. The conspiracy extended far beyond the army to civilian circles on both sides of the political spectrum, even to groups presumed to be close to the Nazi Party.

On the evening of July 20 an overly confident Count Helldorf had averred that the police would not dare lay a finger on him. In fact, the investigators hardly hesitated before pouncing. Other conspirators, like General Eduard Wagner, escaped their fates by committing suicide. Major Hans Ulrich von Oertzen, who had urged the military district headquarters on Hohenzollerndamm to support the uprising, managed in the bedlam that surrounded his arrest to hide two grenades. Shortly before he was to be led away he held one to his head and detonated it. He collapsed on the floor, grievously wounded. With all his remaining strength, he dragged himself to where the second grenade lay hidden, shoved it in his mouth, and pulled the pin. Suicides such as this only extended the circle of suspects to include friends, relatives, and colleagues.

The code of personal honor, always a significant factor in the strange helplessness of the conspirators, influenced their behavior even in defeat. Very few conspirators actually attempted to escape. Most simply arranged their personal affairs and waited calmly for the knock on the door, ready, or so they believed, for anything that might befall them. Many refused to avail themselves of proferred hiding places or even asked to be arrested. Principally they wished to spare their friends and relatives interrogation by the police; but most of them were also operating out of the categorical morality that was the bedrock of their thinking. "Don't flee—stand your ground!" was how Karl Klausing rationalized his decision to give himself up; he did not want, he said, to leave his captured comrades in the lurch. Schlabrendorff also refused to flee, as did Trott, evidently "on account of his wife and children." Tresckow's brother Gerd knew about the conspiracy, but as a lieutenant colonel in a division on the Italian front he was too far away from the scene to arouse suspicion. Nevertheless, he went and confessed to his superior officers and, when told to forget about it, insisted on his culpability. He was finally arrested and incarcerated in the Gestapo prison on Lehrterstrasse, where, in a state of physical and mental depletion, he took his life in early September 1944.[4]

Time and again, fugitives sought by the police turned themselves in out of a feeling that can best be described as part pride and part exhaustion. They were no longer willing or able to hide out or to continue the duplicitous life they had led for far too long, at the cost, they believed, of their self-respect. Ulrich von Hassell left his home in Bavaria and traveled to Berlin by a circuitous route, making many stops. For a few days he roamed restlessly through the streets of the capital, then went to his desk and waited calmly for the Gestapo to arrive. Theodor Steltzer, who was already in Norway, refused to flee across the border to Sweden, returning instead to Berlin, where he acted on his belief that a Christian cannot tell a lie, even to a Gestapo interrogator or before the People's Court.[5]

The motivation behind these and many other unrealistic if honorable gestures was certainly the expectation that the impending trials could be used as a forum for denouncing the Nazis. As the curtains fell on their lives, these brave men hoped for one last chance to expose the true nature of the regime, much as some of them had fervently hoped to do in criminal proceedings against Hitler. The illusion that they would be allowed to speak their minds freely at their trials was soon shattered, however, as was the belief, cherished primarily by the military men, that every legal formality would be observed and that they would be treated in a manner befitting their standing in society.

Although the investigators found themselves groping in the dark at first, over the next few months, they succeeded in arresting some six hundred suspects beyond those immediately implicated in the plot. A second wave of arrests in mid-August, known as Operation Thunderstorm, put five thousand putative opponents of the regime behind bars; most of these people had been connected to various political parties and organizations in the Weimar Republic. Again, even when under interrogation, some of the accused strove more to demonstrate the high moral principle behind their actions than to save their lives, so that the head of the special investigatory commission was soon able to say that "the manly attitude of the idealists immediately shed some light in the darkness."[6]

Although much of this courageous and self-sacrificing spirit may seem naive, it was perhaps the only defense to which the regime had no answer. Apparently Hitler had originally intended to stage a great spectacle modeled on the Soviet show trials of the 1930s, with radio and film coverage and lengthy press reports, but he was soon forced to abandon all such plans. Schulenburg, for example, declared before the court: "We resolved to take this deed upon ourselves in order to save Germany from indescribable misery. I realize that I shall be hanged for my part in it, but I do not regret what I did and only hope that someone else will succeed in luckier circumstances." Similar declarations from numerous defendants increasingly put the authorities on the defensive, and on August 17, 1944, Hitler forbade any further reporting of the trials. In the end, not even the executions were publicly announced.[7]

The Gestapo had considerable difficulty determining the breadth of the conspiracy. It is known, for instance, that Stieff and Fellgiebel held out for at least six days under torture without revealing anything. Contrary to legend, no list of conspirators or a projected cabinet was ever found, and as late as August 8 Yorck was able to tell prison chaplain Harald Poelchau that the Gestapo still knew nothing about the Kreisau Circle. Moltke's name was not uttered until Leber's interrogation on August 10.[8] Schlabrendorff, who survived the war to write a detailed account of the four types of torture employed—beginning with a device to screw spikes into the fingertips and progressing to spike-lined "Spanish boots," the rack, and other horrors—did not

"I want them to be hanged, strung up like butchered cattle," Hitler ordered Roland Freisler (center), the president of the People's Court. Freisler handled the trials in anything but an orderly fashion, constantly interrupting the defendants and bellowing at them. Nevertheless, the impression he left on a man like Moltke, who loved debate, was not entirely negative. Moltke wrote to his wife that he and Freisler enjoyed their verbal jousting. Freisler, according to Moltke, was "gifted, something of a genius, but not wise, and all this in the highest degree."

Above: Freisler shows evidence to the conspirators' publicly appointed attorneys.

reveal the names of his co-conspirators at Army Group Center, even when the mutilated corpse of his friend Tresckow was exhumed and shown to him. Despite severe torments, not much more than was already known could be dragged out of Jessen, Langbehn, Oster, Kleist-Schmenzin, and Leuschner. But what these men refused to reveal in so-called intensified interrogation—in which all the horror and vengeful fury were brought to bear on them—the Allies now did. As if eager to do one last favor for Hitler, British radio began regularly broadcasting the names of people alleged to have had a hand in the coup. Roland Freisler, the president of the People's Court, was even able to show Schwerin von Schwanenfeld an Allied leaflet that heaped scorn on the conspirators, just as the Nazis' propaganda was doing.[9]

The military "court of honor" that Hitler had demanded met on August 4, with Field Marshal Rundstedt presiding and Field Marshal Keitel, General Guderian, and Lieutenant Generals Schroth, Specht, Kriebel, Burgdorf, and Maisel serving as associates. Without any hearings or presentation of evidence, they drummed twenty-two officers out of the Wehrmacht, thus depriving them of the legal protections of a court-martial, just as Hitler wanted. However extreme this step may have appeared to be, it was actually only the final act in a lengthy process that had revealed to all that the unity and cohesiveness of the army had long since been shattered. It was the last of many gestures of submission to Hitler's will.

Responsibility for trying the accused officers and the other participants in the attempted coup fell now to the People's Court, which had been specially constituted in 1934 to judge "political crimes." Hitler ordered the cases to be heard in closed chambers before a small, select audience. He invited Freisler and—if the reports are accurate—even the executioner to Führer headquarters, where he instructed them to refuse the condemned men all religious and spiritual comfort. "I want them to be hanged, strung up like butchered cattle," Hitler said.[10]

The trials began on August 7 in the great hall of the Berlin People's Court, which was hung with Nazi flags for the occasion. The accused were Witzleben, Hoepner, Stieff, Hase, Bernardis, Klausing, Yorck, and Hagen. To further humiliate the conspirators, they were forbidden to wear neckties, and Witzleben was even denied suspenders for his trousers. Hoepner was dressed in a cardigan. All bore the signs, as one witness reported, of the "tortures they had suffered while in custody."[11] Presiding over the scene was Roland Freisler, attired in his red judicial robes and seated beneath a bust of the Führer.

Freisler had been appointed president of the People's Court two years earlier, and in him the regime found a man very much in its own image. Hitler always felt a certain distrust toward Freisler, how-

Erich Hoepner (right), a tank general, was dishonorably discharged from the army for refusing to obey Hitler's orders to stand firm during the winter campaign outside Moscow. The conspirators enlisted him to replace Friedrich Fromm and assume command of the home, or reserve, army. He was present on Bendlerstrasse on July 20, 1944, and was arrested that night and executed in Plötzensee prison on August 8, 1944.

Above: *Hoepner during his trial. His execution followed the same day.*

ever, and his likening of him to Andrei Vishinsky, the chief prosecutor in the Moscow show trials, suggests the reason: Freisler had been taken prisoner by the Russians during the First World War and had become a Soviet commissar after the October Revolution; he liked to boast that he had begun his career as a diehard Communist. With his cynical bent and taste for radical politics, he joined the Nazis in 1925, throwing himself into political and journalistic tasks on behalf of the party and reaping his reward with an appointment as state secretary in the Ministry of Justice. Seizing on a comment by Hitler in his address to the Reichstag justifying the Night of the Long Knives, he made himself a vocal advocate of *Gesinnungsstrafrecht*, harsh laws that called for defendants in political cases to be punished not so much for their deeds as for the convictions underlying those deeds.

His loud, bullying style—intended, he occasionally conceded, to "atomize" the defendants—was matched by his theatrical temperament, his fondness for adopting extravagant poses, and his pleasure in exercising power over life and death. The psychological corollary to all this was his fawning subservience to Hitler. He played his roles to the hilt, outraged one moment, then cutting, then affable, now and again seeming to enjoy sharp-witted repartee. All in all he was the kind of man who rises to the top in turbulent times, when all values and principles are placed in doubt. The first chief of the Prussian Gestapo, Rudolf Diels, called Freisler "more brilliant, adaptable, and fiendish than anyone in the long line of revolutionary prosecutors." Despite his repellent characteristics and the clear delight he took in humiliating and defaming those who appeared before him, few were immune to his remarkable charisma. Helmuth von Moltke wrote after his trial that Freisler was "gifted, something of a genius, but not wise, and all this in the highest degree." According to Freisler's predecessor, Otto Thierack, he was simply mentally ill.[12]

Freisler opened the first day of proceedings by remarking that the court would be ruling on "the most horrific charges ever brought in the history of the German people." He heaped scorn on the accused, continually referring to them as "rabble," "criminals," and "traitors," men with the "character of pigs"; Stauffenberg he called a "murderous scoundrel." Freisler's role was to express boundless moral outrage. The proceedings focused strictly on the deeds that had been committed; any attempt by the accused to introduce the issue of their motives was immediately interrupted. Stieff came before the court first, and when he tried to raise the issue Freisler informed him that as a soldier he needed only "to obey, triumph, and die, without looking either left or right" and added, "We don't want to hear any more from you about that." None of the accused was allowed an opportunity to address the court at length or even to reach any sort of under-

Count Ulrich Wilhelm Schwerin von Schwanenfeld was a long-time friend of Peter Yorck von Wartenburg and Adam von Trott zu Solz. As early as 1935 he advocated overthrowing Hitler by force to bring about a Christian renewal in Germany. When war broke out in 1939 he was sent to Poland, where he became adjutant to Field Marshal Erwin von Witzleben, and where he learned of the atrocities committed by the German Einsatzgruppen. He condemned these crimes openly before the People's Court on September 8, 1944. When Freisler asked if he felt ashamed of the brazen allegations he was making, he answered emphatically, "No!"

standing with their attorneys, who were seated some distance away. Not all but a good many of these attorneys openly supported the prosecution's case. Witzleben's lawyer, for instance, a Dr. Weissmann, stated in his final summation that the court's decision had in effect already been rendered by "heavenly Providence when, in a miraculous act of deliverance, it protected the Führer from destruction for the sake of the German people." Weissmann concluded, "The deed of the accused stands, and the guilty perpetrator will go down with it." Freisler sentenced all eight defendants to be hanged, ending the proceedings with the words "We return now to life and to the struggle. We have nothing more in common with you. The *Volk* has purged itself of you and remains pure. We fight on. The Wehrmacht cries, 'Heil Hitler!' We all cry, 'Heil Hitler!' We fight together with our Führer, following him, for Germany's sake!"[13]

Thus the trials proceeded, case after case. The next session was held on August 10, when Fellgiebel, Berthold von Stauffenberg, Alfred Kranzfelder, and Fritz von der Schulenburg were paraded before the People's Court. Freisler seemed particularly irritated by the quiet dignity and disdain of Schulenburg. Josef Wirmer was arraigned not long afterward. When Freisler remarked that Wirmer would soon find himself roasting in hell, Wirmer bowed curtly and riposted, "I'll look forward to your own imminent arrival, your honor!" Freisler did not always succeed in interrupting the defendants in time. Hans-Bernd von Haeften managed to interject a comment about Hitler's "place in world history as a great perpetrator of evil"; Kleist-Schmenzin announced that he had been determined to commit treason ever since January 30, 1933, and spoke of it as a "command from God"; Schwerin managed to mention "all the murders committed at home and abroad" and, when asked by an angry Freisler if he was not ashamed to be making such a base allegation, retorted, "No!" During the examination phase of the proceedings, Cäsar von Hofacker claimed that he had acted with as much right on July 20 as Hitler had on November 9, 1923, the day of the "beer-hall putsch." He regretted, he said, that he had not been chosen to carry out the assassination, because then it would not have failed. Later he managed to cut Freisler off during one of the judge's own numerous interruptions: "Be quiet now, Herr Freisler, because today it's my neck that's on the block. But in a year it will be yours!" Fellgiebel even advised Freisler that he had better hurry lest he himself hang before he hung the accused.[14]

On the afternoon of August 8, immediately following their trials, the first group of condemned men was transported to the execution grounds in Plötzensee prison. Although Hitler had expressly forbidden any spiritual consolation, the prison chaplain, Harald Poelchau,

The lawyer Josef Wirmer, a leftist member of the Catholic Center Party, became a close confidant of Jakob Kaiser, who served on the executive of the Christian trade union movement. Wirmer's apartment in Berlin became a meeting place for the opposition, and he himself worked largely on forging ties between the trade unions and the civilian resistance. Wirmer was arrested following the events of July 20 and hanged in Plötzensee prison.

did manage to "speak quickly" with Witzleben and Hase. But according to his own report, as he approached Yorck "the conversation was violently interrupted. SS men with floodlights stormed into the cells and filmed the various prisoners before they were hauled away to be executed. The resulting movie, made at the express wish of the Führer, was supposed to show all phases of the entire process, at length and in full detail."[15]

Once inside Plötzensee, the prisoners were allowed only enough time to change into prison garb. One by one, in accordance with prison drill procedures, they crossed the courtyard in wooden shoes, under the ever-present gaze of a camera, and entered the execution chamber through a black curtain. Here, too, a camera recorded their every step as they arrived and were led to the back of the chamber to stand under hooks attached to a girder running across the ceiling. Floodlights brilliantly illuminated the scene. A few observers were standing around: the public prosecutor, prison officials, photographers. The executioners removed the prisoners' handcuffs, placed short, thin nooses around their necks, and stripped them to the waist. At a signal, they hoisted each man aloft and let him down on the tightened noose, slowly in some cases, more quickly in others. Before the prisoner's death throes were over, his trousers were ripped off him. After each execution the chief executioner and his assistants went to the table at the front of the room and fortified themselves with brandy until the sound of steps announced the arrival of the next victim. Every detail was recorded on film, from the first wild struggle for breath to the final twitches.

Hitler had already "eagerly devoured" the arrest reports, information on new groups of suspects, and the statements recorded by interrogators. Now, on the very night of the first trials and executions, the film of the proceedings arrived at the Wolf's Lair for the amusement of the Führer and his guests. The putsch, he announced to his assembled retinue, was "perhaps the best thing that could have happened for our future." He could not get enough of watching his foes go to their doom. Days later, photographs of the condemned men dangling from hooks still lay about the great map table in his bunker. As his horizons shrank on all sides, Hitler took great satisfaction from this, his last great triumph.[16]

. . .

The excess so characteristic of the Nazi regime expressed itself not only in the savageness of the retribution but also in its broad sweep: even distant relatives of the conspirators fell victim to a lust for revenge worthy of the ancient Teutonic tribes. Himmler discussed the failed coup at length at a meeting of gauleiters in Posen two weeks after the event, declaring that he would "introduce absolute responsibility of kin . . . a very old custom practiced among our forefathers." One had only to read the Teutonic sagas, he said: "When they placed a family under the ban and declared it outlawed or when there was a blood feud in a family, they were utterly consistent. . . . This man has committed treason; his blood is bad; there is traitor's blood in him; that must be wiped out. And in the blood feud the entire clan was wiped out down to the last member. And so, too, will Count Stauffenberg's family be wiped out down to the last member."[17]

Accordingly, Himmler ordered relatives of the Stauffenberg brothers arrested, from their wives all the way to a three-year-old child and the eighty-five-year-old father of a cousin. A third Stauffenberg brother, Alexander, was not involved in the plot but was nevertheless returned from Athens to Berlin, interrogated at length, and dispatched to a concentration camp. The property of all relatives was seized. After an interrogation that yielded nothing of interest, Countess Stauffenberg was sent to the Ravensbrück concentration camp, as was her mother. Her children were placed in an orphanage and given the new surname Meister, which had been dreamed up by the Gestapo, perhaps in an ironic allusion to the Stefan George circle, whose members referred to their mentor as "master." Similar fates befell the families of Goerdeler, Tresckow, Lehndorff, Schwerin, Kleist, Oster, Trott, Haeften, Popitz, Hammerstein, and many others. While the persecution was extensive, it was also arbitrary: Princess Elisabeth Ruspoli, the mistress of General Alexander von Falkenhausen, was arrested, for example, but Moltke's family was left largely undisturbed.

In the tumultuous weeks preceding the final collapse of the Third Reich, most of these family members and other "prominent" prisoners were gathered together and dispatched on a nerve-wracking odyssey from one concentration camp to the next. In the late afternoon of April 28, 1945, the convoy arrived in Niederdorf in the Puster valley of Tyrol. Under the watch of some eighty SS men the trucks disgorged, among others, Hjalmar Schacht; the former French prime minister Léon Blum and his wife; Franz Halder; Kurt von Schuschnigg, the last chancellor of Austria; Martin Niemöller; Falkenhausen; the former Hungarian prime minister Count Nicholas Kállay; a nephew of Vyacheslav Molotov; some British secret service men; and a number of generals from countries formerly allied with Germany—160 people in all. The convoy commander, SS Obersturmführer Stiller, had top-priority orders to lead the prisoners to the nearby Pragser valley, where they would be shot and their bodies disposed of in the adjacent Wildsee. When one of the SS men disclosed to the throng that they were at "the final stop before the end," panic broke out. In the midst of the ensuing pandemonium one of the prisoners, Colonel Bogislav von Bonin, managed to contact the general staff of the commander in chief in the Southwest, stationed in Bozen, who asked Captain Wichard von Alvensleben to investigate "what's going on." But Alvensleben took it upon himself to go much further. The next morning he showed up with a quickly assembled contingent of troops and freed the prisoners, much to the anger of his superiors.[18]

The investigation of the failed coup received new impetus and much new information when Carl Goerdeler was finally arrested on August 12. For three weeks devoted friends had kept him in hiding, largely in and around Berlin, despite the bounty of a million marks on his head. True to form, he wrote yet another report during this time, as if obsessed with a mission that would never end. After a long, exhausting period of vacillation over whether he should continue hiding or attempt to flee the country, he seemed to abandon all hope of survival and simply set out to see his West Prussian homeland one last time. After a perilous three-day journey and much camping out in the open forest, he managed to reach Marienwerder. On his way to visit the graves of his parents, however, he was recognized by a woman who followed him so doggedly that he was forced to turn back. After another night under open skies, he was so drained that in the morning he sought refuge at an inn. Here he was recognized again, this time by a Luftwaffe employee who at one time had frequented his parents' house. She denounced Goerdeler to the police, apparently more out of eagerness to be involved in important goings-on than out of any particular ill will toward Goerdeler or even desire for the million-mark reward.

In the very first sentence he uttered in his initial interrogation session, Goerdeler admitted involvement in planning the coup. But he was eager to distance himself from the attempt on Hitler's life, describing Stauffenberg's failure as a "judgment by God." A few days after the attempt he had admonished an acquaintance he encountered in a Berlin metro station with the words "Thou shalt not kill."[19] Otherwise though, he spoke volubly about the leading role he had played in the opposition and about the widespread involvement of civilians, all to the great astonishment of his interrogators, who had continued to imagine that they were dealing with a military putsch and now learned for the first time about the civilian aspect—from no other authority than Goerdeler himself.

The willingness with which the former mayor of Leipzig disclosed the names of implicated businessmen, union leaders, and churchmen and detailed their motives and goals made him a traitor in the eyes of many of his fellow prisoners. It has also posed unsettling questions for his biographers. But one needs to make allowances for the shock he felt on being imprisoned, for his shattered nerves, and for the fact that he was held, heavily chained, in solitary confinement far longer than any of the other prisoners. He was dragged through endless interrogations and forced to pass night after night under brilliant floodlights, the door to his cell open and a guard posted outside; still, he did not recant his devotion to the cause. In the notes he wrote during these weeks he described Hitler as a "vampire" and a "disgrace to humanity," referred to the "bestial murder of a million Jews," and lamented the cowardice of those who allowed such things to happen "partly without realizing it and partly out of despair."[20] There were numerous friends and co-conspirators whom Goerdeler actually saved from arrest, and it is likely that he was also attempting to confuse the Gestapo by inundating them with an avalanche of facts and details.

Primarily, though, Goerdeler was simply acting in accordance with his lifelong belief that truth and reason would prove persuasive, even to Gestapo agents. This time, however, his belief would cost many lives. Thinking that the special commission must already know the general outlines of the plot, Goerdeler never thought to minimize things, to portray the monumental efforts of the resistance as merely the ravings of a few disgruntled malcontents. He still believed he had a duty to open Hitler's eyes to the fact that he was leading Germany into the abyss; he may even have hoped to initiate a dialogue with him. Goerdeler's "extraordinarily far-reaching account," as described in the Kaltenbrunner reports, thoroughly rebutted Hitler's notion of a "very small clique of ambitious officers." Goerdeler's candor was as admirable as it was fatal. His biographer Gerhard Ritter comments:

The surviving diaries of Ulrich von Hassell are one of the most important sources of information about the resistance to Hitler. Until he was dismissed from his position as ambassador to Rome in 1938, he was a prominent member of the conservative opposition. Respected by all, he was included on every cabinet list drawn up by the resistance after January 1943.
Above: *Hassell before the People's Court on September 8, 1944.*

He wanted not to play down what had been done but rather to make it appear as large, significant, and menacing to the regime as possible. For Goerdeler, this was absolutely not an officers' putsch . . . but an attempted uprising by an entire people as represented by the best and most noble members from all social strata, the entire political spectrum, and both the Catholic and Protestant churches. He himself stood up valiantly for what he had done, and he presumed his friends would do the same. In the shadow of the gallows, he still thought only of bringing the entire, unvarnished truth to light and hurling it in the faces of the authorities. This was impossible at the public show trials, as the shameful proceedings against Field Marshal Witzleben had made chillingly apparent. And so Goerdeler sought to speak out all the more clearly, forcefully, and exhaustively in the interrogations.[21]

The futility of this gesture, on which he had apparently based great hopes, was made clear to him scarcely four weeks after his incarceration at Gestapo headquarters on Prinz-Albrecht-Strasse. On September 8 he stood before the People's Court with Ulrich von Hassell, Josef Wirmer, lawyer Paul Lejeune-Jung, and Wilhelm Leuschner. Their trials proceeded like all the rest, with a raving, wildly gesticulating Freisler constantly interrupting and refusing to allow any of the accused to explain their motives. In the end Goerdeler was condemned as a "traitor through and through, . . . a cowardly, disreputable traitor, consumed with ambition, and a political spy in wartime." While Wirmer, Lejeune-Jung, and Hassell were executed that same day and Leuschner was dispatched two weeks later, Goerdeler was kept alive for almost five months. He was probably spared so that further information could be extracted from him and so that his skills as a master administrator could be exploited for drawing up plans for reform and reconstruction after the war. The decisive factor in the delay, however, was presumably Himmler's desire to have Goerdeler as a negotiator in the event that his insane scheme of making contact with the enemy behind Hitler's back succeeded. This supposition is supported by the fact that Popitz's life was also spared for some time, even though he had been sentenced to die on October 3.[22]

Goerdeler hoped that his date with the executioner would be delayed until the war had ended, saving him and his fellow prisoners. Meanwhile, however, the Allied advance into central Germany was stalled, and Justice Minister Otto Thierack began asking more and more pointed questions as to why Goerdeler and Popitz were still alive. Like so many of his previous fantasies, Goerdeler's last hope finally burst on the afternoon of February 2, 1945, when bellowing SS men barged into his cell and led him away.

Gerhard Ritter has painted a profound and compelling portrait of Goerdeler as someone whose very relentlessness in the struggle against Hitler was symptomatic of a lack of realism. Arrested as a member of the Freiburg group of professors, Ritter found himself face to face with Goerdeler in prison in January 1945: "A suddenly aged man stood before me," Ritter later recounted, "chained hand and foot and wearing the same light summer clothing—now shabby and collarless—in which he had been arrested." What shook Ritter most, however, were Goerdeler's eyes. Always so luminous in the past, they had now become "the eyes of a blind man."[23]

. . .

On September 15, 1944, Ernst Kaltenbrunner reported that the investigations had been largely completed and that no further revelations could be expected. Then, just eight days later, papers fell into the hands of Reich Security Headquarters that proved him wrong. Lieutenant Colonel Werner Schrader, a close confidant of Hans Oster's at Military Intelligence, had committed suicide, and his driver, feeling despondent and abandoned, approached police inspector Franz Xaver Sonderegger and described to him a bundle of papers that had been deposited in the Prussian State Bank in 1942 and later taken to Zossen, where they were stored in a safe. His curiosity aroused, Sonderegger went to Zossen and opened the safe. What he found were the materials that Beck, Oster, and Halder had produced for the coup attempt in the late 1930s and that Hans von Dohnanyi had gathered together: minutes of meetings, plans for military operations, addresses, notes on the Blomberg and Fritsch affairs, loose sheets of paper—all of it carefully filed. There were even a few pages from the long-sought diaries of Admiral Canaris.

The discovery brought to light the activities of Halder, Brauchitsch, Thomas, Nebe, and others, but what was much more devastating to the regime was the sudden realization once again that the assumption underlying the entire investigation was false. The conspiracy of July 20 was plainly not the work of a few disgruntled, resentful, or exhausted officers, unhappy with the reversal in the tide of war. Quite to the contrary, the roots of the conspiracy reached as far back as 1938, the highest echelons of the Wehrmacht were involved, and the motives of the conspirators were much more complex than anyone had suspected. Kaltenbrunner's next report spoke of the conspirators' desire to prevent the outbreak of war, their widespread criticism of the "handling of the Jewish question," the Nazis' policy toward the churches, and the generally "harmful influence" of

Himmler and the Gestapo.[24] Hitler was so alarmed that he ordered that none of the documents was to be entered into evidence in the trials before the People's Court without his specific approval. He also insisted that the investigation of the new revelations be strictly separate and that the arrest of General Halder and his incarceration on Prinz-Albrecht-Strasse be kept secret from all the other prisoners.[25]

The Nazis' belief in the unity of *Volk* and Führer could not survive the Zossen documents and the information they revealed. As one high official in the Ministry of Justice commented in desperation, "We are being engulfed by July 20. We are no longer masters of the situation."[26] Hitler decided to postpone the trials connected with the newly uncovered conspiracy, and when an American bombing raid destroyed part of Gestapo headquarters he ordered the prisoners implicated in the conspiracy transferred to Buchenwald and then to Flossenbürg in the Upper Palatinate region. It is possible that he even considered sweeping the entire affair under the rug.

On April 4, 1945, the bulk of Canaris's fabled diaries turned up by accident, once again in Zossen. Kaltenbrunner thought the discovery so important that he personally delivered the black notebooks to the Reich Chancellery the very next day. Immersing himself in the revelations they contained, Hitler grew increasingly convinced that his great mission, now under threat from all sides, had been sabotaged from the outset by intrigue, false oaths, deception, and betrayal from within. His anger, hatred, and frustration exploded in a volcanic outburst, which concluded with a terse instruction for the commander of the SS unit responsible for his personal safety, Hans Rattenhuber: "Destroy the conspirators!"[27]

In a farcical procedure, Kaltenbrunner immediately convened two SS kangaroo courts, though they lacked jurisdiction and therefore any veneer of the legality they were meant to display. One court traveled to the Sachsenhausen concentration camp, where Dohnanyi was being held. In order to escape the tortures of his interrogators, he had intentionally infected himself with diptheria bacilli and was still suffering the effects: severe heart problems, frequent cramping, and paralysis. Only semiconscious, he was carried before his judges on a stretcher and, without further ado, condemned to hang. There was not even a written record of the proceedings, though that was strictly required by German law.

Events transpired similarly at Flossenbürg, where, two days later, on April 8, 1945, the second kangaroo court condemned Canaris, Oster, Dietrich Bonhoeffer, Military Intelligence captain Ludwig Gehre, and army judge Karl Sack. While Canaris still sought a way out during the proceedings, Oster reportedly declared, "I can only say what I know. I'm no liar," and defiantly owned up to all that he had done. In the end all the accused were condemned to die. That evening Canaris tapped out a final message to the prisoner in the next cell, a Danish secret service officer: "My days are done. Was not a traitor."[28]

As the skies began to lighten at dawn the next day, the executions began. The victims were taken to a bathing cubicle, where they were forced to strip; then, one by one, they were led naked across the courtyard to the gallows. Hooks had been attached to the rafters of an open wooden structure. The condemned men were ordered to climb a few steps, a noose was placed around their necks, and the steps were kicked aside.

On the stacks of clothing left behind were found the books that the victims had been reading when the end came: on Bonhoeffer's, the Bible and a volume of Goethe's works; on Canaris's, *Kaiser Frederick the Second* by Ernst Kantorowicz. Although Josef Müller had traveled to Rome on a number of occasions at Oster's behest and was also incarcerated in Flossenbürg, for some inexplicable reason he was not tried and condemned with his fellow conspirators. Late that morning he learned from an English prisoner that the bodies of his friends were already being cremated on a pyre behind the camp jail. "Particles floated through the air," he later recalled, "swirling through the bars of my cell . . . little bits of human flesh." Two days later the rumble of the approaching front could be heard in the distance.[29]

■ ■ ■

The more hopeless Germany's military prospects became, the more summary and arbitrary was the regime's great reckoning with its do-

Adam von Trott zu Solz in the dock in the People's Court in Berlin. A few days later, shortly before his death, he said that he regarded his participation in the resistance as an act of loyalty to his country.

mestic opponents, as the courts reached out to punish people only marginally involved in the uprising. In early October 1944 Martin Bormann took it upon himself to remind Hitler that Erwin Rommel, on a visit to Führer headquarters near Margival the previous June, had flatly contradicted Hitler and had subsequently urged him to end the war. Kluge's suicide cast further, though never proven, suspicions on Rommel, whose enormous popularity with the German people only made Hitler more jealous and wary. On October 7, while he was still convalescing at home from the serious war wounds he had suffered, Rommel received orders to present himself in Berlin three days later. On the advice of his doctors, he replied that he was unable to make the journey and asked to send an officer instead. In response, Generals Ernst Maisel and Wilhelm Burgdorf, both members of the military "court of honor," were dispatched to Rommel's residence in Herrlingen near Ulm, where, on October 14, they presented him with an ultimatum: either he took poison and received a state funeral or he would be brought before the People's Court. While this discussion took place, SS units surrounded the village. After Hitler's emissaries left the house Rommel told his wife that he did not shrink from the prospect of a trial but was certain he would never reach Berlin alive. He was also concerned about the consequences for his family if he opted for a trial. And so Rommel decided to take the poison. "I'll be dead in a quarter of an hour," he said before heading out the door to where the two generals were waiting. It was shortly after one o'clock in the afternoon.

About twenty minutes later Maisel and Burgdorf delivered the corpse to a military hospital in Ulm. When the head physician wanted to conduct an autopsy, Burgdorf warned, "Don't touch the body. Everything is being take care of from Berlin." Wilhelm Keitel later said that though Hitler himself first suggested doing away with Rommel, the Führer never revealed the real reasons, even to his closest confidants, and insisted to Göring, Jodl, and Dönitz that the field marshal had died of natural causes.[30]

Meanwhile the political trials had continued, at first at a pace of one a week and later about one every two weeks. On August 15, 1944, Count Helldorf, Hayessen, Hans-Bernd Haeften, and Adam Trott were sentenced to death; on August 21, Thiele, Colonel Jäger, and Schwerin von Schwanenfeld; the next week, Stülpnagel, Hofacker, Linstow, and Finckh. Soon thereafter came Thüngen, Langbehn, Jessen, Meichssner, and General Herfurth (despite his refusal to help on the day of the coup attempt). On October 20, Julius Leber and Adolf Reichwein were condemned, then Captain Hermann Kaiser, General Lindemann, Theodor Haubach, and many others.

Moltke was tried on January 9–10, 1945, along with Alfred Delp, Eugen Gerstenmaier, and a few other friends from the Kreisau Circle. Moltke's connection with the events of July 20 was actually more circumstantial than direct, though he had associated with a number of the rebels. Immediately after the attempted assassination and coup he remarked, "If I had been free, this would not have happened," a reference to the fact that he had already been arrested by that time. At his trial he continued to insist that he was opposed to any acts of violence.

By July 20, 1944, Helmuth von Moltke had already been in custody for half a year. When his connections with the conspirators came to light, however, he was swept up in the trials before the People's Court, even though he had always been opposed to assassinating Hitler. "We are to be hanged because we thought together," he wrote in one of his last letters, almost joyful at the idea that his death sentence represented a testimonial to the power of the mind.

Above: Moltke appearing before the People's Court on January 10, 1945.

Despite his negligible role in the coup, Moltke exemplifies better perhaps than any other opposition figure the deep ambivalence of the German resistance. The records of his trial have been lost, like so many others, but on January 10 and 11, shortly after his trial, he wrote two letters to his wife that were spirited out of his cell by Poelchau, the chaplain. They contain far more than just personal comments. An entire intellectual climate emerges in the love of philosophizing, the distaste for practical action, and the religiously inspired joy at the prospect of death. As one of the early chroniclers of the German resistance commented, Moltke's letters can only be read "with horror and admiration."[31]

The letters begin with an extensive description of his trial, at which Freisler sought to portray not Goerdeler but the Kreisauers—"these

In contrast to most other members of the Kreisau Circle, Eugen Ger-stenmaier always advocated overthrowing Hilter by force. As a Protestant theologian, he maintained close ties with the Ecumenical Council in Geneva and in 1942 met Helmuth von Moltke, who came to value Gerstenmaier's advice on church and foreign policy issues. Summoned by Peter Yorck, he went to Bendlerstrasse on July 20 and was arrested there that evening. He defended himself skillfully before the People's Court and managed to come away with only a prison term.

Above: *Gerstenmaier before the People's Court in January 1945. Helmuth von Moltke is in the background to the right.*

young men"—as the actual "engine" behind the coup. Moltke emphasizes repeatedly that he not only agreed with that assessment but was absolutely delighted by Freisler's decision to drop all specific allegations related to practical preparations for the coup in order to focus on the real crimes: "defeatist" thought and adherence to the Christian and ethical principles to which Moltke and his friends wanted society to return.

"Ultimately," says Moltke in the first of these long letters, "this concentration on the religious aspect corresponds with the inner nature of things and shows that Freisler is a good political judge after all. It gives us the inestimable advantage of being killed for something that (a) we really have done and (b) is worthwhile." He continues, "It is established that we never wanted to use force; it is established that we did not make a single attempt to organize anything, did not promise a single person a future post—though the indictment said otherwise. All we did was think—and really only Delp, Gerstenmaier, and I. . . . And it is before the thoughts of these three isolated men, the mere thoughts, that National Socialism now so trembles that it wants to exterminate everything that is infected by them. If that isn't a compliment of the highest order! After this trial we are free of all the Goerdeler mess; we are free of all practical questions. We are to be hanged because we thought together. Freisler is right, right a thousand times over. If we are to die, then let it be for this. . . . Long live Freisler!"

These few lines distill both what was memorable about the German resistance but what, at the same time, constituted its greatest weakness and the most compelling reason for its failure. The "Goerdeler mess" about which Moltke writes so disparagingly was in fact nothing other than a practical relation to the world, to people, and to the forces at work—in a word, to reality. Virtually all the opposition groups, though some more than others, liked to think of themselves as above the concerns of the grimy everyday world, and that attitude seriously compromised their ability to accomplish anything, especially as the Nazis did not respect the distinction but viewed thought and action as one. On the final judgment against Moltke one contemporary who had read the letters commented curtly, "He did more than just think."

In his second letter, dated January 11, 1945, Moltke returned to his earlier line of reasoning: "Of that entire gang only Freisler recognized me, and of that entire gang only he understands why he must kill me. . . . The key to the trial lay in the words 'Christianity and National Socialism have one thing in common, Count von Moltke, and only one: we both demand the whole person.' Did he realize what he was saying? Just think how wonderfully God prepared this, his most unworthy vessel. At the very moment when I was in danger of being drawn into active preparations for the putsch—when Stauffenberg came to see Peter [Yorck] on the evening of the 19th [of January

1944]—I was taken away, so that I could, and will continue, to remain free of any connection with violence."

Such shifts in tone from factual narration to pious contemplation are already present in the opening, primarily descriptive passages of the letters, but they become more frequent in the more personal parts that follow, until finally spiritual meditations, biblical references, and verses from songs build to a kind of exuberant longing for death that leaves no room for sorrow and farewell, only a sense of divine mission, fulfillment, and the grace of God. Moltke notes on a number of occasions that he feels "exalted and uplifted," even though those around him seem "quite shocked." Toward the end he writes, "I have wept a little, not out of sadness or melancholy, not because I would like to undo what I have done, but because I am thankful and moved by this sign from God. It is not given to us to see him face to face, but we must feel deeply moved when we suddenly realize that he has gone before us our entire lives, a cloud by day and a pillar of fire by night, and that all at once he is allowing us to glimpse this truth. Now nothing more can happen."

On January 12, 1945, Moltke's death sentence was handed down. He was executed eleven days later, on January 23, together with nine other prisoners. Shortly thereafter, on February 3, just as Freisler was launching the proceedings against Fabian von Schlabrendorff, air raid sirens began to howl. In the heaviest aerial attack on Berlin of the entire war, one bomb hit the building on Bellevuestrasse where the People's Court was in session. A falling beam struck Freisler on the head as he clutched the files on Schlabrendorff. Otherwise no one was injured. A passing doctor was summoned from the street, but he could only confirm that Freisler's wounds were fatal. (Ironically, the doctor turned out to be the brother of Rüdiger Schleicher, whom Freisler had condemned to death the previous day.) Schlabrendorff's trial had to be postponed, and when he was brought before the court again in mid-March he was acquitted on a technicality: he had been tortured, in violation of the law.[32]

Some other of the conspirators managed to cheat death as well, including almost all of Tresckow's friends in Army Group Center, among them Philipp von Boeselager, Rudolph-Christoph von Gers-

Arthur Nebe (right) *was one of the most paradoxical figures of the Third Reich, involved in both totalitarian terror and the resistance. As chief of the Office of Criminal Police, which was later absorbed into Reich Security Headquarters, he played a major role in building an omnipresent police state. At the beginning of the Russian campaign, he was named head of Einsatzgruppe B, one of the four mass-murder commandos of the SS. At the same time, he maintained contacts with Oster and Gisevius and funneled important information to them. Serious doubts have been raised about his claim that he ignored Hitler's commands but pretended to have carried them out. Although he was not really part of the resistance, he lost his nerve in late July 1944 and went underground. He was discovered in mid-January 1945 in a mill near Zossen, sentenced to death in early March, and executed.*

Above: Nebe in August 1940 with the chief of the Spanish police, Count Mayalde, and Reinhard Heydrich.

dorff, and Eberhard von Breitenbuch. Several members of the Kreisau Circle—Horst von Einsiedel, Carl Dietrich von Trotha, Otto von der Gablentz, the Jesuit priest Augustin Rösch, and others—also survived. Eugen Gerstenmaier dodged a death sentence by playing the role of the naive theologian baffled and bewildered by the world of politics; so convincing was he that Freisler condemned him to only seven years in prison. Hans Bernd Gisevius managed to escape to Switzerland, thanks to his foreign connections and especially the intervention of Allen W. Dulles, the head of the Office of Strategic Services. Erich Kordt was a safe distance away at a diplomatic posting in China, and Theo Kordt was in Switzerland. Friedrich Wilhelm Heinz was well-acquainted with life underground and numbered among the very few, including Jakob Kaiser and the Hammerstein brothers, Kunrat and Ludwig, who managed to survive the war in hiding. Hans von Boineburg was assigned to an army punishment detail, as was Harald Momm, the colonel who had called for a bottle of champagne in Krampitz on hearing news of the attack on Hitler.[33] Less fortunate was Arthur Nebe, who finally went underground on July 24. Making use of all the evasive ruses at his command, he feigned suicide, leaving fake farewell letters behind. He managed to escape detection until January 16 but was finally arrested, brought before the courts, and executed in March 1945. That same month, so close to the end of the war, Friedrich Fromm was convicted on a charge of cowardice and, in what was viewed as an act of leniency, sentenced to be shot by a firing squad. The execution was carried out on March 12, 1945, in Brandenburg prison.

One month later, as the Red Army girded itself for the final assault on Berlin, Hitler's campaign for revenge was still going strong. The jails were filled to overflowing with political opponents who either had been condemned or were awaiting trial. On April 14 Himmler ordered that none of these prisoners were to survive the war. Earlier, Gestapo chief Heinrich Müller had told Moltke's wife, Freya, "We won't make the same mistake as in 1918. We won't leave our internal German enemies alive."[34]

By this point, however, events were beginning to overtake Himmler, Müller, and the Gestapo in general. On April 21—the same day that an agitated Hitler called General Karl Koller, the chief of staff of the Luftwaffe, to inform him that the heart of Berlin was under artillery bombardment—eleven men who had not yet been sentenced were released. One of them sought, on the spur of the moment, to obtain the release of other prisoners as well. On April 23 his efforts resulted in the freeing of prisoners incarcerated at Moabit prison. The SS, however, had taken charge of liquidating the Gestapo prison on Lehrterstrasse. Here, too, twenty-one inmates facing lesser charges had already been released, among them the lawyer Hans Lukaschek and Kraft von Palombini, who had sheltered Goerdeler. Some of the remaining inmates were informed that they would be released after transfer to headquarters on Prinz-Albrecht-Strasse. They were herded together by SS guards and marched off down Lehrterstrasse in a light rain at about one o'clock in the morning. When they reached the corner of Invalidenstrasse, the guards ordered the prisoners to proceed across a field of rubble. The command "Ready, fire!" rang out and the prisoners fell, all of them shot in the neck. Among those murdered in this fashion were Klaus Bonhoeffer, Rüdiger Schleicher, Friedrich Justus Perels, and Albrecht Haushofer.[35]

The next day some of the remaining inmates were released and the others were turned over to the judicial authorities. After midnight, however, another SS detachment appeared, took away Albrecht von Bernstorff, Karl Ludwig von Guttenberg, and the trade union leader Ernst Schneppenhorst, and murdered them. When day broke, the rest of the prisoners managed to persuade the warden that it was in his own best interest to let them go before the Russian troops arrived. At around six in the evening, the last political prisoners were released from Lehrterstrasse, including Justus Delbrück of Military Intelligence, Professors Gerhard Ritter, Adolf Lampe, and Theodor Steltzer. They fled as the battle for Berlin began in earnest.

■   ■   ■

In the debates that had raged within the resistance for years, Goerdeler had always argued that the first task of the resistance and the one that had the best chance of success was simply to inform the

German people about the crimes of the regime: the fact that the Nazis had set out to provoke war, their enormous corruption, the disgraceful practices of the Einsatzgruppen, the mass murder committed in the concentration camps. Such outrage would be provoked, he imagined, that Hitler and his accomplices would be swept from office.

The failure of the attack on Hitler and the conspirators' lack of opportunity to make their declaration to the people prevented Goerdeler's idea from ever being put to the test. But as the writer Ernst Jünger wrote in his diary following a conversation with Cäsar von Hofacker, Hitler would certainly have emerged the victor in a battle of the airwaves.[36] His psychological hold over the people, although loosening, was still very real, however much the reasons behind it had changed. The masses had lost most of their faith and admiration but still had a dark, fatalistic feeling that their destiny was inextricably bound up with his. The ominous propaganda of the last months of the war and fear of the advancing Red Army drove them into the Führer's arms despite their mounting disgust with the brutality of the regime and with the cowardice, venality, and egotism of its officials. Though they felt suffocated by the pressures of police-state surveillance, informers, and terror, they clung to vague hopes that, as so often in the past, the Führer would find a way to avert catastrophe. On June 16, 1944, the first of his much-heralded "reprisal weapons," V-1 rockets, were launched against London. Immediately following the events of July 20, a Norwegian newspaper reporter observed the general mood in Germany: "The masses are apathetic; they neither see nor hear and therefore remain totally inert. . . . They neither weep nor celebrate nor rage."[37]

And so the German resistance remained what it had always been: an expression of feelings that may well have been widespread but that only a tiny minority was prepared to act on. Ironically, the social isolation of the resistance continued even after the war, for as the end drew near, Nazi propagandists and Allied spokesmen joined forces in a de facto coalition to belittle the accomplishments of the resistance and disparage its motives. In the House of Commons Churchill described the events of July 20 as a murderous internecine power struggle, and in Moscow Rudolf Herrnstadt celebrated the failure of what he termed the final attempt of "the gentlemen's clubs, the reactionaries" to grab power.[38]

These attitudes did not change much even after the fall of the Third Reich in May 1945. The resistance found no more acknowledgment or comprehension after the war than it had under the Nazis themselves, whether in Germany or abroad. On the first anniversary of the execution of Count Schwerin von Schwanenfeld, a church funeral was held but it had to be announced as a service for a "fallen soldier." The family of Fritz-Dietlof von der Schulenburg experienced great difficulty in asserting their rights to his estate, as did the dispossessed families of other conspirators. For a long time the occupation authorities forbade or placed limitations on publications about the German resistance. Ulrich von Hassell's diaries were first published in Switzerland and then in Sweden, while both Fabian von Schlabrendorff's *Offiziere gegen Hitler (Revolt Against Hitler)* and Rudolf Pechel's *Deutscher Widerstand (The German Resistance)* were on the index of books forbidden by the Allies.[39]

Denial and dismissal were common everywhere. When the celebrated English military writer Basil H. Liddell Hart attempted to portray the background to the 1938 coup attempt in a London newspaper, publication was prevented by the government. In American prisoner-of-war and internment camps, officers who had participated in the resistance were locked up indiscriminately with generals and SS men who were still pro-Nazi. The theory of the unity of Führer and *Volk* continued to be upheld. Those who had risked everything in their struggle against the Nazis were held prisoner by the Allies for years—in many cases even longer than their Nazi foes.

In the summer of 1947 the American military administration released Hitler's former army adjutant General Gerhard Engel and a number of general staff officers from prisoner-of-war camps. Meanwhile General Gersdorff, who had undertaken in March 1943 to set off a bomb and kill both Hitler and himself, continued to be held. When he questioned the rationale, he was informed by the camp commandant that "General Engel has demonstrated throughout his military career that he always carries out his orders. He will not engage in any resistance to us in civilian life either, and therefore he poses no threat. You, on the other hand, have shown that you follow your own conscience on occasion and consequently might not obey our orders under certain circumstances. People like you or General Falkenhausen [who also continued to be held prisoner] are therefore dangerous to us. For this reason, you will remain in custody."[40]

. . .

To the many images of the resistance that have been handed down to us, we must add that of Carl Goerdeler sitting alone in his cell in the basement of Reich Security Headquarters. Early in 1945 he made another attempt to break the silence that was beginning to envelop all that he and his fellow conspirators had thought and striven for. In the last of the many papers he wrote, he seems finally to confront the possibility that he took the wrong approach and that everything he had done to prevent Hitler from leading Germany to catastrophe had been in vain. He places hopes in friends who had in fact long since been executed, records a few memories, addresses Germany's youth and future generations, and finally breaks off his musings in the middle of a sentence filled with desperate thoughts about an "indifferent God," the triumph of evil, and the obliteration of goodness, guilt, and righteousness. "Like the psalmist I quarrel with God," he writes, "and this struggle decorates the bare walls of my tiny cell, filling the emptiness with my imaginings and my memories." In the end, he could not continue, finding no answer to the thought to which his mind constantly returned: "Can this be the Last Judgment?"[41]

11

THE WAGES OF FAILURE

No sooner had it collapsed than the German resistance—its thoughts and deeds, its strenuous efforts, its high hopes and crushing disappointments—was almost entirely lost to memory. The stunning events of July 20 overshadowed the movement as a whole, and it has hardly become any better known in the intervening years. Its traces vanished, quickly and inconspicuously, in prison cells, killing fields, concentration camps, execution grounds, and unknown burial sites. It is noted, to be sure, on Germany's informal calendar of memorial events, as a ceremony is held annually in the courtyard of the former army headquarters on Bendlerstrasse. Little about it penetrates the public mind, however, and it has never earned more than grudging respect. It remains, in the words of Fabian von Schlabrendorff, an obscure "episode" of the war.[1]

Curiously enough, Hitler's description of the conspirators as a "very small clique of ambitious officers," a characterization trumpeted by Nazi propagandists, has proved remarkably resilient. By the time of the attack on Hitler all that the conspirators really hoped was that the memory of the resistance would live on. But even this was not to be, thanks both to Allied policy and to Germany's postwar psychological climate of mass repression, born of guilt and a desire to forget.

The quick disappearance of the resistance from public memory was all the more striking in that it seemed to run counter to the sentimental German fondness for lost causes. This penchant was apparently outweighed by the equally traditional deference to authority and by the feeling that the resistance betrayed the fatherland in its hour of need. Germans have found it useful at times to resurrect the resistance in order to disprove the theory of collective guilt, but they have generally adopted Field Marshal Kluge's dismissive view of it as nothing more than a botched coup attempt.

Some writers have even suggested that the opposition decided to act only when it was clear Germany would go down to defeat—and solely for self-seeking reasons. The view that the old aristocracy, dismayed at its waning power, hoped at the last minute to mask its long collusion with the Nazis and thereby retain its privileges, property, position, and influence soon gained currency. Even a superficial knowledge of the resistance shows how misguided and biased that argument is. Probably the most promising of all the plots against Hitler was conceived as early as 1938, in response to his preparations to invade other countries. Furthermore, the planning within Army Group Center for the second attempt on Hitler's life took place before Stalingrad and the great turning point in the war.

The truth is in fact the virtual opposite of what these writers alleged. In view of Hitler's string of political and military triumphs, which were setbacks for the opposition, it is remarkable how tenaciously the resistance continued to plot against him. Apart from Halder, the same men who opposed Hitler in the early days opposed him in the end, their ranks swelled by many new recruits. There is ample reason to conclude that, in the early postwar years at least, disdain for the resistance could be traced to the attitudes of a generation of passive Nazi sympathizers and their descendants, who were not eager to have their own failings highlighted by comparison with the heroism of a group of aristocrats and professional soldiers—a group that had supposedly been consigned to the dustbin of history.

These attitudes stemmed to a certain extent from a fundamental misunderstanding that was created or at least encouraged by some of the early memoirs published by members of the resistance. Today it is well known that—although these accounts seem to imply otherwise—neither the resistance movement as a whole nor the attempt on July

20, 1944, to kill Hitler and stage a coup represented a short-term undertaking by a band of army officers. Many groups, some closely connected to these officers and others linked more indirectly, contributed to the dramatic events of that day. The lists of projected cabinet members of the interim government, which survive in varying versions, all convey the breadth and social pluralism of the resistance, as well as the leading role to be played by civilians.[2] There was never any dispute about the latter point, according to the written sources, which attest to numerous debates and differences of opinion over virtually everything else. The officers who participated in the September conspiracy of 1938, from Oster to Halder and Witzleben, agreed that the officer corps was merely the organized and armed vanguard of the operation and would retreat into the background as soon its work was completed.

Moreover, the motivation of the members of the resistance was not at all a desire to preserve the privileges of social rank. Certainly many of the conspirators saw themselves as members of a social elite, with particular responsibility for providing leadership. That conviction facilitated their decision to oppose the regime and deepened their resolve as the Nazis continued to trample on all traditional principles of law and order. It was not, however, their dominant impulse. Nor can their opposition to the Nazis be said to have sprung solely from a sense of moral outrage, as is often claimed. In reality, the rebels were driven by an array of motives that in most cases arose from professional frustrations and quickly broadened to general political disenchantment. Their motives were further reinforced by moral, religious, or nationalistic convictions, which varied in intensity from one person to the next.

In their interrogations or in their testimony before the People's Court, twenty of the accused conspirators from the various groups— whether civilian or military, national-conservative, middle class, or socialist—mentioned the persecution of the Jews as the primary motive for their opposition.[3] Others emphasized the elimination of civil rights, the arbitrary, dictatorial style of the government, and the assault on the churches. The basic conviction uniting those who acted out of religious belief was best expressed by Hans-Bernd von Haeften, when he stated before the People's Court that Hitler was "a great perpetrator of evil."

Gerstenmaier called this remark "the key to the entire resistance," from which all the rest flowed as a Christian duty.[4]

Those whose resistance was motivated primarily by nationalist concerns were the most torn. Their dilemma stemmed not only from the fact that Hitler shared their nationalism—in however exaggerated a form—but that for a long time his achievements reflected their desires. From the annexation of Austria to the victory over France, notes and reports written at the time by people like Hassell, Stieff, and Schulenburg attest to their divided sentiments: horror at the disgrace heaped on Germany and its good name through incessant criminal acts and yet pride in the growing power and increasing influence of the fatherland. "There is no doubt," wrote Ulrich von Hassell in October 1940, "that if this system emerges victorious, Germany and Europe are headed for terrible times. But if Germany is defeated, the consequences are simply unimaginable."[5]

The kinds of resistance were as varied as the motives, ranging from quiet disapproval and withdrawal to efforts on behalf of the persecuted and finally to active opposition to the Nazi regime, which itself took many forms. Easiest to understand are those people who strongly disapproved of the Nazis from beginning to end, particularly political opponents such as Leber, Mierendorff, the Kreisauers, Hammerstein, and Oster. Somewhat more complicated are those like Mertz von Quirnheim, Jens Peter Jessen, and Fritz-Dietlof von der Schulenburg, whose early enthusiasm for the Nazis turned to disappointment, anger, and finally, bitter rejection. Yet another strand is represented by Ernst von Weizsäcker, the state secretary in the Foreign Office, who traveled a slippery path between conformity and accommodation on the one hand and resistance on the other, with all the attendant illusions and entanglements one might expect. Other cases are stranger, like that of Count Wolf-Heinrich von Helldorf, a rather coarse, boorish man who rose—for good reason—within the ranks of the SA. More unfathomable still was the transformation of SS Gruppenführer Arthur Nebe, who as chief of criminal police in Reich Security Headquarters was one of the architects of the totalitarian police state and later served as commander of Einsatzgruppe B who found his way into resistance circles in the late 1930s after becoming closely acquainted with Oster. No case is the same as the others; each must be looked at in a different light, and all are overshadowed by the darkness of those years.

These brief examples show that the conspirators, though frequently bound together by personal ties and occasionally by ties between the various groups, had no real common denominator or unifying idea, not even a collective name. Far from representing a tightly knit social elite hoping to regain its lost preeminence, the opposition to Hitler consisted of a motley collection of individuals who differed greatly in their social origins, habits of thought, political attitudes, and methods of action. Even the term *resistance* was not used until after the war, and to say that someone "joined" the resistance is misleading. People who were hostile to the regime found their way to one another through friendships, chance encounters, and in some instances persistent searches. Sometimes they remained active in the circles they discovered; at other times they dropped out. They were buffeted by the hazards of war, and they forged new connections whenever circumstances permitted. The extreme diversity of their views is illustrated by the fact that even close friends and philosophical allies could not agree on so basic an issue as whether Hitler should be assassinated.

All that united the resistance were a few fundamental maxims: a refusal to participate in the violence, mindlessness, and injustice on all sides; a strong sense of right and wrong; and, as one member of Tresckow's circle observed, a desire "somehow simply to survive with a sense of decency."[6] In October 1944 Helmuth von Moltke wrote to his two sons from his prison cell: "I have struggled all my life—beginning in my school days—against the narrow-mindedness and arrogance, the penchant for violence, the merciless consistency and the love of the absolute, that seem to be inherent in the Germans and that have found expression in the National Socialist state. I have also done what I could to ensure that this spirit—with its excessive nationalism, persecution of other races, agnosticism, and materialism—is defeated."[7] Hans Oster, writing to his own son from prison, expressed similar sentiments, though couched in simpler terms reminiscent of an earlier era; the important thing, he wrote, is to remain "to your last breath the decent sort of fellow you were taught to be in the nursery and in your training as a soldier."[8]

Their clear sense of conscience and morality lent the conspirators an uncompromising, categorical outlook that was the source of much of their inner strength. But coupled with their fondness for abstract theorizing and elaborate intellectualism, it tended to impede action. Well after they had finally decided to resort to violence—indeed on the afternoon of July 20—they nevertheless renounced the use of firearms in army headquarters so as not to besmirch the righteousness of their cause; this was an expression more of their romantic impracticality and their inconsistency than of their high moral purpose. Eugen Gerstenmaier, who had always favored killing Hitler, turned up at army headquarters carrying both a revolver and a Bible, as if hoping to demonstrate the compatibility of religious faith and tyrannicide. He urged the conspirators to take up arms as a visible sign of their determination, arguing that rebels who failed to go the limit were not rebels at all but sacrificial lambs.[9]

But lofty moral principles had in fact come into play much earlier. For instance, General Alexander von Falkenhausen was not admitted into the inner circle of conspirators because he had a mistress. Similarly, Helldorf was kept at arm's length because of misgivings about his moral fiber, and it was possibly for this reason that he was left without instructions on July 20. Although Rommel certainly had reservations of his own about the conspiracy, the rebels made little attempt to win him over, because he clearly had little sympathy for their strict moral imperatives, ethics, and concern with matters of conscience. Nor were they swayed by the fact that Rommel was the only public figure with sufficient authority to challenge Hitler. They would permit no outsider to taint the purity of the new beginning they were proposing. Throughout the struggle there were similar moral gestures, including the determination of the Stauffenberg brothers to turn themselves over to the courts for judgment if the coup proved successful.[10]

■　■　■

None of the leading participants felt at ease with the role of conspirator. Born and raised in secure circumstances with a solid core of values and beliefs, extensive social ties, and firm loyalties, they had known only sheltered existences, and they had difficulty even comprehending what Hitler had done to their ostensibly reliable world. Ernst von Weizsäcker, asked if he had a pistol in case worst came to worst, replied, "I'm sorry, but I was not brought up to kill anyone."[11] For a while, most of the conspirators concealed or simply endured their torn loyalties. Henning von Tresckow, for example, threw himself into planning troop movements for the invasion of Czechoslovakia at a time when he had already urged that forceful measures be taken against the SS and the Gestapo. Such inconsistencies grew increasingly hard to live with, however, and eventually compelled the opposition to confront the fact that fighting for their country meant advancing the very brutality they despised.

Only a minority freed themselves from this quandary by deciding to resist actively. The majority, even of those senior officers who disliked the regime or privately expressed their outrage at it, grew resigned early on and adopted the posture of morally neutral specialists in military affairs. No less a figure than Franz Halder said after the war that he was "astonished beyond belief" at the suggestion that people "who were duty-bound by a specific oath to a particular kind of obedience" could be expected to support the coup.[12]

Of course, many who thought of themselves purely as "professional soldiers" supported the regime and were even devoted to it, at first often out of an illusory self-interest and later out of subservience and a need to conform. In his diary, Hassell bitterly parodied the attitude of a leading general with this jingle: "Turn your collar up and say, 'I'm a soldier and must obey!'"[13] But far from being an exception, that attitude was much closer to the norm. In that light the history of the Hitler years amounted to a depressing series of evasions and gestures of abject submission, broken only occasionally by halfhearted protests.

As always in times of rapid political and social change, the period was marked by opportunism and shortsightedness, aggravated in this case by the continuing disintegration of the traditional value system, a process begun with the First World War and the Treaty of Versailles, if not earlier. To explain such a breakdown solely in terms of individual frailty, however, is to ignore the deeper reasons for the failure of the vast majority of German officers to resist the Nazis. For these, one must turn to the explanations that the participants themselves advanced.

Chief among them is the myth that the German army had a tradition of nonintervention in politics, a leitmotif that runs through numerous apologia written after the war. The authors of these accounts complain that their critics want to have it both ways, accusing the army of having intervened in politics during the Weimar Republic and under Kaiser Wilhelm and then claiming that it had not done so under Hitler. General Fritsch's pathetic lament in the turbulent days following his dismissal—"I just wasn't cut out for politics!"—aptly sums up the attitude of these apologists.[14]

Their argument misses the point. The Reichswehr was far from apolitical; it frequently interfered in politics to defend its own interests. Many of the concessions it made to Hitler were in fact motivated by political calculation. In any event, critics of the army do not focus so much on its failure to intervene as on its inadequate powers of moral discernment. In return for short-term influence and the right to be "sole bearer of arms," the Reichswehr abandoned basic principles and traditions. The Röhm affair, the silent acceptance of the murders of Schleicher and Bredow, and the army's precipitous order—issued voluntarily from within its own ranks—that every soldier swear a personal oath to Hitler were all part of a concerted attempt to win influence, an effort on which the army staked more and more in return for less and less. The Fritsch affair determined the final outcome; all that remained was to play out the hands.

It was not until the Fritsch affair, or until the outbreak of war, at the latest, that most officers adopted the pose of apolitical professionals. They were motivated less by resigned acceptance of Hitler's victory over them than by an active desire to evade the code of standards and rules by which war is traditionally waged. More often than can be justified, the army was deaf to appeals for humane assistance in areas under its control, especially when it came to the actions of the Einsatzgruppen. Insofar as the army considered its toleration of SS atrocities a final concession to Hitler for which it deserved to be rewarded, it would only be disappointed once again: the last thing Hitler wanted Nazi officers to be was protean. In 1941, shortly before the campaign against the Soviet Union, he excoriated Reichenau for being "pliable," in contrast to a foe like Hammerstein, who at least remained true to his hatred for Hitler and to his own worldview. Later the Führer commented that he often bitterly regretted not having purged his officer corps the way Stalin did.[15] The excesses of Hitler's retaliation after July 20 can probably be ascribed not least of all to his desire to compensate for the purge he failed to carry out earlier.

Nothing illuminates Hitler's continuing rancor toward the officer corps more than his appointment on July 20, 1944, of its most deadly rival, Heinrich Himmler, as the new commander of the reserve army, a well-calculated gesture of contempt. Himmler immediately set about reorganizing the German army into a National Socialist "people's army." He banned all references to the theory that the state rested on twin pillars, the Nazi Party and the army, a theory in which Blomberg and Reichenau had placed great stock. The German people did not consist of pillars, Himmler explained, and the army merely "carried out the functions of the party." The army had been thoroughly degraded, yet more was to come.[16] By the end of the war, the Waffen-SS had mushroomed to over seventeen divisions.

Another reason for the unwillingness of many officers to engage in any sort of resistance was their profound aversion to revolt against the state. That feeling was greatly reinforced by fear for the soldiers under them, who were already being badly beaten at the fronts and whose ability to defend themselves might well be further weakened by a coup. There is no question that many officers were tormented by the pressures placed on them and by concerns about justifying their actions. In this, they had much in common with the conspirators. As can be seen in the example of Tresckow, even officers who were absolutely determined to stage a coup were troubled by the fact that everything they were contemplating would inevitably be seen by their troops as dereliction of duty, as irresponsible arrogance, and, worst, as capable of triggering a civil war.

Scarcely less inhibiting, even to many of the conspirators themselves, was the idea of murdering the head of state. One could point, as Stauffenberg did, to the immense number of fatalities incurred every day in Hitler's war and to his slaughter of entire populations. Psychologically, however, there is a great difference between the murder of one person and the killing of many, a difference difficult to comprehend and perhaps essentially symbolic in nature.[17] Virtually none of the plotters was able to overcome these inhibitions, and in all likelihood not even Stauffenberg was prepared to dispatch Hitler "as if he were a mad dog," as Gersdorff put it. The indecision over what to do with Hitler that marked the conspiracy of September 1938 and was even more acutely evident in November 1939 reflects the scruples the conspirators had to overcome.

The same problem plagued the planning for July 20, influencing events in almost imperceptible ways. The conspirators' euphemistic reference to the murder of Hitler as the "initial spark" tended to minimize the importance of the act, making it seem a mere prelude when in fact it was the key event. Perhaps that is why the conspirators devoted much less time and attention to planning the action at the Wolf's Lair than to the deception and surprise attacks of Operation Valkyrie. Not every detail of the assassination attempt could be foreseen, of course, but even so at noon on July 20, 1944 Stauffenberg found himself forced to make many more hasty last-minute decisions than were really necessary. The questions that continually puzzle observers—Why didn't Haeften arm the bomb? Why wasn't Stauffenberg adequately informed about the reduced power the bombs would have in a wooden hut? Why was the second bomb left unused and simply thrown out of the car on the way to the airfield?—are best answered with reference to the unconscious aversion to the murder of a head of state.

Many highly placed officers were also dissuaded from joining the opposition by their vivid memories of Hitler's amazing string of triumphs both before the war and in its early years. They belonged to a generation that had known nothing but defeat and humiliation, from the First World War to Versailles to the never-ending insults of the Weimar Republic. They were therefore all the more impressed by Hitler's victories, scored time and again in flagrant defiance of the warnings and advice of experts. Hitler's uncanny success did much to undermine the officers' confidence in their own judgment, especially as they had been trained and were accustomed, like military strategists in all other countries, to think strictly in terms of outcome.

A number of officers were also cool toward the resistance because, by the time war broke out, the notion of *Hochverrat*, or betrayal of the head of state, had become conflated with the odious crime of *Landesverrat*, betrayal of one's country, for which there was absolutely no tolerance within the army. The complete isolation of Hans Oster, notwithstanding the personal respect accorded him, was a case in point. Even Stauffenberg remarked at the beginning of the Russian campaign that a putsch was unthinkable in time of war.[18] Halder expressed similar sentiments, and it is no accident that he helped plan coups only before the war or, in the case of the 1939 plot, at a time when it seemed the conflict could still be prevented from escalating into a world war.[19]

These were the dilemmas facing men like Rundstedt, Leeb, Sodenstern, and Kluge as they decided how they would respond to the impending assassination attempt and coup. They were by no means typical Nazi generals and they did not betray the conspirators, but neither did they provide encouragement or support. "Just do it!" is how General Heusinger responded on a number of occasions to requests from Tresckow's circle to join the conspiracy.[20] Like many others, Heusinger himself preferred to withdraw into a posture of more or less blind—or at least silent—obedience. A considerable number of these officers were capable of realizing that adherence to abstract ideals about a soldier's duty would ultimately bring catastrophe on Germany and some, including Manstein and Bock, were expressly told as much by colleagues in the opposition. Most of them, however, continued to shrug their shoulders and seek solace in rationalizations, all the while nurturing the hope that disaster would ultimately be avoided, as it had been so many times in the past.

There were also those who, though they did not join the resistance, found the conflict of values unbearable and sought escape in death. This is the only way that Gerd von Tresckow's insistence on incriminating himself can be understood. The commanding general at Cherbourg, Erich Marcks, was acting on a similar impulse when he headed into the front lines, telling those around him that a soldier's death was the best a man could meet. Field Marshal Walter Model served the regime loyally for many years, but in mid-April 1945, while commanding his army group in the Ruhr valley, he was suddenly seized by the conviction that he had been serving a false master and a false cause; in despair, he committed suicide. His successor, Albert Kesselring, returned to business as usual; he inaugurated his command by complaining to his general staff that nowhere on his journey through the army area had he seen a hanged deserter, a sure sign of ineffective military leadership.[21]

A final reason for the reluctance of most officers to assist the resistance was its lack of support among the general population, a state of affairs continually lamented by voices in the army ranging from Chief of General Staff Halder to General Wagner. The upper echelons of the military were staffed largely by men of high social rank who had little truck with the common people, and in the wake of the Reichenau and Fritsch affairs, nothing so impressed them as Hitler's ability to sway the masses and make himself their wildly acclaimed spokesman. An attempt was made to use Wilhelm Leuschner's network of former trade union members to bring the opposition message to the people, but this single initiative was not enough to break the social isolation of the rebels. Inquiries conducted primarily by Julius Leber and Alfred Delp in late 1943 indicated that most industrial workers remained loyal to the regime, even as the war ground on. Security Service reports on the mood of the people in the days following July 20 concluded that Hitler was increasingly popular even in such traditionally "red" areas as Berlin's Wedding, a heavily working-class district.[22] Although the resistance had for years been concerned with the problem of how to reach the general population and enlighten it as to the criminality of the Nazi regime, a satisfactory solution was never found.

This was one of the main differences between the resistance in Germany and its counterparts in the occupied countries. These groups, too, represented only tiny minorities (not until after the war did everyone claim membership, as national pride demanded). Nevertheless they built genuine, viable resistance movements, which, unlike the opposition in Germany, could count on support from the general population. They had an infrastructure, bases, and battle-ready units. They also had a clear and simple purpose: to drive the enemy from the motherland. There were no torn loyalties, broken oaths, or concerns about treason, no need to engage in esoteric debates about the new order to be instituted after the Nazis were driven out. In short, the resistance movements in the occupied countries found moral, political, or nationalist justifications within themselves.

In addition, they enjoyed psychological and material support from the Allies. When Anthony Eden told Bishop George Bell in the summer of 1943 that the German resistance, in contrast to the movements elsewhere, had never demonstrated a thoroughgoing determination to oppose the regime, Bell responded that the others had been promised liberation in return for their efforts while the Germans were offered nothing more than unconditional surrender.[23] Although the clear aim of all resistance movements was the overthrow of Nazi rule, for the Germans that meant surrendering their homeland to bitter foes, not only from the West but also, and much more terrifying, from the East. It is hard not to appreciate the psychological torment of those Germans who abhorred Hitler and were horrified by his crimes yet knew what Stalin had proved capable of, from the Red Terror to mass murders in the forest of Katyn.

The view toward the West was different, but as we have seen, there was never a meeting of minds between the German resistance and the American and British governments. The objections raised by Eden were undoubtedly justified. But the psychological warfare waged by the West, the most important manifestation of which was the bombing campaign, has been rightly deplored.[24] Contrary to expectations, it did not demoralize the German people but rather tended to rally them around the Nazis in a gesture of defiance that benefited the regime at a time when it had grown increasingly concerned about the atmosphere of anxiety, apathy, and war weariness following the reversals of the winter of 1942–43. Paradoxically, the Allied bombing campaign only succeeded in driving the people back into the arms of the regime, as they heeded the instinct to stand together in times of mortal danger. Meanwhile the opposition grew even more isolated.

* * *

Thus, the decision to join the resistance also meant, for a German, withdrawal from the social mainstream and personal loneliness. It meant the rearrangement of one's entire life and reliance on the few people who shared one's views. Long-term friendships were severed and relations with the outside world were necessarily tainted by suspicion, deception, and duplicity. Deciding to resist the Nazis meant placing one's family and friends in serious danger. Writing to his British friend Lionel Curtis in June 1942, Moltke described the awkward lengths to which he and all the other conspirators had to go in their daily lives. Oster and Tresckow never once dared to meet or to speak directly, for example, despite the countless questions they had to resolve or clarify.[25]

All these special circumstances gave the resistance its highly individualistic, insular character. Postwar analyses have blamed the bourgeoisie, the army, the churches, the traditional curriculum in the schools, and various other social factors for the Germans' failure to resist the Nazis more resolutely. In actual fact, no institution, no ideological current from either the left or the right, no tradition, nor any social class proved sufficient to confer on its members or adherents immunity from Nazi blandishments. Resistance was entirely a matter of personal character, whether it occurred in the bourgeoisie, the unions, or the army. The conspirators' social background or intellectual training provided them at most with support against occasional doubts or the temptation to give up. The German resistance has thus quite properly been called a "revolt of conscience."[26]

The large role played by personal determination and individual strength of character turned out, ironically, to be one of the reasons the resistance failed. It explains the lack of a unifying ideology, the disagreements, and the characteristic indecision. One person's views were apt to raise the hackles of someone else, whose convictions would in turn be denounced by still others. The ensuing rounds of discussion and debate soon degenerated into arguments over basic philosophies that demanded to be resolved, everyone seemed to believe, rather than simply papered over with easy compromises. The result was the inaction that in retrospect makes the German resistance look like nothing more than a passionate debating society. Moltke's elation at Freisler's conclusion that Moltke did nothing, arranged nothing, and planned no violent acts—that he merely *thought*—remains one of the keys to understanding the resistance.

German philosophy is often said to be rather removed from reality, and this characterization certainly holds true for the German resistance. All the discussion papers, draft constitutions, cabinet lists, and endless debates about a new order were at least partially an escape from the practical needs of the moment. Only a few conspirators avoided the temptation to indulge in theorizing. Indeed, it seems likely that if Stauffenberg had not appeared on the scene the conspirators would have spent the rest of the war discussing with great profundity the many insurmountable problems impeding them.

Closer examination also reveals that a deep melancholy settled over the conspirators as a whole (excluding, of course, the indomitably optimistic Goerdeler). Even Tresckow was said to suffer from it; Yorck was described at one point as having been "very serious and sad the last few weeks," and Trott observed just before the assassination attempt: "If this colossus Hitler falls, he will drag us all into the abyss."[27] At some deeper level, the conspirators all seemed to realize that their chances of success were small. The assassination of Hitler would not necessarily liberate Germany from Nazi tyranny. All it would do for certain was free German soldiers from their loyalty oaths and possibly rouse some senior officers from their moral slumber. But those results would not necessarily have been any more decisive than the successful launch of Operation Valkyrie. The real struggle would have only then begun, and its outcome would by no means have been certain. Goerdeler's objections to violence were based not only on moral principles but on practical political considerations as well: he feared it might lead to civil war, thereby destroying the last of the conspirators' hopes; to defeat on the battle fronts, especially in the East; and to chaos and lawlessness. Finally, Germany might be forced to surrender unconditionally, a result he hoped to the end to avoid.

Goerdeler may well have understood the uncertain consequences of Hitler's assassination better than those who advocated it. Stauffenberg, however, thought in different terms. Determined to overthrow the Nazi regime, he knew that there was no realistic alternative to violence. He felt it was absurd to attempt, as Carl Langbehn and Johannes Popitz had, to turn the Nazis against one another or to undermine the system from within. No less unrealistic, to his mind, was Goerdeler's hope that a public debate with Hitler would trigger a broad popular uprising. If there were no alternatives worth discussing, then the only way to break out of the conspirators' "little debating circle," as Stauffenberg called it, was clearly to assassinate Hitler and stage a coup.

Like Goerdeler, Stauffenberg was still confident that an anti-Nazi government would be able to work out an arrangement with the Allies and avoid unconditional surrender. Julius Leber sought in vain to disabuse him of this illusion. In a paper apparently written by Stauffenberg himself and left behind in army headquarters on Bendlerstrasse on July 20, the hope was expressed that Germany would remain a "significant factor in the constellation of powers" and that the Wehrmacht would be an "effective instrument" in bringing about negotiations "on an equal footing" with the Allies.[28] The tenacity with which Stauffenberg clung to this misconception has often been noted. Perhaps, as some commentators have speculated, he needed it as much as he needed his moral outrage in order to take action.[29] After all, any clearheaded assessment of the situation could only have led to the conclusion that events should be allowed to play themselves out to the bitter end. The historian Gordon Craig regards the German conspirators as incurable "romantics," and his characterization is probably apt, even in respect to Stauffenberg. But the critical undertone of that judgment denies them the dignity of their efforts, however desperate, impulsive, and irrational they may have been.

The particular heroism of the German resistance resides precisely in the hopelessness of the conspirators' position, in what one historian calls the "last hurrah of a lost cause."[30] Utterly without support or encouragement from within or without, they carried on the struggle even though, by the end, no national or tangible political interest could be advanced. Thus the assassination attempt of July 20 was launched in the spirit of Tresckow's words to Stauffenberg: *"coûte que coûte"*—do it "whatever the cost." Stauffenberg surely knew that the political goals he was serving by killing Hitler were now a mere fantasy. To the Allied demand for unconditional surrender he and his friends responded with an equally unconditional determination to act, motivated at this point by only the most abstract and general ideals: the dignity of humankind, justice, responsibility, self-respect. It is revealing that all discussion of the "right psychological moment," which had played so prominent a role in the debates of previous years, had long since ceased.

In the end success or failure no longer mattered very much. All that remained was to make a dramatic gesture disavowing Hitler and everything his regime stood for. Tresckow's words to Stauffenberg have become the most memorable phrase of the resistance because they convey this idea in its most forceful form and express the need for action regardless of the political or practical consequences.

The July 20 attack was, therefore, primarily a symbolic act. Those who point disparagingly to the hopelessness of the conspirators' undertaking or the inadequateness of their planning fail to see the real significance. It is only a slight exaggeration to say that the decision to attack was a decision for martyrdom. Schulenburg made this explicit late in the evening of July 20 when the idea of taking flight came up again: "We must drain this cup to the dregs," he said to Hans Fritzsche, "we must sacrifice ourselves."[31]

Given that spirit, accusations of treason and disloyalty weighed relatively lightly on the conspirators, and concerns about the success of their mission could no longer hold them back. A few days before the coup attempt Tresckow confided to a friend that "in all likelihood everything will go wrong"; asked if the action was necessary nevertheless, he replied simply, "Yes, even so."[32] That is the key without which nothing can be understood. The purpose of July 20 was the gesture itself; it was its own justification. The conspirators believed that failure would not detract from the idea behind the attack. Some seem to have believed that failure would actually cast their actions in an even purer light. As Stieff replied when asked what had driven him to do what he had done, "We were purifying ourselves."[33]

It is fitting that the conspirators had their great moment in court, when, free of the burden of reality, they could focus on their thoughts, principles, and beliefs. They utilized fully the few opportunities that the raging Freisler allowed them. Despite his efforts at humiliation, they managed to prevent the regime from using the trials as a crowd-pleasing spectacle. Public reports of the trials were quickly cut back and then stopped entirely in what was probably the most searing propaganda defeat the regime had ever suffered.

The German resistance has been called a unique phenomenon because it sought, in an era still imbued with nationalistic fervor, to oppose the policies of its own government—and at a moment when that government was enjoying one victory after another. To counter those triumphs, the resistance could offer only its conviction that no amount of success justified the government's crimes.[34] Also remarkable was the evolution that the thinking of many members of the resistance was forced to undergo in extremely trying circumstances: despite the considerable power of tradition, conservatives and others began to question and ultimately to abandon such narrow concepts as the nation-state, a process that never advanced, however, beyond the initial stages. But the laudatory early accounts of the resistance tended to ignore the sympathy that many opponents of the regime originally felt for Hitler, or at least for some of his aims, and depicted these men as timeless heroes, divorced from their times. These accounts miss the drama that shapes so many of the conspirators' lives. More to the point, they make the participants stranger and even more remote than they may already have seemed.

■   ■   ■

The aura of failure that surrounded the German resistance from the outset continued after its demise. As we have seen, some of the conspirators, especially those in the Kreisau Circle, entertained the idea of a united Europe, but they can hardly be said to have laid its foundations, since no one built on their work or even referred to it. If the resistance had any legacy at all, it was the aversion to totalitarianism that characterized all political parties in the early days of the German Federal Republic, regardless of their other differences. Although this sentiment was a reaction to the entire experience of the Hitler years, it was the resistance that did most to bolster and legitimize it.

Among the enduring lessons of the failed resistance is that it is virtually impossible to overthrow a totalitarian regime from within.

Even the events in the Communist world in 1989–90 do little to challenge this point. The most promising act of resistance was actually undertaken before the fact, when Kurt von Hammerstein, the chief of army command, went to see Hindenburg on the morning of January 26, 1933, to voice his grave misgivings about Hitler's appointment as chancellor. All the later plans, deeds, and sacrifices of the resistance may have represented moral victories, but politically they were condemned to failure.

The question has periodically been raised as to what would have happened if either the July 20 assassination attempt or the coup had succeeded. The sobering—and virtually unanimous—consensus is that nothing would have changed. The Allies would not have altered their aims, abandoning their demand for unconditional surrender, nor would they have modified the decision made later at Yalta to occupy and divide Germany. It is also unlikely that the myth that Germany had been sabotaged from within would yet again have arisen, as many feared it would. There is little reason to share Goerdeler's optimism that, if he and his colleagues had gained access to the radio waves "for just twenty-four hours" and freely proclaimed the truth about the Nazis, a wave of indignation would have swept the Reich. Even less justified was his hope that Hitler could then have been deposed without violence. There is, however, at least a grain of truth to Goerdeler's version of events: although many individuals have published defenses of their activities during the Hitler years, no significant attempt has ever been made to exculpate the Third Reich itself. Public horror over the depth and extent of its crimes—the thing Goerdeler always counted on—has not permitted such forgiveness. The Nazi regime, like totalitarian governments everywhere, proved unable to generate a sustaining mythology, except among the few diehards whose fate was linked to Hitler.

In the final analysis, the German resistance cannot be measured by the futility of its efforts or by its unfulfilled hopes. Although it had very little influence on the course of history, it nevertheless radically changed how we view those years. History consists not only of those dates and great events we commemorate but also, and perhaps more tellingly, of deeds motivated by self-respect and moral commitment.

Beck, Schulenburg, Goerdeler, and others believed that the issue of whether the Nazi regime was ultimately brought down from without or overthrown from within would have an enormous effect on Germany's reputation and reacceptance into the ranks of civilized nations.[35] On a moral plane, failing in the attempt is as worthy as succeeding.

The importance of the resistance cannot seriously be challenged. Opinions continue to vary on almost every facet of it: its alliances, its view of society, its illusions, its passivity, and the resolve it finally mustered. The main questions about it, though, were raised early on. The day after the attack on Hitler, Emmi Bonhoeffer returned to Berlin to find her husband, Klaus, and her brother, Justus Delbrück, clearing the wreckage of a neighbor's house. When they sat down to rest amid the ruins, she asked whether the two men could draw any lesson at all from the failure of the plot. There was a momentary pause while they weighed their answer. Finally Delbrück responded in a way that captured the pathos and paradox of the resistance: "I think it was good that it happened, and good too, perhaps, that it did not succeed."[36]

NOTES

Preface

1. Among the major titles discussed here are Hans Bernd Gisevius, *Bis zum bittern Ende* (Zurich, 1954); Helmuth Groscurth, *Tagebücher eines Abwehroffiziers, 1938–1940* (Stuttgart, 1970); Ulrich von Hassell, *Die Hassell-Tagebücher 1938–1944: Aufzeichnungen vom Andern Deutschland*, ed. Friedrich Hiller von Gaertingen, rev. and exp. ed. (Berlin, 1988); and Hans Rothfels, *Deutsche Opposition gegen Hitler: Eine Würdigung*, exp. ed. (Tübingen, 1969). See also A Note on the Texts at the end of this volume.

2. Alexander Stahlberg, *Die verdammte Pflicht: Erinnerungen, 1932–1945* (Berlin and Frankfurt, 1994), 456ff.

3. Karl Dietrich Bracher, *Das deutsche Dilemma: Leidenswege der politischen Emanzipation* (Munich, 1971), 158.

4. Peter Hoffmann lists a large number of these organizations in *Widerstand, Staatsstreich, Attentat: Der Kampf der Opposition gegen Hitler*, 3rd ed. (Munich, 1979), 34ff., 226ff. The motives, goals, and activities of some of them, however, remain virtually unknown.

1. The Resistance That Never Was

1. Walter Frank, "Zur Geschichte des Nationalsozialismus," *Wille und Macht* (1934), 1.

2. Count Harry Kessler, *Tagebücher, 1918–1937* (Frankfurt, 1962), 702. For more about Hitler's seizure of power, about which only a little can be said here, see Karl Dietrich Bracher, *Die deutsche Diktatur: Entstehung, Struktur, Folgen des Nationalsozialismus* (Cologne and Berlin, 1969), 209ff.

3. Wilhelm Hoegner, *Flucht vor Hitler* (Munich, 1977), 56.

4. Goebbels's introduction to Hitler's speech in the Berlin Sportpalast on Feb.

10, 1933; rpt. in *Hitlers Machtergreifung*, by Josef and Ruth Becker (Munich, 1983), 59–60.

5. See Heinz Höhne, *Die Machtergreifung: Deutschlands Weg in die Hitlerdiktatur* (Reinbek, 1983), 279ff.

6. Fritz Stern, "Der Nationalsozialismus als Versuchung," *Der Traum vom Frieden und die Versuchung der Macht: Deutsche Geschichte im 20. Jahrhundert* (Berlin, 1988).

7. Qtd. in Dorothea Beck, *Julius Leber: Sozialdemokrat zwischen Reform und Widerstand* (Berlin, 1983), 257.

8. Hoegner, *Flucht*, 111ff., esp. 122–23.

9. Letter to her parents, Jan. 30, 1933; qtd. in Ger van Roon, "Widerstand und Krieg," *Der Widerstand gegen den Nationalsozialismus: Die deutsche Gesellschaft und der Widerstand gegen Hitler*, ed. Jürgen Schmädecke and Peter Steinbach (Munich, 1986), 55.

10. Martin H. Sommerfeldt, *Ich war dabei: Die Verschwörung der Dämonen* (Darmstadt, 1949), 42.

11. See Peter Hoffmann, *Widerstand, Staatsstreich, Attentat: Der Kampf der Opposition gegen Hitler*, 3rd ed. (Munich, 1979), 31–32.

12. Qtd. in André François-Poncet, *Botschafter in Berlin, 1931–1938* (Berlin and Mainz, 1962), 136.

13. Heinrich Brüning, *Memoiren, 1918–1934* (Stuttgart, 1970), 657.

14. Julius Leber, qtd. in Hagen Schulze, *Weimar: Deutschland, 1917–1933* (Berlin, 1982), 313.

15. Breitscheid qtd. in Fabian von Schlabrendorff, *Offiziere gegen Hitler* (Frankfurt and Hamburg, 1959), 12; Leber, *Ein Mann geht seinen Weg: Schriften, Reden und Briefe von Julius Leber* (Berlin, 1952), 123–24.

16. *Prozess gegen die Hauptkriegsverbrecher vor dem Internationalen Militärgerichtshof Nürnberg, 14. November 1945–1. Oktober 1946* (Nuremberg, 1949), vol. 41, 267.

17. Qtd. in Count Lutz Schwerin von Krosigk, *Es geschah in Deutschland. Menschenbilder unseres Jahrhunderts* (Tübingen and Stuttgart, 1951), 147; *Politische Studien* 10 (1959): 92.

18. See Erich Mathias and Rudolf Morsey, eds., *Das Ende der Parteien 1933* (Düsseldorf, 1960), 152ff.

19. Mathias and Morsey, *Ende*, 175ff.

20. Mathias and Morsey, *Ende*, 692, 698.

21. The term is Günther Weisenborn's.

22. Karl Otmar von Aretin, qtd. in Ulrich Cartarius, *Opposition gegen Hitler* (Berlin, 1984), 14.

23. Konrad Heiden, *Geburt des Dritten Reiches: Die Geschichte des Nationalsozialismus bis Herbst 1933*, 2nd ed. (Zurich, 1934), 260.

24. Qtd. in Wilfried Berghahn, *Robert Musil in Selbstzeugnissen und Bilddokumenten* (Hamburg, 1963), 123.

25. Notes of Albert Grzesinski, Prussian minister of state and prefect of the Berlin police until 1933, qtd. in Mathias and Morsey, *Ende*, 160.

26. Qtd. in Hans Rothfels, *Deutsche Opposition gegen Hitler: Eine Würdigung,* exp. ed. (Tübingen, 1969), 59.

27. Hans Mommsen, "Der Widerstand gegen Hitler und die deutsche Gesellschaft," Schmädecke and Steinbach, *Widerstand,* 8.

28. Qtd. in Michael Krüger-Charlé, "Carl Goerdelers Versuche der Durchsetzung einer alternativen Politik 1933 bis 1937," Schmädecke and Steinbach, *Widerstand,* 385.

29. Helmut Krausnick, "Vorgeschichte und Beginn des militärischen Widerstandes gegen Hitler," *Die Vollmacht des Gewissens* (Berlin and Frankfurt, 1960), vol. 1, 208.

2. The Army Succumbs

1. Christian Müller, *Oberst i.G. Stauffenberg: Eine Biographie* (Düsseldorf, 1970), 93ff. For von Tresckow and Mertz von Quirnheim, see Bodo Scheurig, *Henning von Tresckow: Eine Biographie* (Frankfurt and Berlin, 1980), 44.

2. Baron Rudolph-Christoph von Gersdorff, *Soldat im Untergang: Lebensbilder* (Frankfurt and Berlin, 1979), 51.

3. Report by Horst von Mellenthin, at the time second adjutant to Hammerstein, in *Zeugenschrifttum des IfZ München,* no. 105, 1ff.

4. Notes of Major General Curt Liebmann. See Thilo Vogelsang, "Neue Dokumente zur Geschichte der Reichswehr, 1930–1933," *Vierteljahrshefte für Zeitgeschichte* (1954), no. 2, 434–35.

5. Herman Foertsch, *Schuld und Verhängnis: Die Fritsch-Krise im Frühjahr 1938 als Wendepunkt der nationalsozialistischen Zeit* (Stuttgart, 1951), 33.

6. Rudolf Diels, *Lucifer ante portas . . . Es spricht der erste Chef der Gestapo* (Stuttgart, 1950), 278.

7. Qtd. in Klaus-Jürgen Müller, *Das Heer und Hitler: Armee und nationalsozialistisches Regime, 1933–1940* (Stuttgart, 1969), 53.

8. Heinz Höhne, *Mordsache Röhm: Hitlers Durchbruch zur Alleinherrschaft* (Reinbek, 1984), 168.

9. Helmut Krausnick, *20. Juli 1944,* ed. Erich Zimmerman and Hans-Adolf Jacobsen, special ed. of *Das Parlament,* 3rd ed. (Bonn, 1960), 319.

10. Gerhard Rossbach, *Mein Weg durch die Zeit* (Weilburg, 1959), 150.

11. Röhm's words as reported to the commanders by Brigadier General Weichs. Reichenau, in an act of "effective direction," may, however, have given an interpretive twist to the key sentences in Röhm's memorandum. See Müller, *Heer,* 97, n. 53.

12. Müller, *Heer,* 59.

13. Ludwig von Hammerstein, personal interview, December 20, 1983.

14. Exceptions were made for people who were civil servants before the First World War or who fought at the front, as well as for civil servants whose fathers or sons had fallen in the war. In the army, seventy officers and men came under this provision.

15. Helmut Krausnick, "Vorgeschichte und Beginn des militärischen Wider-

standes gegen Hitler," *Die Vollmacht des Gewissens* (Berlin and Frankfurt, 1960), vol. 1, 319.

16. Franz von Papen, *Der Wahrheit eine Gasse* (Munich, 1952), 344.

17. For a fuller account of the events of June 30–July 1, see Müller, *Heer*, 88ff.; Höhne, *Röhm*, 247ff.; and Krausnick, "Vorgeschichte."

18. Walter Görlitz, *Kleine Geschichte des deutschen Generalstabs*, 2nd ed. (Berlin, 1977), 298.

19. See Theodor Eschenburg, "Zur Ermordung des Generals Schleicher," *Vierteljahrshefte für Zeitgeschichte* (1953), no. 1, 71ff.

20. Krausnick, "Vorgeschichte," 234.

21. Krausnick, "Vorgeschichte," 243, 336–37.

22. Hans Bernd Gisevius, qtd. in Müller, *Heer*, 136. See also pp. 136ff.

23. Gersdorff, *Soldat*, 56ff.

24. André François-Poncet, *Botschafter in Berlin, 1931–1938* (Berlin and Mainz, 1962), 264.

25. Friedrich Hossbach, *Zwischen Wehrmacht und Hitler, 1934–1938* (Wolfenbüttel and Hannover, 1949), 219. For the idea that the military leaders, in their impatience to rearm, created the time pressures that Hitler now cited, see Klaus-Jürgen Müller, "Deutsche Militär-Elite in der Vorgeschichte des Zweiten Weltkrieges," *Die deutschen Eliten und der Weg in den Zweiten Weltkrieg*, ed. Martin Broszat and Klaus Schwabe (Munich, 1989), 263ff.

26. Fabian von Schlabrendorff, *Offiziere gegen Hitler* (Frankfurt and Hamburg, 1959), 49.

27. Qtd. in Gert Buchheit, *Ludwig Beck, ein preussischer General* (Munich, 1964), 106. For the entire Blomberg affair, including the arguments as to whether it was at least partially the result of an intrigue, see Harold C. Deutsch, *Das Komplott oder die Entmachtung der Generäle Blomberg- und Fritsch-Krise: Hitlers Weg zum Krieg* (Munich, 1974).

28. Walter Görlitz and Herbert A. Quint, *Adolf Hitler: Eine Biographie* (Stuttgart, 1952), 489.

29. Qtd. in Count Romedio Galeazzo von Thun-Hohenstein, *Der Verschwörer: General Oster und die Militäropposition* (Berlin, 1982), 70.

30. Thun-Hohenstein, *Verschwörer*, 71.

31. See Müller, *Heer*, 269–70.

32. Karl Dietrich Bracher, *Die deutsche Dikatur: Entstehung, Struktur, Folgen des Nationalsozialismus* (Cologne and Berlin, 1969), 428.

33. Qtd. in Michael Krüger-Charlé, "Carl Goerdelers Versuche der Durchsetzung einer alternativen Politik 1933 bis 1937," *Der Widerstand gegen den Nationalsozialismus: Die deutsche Gesellschaft und der Widerstand gegen Hitler*, ed. Jürgen Schmädecke and Peter Steinbach (Munich, 1960), 387.

34. Scheurig, *Tresckow*, 59.

35. Qtd. in Thun-Hohenstein, *Verschwörer*, 90. The reference to "rule by the bosses" was directed against the party and that to "Cheka methods" (those of the Soviet political police) against the SS.

3. The September Plot

1. See Klemens von Klemperer, *Die verlassenen Verschwörer: Der deutsche Widerstand auf der Suche nach Verbündeten, 1938–1945* (Berlin, 1994), which provides an extensive and highly informative description of the attempts to prompt France and especially Britain to adopt a clear, unyielding attitude toward Hitler. An overview can also be found in Peter Hoffmann, *Widerstand, Staatsstreich, Attentat: Der Kampf der Opposition gegen Hitler*, 3rd ed. (Munich, 1979), 79ff.

2. Qtd. in Count Romedio Galeazzo von Thun-Hohenstein, *Der Verschwörer: General Oster und die Militäropposition* (Berlin, 1982), 93. According to Hans Rothfels, neither Fabian von Schlabrendorff nor Kleist's son confirmed the wording of Beck's statement, so some question remains (*Deutsche Opposition gegen Hitler: Eine Würdigung*, exp. ed. [Tübingen, 1969], 73).

3. Erich Kordt, *Nicht aus den Akten . . . Die Wilhelmstrasse in Frieden und Krieg: Erlebnisse, Begegnungen, und Eindrücke, 1928–1945* (Munich, 1949), 248.

4. See Hoffmann, *Widerstand*, 92.

5. Carl J. Burckhardt, *Meine Danziger Mission, 1937–1939* (Zurich and Munich, 1960), 182.

6. See Hoffmann, *Widerstand*, 81.

7. Sebastian Haffner, *Winston Churchill in Selbstzeugnissen und Bilddokumenten* (Reinbek, 1979), 102.

8. Otto Hintze to Friedrich Meinecke; see *Die deutsche Katastrophe* (Wiesbaden, 1955), 89.

9. Vansittart qtd. in Lothar Kettenacker, "Der nationalkonservative Widerstand aus angelsächsischer Sicht," *Die Widerstand gegen den Nationalsozialismus: Die deutsche Gesellschaft und der Widerstand gegen Hitler*, ed. Jürgen Schmädecke and Peter Steinbach (Munich, 1986), 715; Dalton qtd. in Hevda Ben-Israel, "Im Widerstreit der Ziele: Die britische Reaktion auf den deutschen Widerstand," Schmädecke and Steinbach, 739.

10. Hans Frank, *Im Angesicht des Galgens* (Neuhaus, 1955), 209.

11. Ulrich Schlie, "Das Ausland und die deutsche Opposition gegen Hitler: Widerstandsforschung und politische Gegenwart seit 1945," *Militärgeschichtliche Mitteilungen* 52 (1993): 166.

12. Rainer Hildebrand, *Wir sind die Letzten* (Neuwied and Bern, 1949), 92.

13. Beck's report as well as a related "note" are reprinted in *Ursachen und Folgen: Vom deutschen Zusammenbruch 1918 und 1945 bis zur staatlichen Neuordnung Deutschlands in der Gegenwart. Eine Urkunden- und Dokumentensammlung zur Zeitgeschichte*, ed. Herbert Michaelis and Ernst Schraepler, vol. 12 (Berlin), 206ff.

14. Klaus-Jürgen Müller, *Das Heer und Hitler: Armee und nationalsozialistisches Regime, 1933–1940* (Stuttgart, 1969), 336.

15. Müller, *Heer*, 343.

16. Harold C. Deutsch, *Verschwörung gegen den Krieg: Der Widerstand in den Jahren 1939–1940* (Munich, 1969), 95. For Manstein's comment in a letter, see Müller, *Heer*, 333.

17. Christine von Dohnanyi (widow of Hans von Dohnanyi), qtd. in Kurt

Sendtner, "Die deutsche Militäropposition im ersten Kriegsjahr," *Die Vollmacht des Gewissens,* vol. 1 (Berlin and Frankfurt, 1960), 441.

18. Ulrich von Hassell, *Die Hassell-Tagebücher, 1938–1944: Aufzeichnungen vom anderen Deutschland,*ed. Friedrich Hiller von Gaertingen, rev. and exp. ed. (Berlin, 1988), 289 (entry of Dec. 21, 1941); see also 345, 382.

19. Hans Bernd Gisevius, *Bis zum bittern Ende* (Zurich, 1954), 318.

20. Hoffmann, *Widerstand,* 96.

21. Gisevius, *Ende,* 324.

22. Qtd. in Gerhard Ritter, *Carl Goerdeler und die deutsche Widerstandsbewegung* (Stuttgart, 1984), 190. For Halder's personality see the informative portrait in Helmut Krausnick, "Vorgeschichte und Beginn des militärischen Widerstandes gegen Hitler," *Die Vollmacht des Gewissens,* vol. 1, 336ff.

23. Müller, *Heer,* 349.

24. Friedrich Wilhelm Heinz, qtd. in Hoffmann, *Widerstand,* 125. There are still a number of gaps in the literature on the so-called September plot and especially on the Heinz task force.

25. Gisevius, *Ende,* 332.

26. Krausnick, "Vorgeschichte," 345.

27. Gisevius, *Ende,* 340.

28. Friedrich Hossbach, *Zwischen Wehrmacht und Hitler, 1934–1938* (Wolfenbüttel and Hannover, 1949), 136.

29. Gisevius, *Ende,* 350.

30. Ivone Kirkpatrick, *Im innern Kreis: Erinnerungen eines Diplomaten* (Berlin, 1964), 462; see also Paul Schmidt, *Statist auf diplomatischer Bühne, 1923–1945* (Bonn, 1950), 409.

31. Kordt, *Akten,* 262.

32. William L. Shirer, *The Rise and Fall of the Third Reich* (New York, 1959), 399.

33. Helmuth Groscurth, *Tagebücher eines Abwehroffiziers, 1938–1940* (Stuttgart, 1970), 35. Contrary to the widespread assumption, the brothers must have met not in mid-September but on the evening of September 27. In the middle of the month the actions of the task force had not yet been decided on in detail, if the dates we have are accurate. On the other hand, if we accept the later date, it is difficult to understand why Groscurth said that Hitler would be arrested "tonight," since the deadline would not have been reached until the next day at 2:00 p.m. In either case there was probably a lapse of memory. The evening of September 27, however, seems the likeliest date.

34. Gisevius, *Ende,* 360; see also Kordt, *Akten,* 270–71. Brauchitsch himself stated after the war that he never intended to issue orders for a coup and even denied that Halder, Witzleben, or anyone else ever approached him with plans to overthrow Hitler. See Hoffmann, *Widerstand,* 128, and the related note.

35. Gisevius, *Ende,* 169.

36. Qtd. in Fabian von Schlabrendorff, *Offiziere gegen Hitler* (Frankfurt and Hamburg, 1959), 169.

37. *Le Testament politique de Hitler,* ed. Hugh R. Trevor-Roper (Paris, 1959),

118–19. For Schacht's statement, see *Prozess gegen die Hauptkriegsverbrecher vor dem Internationalen Militärgerichtshof Nürnberg, 14. November 1945–1. Oktober 1946* (Nuremberg, 1949), vol. 13, 4.

38. Gisevius, *Ende*, 362.

39. *Hassell-Tagebücher*, 71 (entry of Dec. 18, 1938). For Halder's comment see Krausnick, "Vorgeschichte," 370.

40. Qtd. in Schlabrendorff, 168–69.

41. Gisevius, *Ende*, 362; see also Rothfels, *Opposition*, 91.

42. Hoffmann, *Widerstand*, 317–18 and 50 (for Römer).

43. Hildegard von Kotze, ed., *Heeresadjutant bei Hitler, 1938–1943: Aufzeichnungen des Majors Engel* (Stuttgart, 1974), 39.

4. From Munich to Zossen

1. Speech on February 10, 1939, in the Kroll Opera House before the army group commanders. See Klaus-Jürgen Müller, *Das Heer und Hitler: Armee und nationalsozialistisches Regime, 1933–1940* (Stuttgart, 1969), 379ff.

2. Müller, *Heer*, 271. "Red pants" refers to the red stripe on the trousers of members of the general staff. For the quotation from Jodl that follows, see 382. In the interrogations conducted by the Gestapo after July 20, 1944, Fritz-Dietlof von der Schulenburg pointed to the Fritsch affair as the beginning of the division in the officer corps; see Archiv Peter, ed., *Spiegelbild einer Verschwörung: Die Kaltenbrunner-Berichte über das Attentat vom 20. Juli 1944* (Stuttgart, 1961), 273–74.

3. For Keitel, see Hans Bernd Gisevius, *Bis zum bittern Ende* (Zurich, 1954), 39–40. For Manstein and Guderian, see Fabian von Schlabrendorff, *Offiziere gegen Hitler* (Frankfurt and Hamburg, 1959), 99–100. Reichenau's earlier disparagement of Beck is another example. Similarly, General Fritz Fromm, who played an inglorious role on July 20, 1944, recorded in his army diary Halder's thoughts about a coup in the fall of 1939 (Harold C. Deutsch, *Verschwörung gegen den Krieg: Der Widerstand in den Jahren 1939–1940* [Munich, 1969], 226–27).

4. Helmut Krausnick, "Vorgeschichte und Beginn des militärischen Widerstandes gegen Hitler," *Die Vollmacht des Gewissens*, vol. 1 (Berlin and Frankfurt, 1960), 373.

5. Krausnick, "Vorgeschichte," 373; see also Erich Raeder, *Mein Leben* (Tübingen, 1956–57), vol. 2, 133ff.

6. Christian Müller, *Oberst i.G. Stauffenberg: Eine Biographie* (Düsseldorf, 1970), 148; see also K.-J. Müller, *Heer*, 387.

7. Galeazzo Ciano, *Tagebücher, 1939–1943* (Bern, 1946), 225. For the confused feelings of the opposition, see the comments of Eduard Wagner in Müller, *Heer*, 389.

8. This to the former Austrian minister Claise von Horstenau, qtd. in Ulrich von Hassell, *Die Hassell-Tagebücher, 1938–1944: Aufzeichnung vom anderen Deutschland*, ed. Friedrich Hiller von Gaertingen, rev. and exp. ed. (Berlin, 1988), 59 (entry of Oct. 15, 1938).

9. A total of six versions of this address have been preserved. Although differing in emphasis, they convey the same basic message. The version quoted here can be found in *Prozess gegen die Hauptkriegsverbrecher vor dem Internationalen*

Militärgerichtshof Nürnberg, 14. November 1945–1. Oktober 1946 (Nuremberg, 1949), vol. 26, PS-798 (part 1) and PS-1014 (part 2). For the atmosphere of the meeting, see Halder's remarks in Krausnick, "Vorgeschichte," 381.

10. Franz Halder, *Kriegstagebuch: Tägliche Aufzeichnungen des Chefs des Generalstabs des Heeres, 1939–1942*, 3 vols. (Stuttgart, 1962–64), vol. 1, 34. For Halder's comments to Henderson, see Krausnick, "Vorgeschichte," 377.

11. Gisevius, *Ende*, 401ff. For Oster's directions to the members of Heinz's task force, see Peter Hoffmann, *Widerstand, Staatsstreich, Attentat: Der Kampf der Opposition gegen Hitler*, 3rd ed. (Munich, 1979), 142.

12. Nikolaus von Vormann, Hitler's OKH liaison officer, qtd. in Müller, *Heer*, 420.

13. Qtd. in Müller, *Heer*, 419. I am also grateful to Müller for pointing out that this was just the situation the conspirators had been waiting for.

14. Gisevius, *Ende*, 408.

15. Müller, *Heer*, 425.

16. Helmuth Groscurth, *Tagebücher eines Abwehroffiziers, 1938–1940* (Stuttgart, 1970), 201 (entry of Sept. 8, 1939); see also Martin Broszat, *Nationalsozialistische Polenpolitik, 1939–1945* (Stuttgart, 1961), 28.

17. Note on the documents by Canaris on Sept. 14, 1939; qtd. in Müller, *Heer*, 428.

18. See Hans-Adolf Jacobsen, *1939–1945: Der zweite Weltkrieg in Chronik und Dokumenten* (Darmstadt, 1961), 607. See also Count Romedio Galeazzo von Thun-Hohenstein, *Der Verschwörer: General Oster und die Militäropposition* (Berlin, 1982), 143.

19. See *Hitler's Secret Book* (New York, 1962), with its continual criticism of the Prussian and bourgeois-nationalist policy toward Poland under the kaisers. The so-called *Table Talk* (London, 1953) also contains voluminous material on this topic.

20. Manfred Messerschmidt, "Militärische Motive zur Durchführung des Umsturzes," *Der Widerstand gegen den Nationalsozialismus: Die deutsche Gesellschaft und der Widerstand gegen Hitler*, ed. Jürgen Schmädecke and Peter Steinbach (Munich, 1986), 1023.

21. *Prozess*, vol. 26, PS-864, 381–82.

22. Hildegard von Kotze, ed., *Heeresadjutant bei Hitler, 1938–1943: Aufzeichnungen des Majors Engel* (Stuttgart, 1974), 68 (entry of Nov. 18, 1939).

23. This according to Colonel (later General) Eduard Wagner, who was already beginning to draft plans for martial law, and Quartermaster General Tippelskirch; see Groscurth, *Tagebücher*, 231 (entry of Nov. 14, 1939). For Blaskowitz's report to Brauchitsch, see Groscurth, *Tagebücher*, 426.

24. Jacobsen, *1939–1945*, 606–07; also see Groscurth, *Tagebücher*, 426, n. 230.

25. Halder, *Kriegstagebuch*, 160ff. (entry of Jan. 18, 1940).

26. See Hassell, *Hassell-Tagebücher*, 152 (entry of Dec. 25, 1939). For Tresckow's comment, see Bodo Scheurig, *Henning von Tresckow: Eine Biographie* (Frankfurt and Berlin, 1980), 76.

27. Jodl reported Hitler's reaction to Halder: "Distrust. Bitter that the soldiers don't follow him." See Halder, *Kriegstagebuch*, 97–98 (entry of Oct. 4, 1939).

28. Halder, *Kriegstagebuch*, 105 (entry of Oct. 14, 1939).

29. Quoted in Thun-Hohenstein, *Verschwörer*, 158.

30. Groscurth, *Tagebücher*, 218 (entry of Oct. 16, 1939): "Admiral visited Halder. Came back deeply shaken. Total nervous collapse. Brauchitsch also at wit's end. Führer demands invasion. Closed to any factual objections. Just bloodthirsty."

31. Hassell, *Hassell-Tagebücher*, 133 (entry of Oct. 19, 1939).

32. A thought of the former German ambassador in Paris, Count Johannes von Welczeck; see Hassell, *Hassell-Tagebücher*, 131 (entry of Oct. 16, 1939).

33. Groscurth, *Tagebücher*, 498ff.

34. Groscurth, *Tagebücher*, 223 (entry of Nov. 1, 1939). The description of the various, generally separate "centers of gravity" that came together only after Halder's decision to take action is based on the presentation in Müller, *Heer*, 494ff.

35. Hoffmann, *Widerstand*, 320–21.

36. Gisevius, *Ende*, 418.

37. Keitel's account; see Müller, *Heer*, 521.

38. See the statement that Army Adjutant and later General Gerhard Engel provided to the Institut für Zeitgeschichte, qtd. in Groscurth, *Tagebücher*, 225, n. 589.

39. This is the version provided by Halder after the war to Gerhard Ritter, *Carl Goerdeler und die deutsche Widerstandsbewegung* (Stuttgart, 1984), 504–05. For the rest, see Groscurth, *Tagebücher*, 225 (entry of Nov. 5, 1939), 246 (entry of Feb. 14, 1940). For Brauchitsch's comment, see Gisevius, *Ende*, 420.

40. See Deutsch, *Verschwörung*, 259; for V. Müller, see Müller, *Heer*, 534. The description in Gisevius, *Ende*, 423ff., is quite different.

41. Leeb said this after the war in his statement for the Military History Research Bureau; see Müller, *Heer*, 543. For Halder's comments, see Groscurth, *Tagebücher*, 236 (entry of Dec. 10, 1939), 233 (entry of Nov. 17, 1939).

42. Together with Popitz and possibly also with Oster, Beck, and Schacht, Goerdeler had developed the plan of dropping off a few divisions in Berlin during their transfer and then having Witzleben appear and use them to disarm the SS. At the same time, Beck would drive to Zossen to "assume supreme command from the weak hands of Brauchitsch." Hitler, according to the plan, would be "certified unfit to govern by a medical statement and kept in a safe place. Then an appeal to the people. . . ." Qtd. in Hassell, *Hassell-Tagebücher*, 153 (entry of Dec. 30, 1939).

43. Groscurth, *Tagebücher*, 232 (entry of Nov. 16, 1939) and 233, nn.

44. Erich Kordt, *Nicht aus den Akten . . . Die Wilhelmstrasse in Frieden und Krieg: Erlebnisse, Begegnungen, und Eindrücke, 1928–1945* (Munich, 1949), 377. Hitler's speech of November 23, 1939, was recorded and preserved by a number of different participants, who agree on its import. See *Prozess*, vol. 26, PS-789, 327ff.; also Groscurth, *Tagebücher*, 414ff. (document 40).

45. Qtd. in Paul Seabury, *Die Wilhelmstrasse: Die Geschichte der deutschen Diplomatie 1930–1945* (Frankfurt, 1956), 149. (Rosenheim is a provincial city in the far south of Germany; Eydtkuhnen is in the north.)

46. I am grateful to Jerzy W. Borejsza for this association; see "Der 25. Juli 1943 in Italien und der 20. Juli 1944 in Deutschland: Zur Technik des Staatsstreichs im totalitären System," Schmädecke and Steinbach, *Widerstand*, 1085.

47. Gert Buchheit, *Ludwig Beck, ein preussicher General* (Munich, 1964), 228. See also Ritter, *Goerdeler,* 267.

48. Hans Oster, qtd. in Deutsch, *Verschwörung,* 104.

5. The New Generation

1. S. Haffner, "The Day That Failed to End the War," *Contact* (London, 1947), 42. Haffner's bent for original points of view as well as the early date of this publication explain many of his excesses; his interpretation does, however, shed some light on the sociology of the resistance, a controversial subject.

2. Ulrich von Hassell, *Die Hassell-Tagebücher, 1938–1944: Aufzeichnung vom anderen Deutschland,* ed. Friedrich Hiller von Gaertingen, rev. and exp. ed. (Berlin, 1988), 289 (entry of Dec. 21, 1941). "The old-timers' revolution" comes from a conversation between Stauffenberg and Leber; see Eberhard Zeller, *Geist der Freiheit: Der zwanzigste Juli* (Munich, 1963), 297.

3. Harold C. Deutsch, *Verschwörung gegen den Krieg: Der Widerstand in den Jahren 1939–1940* (Munich, 1969), 104. For the "Oster problem," see Kurt Sendtner, "Die deutsche Militäropposition im ersten Kriegsjahr," *Die Vollmacht des Gewissens,* vol. 1 (Berlin and Frankfurt, 1960), 507ff.

4. Gerhard Ritter, *Carl Goerdeler und die deutsche Widerstandsbewegung* (Stuttgart, 1984), 271.

5. Apparently the atrocities in Poland also played a part in Reichenau's readiness to commit treason. H. C. Deutsch was the first to note this remarkable episode; see *Verschwörung,* 76ff.

6. Deutsch, *Verschwörung,* 105.

7. Hassell, *Hassell-Tagebücher,* 207 (entry of Aug. 10, 1940).

8. Heinz Höhne, *Canaris: Patriot im Zwielicht* (Munich, 1976), 403.

9. Klaus-Jürgen Müller, *Das Heer und Hitler: Armee und nationalsozialistisches Regime, 1933–1940* (Stuttgart, 1969), 452–53.

10. Ritter, *Goerdeler,* 274.

11. Qtd. in Ritter, *Goerdeler,* 47–48. For the earlier characterizations of Goerdeler, see Margret Boveri, *Für und gegen die Nation,* vol. 2 of *Der Verrat in XX. Jahrhundert* (Hamburg, 1956), 26.

12. See Ritter, *Goerdeler,* 272ff.; Hans Rothfels, *Opposition gegen Hitler: Eine Würdigung* (Frankfurt, 1958), 104ff.; and Hans Mommsen, "Gesellschaftsbild und Verfassungspläne des deutschen Widerstands," *Der deutsche Widerstand gegen Hitler,* ed. Walter Schmitthenner and Hans Buchheim (Cologne and Berlin, 1966), 73ff. For Hassell's contribution, see Gregor Schöllgen, *Ulrich von Hassell, 1881–1944: Ein Konservativer in der Opposition* (Munich, 1990), 136ff.

13. Mommsen, "Gesellschaftsbild," 83.

14. See George K. Romoser, "The Politics of Uncertainty: The German Resistance Movement," *Social Research* (1964), vol. 31, 73ff.; Hannah Arendt, *Eichmann in Jerusalem: A Report on the Banality of Evil,* rev. and enl. ed. (New York, 1965), 97ff.; and Ralf Dahrendorf, *Gesellschaft und Demokratie in Deutschland* (Munich, 1965), 441f.

15. Mommsen points this out and mentions Wilhelm Leuschner as the sole exception, although he can only be viewed to a limited extent as a typical representative of the Weimar Republic ("Gesellschaftsbild," 76).

16. Qtd. in Mommsen, "Gesellschaftsbild," 134–35.

17. Hassell, *Hassell-Tagebücher*, 293–94 (entry of Jan. 24, 1942).

18. For an overall assessment of these proposals, see Mommsen, "Gesellschaftsbild," 161ff.

19. See Dorothee von Meding, *Mit dem Mut des Herzens: Die Frauen des 20. Juli* (Berlin, 1992), 135 (Freya von Moltke) and 198 (Marion Yorck von Wartenburg).

20. Ger van Roon, *Neuordnung und Widerstand: Der Kreisauer Kreis innerhalb der deutschen Widerstandsbewegung* (Munich, 1967), 187.

21. Freya von Moltke, qtd. in Meding, *Mut*, 135.

22. Heinrich Stehkämper, *Protest, Opposition, und Widerstand im Umkreis der (untergegangenen) Zentrumspartei: Ein Überblick* part 2, in *Der Widerstand gegen den Nationalsozialismus: Die deutsche Gesellschaft und der Widerstand gegen Hitler*, ed. Jürgen Schmädeke and Peter Steinbach (Munich, 1986), 895. See also Peter Hoffmann, *Widerstand, Staatsstreich, Attentat: Der Kampf der Opposition gegen Hitler*, 3rd ed. (Munich, 1979), 444. Moltke's remark about "that Goerdeler mess" appears only in his next-to-last letter from prison, but it hints at the reservations that always existed.

23. Marion von Yorck von Wartenburg, qtd. in Meding, *Mut*, 203.

24. Qtd. in Christian Müller, *Oberst i.G. Stauffenberg: Eine Biographie* (Düsseldorf, 1990), 368. For the letter to Lionel Curtis, see Klemens von Klemperer et al., *Für Deutschland: Die Männer des 20. Juli* (Frankfurt and Berlin, 1994), 170–71.

25. Qtd. in Hermann Graml's groundbreaking study "Die aussenpolitische Vorstellungen des deutschen Widerstands," Schmitthenner and Buchheim, *Widerstand*, 15 and 22.

26. Graml, "Vorstellungen," 40.

27. Van Roon, *Neuordnung*, 271. See also Hassell, *Hassell-Tagebücher*, 335–36 (entry of Jan. 22, 1943). The comment about a "Kerensky solution" refers to Alexander F. Kerensky, the prime minister of Russia after the Russian Revolution of February 1917, whose halfhearted policies seeking compromise solutions cleared the way for the Bolsheviks. Conceivably Moltke thought that Goerdeler would be a transitional figure who would clear the way for the Kreisauers.

28. Rothfels, *Opposition*, 187.

29. Hans Bernd Gisevius, *Bis zum bittern Ende* (Zurich, 1954), 455.

30. Gisevius, *Ende*, 471.

31. Deutsch, *Verschwörung*, 385–86; see also Oscar Reile, *Geheime Westfront: Die Abwehr, 1935–1945* (Munich, 1962), 387.

32. Höhne, *Canaris*, 201.

6. The Army Groups

1. Karl Klee, *Das Unternehmen "Seelöwe"* (Göttingen, 1985), 189–90.

2. Franz Halder, *Kriegstagebuch: Tägliche Aufzeichnungen des Chefs des*

Generalstabs des Heeres, 1939–1942, 3 vols. (Stuttgart, 1962–64), vol. 2, 121. For the conversation with Jodl, see vol. 1, 996 (Dec. 17, 1940); for the comment to Mussolini, see vol. 1, 275 (Jan. 20, 1941). That preparations for a war against the Soviet Union were quite open is evidenced in the fact that Hassell heard about them as early as the beginning of August (*Die Hassell-Tagebücher, 1938–1944: Aufzeichnungen vom anderen Deutschland,* ed. Friedrich Hiller von Gaertingen, rev. and exp. ed. [Berlin, 1988], 206 [entry of Aug. 10, 1940]).

3. Halder, *Kriegstagebuch,* vol. 2, 335ff.

4. Gerhard Ritter, *Carl Goerdeler und die deutsche Widerstandsbewegung* (Stuttgart, 1954), 323. For Jodl's statement at Nuremberg, see *Prozess gegen die Hauptkriegsverbrecher vor dem Internationalen Militärgerichtshof Nürnberg, 14. November 1945–1. Oktober 1946* (Nuremberg, 1949), vol. 15, 339.

5. The meeting, described by Ulrich Hassell, took place on April 8, *Hassell-Tagebücher,* 248 (entry of May 4, 1941). For the guidelines themselves, see Hans-Adolf Jacobsen, "Kommissarbefehl und Massenexekutionen sowjetischer Kreigsgefangener," *Anatomie des SS-Staates,* by Hans Buchheim et al. (Olten and Freiburg, 1965), vol. 2, 223–24 and 225ff.

6. Archiv Peter, ed., *Spiegelbild einer Verschwörung: Die Kaltenbrunner-Berichte über das Attentat vom 20. Juli 1944* (Stuttgart, 1961), 368.

7. Bodo Scheurig, *Henning von Tresckow: Eine Biographie* (Düsseldorf, 1970), 70.

8. Scheurig, *Tresckow,* 84.

9. Rudolph-Christoph von Gersdorff, *Soldat im Untergang: Lebensbilder* (Frankfurt and Berlin, 1979), 87.

10. Gersdorff, *Soldat,* 87ff. Gersdorff records many further vivid details. The inkwell scene was probably meant figuratively.

11. See Hans-Adolf Jacobsen, "Kommissarbefehl," 153, and Heinrich Uhlig, "Der verbrecherische Befehl," *Die Vollmacht des Gewissens* (Berlin and Frankfurt, 1960), vol. 2, 320ff. Christian Streit takes a more critical view of the generals in *Keine Kameraden: Die Wehrmacht und die sowjetischen Kriegsgefangenen, 1941–1945* (Stuttgart, 1978), 83ff. Gersdorff wrote in the army group war diary: "In all longer conversations with officers, I was eventually asked about the shooting of Jews, without my having mentioned them in any way. I got the impression that virtually the entire officer corps opposed the shooting of Jews, prisoners, and commissars. They opposed the shooting of commissars especially because it strengthened the enemy's will to fight. The shootings are seen as a blot on the honor of the German army and especially of the German officer corps" (qtd. in Peter Hoffmann, *Widerstand, Staatsstreich, Attentat: Der Kampf der Opposition gegen Hitler,* 3rd. ed. [Munich, 1979], 334). For Arthur Nebe, see Hermann Graml, "Die deutsche Militäropposition vom Sommer 1940 bis zum Frühjahr 1943," *Vollmacht des Gewissens,* vol. 2, 442. Gersdorff said he noticed that Nebe carried out the ordered mass executions much more often than he admitted to the army group.

12. Hassell, *Hassell-Tagebücher,* 256 (entry of May 29, 1941).

13. The staff officer was Friedrich Olbricht (*Süddeutsche Zeitung,* Aug. 7, 1986). See Heinz Boberach, ed., *Meldungen aus dem Reich: Auswahl aus den geheimen*

Lageberichten des Sicherheitsdienstes der SS, 1939–1941 (Neuwied and Berlin, 1965), 155ff. See also Marlis G. Steinert, *Hitlers Krieg und die Deutschen: Stimmungen und Haltung der deutschen Bevölkerung im Zweiten Weltkrieg* (Düsseldorf and Vienna, 1970), 206ff., which cites the observation of the chief public prosecutor of Bamberg that "much of the population was still incapable of understanding that Germany would assume the role in the world as the leading country in Europe through the direct absorption of the eastern territories."

14. Horst Mühleisen, ed., *Helmuth Stieff: Briefe* (Berlin, 1991), 127 (Sept. 5, 1941) and 138 (Nov. 24, 1941); Hans Meier-Welcker, *Aufzeichnungen eines Generalstabsoffiziers, 1939–1942* (Freiburg, 1982), 121. The pogrom in Kovno, ordered by Heydrich, took place between June 25 and June 29, 1941.

15. See the extensive description in Gersdorff, *Soldat*, 96ff. Gersdorff, too, reported the incident to the OKH. A notation on the original document indicates that it was shown to Brauchitsch, although after the war he claimed he could "not remember anymore."

16. *Hitler's Table Talk, 1941–1944* (London, 1953), 44.

17. See Gersdorff, *Soldat*, 84 and 99; for Stauffenberg, see Christian Müller, *Oberst i.G. Stauffenberg: Eine Biographie* (Düsseldorf, 1970), 203–04. For the importance of the mass murders in the East as a motivation for the resistance, see also the so-called Kaltenbrunner reports, *Spiegelbild*, 424ff.

18. Mühleisen, *Stieff*, 123 (Aug. 23, 1941): "This bloody amateurism, which is still supported by such glorious representatives as Keitel and Jodl, may well, God knows, cost us the war."

19. Hassell, *Hassell-Tagebücher*, 278 (entry of Oct. 4, 1941).

20. Hassell, *Hassell-Tagebücher*, 280 (entry of Nov. 1, 1941).

21. Peter Bor, *Gespräche mit Halder* (Wiesbaden, 1950), 214.

22. See Gersdorff, *Soldat*, 93; Henry Pickler, *Hitlers Tischgespräche im Führerhauptquartier, 1941–1942* (Stuttgart, 1965), passim; and Werner Jochmann, ed., *Adolf Hitler: Monologe im Führerhauptquartier, 1941–1944* (Hamburg, 1980), passim.

23. Mühleisen, *Stieff*, 150 (Jan. 10, 1942); Hassell, *Hassell-Tagebücher*, 283 (entry of Nov. 30, 1941).

24. Karl Silex, cited in Scheurig, *Tresckow*, 125–26.

25. Hassell, *Hassell-Tagebücher*, 307 (entry of March 28, 1942). Gerhard Ritter already speaks in the winter of 1941–42 of a troika consisting of Beck, Goerdeler, and Witzleben that will form the provisional government after a coup (*Goerdeler*, 348).

26. It was Olbricht's widow who called attention to this maxim. She set herself the admirable task of filling in the blanks in research on the resistance and correcting the neglect from which Olbricht has always suffered and the errors that studies of July 20 have made in assigning credit. See Helena P. Page, *General Friedrich Olbricht: Ein Mann des 20 Juli* (Bonn and Berlin, 1992).

27. Fabian von Schlabrendorff, *Offiziere gegen Hitler* (Frankfurt and Hamburg, 1959), 55–56. See also Gersdorff, *Soldat*, 124–25.

28. Schlabrendorff, *Offiziere*, 55.

29. Hans Bernd Gisevius, *Bis zum Bittern Ende* (Zurich, 1954), 389.

30. Gisevius, *Ende,* 508. Goerdeler informed Gerhard Ritter in late 1942 of the various views on arresting Hitler *(Goerdeler,* 535, n. 14).

31. Hoffmann, *Widerstand,* 338.

32. Qtd. in Scheurig, *Tresckow,* 133.

33. H. Kaiser, qtd. in Count Romedio Galeazzo von Thun-Hohenstein, *Der Verschwörer: General Oster und die Militäropposition* (Cologne and Berlin, 1969), 224.

34. Count Detlef von Schwerin, *Dann sind's die besten Köpfe, die man henkt: Die junge Generation im deutschen Widerstand* (Munich, 1991), 289.

35. The available information about why the Boeselager plan was not carried out is contradictory, and it is probably impossible now to clarify the course of events. See Hoffmann, *Widerstand,* 351, and his *Die Sicherheit des Diktators: Hitlers Leibwachen, Schutzmassnahmen, Residenzen, Hauptquartiere* (Munich, 1975), 165–66. Scheurig does not discuss the plan. For the course of the visit to Smolensk, see in addition to the works cited above Schlabrendorff, *Offiziere,* 71ff. After the war Schlabrendorff said that Kluge could not be persuaded to agree to an assassination attempt by the Boeselager unit; see Thun-Hohenstein, *Verschwörer,* 230.

36. See Hoffmann, *Widerstand,* 353 and 760, n. 93, and Schlabrendorff, *Offiziere,* 74–75.

37. Gersdorff, *Soldat,* 128–29.

38. Gersdorff, *Soldat,* 132–33.

39. Hassell, *Hassell-Tagebücher,* 347 (entry of Feb. 14, 1943).

40. Qtd. in Hoffmann, *Widerstand,* 370. For Groscurth's message from encircled Stalingrad, see his *Tagebücher eines Abwehroffiziers, 1938–1940* (Stuttgart, 1970), 93. Groscurth was taken prisoner along with the remnants of the Sixth Army, soon contracted typhus, and died on April 7, 1943, in the Frolov camp.

41. Christian Petry, *Studenten aufs Schafott: Die Weisse Rose und ihr Scheitern* (Munich, 1968), 122.

42. Gersdorff, *Soldat,* 133.

43. Gersdorff, *Soldat,* 134ff.

44. Müller, *Stauffenberg,* 279–80.

7. Stauffenberg

1. Ulrich von Hassell, *Die Hassell-Tagebücher, 1938–1944: Aufzeichnungen vom anderen Deutschland,* ed. Friedrich Hiller von Gaertingen, rev. and exp. ed. (Berlin, 1988), 362 (entry of April 20, 1943) and 331 (entry of Sept. 26, 1942).

2. Fabian von Schlabrendorff, *Offiziere gegen Hitler* (Frankfurt and Hamburg, 1959), 107. For the reasons why Jäger and Schulenburg were suspected, see Peter Hoffmann, *Widerstand, Staatsstreich, Attentat: Der Kampf der Opposition gegen Hitler,* 3rd ed. (Munich, 1979), 363. Jäger was released after just a few days and Schulenburg managed to assuage his interrogators in the very first interview.

3. Hoffmann, *Widerstand,* 363ff.; Count Romedio Galeazzo von Thun-Hohenstein, *Der Verschwörer: General Oster und die Militäropposition* (Berlin, 1982), 236ff.; and Heinz Höhne, *Canaris: Patriot in Zwielicht* (Munich, 1976), 472ff.

1. Höhne, *Canaris*, 495.

5. See the numerous references in Hassell's diaries. For "the crux of the matter," see 405 (entry of Nov. 13, 1943).

6. Hassell, *Hassell-Tagebücher*, 291 (entry of Dec. 21, 1941), and 345 (entry of Jan. 22, 1943).

7. Hans Rothfels, *Deutsche Opposition gegen Hitler: Eine Würdigung*, exp. ed. (Tübingen, 1969), 163.

8. Cited in Patricia Meehan, *The Unnecessary War: White Hall and the German Resistance to Hitler* (London, 1992), 337. For a balanced study reflecting the recent tendency in British historiography to do justice to the German resistance and its attempts to win over the Western Allies, see Richard Lamb, *The Ghosts of Peace, 1935–1945* (London, 1987).

9. Qtd. in Ger van Roon, *Neuordnung und Widerstand: Der Kreisauer Kreis innerhalb der deutschen Widerstandsbewegung* (Munich, 1967), 316.

10. Rothfels, *Opposition*, 187.

11. Alfred Vagts, "Unconditional Surrender—vor und nach 1943," *Vierteljahrshefte für Zeitgeschichte* (1959), 298–99.

12. Rothfels, *Opposition*, 161–62. For the larger context, see also Klemens von Klemperer, *Die verlassenen Verschwörer: Der deutsche Widerstand auf der Suche nach Verbündeten, 1938–1945* (Berlin, 1994), 209ff.

13. Bodo Scheurig, *Ewald von Kleist-Schmenzin: Ein Konservativer gegen Hitler* (Oldenburg and Hamburg, 1968), 183. For Trott's comment, see Rothfels, *Opposition*, 158.

14. Van Roon, *Neuordnung*, 317.

15. Thun-Hohenstein, *Verschwörer*, 228. For Manstein and Röhricht, see Bodo Scheurig, *Henning von Tresckow: Eine Biographie* (Frankfurt and Berlin, 1980), 182 and 185. For Fritsch, see Hassell, *Hassell-Tagebücher*, 71 (entry of Dec. 18, 1938). For Canaris and his "profound fatalism," see Harold C. Deutsch, *Verschwörung gegen den Krieg: Der Widerstand in den Jahren 1939–1940* (Munich, 1969), 386; see also Margret Boveri, *Für und gegen die Nation*, vol. 2 of *Der Verrat im XX. Jahrhundert* (Hamburg, 1956), 51.

16. Hassell, *Hassell-Tagebücher*, 350 (entry of March 6, 1943).

17. Scheurig, *Tresckow*, 243, n. 83.

18. Archiv Peter, ed., *Spiegelbild einer Verschwörung: Die Kaltenbrunner-Berichte über das Attentat vom 20. Juli 1944* (Stuttgart, 1961), 412; for the message to J. Wallenberg, see Gerhard Ritter, *Carl Goerdeler und die deutsche Widerstandsbewegung* (Stuttgart, 1984).

19. Joachim Kramarz, *Claus Graf Stauffenberg, 15. November 1907–20 Juli 1944: Das Leben eines Offiziers* (Frankfurt, 1965), 131.

20. Eberhard Zeller, *Geist der Freiheit: Der zwanzigste Juli* (Munich, 1963), 242; Christian Müller, *Oberst i.G. Stauffenberg: Eine Biographie* (Düsseldorf, 1970), 239.

21. Müller, *Stauffenberg*, 235; Zeller, *Freiheit*, 244.

22. Ritter, *Goerdeler*, 367.

23. Kramarz, *Stauffenberg*, 113.

24. Zeller, *Freiheit*, 246–47.

25. See Müller, *Stauffenberg*, 14ff., which describes briefly but thoroughly the emergence and step-by-step transformation of a few doubtful memories, later recanted, and a few prejudices into a historical legend of considerable influence. The Soviet version was well known in the Federal Republic and was enthusiastically embraced as a contribution to détente by Daniel Melnikov, *20. Juli 1944: Legende und Wirklichkeit* (Hamburg, 1968). See also Hoffmann, *Widerstand*, 304ff. and 744, n. 139.

26. Kramarz, *Stauffenberg*, 147–48.

27. Helena P. Page, *General Friedrich Olbricht: Ein Mann des 20 Juli* (Bonn and Berlin, 1992), 246.

28. Hans Bernd Gisevius, *Bis zum bittern Ende* (Zurich, 1954), 582.

29. Schlabrendorff, *Offiziere*, 99–100.

30. Zeller, *Freiheit*, 334.

31. Hoffmann, *Widerstand*, 405.

32. *Prozess gegen die Hauptkriegsverbrecher vor dem Internationalen Militärgerichtshof Nürnberg, 14. November 1945–1. Oktober 1946* (Nuremberg, 1949), vol. 33, 330ff.

33. Scheurig, *Kleist*, 187. Ewald Heinrich von Kleist described these events on a television program produced by Hava K. Beller entitled "The Restless Conscience," London, 1992. See also Zeller, *Freiheit*, 190 and 337 (for the conversation between Stauffenberg and Kleist).

34. Baron Rudolph-Christoph von Gersdorff, *Soldat im Untergang: Lebensbilder* (Frankfurt and Berlin, 1979), 143.

35. Hoffmann, *Widerstand*, 410.

36. Schlabrendorff, *Offiziere*, 105.

37. Van Roon, *Neuordnung*, 131.

38. Hassell, *Hassell-Tagebücher*, 421 (entry of Feb. 23, 1944). See also 400 (entry of Nov. 13, 1943) and 411 (entry of Dec. 27, 1943). It was Hassell who described Popitz's initiative as an "act of desperation" (333 [entry of Oct. 10, 1942]). See also Ritter, *Goerdeler*, 362 and 370. For a succinct, accurate summary of the entire Popitz affair, see Karl Dietrich Bracher, *Die deutsche Diktatur: Entstehung, Struktur, Folgen des Nationalsozialismus* (Cologne and Berlin, 1969), 485–86.

39. Ulrich von Hassell spoke of a "band of brothers" in melancholy recollections recorded in December 1943 (*Hassell-Tagebücher* 408). For Goerdeler's request to Zeitzler, see *Spiegelbild*, 56, 112, and 178. Kunrat von Hammerstein writes in *Spähtrupp* (Stuttgart, 1963) that Zeitzler told him in 1956 that he was never informed about Goerdeler's suggestion (243–44).

40. Elfriede Nebgen, qtd. in Müller, *Stauffenberg*, 385.

41. Müller, *Stauffenberg*, 393.

42. Müller, *Stauffenberg*, 374.

43. *Spiegelbild*, 502.

44. Hoffmann, *Widerstand*, 305.

45. Van Roon, *Neuordnung*, 288–89. For Stauffenberg's view, see Hoffmann, *Widerstand*, 308. For doubts about Stauffenberg's agreement on making contact, see Müller, *Stauffenberg*, 419.

46. Schlabrendorff, *Offiziere*, 109. The version in the older paperback edition is somewhat different.

8. The Eleventh Hour

1. Eberhard Zeller, *Geist der Freiheit: Der zwanzigste Juli* (Munich, 1963), 346.

2. Albert Speer, *Inside the Third Reich*, trans. Richard and Clara Winston (New York: Collier), 378. At first Mertz von Quirnheim was unhappy about being transferred from the front, but soon he felt "liberated" because he was close to Stauffenberg and the conspiracy; see Peter Hoffmann, *Claus Schenk Graf von Stauffenberg und seine Brüder* (Stuttgart, 1992), 386–87.

3. Peter Hoffmann, *Widerstand, Staatsstreich, Attentat. Der Kampf der Opposition gegen Hitler*, 3rd ed. (Munich, 1979), 468.

4. Ferdinand Sauerbruch, *Das war mein Leben* (Munich, 1976), 432–33.

5. Zeller, *Freiheit*, 506, n. 9.

6. Dorothee von Meding, *Mit dem Mut des Herzens: Die Frauen des 20. Juli* (Berlin, 1992), 255–56. A report quoted in Hoffmann's *Widerstand* shows that Werner von Haeften himself "suffered" from the idea of assassinating someone (777, n. 67).

7. Joachim Kramarz, *Claus Graf Stauffenberg, 15. November 1907–20. Juli 1944: Das Leben eines Offiziers* (Munich, 1963), 201; see also Hoffmann, *Stauffenberg*, 338.

8. Gerhard Ritter, *Carl Goerdeler und die deutsche Widerstandsbewegung* (Stuttgart, 1984), 408.

9. Harald Poelchau, *Die letzten Stunden: Erinnerungen eines Gefängnispfarrers* (Cologne, 1987), 117. See also Hoffmann, *Widerstand*, 465. For Captain Gehre, see Helena P. Page, *General Friedrich Olbricht: Ein Mann des 20 Juli* (Bonn and Berlin, 1992), 261. For the current rumors, see Marie Wassiltschikow, *Die Berliner Tagebücher der "Missie" Wassiltschikow, 1940–1945* (Berlin, 1987), 229–30 and 232.

10. Kunrat von Hammerstein, *Spähtrupp* (Stuttgart, 1963), 262. For Stauffenberg's comments about Stieff, see Archiv Peter, ed., *Spiegelbild einer Verschwörung: Die Kaltenbrunner-Berichte über das Attentat vom 20 Juli 1944* (Stuttgart, 1961).

11. Zeller, *Freiheit*, 327ff.

12. Hans Speidel, *Invasion 1944* (Stuttgart, 1949), 138–39. Christian Müller also points out the distance between Rommel and the resistance, legends to the contrary. The field marshal was actually only identified with the resistance as a result of his forced suicide (*Oberst i.G. Stauffenberg: Eine Biographie* [Düsseldorf, 1970], 422).

13. Berthold von Stauffenberg was interrogated on July 22, 1944; see *Spiegelbild*, 21. For the statement to Klausing, see *Spiegelbild*, 131. For another version of events and Stauffenberg's reasons for holding off, see Hoffmann, *Widerstand*, 473, and *Stauffenberg*, 417ff. Hoffmann emphasizes the "unbelievable" action of Stieff, Fellgiebel, and Wagner, whom he sees as effectively withdrawing their support for the entire uprising by insisting on Himmler's presence. He seems to go too far, however, in view of the fact that all three generals were without doubt strongly

opposed to the regime and that they supported the assassination attempt of July 20 even though Himmler was again absent.

14. The source of the quotation is Captain Eberhard Siebeck, whom Mertz von Quirnheim had summoned to Berlin for a few days to support the coup. He is also the source of the comment that follows about the relaxed atmosphere on Bendlerstrasse after the assassination attempt was canceled. When Stauffenberg asked Mertz von Quirnheim what he personally thought about an assassination attempt if Himmler was not present, the reply was terse: "Do it!" See Hoffmann, *Widerstand*, 474–75. See also Page (*Olbricht*), who casts doubt, not without good reason, on the thesis advanced mainly by Hoffmann that Stauffenberg hesitated at the last moment. That thesis is based on accounts by Hans Bernd Gisevius, who was of course biased, and Mertz von Quirnheim's wife. In Page's view, it may be just a matter of confusing the events of July 15 with those of July 11. Although her view seems plausible, the intervention of Fellgiebel, Stieff, and Wagner is not mentioned.

15. According to Gisevius, it was Helldorf who reported the "euphoric mood," commenting that "a stone seemed to have been lifted from Olbricht's heart" (*Bis zum bittern Ende* [Zurich, 1954], 589). Page (*Olbricht*) expresses well-founded doubts about the "euphoria" as well.

16. See Zeller, *Freiheit*, 373, although there is no indication of source.

17. Count Romedio Galeazzo von Thun-Hohenstein, *Der Verschwörer: General Oster und die Militäropposition* (Berlin, 1982), 256.

18. *Spiegelbild*, 217. It may be that at the time he spoke to Goerdeler Stauffenberg still did not know for sure that he would be making a presentation at Führer headquarters on July 20.

19. Ursula von Kardoff, *Berliner Aufzeichnungen, 1942–1945* (Munich, 1992), 209 (entry of July 18, 1944).

20. *Spiegelbild*, 117.

21. *Spiegelbild*, 146.

22. Cäsar von Hofacker assessed the chances of the coup attempt as "only ten percent"; see Walter Bargatzky, *Hotel Majestic: Ein Deutscher im besetzten Frankreich* (Freiburg, 1987), 131. For Schulenburg and Berthold von Stauffenberg, see Hoffmann, *Widerstand*, 479; for Beck, see 462. For Stauffenberg, see Müller, *Stauffenberg*, 460.

23. Ritter, *Goerdeler*, 408.

9. July 20, 1944

1. The most thorough studies of the assassination attempt are Peter Hoffmann, *Widerstand, Staatsstreich, Attentat: Der Kampf der Opposition gegen Hitler*, 3rd. ed. (Munich, 1979), 496ff. and 813ff., and Christian Müller, *Oberst i.G. Stauffenberg: Eine Biographie* (Düsseldorf, 1970), 477ff., 484–85, and 613ff. See also Archiv Peter, ed., *Spiegelbild einer Verschwörung: Die Kaltenbrunner-Berichte über das Attentat vom 20. Juli 1944* (Stuttgart, 1961), 85–86. The widespread belief that the assassination attempt failed because the briefing was suddenly shifted to a "barracks" is unfounded. In actual fact, the "noon briefings" had been held for quite some time in

what was known as the "Speer barracks" while the "evening briefing" was always held in the bunker. It is true that if the explosion had occurred in the bunker, with its cement walls, everyone present would have been killed because of the much greater concentrating effect.

2. Peter Hoffmann, *Claus Schenk Graf von Stauffenberg und seine Brüder* (Stuttgart, 1992), 425-26.

3. Albert Speer, *Inside the Third Reich*, trans. Richard and Clara Winston (New York, 1981), 389.

4. See Müller, *Stauffenberg*, 487, for an enlightening description of the situation in which Fellgiebel found himself.

5. Hoffmann, *Widerstand*, 504.

6. Bernd Wehner, on Hava K. Beller's television program "The Restless Conscience," London, 1992.

7. Views differ considerably as to when and through whom Olbricht learned about the failure of the assassination attempt. Peter Hoffmann thinks that Thiele informed Olbricht shortly after the news from Fellgiebel arrived (*Stauffenberg*, 427, and *Widerstand*, 464-65). Helena P. Page, on the other hand, believes that Olbricht was not informed by Thiele until 3:15 p.m. (*General Friedrich Olbricht: Ein Mann des 20 Juli* [Bonn and Berlin, 1992], 276ff). According to her, Olbricht, accompanied by General Hoepner, went home at 1:00 p.m. as usual for lunch in order not to arouse suspicion. He returned to Bendlerstrasse shortly after 2:00 but still did not know what had happened in Rastenburg. There are some indications that General Wagner, who informed the conspirators in Paris around 2:00 p.m., also contacted Bendlerstrasse (see Eberhard Zeller, *Geist der Freiheit: Der zwanzigste Juli* [Munich, 1963], 435-36).

8. Müller, *Stauffenberg*, 490. Whether the decision to issue the Valkyrie orders was made before or after Haeften's telephone call is still a matter of controversy; see Müller, 606.

9. According to Schulenburg; see *Spiegelbild*, 97.

10. Hoffmann, *Widerstand*, 516.

11. *Prozess gegen die Hauptkriegsverbrecher vor dem Internationalen Militärgerichtshof Nürnberg, 14. November 1945-1. Oktober 1946* (Nuremberg, 1949), vol. 33, 404.

12. Hans Bernd Gisevius, *Bis zum bittern Ende* (Zurich, 1954), 631.

13. Speer, *Inside*, 383.

14. Kunrat von Hammerstein, *Spähtrupp* (Stuttgart, 1963), 280, and Hoffmann, *Widerstand*, 592.

15. Hoffmann, *Widerstand*, 608 and 507.

16. Müller, *Stauffenberg*, 498. Müller accurately characterizes Hoepner's behavior as "frightful," given the crucial role he was supposed to play in the coup. For the apathetic way in which Hoepner gave out information over the telephone at a very early point, see Schulenburg's statements in *Spiegelbild*, 97.

17. Hoffmann, *Widerstand*, 601; Gisevius, *Ende*, 634-35.

18. *Spiegelbild*, 22 and 336.

19. For accounts of the events in general, see Hoffmann, *Widerstand,* 619ff., and Müller, *Stauffenberg,* 505–06.

20. Gisevius, *Ende,* 649. My presentation of events from Fromm's reemergence to the proclamation of the court-martial decision largely follows the account Erich Hoepner provided to the People's Court; see *Prozess,* vol. 33 (PS-3881), 417ff. and 505ff.

21. There has been controversy from the outset as to what Stauffenberg shouted into the salvo. Some witnesses understood him to say, "Long live sacred Germany," while others heard only "Holy Germany" and still others "Long live Germany." An informative overview, with the relevant sources, can be found in Hoffmann, *Widerstand,* 862–63.

22. *Spiegelbild,* 76.

23. Hans Speidel, *Aus unserer Zeit: Erinnerungen* (Berlin, 1977), 191.

24. Hoffmann, *Widerstand,* 586–87.

25. Walter Bargatzky, *Hotel Majestic: Ein Deutscher im besetzten Frankreich* (Freiburg, 1987), 127ff.

26. Count Dankwart von Arnim, *Als Brandenburg noch die Mark hiess: Erinnerungen* (Berlin, 1991), 208. The address Hitler delivered on the night of July 20–21, 1944, is reprinted in Max Domarus, *Hitler: Reden und Proklamationen, 1932–1945,* vol. 2 (Würzburg, 1963), 2127.

27. Zeller, *Freiheit,* 415ff.

28. Günther Blumentritt, in B. H. Lidell Hart, *Jetzt dürfen sie reden: Hitlers Generale berichten* (Stuttgart and Hamburg, 1950), 527.

29. Ernst Jünger, *Strahlungen* (Tübingen, 1949), 540 (entry of July 21, 1944).

30. Bargatzky, *Majestic,* 139. For Kluge's denunciation, see Wilhelm von Schramm, *Der 20. Juli in Paris* (Bad Wörishofen, 1953), 222.

31. Margret Boveri, *Für und gegen die Nation,* vol. 2 of *Der Verrat im XX. Jahrhundert* (Hamburg, 1956), 51. For the accusation of "amateurism," with its unmistakable undertones of animosity toward Stauffenberg and the "count group," see Gisevius, *Ende,* 647.

32. Speer, *Inside,* 388.

33. Dietrich Ehlers, *Technik und Moral einer Verschwörung: Der 20. Juli 1944* (Frankfurt and Bonn, 1964), 107.

34. Fabian von Schlabrendorff, *Offiziere gegen Hitler* (Frankfurt and Hamburg, 1959), 128–29.

35. Zeller, *Freiheit,* 416.

36. Gert Buchheit, *Hitler der Feldherr: Die Zerstörung einer Legende* (Rastatt, 1958), 439.

37. Chester Wilmot, *Der Kampf um Europa* (Frankfurt, 1954), 780–81.

38. Rudolph-Christoph von Gersdorff, *Soldat im Untergang: Lebensbilder* (Frankfurt and Berlin, 1979), 151–52.

10. Persecution and Judgment

1. Eberhard Zeller, *Geist der Freiheit: Der zwanzigste Juli* (Munich, 1963), 435. See also Peter Hoffmann, *Widerstand, Staatsstreich, Attentat: Der Kampf der Opposition gegen Hitler,* 3rd ed. (Munich, 1979), 632.

2. W. Scheidt, *Gespräche mit Hitler,* qtd. in Zeller, *Freiheit,* 538. See also *Hitlers Lagebesprechungen: Die Protokollfragmente seiner militärischen Konferenzen, 1942–1945* ed. Helmut Heiber (Stuttgart, 1962), 588.

3. Zeller, *Freiheit,* 451.

4. Bodo Scheurig, *Henning von Tresckow: Eine Biographie* (Frankfurt and Berlin, 1980), 209–10. For Klausing, see Dietrich Ehlers, *Technik und Moral einer Verschwörung: Der 20. Juli 1944* (Frankfurt and Bonn, 1964), 31–32. For Trott, see Marie Wassiltschikow, *Die Berliner Tagebücher der "Missie" Wassiltschikow, 1940–1945* (Berlin, 1987), 243–44.

5. Ger van Roon, *Neuordnung und Widerstand: Der Kreisauer Kreis innerhalb der deutschen Widerstandsbewegung* (Munich, 1967), 139, and Hoffmann, *Widerstand,* 457.

6. Georg Kiessel, qtd. in Hoffmann, *Widerstand,* 628.

7. Werner Fiedler, a journalist for the *Deutsche Allgemeine Zeitung,* memorized Schulenberg's words—as recorded by the newspaper's court reporter—and passed them along to his family; see Elisabeth Ruge, ed., *Charlotte Gräfin von der Schulenburg zur Erinnerung,* privately printed, n.d., 38. For Hitler's prohibition on reporting, see Count Detlef von Schwerin, *Dann sind's die besten Köpfe, die man henkt: Die junge Generation im deutschen Widerstand* (Munich, 1991), 425, and Zeller, *Freiheit,* 465.

8. Freya von Moltke, Michael Balfour, and Julian Frisby, *Helmuth James von Moltke, 1907–1945: Anwalt der Zukunft* (Stuttgart, 1975), 298. See also Archiv Peter, ed., *Spiegelbild einer Verschwörung: Die Kaltenbrunner-Berichte über das Attentat vom 20. Juli 1944* (Stuttgart, 1961), 188–89. In the cleanup following a bombing raid, an envelope was found in Goerdeler's destroyed hotel, the Hospiz on Askanischer Platz. It had been placed in a safe before the raid and never retrieved. Various documents were found in it, including Goerdeler's inaugural address.

9. Wassiltschikow, *Tagebücher,* 267, and Schwerin, *Köpfe,* 44–45.

10. Ehlers, *Technik,* 113.

11. Zeller, *Freiheit,* 461–62.

12. See Walter Wagner's portrait of Freisler in "Der Volksgerichtshof im nationalsozialistischen Staat," *Die Justiz und der Nationalsozialismus,* Institut für Zeitgeschichte (Stuttgart, 1974), esp. 832ff. See also Rudolf Diels, *Lucifer ante portas . . . Es spricht der erste Chef der Gestapo* (Stuttgart, 1950), 295, and Helmuth James von Moltke, *Letters to Freya, 1939–1945,* ed. and trans. Beate Ruhm von Oppen (New York, 1990), 399.

13. *Prozess gegen die Hauptkriegsverbrecher vor dem Internationalen Militärgerichtshof Nürnberg, 14. November 1945–1. Oktober 1946* (Nuremberg, 1949), vol. 33, PS-3881, 299ff. Freisler's concluding words are on 529. The text is one of the few surviving records of the trials before the People's Court. Unlike the text of the introductory comments, it is not a word-for-word transcript since, as a few sequences

in some films of the trial show, Freisler's cursing in particular is omitted. In all likelihood, the defendants' statements of what they believed were also omitted. Detlef von Schwerin points out that according to the transcript Witzleben responded, "I approved of that," when asked whether he assented to the new regime's arresting Nazi functionaries and liberating political prisoners. In actual fact, as can be seen in other documentation, Witzleben replied in much more definite tones: "But of course I approved of that" (*Köpfe*, 422–23).

14. Hoffmann, *Widerstand*, 647–48 (for Wirmer and Haeften); Hans Rothfels, *Deutsche Opposition gegen Hitler: Eine Würdigung*, exp. ed. (Tübingen, 1969), 108 (for Kleist-Schmenzin); Schwerin, *Köpfe*, 426 (for Schwerin); Peter Hoffmann, *Claus Schenk Graf von Stauffenberg und seine Brüder* (Stuttgart, 1992), 445, and Zeller, *Freiheit*, 296 (for Hofacker); Hoffmann, *Widerstand*, 648 (for Fellgiebel and for other comments of the accused).

15. Harald Poelchau, *Die letzten Stunden: Erinnerungen eines Gefängnispfarrers* (Cologne, 1987), 101.

16. See Gerhard Ritter, *Carl Goerdeler und die deutsche Widerstandsbewegung* (Stuttgart, 1984), 9 and 423, and Albert Speer, *Inside the Third Reich*, trans. Richard and Clara Winston (New York, 1981), 395. For an extensive discussion of different versions of the executions and of the reactions in Führer headquarters, see Hoffmann, *Widerstand*, 871ff.

17. Qtd. in *Ursachen und Folgen: Vom deutschen Zusammenbruch 1918 und 1945 bis zur staatlichen Neuordnung Deutschlands in der Gegenwart. Eine Urkunden und Dokumentensammlung zur Zeifgeschichte*, ed. Hebert Michaelis and Ernst Schraepler, vol. 21 (Berlin, 1970), 505–06.

18. Lothar Meissner, "Handstreich im Pustertal: Ein Zeitdokument," rpt. in *Hannoversche Allgemeine Zeitung*, June 5, 1964, 12–13.

19. Ritter, *Goerdeler*, 416.

20. Ritter, *Goerdeler*, 432 and 440.

21. Ritter, *Goerdeler*, 422.

22. For a lengthy discussion of the delays, see Ritter, *Goerdeler*, 426ff. Photocopies of the judgments against Goerdeler and others were made available to the author in documents numbered 1 L 316/44, O J 17/44 gRs.

23. Ritter, *Goerdeler*, 441.

24. *Spiegelbild*, 430.

25. For informative details of the discovery of the documents in Zossen, see Heinz Höhne, *Canaris: Patriot im Zwielicht* (Munich, 1976), 552ff.

26. Zeller, *Freiheit*, 472.

27. Gert Buchheit, *Der deutsche Geheimdienst* (Munich, 1966), 445.

28. Höhne, *Canaris*, 566; see also Count Romedio Galeazzo von Thun-Hohenstein, *Der Verschwörer: General Oster und die Militäropposition* (Berlin, 1982), 271.

29. Höhne, *Canaris*, 569; Josef Müller, *Bis zur letzten Konsequenz* (Munich, 1975), 252. According to Fabian von Schlabrendorff, the crematorium in Flossenbürg was not working at that time, and the daily toll of executed prisoners had to be burned on specially constructed pyres (*Offiziere gegen Hitler* [Frankfurt and Hamburg, 1959], 155).

30. Zeller, *Freiheit*, 468–69.

31. Zeller, *Freiheit*, 463. See also Freya von Moltke et al., *Moltke*, 303ff., where extended passages from both letters are printed. For a complete version, see Helmuth James von Moltke, *Letters*, 398ff.

32. Schlabrendorff, *Offiziere*, 153–54. The doctor who was summoned was Rolf Schleicher. His brother Rüdiger worked at the Institute for the Law of the Sky on Leipziger Platz, which he turned into a meeting place for the opposition. Rüdiger was related by marriage to Hans von Dohnanyi and Dietrich Bonhoeffer. In reaction to the death sentence Freisler had handed down, Rolf Schleicher refused to issue a death certificate for him.

33. Momm told the Gestapo that he said not "swine" but "sow," which he alleged was a proper hunting term and not at all derogatory. Despite this flimsy explanation, he received only relatively mild punishment and a demotion. He later regained his former rank. See Hoffmann, *Widerstand*, 838, n. 170.

34. Freya von Moltke et al., *Moltke*, 300.

35. Hoffmann, *Widerstand*, 652ff. See also *20. Juli 1944*, ed. Erich Zimmerman and Hans-Adolf Jacobsen, special ed. of *Das Parlament*, 3rd ed. (Bonn, 1960), 212–13.

36. Ernst Jünger, *Strahlungen* (Tübingen, 1949), 496 (entry of March 3, 1944).

37. Heinz Boberach, "Chancen eines Umsturzes im Spiegel der Berichte des Sicherheitsdienstes," in *Der Widerstand gegen den Nationalsozialismus: Die deutsche Gesellschaft und der Widerstand gegen Hitler*, ed. Jürgen Schmädecke and Peter Steinbach, (Munich, 1968), 820.

38. On August 2, 1944, Churchill told the House of Commons that the "highest personalities in the German Reich are murdering one another, or trying to, while the avenging Armies of the Allies close upon the doomed and ever-narrowing circle of their power." The events in Germany were, he continued, a manifestation of "internal disease." For Herrnstadt, see Christian Müller, *Oberst i.G. Stauffenberg: Eine Biographie* (Düsseldorf, 1970), 417–18.

39. The ban was broken when Hans Rothfels, who had emigrated to the United States, published *The German Opposition to Hitler* there in 1948. One year later it was published in Germany.

40. Baron Rudolph-Christoph von Gersdorff, *Soldat im Untergang: Lebensbilder* (Frankfurt and Berlin, 1979), 203–04.

41. Ritter, *Goerdeler*, 441ff.

11. The Wages of Failure

1. Fabian von Schlabrendorff, *Offiziere gegen Hitler* (Frankfurt and Hamburg, 1959), 13.

2. Peter Hoffmann, *Widerstand, Staatsstreich, Attentat: Der Kampf der Opposition gegen Hitler*, 3rd ed. (Munich, 1979), 453–54

3. Peter Hoffmann, "Motive," *Der Widerstand gegen den Nationalsozialismus: Die deutsche Gesellschaft und der Widerstand gegen Hitler*, ed. Jürgen Schmädecke and Peter Steinbach (Munich, 1986), 1089.

4. Dorothee von Meding, *Mit dem Mut des Herzens: Die Frauen des 20. Juli* (Berlin, 1992), 244.

5. Ulrich von Hassell, *Die Hassell-Tagebücher, 1938–1944: Aufzeichnungen vom anderen Deutschland*, ed. Friedrich Hiller von Gaertingen, rev. and exp. ed. (Berlin, 1988), 211 (entry of Oct. 8, 1940).

6. Meding, *Mut*, 11.

7. Freya von Moltke, Michael Balfour, and Julian Frisby, *Helmuth James von Moltke, 1907–1945: Anwalt der Zukunft* (Stuttgart, 1975), 315.

8. Eberhard Zeller, *Geist der Freiheit: Der zwanzigste Juli* (Munich, 1963), 36.

9. Hoffmann, *Widerstand*, 524.

10. Dietrich Ehlers, *Technik und Moral einer Verschwörung: Der 20. Juli 1944* (Frankfurt and Bonn, 1964), 123.

11. Erich Kordt, *Nicht aus den Akten . . . Die Wilhelmstrasse in Frieden und Krieg: Erlebnisse, Begegnungen, und Eindrücke, 1928–1945* (Munich, 1949), 370.

12. Peter Bor, *Gespräche mit Halder* (Wiesbaden, 1950), 79.

13. Hassell was speaking of Walther von Brauchitsch (*Hassell-Tagebücher*, 54 [entry of Sept. 29, 1938]).

14. Hoffmann, *Widerstand*, 43. Despite the humiliation he suffered, Fritsch learned virtually nothing, as can be seen in a letter he wrote on December 11, 1938, ten months after his dismissal. He says that after the First World War he realized that Germany would have to fight "three victorious battles" in order to become powerful again: one against the working class—as Hitler, he added, had already largely done— one against the Catholic Church, and one against the Jews. "We are still in the midst of these struggles," he continued. "And the struggle against the Jews is the hardest." See Nicholas Reynolds, "Der Fritsch-Brief vom 11. Dezember 1938," *Vierteljahrshefte für Zeitgeschichte* (1980), 358ff.

15. Adolf Heusinger, *Befehl im Widerstreit* (Tübingen and Stuttgart, 1950), 367. For Reichenau and Hammerstein, see Hildegard von Kotze, ed. *Heeresadjutant bei Hitler, 1938–1943: Aufzeichnungen des Majors Engel* (Stuttgart, 1974), 107 (entry of May 23, 1941).

16. Helmut Krausnick, "Stationen des nationalsozialistischen Herrschaftssystems," *Stationen der deutschen Geschichte, 1919–1943*, ed. Burghard Freudenfeld (Stuttgart, 1962), 135–36. See also Archiv Peter, ed., *Spiegelbild einer Verschwörung: Die Kaltenbrunner-Berichte über das Attentat vom 20. Juli 1944* (Stuttgart, 1961), 281ff.

17. Ehlers, *Technik*, 120.

18. Christian Müller, *Oberst i.G. Stauffenberg: Eine Biographie* (Dusseldorf, 1970), 462.

19. Bor, *Gespräche*, 125; see also Hoffmann, *Widerstand*, 185.

20. Ehlers, *Technik*, 66.

21. Count Rudolph-Christoph von Gersdorff, *Soldat im Untergang: Lebensbilder* (Frankfurt and Berlin, 1979), 176–77. For Erich Marcks, see Hans Rothfels, *Deutsche Opposition gegen Hitler: Eine Würdigung*, exp. ed. (Tübingen, 1969), 92.

22. Hans Mommsen, "Der Widerstand gegen Hitler und die deutsche Gesell-

schaft," Schmädecke and Steinbach, *Widerstand*, 14. See Mommsen for suggested further reading as well.

23. Rothfels, *Opposition*, 165.

24. Hermann Graml, "Die deutsche Militäropposition vom Sommer 1940 bis zum Frühjahr 1943," *Die Vollmacht des Gewissens* (Berlin and Frankfurt), vol. 2, 509–10.

25. Schlabrendorff, *Offiziere*, 65. For Moltke's letter, see Richard Lamb, *The Ghosts of Peace, 1935–1945* (London, 1987), 262.

26. Probably the first to do so was Gerhard Ritter, in *Carl Goerdeler und die deutsche Widerstandsbewegung* (Stuttgart, 1984), 13.

27. Marion Yorck von Wartenburg, *Die Stärke der Stille: Erzählungen eines Lebens aus dem deutschen Widerstand* (Cologne, 1984), 70.

28. *Spiegelbild*, 34.

29. Manfred Messerschmidt, "Militärische Motive zur Durchführung des Umsturzes," Schmädecke and Steinbach, *Widerstand*, 1034.

30. Rüdiger Altmann, *Der wilde Frieden: Notizen zu einer politischen Theorie des Scheiterns* (Stuttgart, 1987), 200.

31. Zeller, *Freiheit*, 531.

32. Alexander Stahlberg, *Die verdammte Pflicht: Erinnerungen, 1932–1945* (Berlin and Frankfurt, 1994), 456ff.

33. Rothfels, *Opposition*, 87.

34. Karl Otmar von Aretin, cited in Ulrich Cartarius, *Opposition gegen Hitler* (Berlin, 1984), 26.

35. Kunrat von Hammerstein, *Spähtrupp* (Stuttgart, 1963), 295.

36. Meding, *Mut*, 52. Stauffenberg's widow, Countess Nina Schenk von Stauffenberg, said something similar: "On the whole, what happened was probably best for the cause" (288).

A NOTE ON THE TEXTS

The following works cited in their German editions in the notes are available in English translation.

Balfour, Michael, and Julian Frisby. *Helmuth von Moltke: A Leader against Hitler.* London, 1972.

Bracher, Karl Dietrich. *The German Dictatorship: The Origins, Structure, and Effects of National Socialism.* New York, 1970.

Buchheim, Hans, et al. *Anatomy of the SS State.* Trans. Richard Barry, Marian Jackson, and Dorothy Lang. New York, 1968.

Ciano, Galeazzo. *The Ciano Diaries, 1939–1943.* Ed. Hugh Gibson. New York, 1947.

Domarus, Max. *Hitler: Speeches and Proclamations, 1932–1945.* London, 1990.

Fest, Joachim, *Hitler.* Trans. Richard and Clara Winston. New York, 1973.

———. *The Face of the Third Reich.* Trans. Michael Bullock. New York, 1970.

François-Poncet, André. *The Fateful Years: Memoirs of a French Ambassador in Berlin, 1931–1938.* New York, 1949.

Gisevius, Hans Bernd. *To the Bitter End.* Trans. Richard and Clara Winston. Boston, 1947.

Halder, Franz. *The Halder War Diary, 1939–1942.* Ed. Charles Burdick and Hans-Adolf Jacobsen. Novato, 1988.

Hassell, Ulrich von. *The von Hassell Diaries: The Story of the Forces against Hitler inside Germany, 1938–1944.* Boulder, 1944.

Hoffmann, Peter. *German Resistance to Hitler.* Cambridge, Mass., 1988.

———. *Hitler's Personal Security.* Cambridge, Mass., 1979.

Höhne, Heinz. *Canaris: A Biography of Hitler's Chief of Espionage.* Trans. J. Maxwell Brownjohn. New York, 1979.

Kramarz, Joachim. *Stauffenberg: The Architect of the Famous July 20th Conspiracy to Assassinate Hitler.* Trans. R. H. Barry. New York, 1967.

Moltke, Helmuth James von. *Letters to Freya, 1939–1945.* Ed. and trans. Beate Ruhm von Oppen. New York, 1990.

Rothfels, Hans. *The German Opposition to Hitler: An Appraisal.* Chicago, 1962.

Schlabrendorff, Fabian von. *Revolt against Hitler.* New York, 1982.

Schöllgen, Gregor. *A Conservative against Hitler: Ulrich von Hassell, Diplomat in Imperial Germany, the Weimar Republic, and the Third Reich, 1881–1944.* Trans. Louise Willmot. New York, 1991.

Speidel, Hans. *Invasion 1944: Rommel and the Normandy Campaign.* Chicago, 1950.

Stahlberg, Alexander. *Bounden Duty: The Memoirs of a German Officer, 1932–1945.* Trans. Patricia Crampton. New York, 1990.

Steinert, Marlis G. *Hitler's War and the Germans: Public Mood and Attitude during the Second World War.* Ed. and trans. Thomas E. J. de Witt. Athens, Ohio, 1977.

Stern, Fritz. *Dreams and Delusions: The Drama of German History.* New York, 1987.

Trial of Major War Criminals before the International Military Tribunal. 42 vols. Nuromberg, 1947–49.

van Roon, Ger. *German Resistance to Hitler: Count von Moltke and the Kreisau Circle.* Trans. Peter Ludlow. New York, 1971.

Vassiltchikov, Maria. *Berlin Diaries, 1940–1945.* London, 1986.

Wilmot, Chester. *The Struggle for Europe.* Westport, 1972.

Zeller, Eberhard. *The Flame of Freedom: The German Struggle against Hitler.* Trans. R. P. Heller and D. R. Masters. London, 1967.

CHRONOLOGY

1933

Jan. 30	Hitler appointed chancellor
Feb. 3	Hitler meets with commanders of the Reichswehr for the first time
Feb. 27–28	Reichstag fire. Government issues emergency decree "to protect the people and the state"
March 5	Reichstag elections. Nazis receive 43.9 percent of the vote
March 21	Potsdam Day celebrations, intended to show unity of Prussianness and National Socialism
March 23	Enabling Act passed
Apr. 1	Boycott of Jewish businesses
Apr. 7	Act to Restore a Professional Public Service passed
May 2	Trade unions disbanded and German Labor Front founded
June–July	Political parties dissolved
July 20	Concordat with Vatican signed

1934

April 24	People's Court established
June 30	Night of the Long Knives. Liquidation of SA leaders and other political opponents begins
Aug. 2	Hindenburg dies. General Werner von Blomberg orders Reichswehr to swear loyalty to Hitler. Hitler granted unlimited power as "Führer and chancellor"

1935

Jan. 2	Admiral Wilhelm Canaris takes over as chief of Military Intelligence
March 4–5	Synod of the Confessional Church decides to denounce Nazi racial theories and the "new heathens" from the pulpit. Seven hundred pastors arrested
March 16	Reintroduction of universal conscription
Aug. on	Wave of arrests directed against socialist resistance group Beginning Anew
Sept. 15	Nuremberg laws enacted
Oct.	Wave of arrests by the Gestapo. By May 1936, over seven thousand seized for political reasons

1936

March 7	German troops march into the demilitarized Rhineland
May 26	Campaign against monasteries and convents. Morals charges brought against 276 members of religious orders for alleged homosexuality
May 28	Whitsun declaration of the Confessional Church condemns Nazi racial policies
Aug.	The Socialist Front in Hannover, one of the largest northern German resistance groups, headed by Werner Blumenberg, broken up by Gestapo

Nov. Gestapo arrests members of the left-wing socialist organization Red Fighters

1937

Jan. 30 Enabling Act extended for four years. Hitler withdraws Germany's signature from the discriminatory clauses of the Treaty of Versailles

March 14 Papal encyclical *Mit brennender Sorge (With Deepest Anxiety)* condemns Nazi policy toward the church. Mass arrest of clergymen, expropriation of church publishing houses and presses

July 1 Pastor Martin Niemöller arrested and sent to a concentration camp

Nov. 5 Hitler announces war plans to the military leadership and the foreign minister. Immediate targets: Austria and Czechoslovakia

Dec. Large-scale operation mounted in many major cities against left-wing resistance organizations

1938

Feb. 4 Dismissal of Blomberg and Army Commander in Chief Fritsch. Hitler creates the High Command of the Armed Forces (OKW) under Wilhelm Keitel. Walther von Brauchitsch named commander in chief of the army. Hitler himself takes over as supreme commander of the entire armed forces (Wehrmacht)

March 12 Annexation of Austria

March 13 Law proclaiming the *Anschluss* passed

May 30 Directive from Hitler announcing the invasion of Czechoslovakia

Aug. 18 Chief of General Staff Ludwig Beck resigns in protest of Hitler's aggression. Franz Halder appointed as successor

Summer	Conspiracy of civilian and military resistance groups launched. Main participants are Halder, Hans Oster, and Erwin von Witzleben
Sept. 28	Oster and Friedrich Wilhelm Heinz's plan for a task force to invade the Chancellery and kill Hitler fails
Sept. 29	Munich conference grants Sudetenland to Germany
Oct. 21	Hitler issues secret orders to prepare "to eliminate the rest of Czechoslovakia"
Nov. 9	*Kristallnacht*, a "spontaneous" pogrom against Jews. Police forbidden to intervene

1939

March 15	Entry into Czechoslovakia. Under pressure from Germany, Slovakia declares its independence
April 3	Hitler issues directive to prepare for the invasion of Poland
May 23	Hitler explains invasion plans to his generals
Summer	Civilian and military resistance circles plan to remove Hitler from power to prevent war. Opposition groups around Harro Schulze-Boysen and Arvid and Mildred Harnack form the Red Orchestra
Aug. 23	Hitler-Stalin pact divides Poland and Eastern Europe into spheres of interest
Sept. 1	Outbreak of the Second World War with invasion of Poland
Sept. 21	Reinhard Heydrich issues guidelines for the Einsatzgruppen in occupied Poland
Sept. 27	Warsaw surrenders
Oct. 9	Hitler announces his intention to launch an invasion in the West by November 12
Oct.–Nov.	Preparations made for Erich Kordt's attempt to assassinate Hitler with a bomb
Nov. 8	Acting alone, Georg Elser fails to kill Hitler in Munich

1940

April 9	Beginning of operation that will lead to occupation of Denmark and Norway
May 10	Beginning of the campaign in the West. Capitulation of Holland (May 15) and Belgium (May 28) and truce with France (June 22)
Dec. 18	Directive from Hitler for Operation Barbarossa: "Before the end of the war against England," the Wehrmacht is to defeat the USSR in "a quick campaign"

1941

March 30	Hitler declares to his generals that the Russian campaign will be a "struggle of annihilation"
Spring	Henning von Tresckow organizes a group of conspirators within Army Group Center
May 13	Hitler cancels the jurisdiction of the military courts over the areas of the Soviet Union that will be occupied. Illegal acts against Soviet civilians no longer punishable; crimes against the occupying Germans to be punished extrajudicially
June 6	Commissar Order calls for the liquidation of political commissars in the Soviet Union
June 22	Beginning of the Russian campaign. The three army groups are followed by four Einsatzgruppen of security police and the SD
Nov.–Dec.	The Russian winter destroys Hitler's plans for blitzkrieg against the Soviet Union
Dec. 19	Hitler dismisses Field Marshal Walther von Brauchitsch and assumes supreme command of the army himself

1942

Feb.	The revolutionary left-wing resistance organization led by Beppo Römer and Robert Uhrig is broken up in Berlin. Forty-five death sentences issued
March 22	Pastoral letter of Catholic bishops on the "Struggle against Christianity and the Church"
Spring	The resistance organization Revolutionary Socialists broken up in Bavaria and Austria
Aug. 20	Roland Freisler named president of the People's Court
Sept. 24	Franz Halder replaced as chief of general staff by Kurt Zeitzler
Fall	Gestapo breaks up the Red Orchestra
Nov. 22	The Sixth Army (some 250,000 troops) cut off near Stalingrad

1943

Jan. 24	Franklin D. Roosevelt and Winston Churchill announce at the Casablanca Conference (Jan. 14–26) their demand for "unconditional surrender"
Feb. 2	Capitulation of the Sixth Army in Stalingrad
Feb. 18	Flyers distributed in Munich by White Rose, a student resistance group with Catholic and youth-organization roots
March 13	Attempt by conspirators in Army Group Center to blow up Hitler fails
March 21	Colonel Rudolph-Christoph von Gersdorff's assassination attempt in the Berlin Zeughaus fails
April 5	Arrest of Hans von Dohnanyi, Dietrich Bonhoeffer, Josef Müller, and other members of the resistance group within Military Intelligence. Hans Oster's activities are curtailed
July 12–13	Establishment of the National Committee for a Free Germany in Krasnogorsk, near Moscow

Summer	Friedrich Olbricht, Tresckow, and Claus Schenk von Stauffenberg begin to rework the Valkyrie plans for a coup
Oct. 1	Stauffenberg assumes his position as chief of staff in the General Army Office under General Olbricht
Nov. 28–Dec. 12	Teheran Conference. Roosevelt, Stalin, and Churchill agree in principle on the division of Germany

1944

Jan. 19	Helmuth von Moltke and members of the Solf Circle arrested
Jan.–March	Captain Axel von dem Bussche, Lieutenant Ewald von Kleist-Schmenzin, and Cavalry Captain Eberhard von Breitenbuch all fail in various plans to assassinate Hitler
Feb. 12	Admiral Wilhelm Canaris relieved of his duties. Hitler orders the creation of a "unified German secret information service" under Himmler
June 6	Allied invasion of Normandy commences
June 22	Julius Leber and Adolf Reichwein meet in Berlin with members of the outlawed central committee of the German Communist Party. Beginning of the Soviet offensive on the eastern front in the area of Army Group Center
July 4–5	Adolf Reichwein and Julius Leber arrested
July 11	Stauffenberg plans to assassinate Hitler at Führer headquarters on the Obersalzberg
July 15	Stauffenberg plans to assassinate Hitler at the Wolf's Lair, Führer headquarters in Rastenburg
July 20	Stauffenberg sets off a bomb in the conference barracks at Rastenburg. Hitler survives. Coup attempt in Paris canceled when plans fail at army headquarters in Berlin. Late that night Stauffenberg, Olbricht, Albrecht Mertz von Quirnheim, and Werner von

Haeften are executed in the army courtyard on Bendlerstrasse. A wave of arrests begins

Aug.   Beginning of trials before the People's Court and the
first executions

1945

Feb. 4–11   Yalta Conference
April 25   American and Soviet troops meet near Torgau on the
Elbe
April 30   Hitler commits suicide
May 8   Germany surrenders unconditionally

SHORT BIOGRAPHIES

Beck, Ludwig (1880–1944)
Career officer. In October 1933 named chief of the troop office in the Ministry of Defense and in 1935 army chief of general staff. Attempted in vain in the summer of 1938 to persuade the generals to resign en masse in order to prevent war. Resigned thereafter himself for reasons of conscience and became a central figure in the military-civilian resistance. After some initial reluctance, participated in planning assassination attempts and was supposed to become regent after Hitler's death. After the failure of the coup attempt on July 20, 1944, General Friedrich Fromm demanded that he commit suicide in army headquarters on Bendlerstrasse. He botched the attempt, succeeding only in severely wounding himself, and a sergeant finished the job.

Blaskowitz, Johannes (1883–1948)
Career officer of the old school. Commander in chief of the German occupation forces in Poland. Wrote two memoranda to Walther von Brauchitsch about the atrocities in Poland and the horrified reaction of the troops. Relieved of his command on several occasions during the battle of France. Later, however, took other commands, no longer calling Hitler's policies into question. In January 1945 assigned command of an army group in Holland, where he capitulated to the British on May 5, 1945. Committed suicide on February 5, 1948, by jumping out a window of Nuremberg prison.

Blomberg, Werner von (1878–1946)

Appointed minister of defense in 1933. From 1935 until 1938 minister of war and commander in chief of the Wehrmacht. Became a field marshal in 1936. Nicknamed "the rubber lion" by fellow officers for his ability to adapt. Believed that the Night of the Long Knives was justified because public order was threatened by insurgents; issued a "muzzle edict" forbidding all criticism within the army. Following the death of President Hindenburg on August 2, 1934, facilitated a virtual putsch by ordering all soldiers to swear allegiance to the "Führer Adolf Hitler." Discredited by the Nazis in January 1938, and forced to resign within a few weeks. Died in American custody.

Blumentritt, Günther (1892–1967)

Appointed colonel on the army general staff in 1938. On the general staff of Army Group South during the Polish and French campaigns and appointed chief of staff to the Fourth Army in 1940. Posted to Army Group Center during the Soviet campaign. Became quartermaster general on the army general staff in July 1942. Appointed chief of general staff to the commander in chief in the West. Thanks to his diplomatic skill, the Wehrmacht, the SS, and the SD were able to agree on how to word an official version of events in Paris on the night of July 20–21, 1944. In 1945 was named commander in chief of the Twenty-Fifth Army and then of the First Parachute Army. On April 10, 1945, became commander in chief of the army named after him.

Bock, Fedor von (1880–1945)

Career officer. Promoted to field marshal in 1940. Commander in chief of army groups in Poland, France, and the Soviet Union (Army Group Center). After the attack on Moscow ground to a halt, was posted to Army Group South in January 1942. Dismissed on July 15, 1942, for lack of success. At war's end, placed himself at the disposal of the Dönitz government. Killed during an air raid in early May 1945.

Despite his outrage at the anti-Semitic violence of November 9, 1938, later refused to participate actively in the resistance.

Bonhoeffer, Dietrich (1906–45)

A prominent Protestant theologian, son of the well-known psychiatrist and neurologist Karl Bonhoeffer. Pastor in London between 1933 and 1935. For a time, private lecturer at the university in Berlin. A leading representative of the Confessional Church. In 1940 drafted into the OKW Military Intelligence Office. Helped draft memoranda on the future democratic government of Germany and compiled files on crimes committed by the SS. Important foreign contacts with A. W. Visser 't Hooft—the secretary-general of the provisional World Council of Churches in Geneva—and Bishop George Bell. Arrested on April 5, 1943, for undermining the war effort. Hanged on April 9, 1945, after a summary trial in the Flossenbürg concentration camp.

Brauchitsch, Walther von (1881–1948)
Appointed field marshal in 1940. In 1938 succeeded Werner von Fritsch as commander in chief of the army. Attempted in vain to have Fritsch rehabilitated. Dismissed after the first setbacks on the eastern front in December 1941. Knew about the opposition to Hitler and was critical of his policy of aggression but nevertheless went along with the Führer, largely out of personal weakness. Described the attempted assassination of July 20 as "the mad act of a small number of men who have forgotten all about honor."

Bussche-Streithorst, Baron Axel von dem (1919–93)
Career officer with the rank of major. Witnessed the mass shooting of Jews in Dubno in 1942. Declared thereafter that there were only three ways for an officer to preserve his honor: die in battle, desert, or rebel. Planned in early 1944 to kill both Hitler and himself by detonating a bomb at a public ceremony. Failed when chance events prevented Hitler from coming. Avoided arrest in July 1944. Studied law after 1945. Counselor at the German embassy in Washington from 1954 to 1958.

Canaris, Wilhelm (1887–1945)
Career officer with the rank of admiral. Sympathized with Hitler's resentment of the conditions imposed at Versailles and his anti-Communism but after 1933 came to despise the brutality of the Nazis. Was chief of OKW Military Intelligence from 1935 to 1944. Began to oppose the Nazis actively after the Fritsch affair. Grew resigned, though, after the Munich agreement. In 1939 he and Hans Oster asked Josef Müller, a lawyer, to attempt through the Vatican to sound out the possibilities for maintaining peace.

In late May 1940, when it was discovered that the German offensive in the West had been betrayed, Canaris managed to allay the suspicions directed at his office by portraying them as mere rumor. The SS continued, however, to monitor the group around Canaris and in the spring of 1943 arrested some of his closest collaborators. Dismissed as chief of Military Intelligence in February 1944 and arrested after July 20, 1944. Hanged on April 9, 1945, in the Flossenbürg concentration camp after his diaries were discovered. A controversial personality because he socialized with Heydrich, played a two-faced role as chief of the military secret service, and protected the resistance. Maintained to the end that he was not a traitor.

Dohnanyi, Hans von (1902–45)
In 1929 became personal assistant to the minister of justice, then head of the Bureau of Ministers. Systematically gathered information about the crimes and atrocities of the Nazi regime. Established contacts as early as 1938 with people in the military who opposed the Nazis. Played a leading role in planning the attempted coup of September 1938. As a result of pressure from Nazi Party headquarters in 1938, was transferred to the federal court in Leipzig. Became a special project chief in OKW Military Intelligence in August 1939. Forwarded reports from his brother-in-law, Dietrich Bonhoeffer, about the deportation of Jews to senior military leaders in the hope of spurring them to do something. Helped Jews threatened with deportation to escape. Arrested on April 5, 1943, for alleged currency violations. After July 20, 1944, some of the information he had collected about Nazi crimes and the coup attempts discovered by the Gestapo. Murdered on April 8, 1945, in the Sachsenhausen concentration camp.

Falkenhausen, Alexander von (1878–1966)
General in the infantry. From 1935 to 1938 a military adviser in China. Appointed military commander in Belgium and northern France in 1940. Dismissed on July 18, 1944, on a number of charges and arrested after July 20, 1944. Sent on the odyssey of prominent prisoners from one concentration camp to another in 1945 and then freed. Sentenced in Belgium in 1951 to twelve years of forced labor for the execution of hostages and the deportation of Jews. Released after three weeks when it was revealed he had saved many Belgian citizens from the SS.

Fellgiebel, Erich (1886–1944)
Career officer. Became chief of the army signal corps in August 1938. Closely associated with Beck and Stülpnagel since their days in the Reichswehr and came to the resistance through them. Hitler sensed from the

beginning that this thoughtful, independent, and very observant man was no friend, but Fellgiebel's expertise was absolutely essential. Played a key role in the coup attempt of July 20, 1944, as it was his task to interrupt all communications with Führer headquarters after the assassination. Was one of the first conspirators to be arrested on the evening of July 20–21. Sentenced to death on August 10 and executed on September 4.

Freisler, Roland (1893–1945)
Prisoner of war in Russia during World War I. Became a Bolshevik commissar and returned to Germany as a Communist. Studied law and became a lawyer. Joined NSDAP in 1925. Appointed chief personnel officer in the Prussian Ministry of Justice in 1933. In 1934 became state secretary in the Prussian and then federal Ministry of Justice. Appointed president of the People's Court in August 1942. Killed in an Allied bombing attack in early February 1945.

Fritsch, Baron Werner von (1880–1939)
General and chief of army command from 1934 to 1935. Was outraged at the murder of generals at the time of the Night of the Long Knives but failed to protest. Appointed commander in chief of the army in 1935. Dismissed in 1938 on charges of homosexuality trumped up by the Gestapo. Cleared by a military court of honor but never fully rehabilitated. Had absolutely no inclination or ability to resist and considered Hitler, whom he admired in spite of everything, to be "Germany's destiny." Killed on September 22, 1939, in the German assault on Warsaw while leading his artillery regiment.

Fromm, Friedrich (1888–1945)
Army chief of armaments from 1939 to 1944 and commander of the reserve army. Knew about the conspiratorial activities in his immediate surroundings but, when the coup of July 20 failed, took up the cause of the victors. After a hasty "court-martial," had Claus Schenk von Stauffenberg, who was his chief of staff, and three other conspirators executed at army headquarters on Bendlerstrasse late on the night of July 20, not least of all to conceal his own knowledge of the affair. Was nevertheless condemned by the People's Court and shot.

Gersdorff, Baron Rudolph-Christoph von (1905–80)
Career officer. Graduated from the War Academy in Berlin in 1938–39 and ended up as a brigadier general. Posted to Army Group Center as an intelligence officer in 1941. Attempted in vain to win Erich von Manstein over to the resistance. On March 21, 1943, attempted unsuccessfully to blow both Hitler and himself up with a bomb while the Führer visited an exhibition at a Berlin museum. Chief of staff to the Seventh Army in 1944–45. The Gestapo failed to detect his activities on behalf of the resistance. Described the army's oath of allegiance to Hitler after Hindenburg's death as a "coerced oath."

Gerstenmaier, Eugen (1906–86)
Protestant theologian. In 1933–34 became involved in the church's struggle against the pro-Nazi "German Christians." Held for a short time by the Gestapo. In 1936 appointed consistorial counselor in the Church Office for Foreign Relations under Bishop Theodor Heckel. Traveled abroad on behalf of the resistance. Beginning in 1940 worked in the cultural policy division of the Foreign Office. Participated in the Kreisau Circle. On July 20, 1944, went to Bendlerstrasse to support the coup and was arrested. Following a very skillful defense, was condemned by the People's Court to seven years in prison. After the war became a member of the German Evangelical synod and a leading Christian Democratic Union politician. President of the Bundestag from 1954 to 1969.

Gisevius, Hans Bernd (1904–74)
Lawyer. Accepted a position with the Prussian political police in August 1933. Following the political murders of June 30, 1934, left government service as an assistant secretary in the federal Ministry of the Interior and entered the private sector. Played a leading role in planning the abortive military coup in 1938. In 1939 became chief of special projects for OKW Military Intelligence under Canaris. From 1940 to 1944 was the military intelligence officer in the German consulate general in Zurich. Maintained contacts with the Western Allies on behalf of the military opposition, especially with Allen W. Dulles of the Office of Strategic Services. Shortly before July 20, 1944, traveled to Berlin and, on the appointed day, went to army headquarters ready for action. Managed to flee back to Switzerland after the coup failed. Wrote one of the eyewitness accounts of the German resistance. Testified before the international military tribunal in Nuremberg.

Goerdeler, Carl Friedrich (1884–1945)

Close to the national conservatives. Served as mayor of Leipzig from 1930 to 1937. Was also Reich price commissioner in 1931–32 and 1934–35. Had violent disagreements with the Nazis after 1935. Resigned as mayor in April 1937. Often traveled abroad and used these opportunities to make political contacts. Maintained that foreign powers should adopt a tough line toward Hitler and saw the Munich agreement as "out-and-out capitulation" on the part of the West. Became the spearhead of the civilian resistance, drafting numerous memoranda and outlines for a new political order in Germany. At first argued for maximum German claims in any peace settlement but after 1943 adopted the idea of a "European peace order." Was deeply disappointed at first by the Allied demand for unconditional surrender, since he had been hoping for separate peace negotiations with the Western powers. Chosen by the military-civilian resistance to be the future federal chancellor. Was wanted by the Gestapo even before July 20, 1944, but managed to continue evading capture after the assassination attempt. Was finally denounced to the Gestapo and sentenced to death by the People's Court on September 8. Hanged five months later in Plötzensee prison after lengthy interrogations during which he spoke freely about the plans and the people involved in them.

Groscurth, Helmuth (1898–1943)

Career officer. Colonel on the general staff. Joined Military Intelligence in 1935. Was a driving force in and helped organize the abortive coups in 1938 and 1939 as a liaison officer between OKW Military Intelligence and the OKH. Became OKH chief of military affairs and, in February 1942, chief of general staff to the Eleventh Army Corps in Stalingrad. Taken prisoner there in 1943 and died of typhus in March of that year.

Haeften, Hans-Bernd von (1905–44)

Lawyer. Joined the Confessional Church in 1933. Served in the diplomatic corps in Copenhagen, Vienna, and Bucharest. Became acting head of the Foreign Office's cultural department in 1940. Refused to join the NSDAP. Was the Stauffenberg group's confidant in the Foreign Office and a member of the Kreisau Circle. Slated to become state secretary in the Foreign Office in the future government. Arrested after July 20, 1944, and executed in Plötzensee prison on August 15.

Haeften, Werner von (1908–44)
Younger brother of Hans-Bernd von Haeften. Lawyer for a Hamburg bank. In 1939 became a first lieutenant in the reserves. Took part in the Russian campaign. After recovering from serious wounds, became Stauffenberg's adjutant in reserve army command in November 1943. Flew with Stauffenberg to Führer headquarters in Rastenburg on July 20, 1944, and helped with final preparations for the assassination attempt. Succeeded in getting out of the Restricted Area with Stauffenberg after the bomb went off and flew with him to Berlin. Executed on the night of July 20–21 in the courtyard of army headquarters on Bendlerstrasse.

Halder, Franz (1884–1972)
Career officer. In 1938 succeeded Beck as army chief of general staff, remaining in this post until 1942. In 1938 told members of the opposition that he would support a putsch in order to avert a war in Europe. Toyed with the idea of arresting Hitler if war broke out with Britain and France, a plan that failed because of the Munich agreement. Thereafter made a strong distinction between his personal dislike of Hitler and the loyalty demanded by his position. Contributed substantially to the early German successes on the eastern front. Dismissed on September 24, 1942, for opposing Hitler's decision to withdraw troops from the front so as to concentrate on Stalingrad. Thrown into a concentration camp after July 20, 1944. Toward the end of the war, numbered among the prominent prisoners taken from one camp to another but freed shortly before he was to be executed. From 1946 to 1961 headed the United States Army's court martial research staff. In his book *Hitler als Feldherr* (translated as *Hitler as War Lord*), published in 1949, he criticized the Führer's strategy and his leadership qualities.

Hammerstein-Equord, Baron Kurt von (1878–1943)
Career officer of the old school. Became chief of army command in 1930. In late January 1933 went to Hindenburg to express the command's doubts about Hitler's fitness to become chancellor. Resigned in the fall of 1933. For a short time in 1939 commanded an army division in the West. Was soon relieved of his command because of his negative attitude toward National Socialism. Died of cancer in 1943.

Hassell, Ulrich von (1881–1944)

Lawyer and diplomat who held a number of important posts abroad. Served as German ambassador in Rome from 1932 until recalled in 1938. Later active in private business. From the outset strongly criticized Hitler's foreign policy as leading inevitably to war. After hostilities broke out, used his international contacts to arrange contacts with representatives of Great Britain and the United States. Hoped that a successful coup would soon lead to the conclusion of a peace treaty with the Western Allies. Worked with Goerdeler, Beck, and Popitz on plans for Germany after the coup. Named as prospective foreign minister in all surviving cabinet lists drawn up by the resistance. Arrested on July 28, 1944. Condemned to death by the People's Court on September 8 and executed in Plötzensee prison.

Heinz, Friedrich Wilhelm (1899–1968)

Officer in World War I who later joined the Erhardt Freikorps. Until late 1923 a leader in the SA. Expelled from the NSDAP. From 1925 to 1928 a member of the Stahlhelm's national leadership. Finally a lieutenant colonel in the OKW Military Intelligence division. Was supposed to lead a task force attacking the Chancellery in September 1938. Wanted to prompt a scuffle during this action and shoot Hitler. In 1941 became commander of the Fourth Regiment of the Brandenburg Division. On July 20, 1944, was to lead a task force for the resistance. Though present on Bendlerstrasse, he managed to survive the war by hiding in Berlin. After the end of hostilities, became a municipal politician in the Soviet zone, then a controversial employee in the rearmament office in the West German government.

Helldorf, Count Wolf-Heinrich von (1896–1944)

Fought in World War I and was a member of the Freikorps. Became a National Socialist in 1925 and a member of the Prussian state assembly. In 1931 became the SA leader for Berlin-Brandenburg. Appointed Berlin prefect of police in 1935. After *Kristallnacht* upbraided his police officers for obeying orders to do nothing and stated that if he had been in Berlin he would have issued orders to shoot. Participated in the resistance. Arrested after July 20, 1944, and executed in Plötzensee prison on August 15.

Hofacker, Cäsar von (1896–1944)

Lawyer. Began to work for the Vereinigte Stahlwerke (United Steel) company in Berlin in 1927, rising to considerable prominence there. Joined the

Stahlhelm in 1931. As a lieutenant colonel in the reserve, was drafted into the Wehrmacht in August 1939. Became head of the iron and steel section of the military administrative staff in Paris, and later personal aide to the military commander in France. Acted as messenger between Stülpnagel and Stauffenberg. Attempted to win Rommel over to the conspiracy and later revealed his name under torture, sealing Rommel's fate. Arrested on July 26, 1944, and condemned to death by the People's Court on August 30. Executed in Plötzensee prison on December 20, 1944.

Jessen, Jens Peter (1895–1944)

Professor of political science at Göttingen, Kiel, and Marburg and lived in Berlin starting in 1936. Supported the Nazis before 1933 because he believed that they were the only force that could prevent an imminent Bolshevik takeover in Europe. He said, however, that once the Nazis assumed power he was likely to go into opposition. Was outraged at the abuses and corruption of the new regime. During the war was a captain in the reserves in the office of the quartermaster general of the army. Helped the July 20 conspirators travel. With Popitz and Planck, developed plans for a new constitution that conflicted with those of Goerdeler. Arrested in August 1944. Condemned to death by the People's Court on November 30 for "failure to report treasonous activities" and executed the same day in Plötzensee prison.

Kaiser, Jakob (1888–1961)

Bookbinder. Served from 1924 to 1933 on the executive of the Christian Trade Unions. Became a Center Party deputy in the Reichstag in 1933. With Wilhelm Leuschner attempted, also in 1933, to bring the various trade unions organized along ideological and philosophical lines together into a single union so as to forestall Nazi *Gleichschaltung*. Later, with Josef Wirmer, became one of Carl Goerdeler's most influential advisers. His calm, open-minded, but determined temperament contributed substantially to relieving the tensions between various resistance groups. Went underground after July 20, 1944, and successfully eluded capture. In 1945 helped found the Christian Democratic Union in the Soviet occupation zone and Berlin. Was a West German minister from 1949 to 1957 and acting chairman of the CDU until 1958.

Keitel, Wilhelm (1882–1946)

Career officer. Blomberg's successor as chief of the newly created OKW or high command of the armed forces, serving from 1938 to 1945. Appointed field marshal in 1940. Although originally opposed to an attack on the Soviet Union, he became Hitler's devoted and closest military assistant. Called Hitler the "greatest general of all times," earning himself the nickname Lakaitel (a play on his surname and *Lakai,* the German word for lackey). Sentenced to death at the Nuremberg trials and executed on October 16, 1946.

Kleist-Schmenzin, Ewald von (1890–1945)
Estate owner, lawyer, and conservative politician with strong Christian and monarchical beliefs. Actively combated National Socialism in the dying days of the Weimar Republic. Twice arrested for short periods in May and June 1933. Traveled to London for political discussions in 1938 at the behest of Beck's group. Met Goerdeler in 1942 and 1943 and agreed to support a coup. Was privy to Stauffenberg's plans and approved the assassination attempt. Was the prospective political representative in the Stettin military district. Arrested after July 20 and condemned to death by the People's Court in March 1945. Executed on April 9 in Plötzensee prison.

Kleist-Schmenzin, Ewald Heinrich von (b. 1922)
Son of the above. Lieutenant in the infantry. In early 1944 volunteered, like Bussche, to blow himself and Hitler up during a public ceremony. At the instigation of Fritz-Dietlof von der Schulenburg, went to Bendlerstrasse on July 20 to serve as the conspirators' adjutant. The ensuing preliminary investigation of him was broken off on December 12, 1944, and he was sent to the front, where he managed to survive the war.

Kluge, Hans Günther von (1882–1944)
Career officer. Appointed field marshal in 1940. Commander in chief of Army Group Center from December 1941 to October 1943. Strongly influenced by Tresckow while with Army Group Center but dodged active participation in plans for a coup, although he realized that Germany was headed for catastrophe. In July 1944 became commander in chief in the West and commander in chief of Army Group B. Dismissed on August 18, 1944, because he failed to report the conspiracy and was suspected of seeking to negotiate with the Western Allies. Committed suicide rather than face trial in Germany.

Knochen, Helmut (b. 1910)

SS Standartenführer. Chief of security police in Paris from 1940 to 1944. Clashed with the German military administration in France under Stülpnagel. Held in custody for a while by the conspirators in Paris on July 20, 1944. Condemned to life imprisonment in 1946 by a British military tribunal for having executed captured pilots. Sentenced to death by a military tribunal in Paris in 1954. Granted a pardon in 1962.

Kordt, Erich (1903–70)

Lawyer specializing in administrative law. Diplomat. From 1936 to 1938 counselor in the German embassy in London, where he established political contacts for the resistance. Chief of the Bureau of Ministers in the German Foreign Office from 1938 to 1941. Planned to attack Hitler in November 1939. Was German envoy in Tokyo and Nanjing from 1941 to 1945. Member of the resistance circle within the Foreign Office. Became a private lecturer at the University of Cologne in 1951. Later served in the state government in Düsseldorf.

Kordt, Theodor (1893–1962)

Lawyer specializing in administrative law. Diplomat. Brother of Erich Kordt. Entered the foreign service in 1923. German ambassador in London in 1938–39. Attempted, with his brother, to persuade the British government to make a public statement warning Germany about the danger of a world war. Informed the British of Hitler's intention to go to war, but their efforts, like those of many other members of the resistance, foundered on Britain's appeasement policy. Ambassador in Bern after 1939. Made political contacts for the resistance at his foreign postings. From 1953 to 1958 served as ambassador to Greece for the Federal Republic of Germany.

Leber, Julius (1891–1945)

Social Democratic politician. Volunteered to serve in World War I and became an officer. Deputy in the Reichstag from 1924 to 1933. Official SPD spokesman on defense policy. Imprisoned from 1933 to 1937 in Wolfenbüttel prison and the Esterwegen and Sachsenhausen concentration camps. Worked in the private sector from 1938 to 1944. After the Casablanca Conference in January 1943, maintained, in contrast to many of his friends in the resistance, that the Allies would never drop their demand for unconditional surrender. Was close to the Kreisau Circle and had contacts with other

Social Democrats. Stauffenberg preferred him to Goerdeler as federal chancellor after the coup. Arrested on July 5, 1944, after being betrayed by a Communist resistance circle that had been infiltrated. Sentenced to death by the People's Court on October 20, 1944, and executed in Plötzensee prison on January 5, 1945.

Leuschner, Wilhelm (1888–1944)

Social Democrat and trade union leader. Minister of the interior in Hesse from 1929 to 1933. Acting chairman of the General German Trade Union Federation. Held in a concentration camp in 1933–34. Worked as a small manufacturer in Berlin from 1934 to 1944. Active in the underground. Strove to form a single, united labor union. Chosen in 1944 to become vice-chancellor of the Reich after the coup. When his wife was arrested in August 1944, turned himself over to the Gestapo. Executed in Plötzensee prison on September 29.

Mackensen, August von (1848–1945)

Field marshal. The oldest of the German generals. Attempted to salvage the honor of Generals Kurt von Schleicher and Kurt von Bredow, murdered in the Röhm putsch. Together with Hammerstein wrote a letter of protest to Hindenburg, which apparently was not delivered.

Manstein, Erich von (1887–1973)

Field marshal. From 1935 to 1938 chief of operations on the army general staff. Appointed commander in chief of the Eleventh Army in 1941. Commander in chief of Army Group Don and Army Group South from 1942 to 1944. Dismissed in 1944 when he urged retreat on the eastern front. Considered a leading strategist and field commander. Despite the exhortations of Beck and Stauffenberg, refused to turn against Hitler, even after Stalingrad. Considered himself "just a soldier" who had to obey. In 1949 sentenced by a British court to eighteen years in prison for failing to protect the civilian population. Released in 1953. Later a military adviser to the West German government.

Mertz von Quirnheim, Albrecht Ritter (1905–44)

Career officer with the rank of colonel. Had himself assigned to the SA after the Nazi seizure of power. An early friend of Stauffenberg's and succeeded him in June 1944 as Olbricht's chief of staff. Deeply involved in planning the coup, especially Operation Valkyrie. Present at Bendlerstrasse on the evening of July 20 and executed there that night.

Mierendorff, Carlo (1897–1943)

Politician and journalist. Joined the Social Democrats in 1920. In Hesse became the chief press officer for Interior Minister Wilhelm Leuschner. Became a Reichstag deputy in 1930. Held in a concentration camp from 1933 to 1938. Because of his enormous popularity, which did not fade during his years in the camp, was ordered after his release to take another surname. Inspired by his early enthusiasm for literature, he chose Willemer, the pseudonym of a character in one of Goethe's works. Through Adolf Reichwein met Helmuth von Moltke and the Kreisau Circle, among whom his impressive, forceful personality soon earned him a leading role. Reichwein and others thought he would make the best representative of the new Germany. Killed in December 1943 in an air raid on Leipzig.

Moltke, Count Helmuth James von (1907–45)

Lawyer. The great Prussian field marshal of the same name was his great-granduncle. Thanks to family connections and education, had many ties in England. Became a lawyer in Berlin in 1934. Practiced law in Britain from 1935 to 1938 and planned to take over a law office in London. Undertook a peace mission to London in 1939. Owned the Kreisau estate in Silesia. In September 1939 joined the OKW Military Intelligence branch, where he served as a specialist in international law and law of war. Sought to obtain humane treatment of prisoners of war and compliance with international law. Began writing papers in 1939 arguing for a political change of direction in Germany. Systematically broadened his contacts in the Kreisau Circle to include church leaders and Social Democrats. Communicated with the Allies in 1943. Warned members of the Solf Circle that they were being spied on by the Gestapo and was arrested himself on January 19, 1944. The police investigations following July 20, 1944, uncovered his ties to the innermost circle of conspirators. Condemned to death by the People's Court on January 11, 1945, and executed in Plötzensee prison on January 23.

Oberg, Carl-Albrecht (1897–1965)

SS Obergruppenführer. Senior SS and police commander in occupied France from 1942 to 1945. His appointment brought a sea change in relations between the military administration and the German police, who were made responsible for the security of the troops at their bases. Worked closely with French militiamen and collaborators. Took measures against Jews and the French resistance. Arrested for a short time on July 20, 1944, by army conspirators in Paris. Condemned to death in Germany in 1946, then extradited to France, where in 1954 he was once again sentenced to death. Sentence commuted to life imprisonment in 1958, but Oberg finally pardoned in 1965.

Olbricht, Friedrich (1888–1944)
Career officer. Division commander from 1938 to 1940. Lieutenant general in the infantry. Chief of the OKW General Army Office in Berlin from 1940 to 1944. After 1943 also chief of the reserve section within the OKW. With the groups led by Beck, Goerdeler, and Tresckow developed the Valkyrie plans for seizing control of government. In the fall of 1943 asked to have Stauffenberg appointed chief of staff in his office, but Stauffenberg was transferred in June 1944 to the staff of the commander in chief of the reserve army, Friedrich Fromm. It was Olbricht who gave the signal to launch Operation Valkyrie in Berlin after the assassination attempt of July 20. Executed by firing squad that night in the courtyard of army headquarters on Bendlerstrasse.

Oster, Hans (1888–1945)
Career officer, eventually brigadier general. Led the resistance movement within Military Intelligence. In 1935 joined the counterintelligence division of the Ministry of Defense as a reserve officer with the rank of lieutenant colonel. Played a leading role in the September conspiracy of 1938. In 1940 informed the Dutch military attaché about the impending German invasion of Holland. Became an active officer in 1941. Head of the central division of the OKW Military Intelligence Office. Dismissed on April 16, 1943, on charges of violating currency laws. Supposed to become president of the Reich military court after the coup. Arrested on July 21, 1944. Tried by a kangaroo court and hanged in the Flossenbürg concentration camp on April 9, 1945.

Reichenau, Walter von (1884–1942)
Head of the Bureau of Ministers (later Wehrmacht Office) in the Ministry of Defense and, as such, chief of staff and personal adviser to Blomberg. Saw National Socialism as a mass movement that he could exploit to advance the

interests of the army and enhance the glory and prestige of Germany. Played a key role in integrating the Reichswehr into the Nazi state. After the invasion of Poland in 1939, became critical of Hitler's plans for a hasty offensive in the West. Appointed field marshal in 1940 after the victory over France and finally commander in chief of Army Group South. Covered up the SS bloodbaths in the East. Claimed that German soldiers were imbued with a "relentless racial idea" that was more important than traditional concepts of military honor. Died of a heart attack after crash landing in an airplane.

Reichwein, Adolf (1898–1944)

Educator. Influenced by both socialism and the youth movement. Appointed professor of history and civics in Halle in 1930. Transferred by the Nazis to a rural school in April 1933. Later an educator in the State Museum for German Folklore in Berlin. Maintained contacts with the opposition and was a member of the Kreisau Circle after 1940. His office on Unter den Linden became a meeting place for the opposition. Despite the warnings of fellow conspirators, he and Julius Leber contacted a Communist resistance group that had been infiltrated by the Gestapo. Arrested in early July 1944. Condemned to death by the People's Court on October 20 and executed the same day.

Rommel, Erwin (1891–1944)

Career officer. At first sympathized with the Nazis. Master of tank warfare tactics and a legendary troop commander. From 1941 to 1943 commander of the Africa Corps. Appointed field marshal in 1942. Commander in chief of Army Group B in Italy and northern France in 1944. Sympathized with the conspiracy against Hitler but did not participate. Forced by Hitler to commit suicide on October 14, 1944, after his plans to "open" the western front became known. Would otherwise have been charged with treason before the People's Court.

Schacht, Hjalmar (1877–1970)

Economist. Cofounder of the German Democratic Party. Played a key role in stabilizing the German mark in 1923. Joined the rightist Harzburg Front in 1931. Introduced Hitler to the circles of high finance. President of the Reichsbank from 1923 to 1930 and from 1933 to 1939. Minister of economics from 1934 to 1937. Came into conflict with the Nazi leadership because he wanted to resist devaluation and inflation. Continued as minister without portfolio until 1944. Horrified by the Fritsch affair and Hitler's evident intention to go to war, began to distance himself from the regime and placed himself at the disposal of the conspirators in September 1938. Considered by resistance to be somewhat unreliable. Arrested after July 20, 1944, but nothing could be proved against him. Acquitted at the Nuremberg trials. Became a banker and financial adviser after the war.

Schlabrendorff, Fabian von (1907–80)
Lawyer and first lieutenant in the reserves. Served as Henning von Tresckow's adjutant. In the military resistance, acted as the regular contact between Army Group Center and Beck, Goerdeler, Oster, and Olbricht. Arrested after July 20, 1944. Held in the Flossenbürg and Dachau concentration camps. His trial was delayed when Roland Freisler, president of the People's Court, was killed. Eventually acquitted in March 1945, and released following the war. A judge of the Constitutional Court of the Federal Republic of Germany from 1967 to 1975.

Schulenburg, Count Fritz-Dietlof von der (1902–44)
Lawyer specializing in administrative law. Joined the Nazi Party in 1932. Became deputy prefect of police in Berlin in 1937 and regional commissioner of Upper and Lower Silesia in 1939. Already considered, however, to be "politically unreliable" and was expelled from the Nazi Party in 1940. First lieutenant in the reserves. Contacts with the Kreisau Circle. Held in high esteem by all, thanks to his dynamic personality. Perhaps the most valuable middleman in the resistance, maintaining close contacts with Stauffenberg as well as with Goerdeler, Leber, Popitz, and Moltke. Arrested after July 20, 1944. Executed in Plötzensee prison on August 10.

Schwerin von Schwanenfeld, Count Ulrich Wilhelm (1902–44)
As a student advocated the political renewal of Germany on Christian-socialist foundations and opposed the Nazis from their early days. Convinced as early as 1935 that Germany could only be liberated from the Nazi regime by eliminating Hitler, by force if necessary. Maintained friendly relations with Yorck and Schulenburg and close contacts with Military Intelligence and the Kreisau Circle. One of the most influential intermediaries between military and civilian resistance circles. Conscripted into the Wehrmacht in 1939 and became Field Marshal Witzleben's adjutant in Paris in 1941. Oster managed to have him sent back to Berlin in 1942. Although convinced after 1943–44

that a coup could no longer prevent the necessity of unconditional surrender, continued to advocate assassinating Hitler. Arrested in army headquarters on July 20. Sentenced to death on August 21 and executed in Plötzensee prison.

Stauffenberg, Count Claus Schenk von (1907–44)

Career officer. Member of the south German Catholic nobility but had Prussian ancestors as well. Part of the circle around the poet Stefan George. Joined a cavalry regiment in 1926. In 1938 became staff officer under Major General Erich Hoepner, who numbered among the conspirators led by Witzleben. After the French campaign, posted to the OKH organizational section. In early 1943 joined the Tenth Panzer Division covering Rommel's withdrawal in Africa. Seriously wounded on April 7, 1943. Beginning in the fall of 1943 became the crucial figure in the resistance to Hitler. Named chief of staff in the General Army Office in October 1943 and then chief of staff to the commander of the reserve army. Slated to become secretary of state in the War Ministry after a successful coup. Resolved in the summer of 1944 to carry out the assassination attempt himself, because he had access to Hitler's military briefing conferences. Tried to kill Hitler on July 20, 1944, in the Wolf's Lair near Rastenburg, East Prussia. Thinking he had succeeded, flew to Berlin to help carry out the coup from army headquarters on Bendlerstrasse. Executed there on the night of July 20–21 along with other fellow conspirators.

Stieff, Helmuth (1901–44)

Career officer. Joined the army general staff in 1938. Became chief of the OKH organizational section in October 1942. Wrote many letters during the war, primarily to his wife. Although only a few have survived, they are among the most moving accounts of the period. Recruited into the active resistance by Henning von Tresckow. Although at first volunteered to kill Hitler, reneged after much vacillation. Arrested on the night of July 20–21 at Führer headquarters and brutally tortured at subsequent interrogations. Withstood for several days all attempts to force him to name his fellow conspirators. Condemned to death by the People's Court at the first trial of conspirators on August 8 and executed the same day in Plötzensee prison.

Stülpnagel, Carl-Heinrich von (1886–1944)

Career officer. A friend of Beck's since the early 1930s. Typified a certain kind of cultivated officer, with an interest in science and literature. Participated in the plans for the September conspiracy of 1938. Quartermaster General on the army general staff from 1938 to 1940. Became a general in the infantry and then commander in chief of the Seventeenth Army in 1941, and served as military commander of France from 1942 to 1944. Together with Hofacker, provided support in Paris for the coup by the military resistance. Only in his command area were the conspirators' plans successfully implemented on July 20, 1944. When the failure of the coup became apparent, attempted suicide but succeeded only in blinding and seriously wounding himself. Sentenced to death by the People's Court on August 30 and executed the same day in Plötzensee prison.

Tresckow, Henning von (1901–44)
Career officer, eventually brigadier general. In the late 1920s joined with officers who supported Hitler but soon changed his mind and ultimately proved one of the most courageous opponents of the regime. From 1941 to 1943 was a general staff officer in the high command of Army Group Center. In 1942 became a colonel. Beginning in mid-1942 planned a number of attacks on Hitler. Posted in late July 1943 to the elite "Führer reserve." Worked in Berlin with Stauffenberg on transforming the Valkyrie plans for "internal disturbances" into plans for a coup d'état. Dispatched in the fall of 1943 to the southern wing of the eastern front. In late November 1943 made chief of staff to the Second Army. Maintained his contacts with the conspirators and cited in the Kaltenbrunner reports as the "driving force" and "evil spirit" behind the coup attempt of July 20. When the attempt failed, killed himself at the front with a grenade.

Trott zu Solz, Adam von (1909–44)
Lawyer. Studied at Oxford in 1932–33. Posted to China between 1937 and 1938, traveling by way of the United States. Used that trip and numerous others to establish contacts on behalf of the resistance, sometimes with exiled opponents of the regime. Joined the NSDAP in 1940 to provide a cover. Legation counselor in the Foreign Office's information division. Later worked in the India branch. Foreign policy adviser to the Kreisau Circle. Undertook further travels abroad in 1941 and 1943 to explore the Allied attitude toward a new German government but bitterly disappointed by the indifference of the Western Allies. After the attempted coup of July 20, 1944, not arrested until July 26. Condemned by the People's Court on August 15 and executed in Plötzensee prison.

Wirmer, Josef (1901–44)

Lawyer. Acted before 1933 on behalf of the Catholic Student Unions. Belonged to the left wing of the Center Party. As an opponent of the Nazis from the outset and a frequent legal adviser to persecuted Jews, expelled by the Nazis from the lawyers' syndicate. After 1936, forged friendship with Jakob Kaiser and increasingly close contacts with trade union circles. Established many ties between resistance groups that had been cut off from one another by old differences. His house was one of the most important meeting places of the opposition, frequented not only by Kaiser, Leuschner, and Habermann but also by Goerdeler and the conspirators in Military Intelligence. Arrested on August 4, 1944, and incarcerated in the Ravensbrück concentration camp. Defended himself before the People's Court with great verve and self-assurance. Condemned on September 8 and executed the same day at Plötzensee prison.

Witzleben, Erwin von (1881–1944)

Career officer. In 1934 appointed commander of the Berlin military district. Participated in the coup and assassination plans of 1938–39. In 1940 became a field marshal and commander in chief of Army Group D in the West. From April 1941 until March 1942 commander in chief in the West in France. Retired in March 1942 for health reasons. Took part in preparations for a coup in 1943–44 and agreed to assume command of the Wehrmacht under a new government. On July 20, 1944, did not appear at army headquarters on Bendlerstrasse until the evening. Arrested on July 21. Sentenced to death by the People's Court on August 8 and executed the same day in Plötzensee prison.

Yorck von Wartenburg, Count Peter (1904–44)

Lawyer. From 1936 to 1941 assistant secretary on the staff of the Reich price commissioner. In 1939 a first lieutenant in the reserves. In 1942 joined the OKW Defense Economy Office. The central figure in the Kreisau Circle, along with Helmuth von Moltke. Most of its meetings, including the most important ones, took place in his house on Hortensienstrasse. After long hesitation, was won over to the idea of assassinating Hitler. Maintained close ties with his cousin Stauffenberg. Was expected to become state secretary in the chancellor's office after a successful coup. Went to Bendlerstrasse on July 20, 1944, and was arrested there. Condemned to death by the People's Court on August 8 and executed the same day in Plötzensee prison.

INDEX

Entries in **boldface** *refer to captions and illustrations.*

Acknowledgment is made to the following for permission to use the artwork which appears on the pages listed below.

Archiv der Sozialen Demokratie, Bonn: 152
Archiv für Kunst and Geschichte: 24, 25 (right), 39, 54, 62, 75, 83, 117, 197, 282 (left)
Bayerische Staatsbibliothek, Munich: 64, 97, 96, 155, 300
Bildarchiv Preussischer Kulturbesitz: 44, 47, 85, 99, 106, 123, 147, 147, 154, 156, 182 (right), 190, 205, 207, 239, 251, 256, 280, 282 (right), 296, 312, 314, 315
Bilderdienst Süddeutscher Verlag: 23, 25 (left), 72 (left), 125, 131, 135, 166, 176, 182 (left), 221, 242, 246, 307
Personal Collection: 90, 173, 192, 223, 231
Ullstein Bilderdienst: 15, 41, 72 (right), 80, 92, 216, 248, 250, 259, 278, 286, 298, 302, 318
From Bundeszentrale für Heimatdienst, July, 20, 1944, 3rd ed. (Bonn, 1960: 265 (above left, above right, below)